Latin American Women
and the Search for Social Justice

 Latin American Women

and the Search for Social Justice

Francesca Miller

University Press of New England / Hanover & London

University Press of New England, Hanover, NH 03755
© 1991 by University Press of New England
Printed in the United States of America   5   4   3
CIP data appear at the end of the book

This book is dedicated to
R. Bryan Miller,
Francesca Leona Wellman, and
Arthur Albert Wellman, Jr.

Contents

Acknowledgments

This book is the product of a number of years of research, writing, and the creating and teaching of courses in a previously untaught field of study, the history of women in Latin America. The ideas and concepts presented were developed in the course of discussions with colleagues and students as well as in the many solitary hours spent delving into archival material and communing with my computer. The intellectual heritage drawn upon is apparent in the notes and bibliographies as well as in the text itself.

As all scholars know, there is another book-length story behind the successful completion of a project of this dimension. Here it gives me pleasure to indicate a few of those whose contributions were central to the successful completion of the book. Foremost among them is Gwen Kirkpatrick, who first suggested that my course on the history of women in Latin America contained the elements of a book she would like to read. My other colleagues in the Seminar on Feminism and Culture in Latin America—including Emilie Bergmann, Janet Greenberg, Francine Masiello, Marta Morello-Frosch, Kathleen Newman, and Mary Louise Pratt—were also generous in their comments and suggestions and unfailing in their support of the project. Rollie E. Poppino was always available to discuss ideas, an invaluable resource and colleague. My mother, Francesca Goodell Rappole, read the entire manuscript and offered important critical insights as the writing progressed.

I am grateful to the research assistants who patiently ferreted out obscure references, engaged in lively discussions of the material, and kept me out of library prison, especially Lynn Exe, Karen Boyd, Julianne Keihl, and Debi Tepner Roche, each of whom worked with me for more than a year, and to Kendra Gibson Wellman, Tracy Wallin, Sierra Bruckner, and Theresa Swinehart, who worked on specific short-term projects.

I would like to offer special thanks to Joy Fergoda, librarian of the Women's

Resource and Research Center at the University of California, Davis, for calling new articles to my attention and for facilitating access to the library's holdings. Irene Dempsey offered many insights on the long-term writing process.

There is no question that spousal support enabled the maintenance of home and family during the writing of this book, but it is important to emphasize that the research, travel to archives, hiring of research assistants and of secretarial skills, and the purchase of computer materials and copying services were primarily supported by income from a succession of lectureships in history and women's studies at the University of California, Davis, and in Latin American studies and women's studies at the University of California, Santa Cruz. A series of small grants supported archival research. I am grateful to the Stanford University Center for Latin American Studies; the University of California, Berkeley–Stanford University Joint Center for Latin American Studies; and a Radcliffe College Research Grant for research at the Arthur and Elizabeth Schlesinger Archives on the History of Women. Affiliation as a research associate with the Department of History, UC Davis, afforded me library privileges, including crucial access to interlibrary loan.

I offer special thanks to Elaine Holt, who not only contributed her superb secretarial skills to produce a handsome final draft of the manuscript, but responded to numerous crises (mostly created by the author) with humor and equanimity. The last stages of manuscript preparation—proofreading, writing the bibliographic essay, searching for illustrations, and preparing these acknowledgments—were carried out with the institutional support of the new UC Davis Washington Center, Washington, D.C., where I held a fellowship in 1990/91. The Center and its staff, particularly Melody Johnson, were generous in every way in helping to bring the project to a successful conclusion.

Finally, I offer thanks to those most intimately involved with the completion of the book: my daughter, Francesca Leona Wellman, who was always willing to give a careful reading to a draft; my son, Arthur Wellman; and my husband Bryan, whose substantive, intellectual, and spiritual support was—and is—vital.

May 1991   F.M.

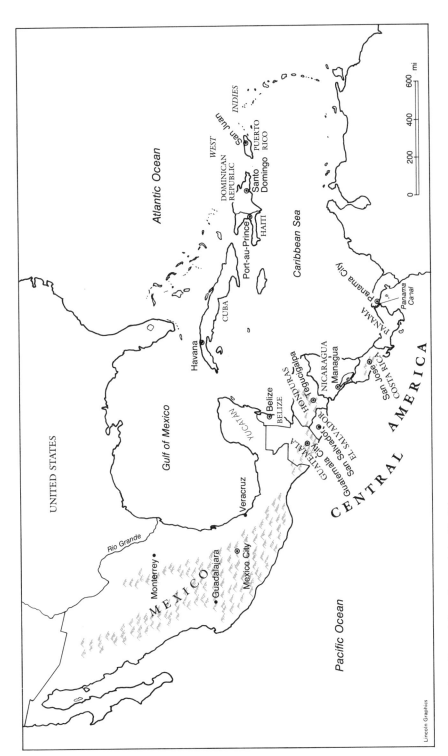

Map 1. Mexico, Central America, and the Caribbean.

Lincoln Graphics

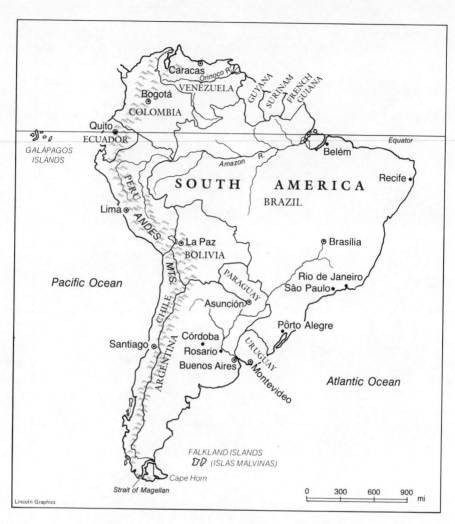

Map 2. South America.

Introduction

Nuestra liberación comenzó en la independencia. ¿Donde terminará? ¿La paz o la guerra sea nuestros medios de liberación?

—Carmen de Goméz Méjia [1]

Every observer of Latin America soon learns that the term "Latin America" serves more to obscure than to illuminate an understanding of the twenty-eight countries and dozen territories that lie between the Rio Grande in the north and Tierra del Fuego in the south. Similarly, it is soon discovered that there is no Latin American woman: factors of time and place, class, race, ethnicity, age, and marital status, among others, are important considerations whether we are speaking of a Mexican woman, a Brazilian, a Haitian, or a woman from Guyana—who would not necessarily be able to speak to one another as their respective national tongues are Spanish, Portuguese, French, and English. Moreover, it is not unlikely that a Guatemalan woman's first language might be Maya or Quiché, not Spanish, that a woman of the Andes might speak only Quechua; a woman of the Amazon, a Tupí dialect.

Additionally, since the late nineteenth century the large Latin American nations have received successive waves of immigrants from Europe and Asia. Italian and German immigrants settled in significant numbers in Mexico, Argentina, Uruguay, Chile, and southern Brazil. Brazil has the largest number of citizens of Japanese descent of any nation other than the United States or Japan itself. Koreans, Chinese, and Southeast Asians also have emigrated to Brazil and other Latin American nations. In the past forty years immigrants from India, Pakistan, Syria, Lebanon, Iran, and Iraq have made their way to South America. Though in some cases the first immigrant generation settled in rural areas—like the Japanese, who established thriving truck farms in the environs of the city of São Paulo—the daughters and granddaughters of these European and Asian and Middle Eastern immigrants live in the cities and should be understood as constituting part of the urban middle class. The historical understanding of women requires a willingness to regard with high skepticism descriptions of women by national category, such as "Mexican women," "Brazilian women."

However, although a consciousness of the diversity of women's historical experience in Latin America is critical to the dispelling of stereotypes and provides the first step toward knowledge, we cannot endlessly atomize; we need themes and categories within which to order our information. Historical analysis allows us to compare and contrast, to see change over time, while remaining aware of the nuances of individuality.

The focus of this book is on the role of Latin American women in the impetus toward change that envisions a fuller empowerment of all people within a society. Historically, this includes the reform-minded female intellectuals of the nineteenth century as well as women leaders of the grass-roots movements of the 1980s. Particular attention is given to the tension between the search for change within the domestic political arena and the transnationalist view that seeks ethical, moral, and substantive support beyond the boundaries of the imagined national community.

Central considerations include the history of the women's movement as influenced by and exerting influence on contemporary social movements (feminism and redemocratization in the Southern Cone and Brazil, women and revolutionary movements in Central America and Peru, for example), with secondary, referential analysis of women's groups that have aligned themselves with the status quo and counterrevolutionary forces. Theoretical insights emerge from the comparison of women's movements as they developed in specific historical contexts; considerations of class and ethnicity as well as of gender inform the analysis.

The examination of women who have sought to make their voices and views heard and who have challenged traditional forms that limit and cripple them because they are women is not, in the Latin American context, a study of the rejection of gender roles. Some of the most powerful articulations of collective anger have arisen from the inability of women, in particular circumstances, to fulfill their sense of self as nurturers and caretakers.[2]

Historically, many women in Latin America have well understood their social and political loci and have acted to change the circumstances—economic, political, cultural—that disempower them. The concepts of *abertura*, which means "opening" in Portuguese and came into use to describe the precarious and gradual retreat of the military from the executive branch of government in Brazil between 1974 and 1984, and *parenthèse*, or parenthesis, a Haitian term connoting a brief break but little change in politics as usual, are useful in the attempt to discern themes and trends in the history of women's political engagement in Latin America. Women activists have taken advantage of whatever political space presented itself in periods of *abertura* to advance their program, and in different places at different times they have worked successfully to create political openings.

The patterns that emerge suggest that the presence or absence of a gendered positing of the current political question—for example, the demand for full citizenship for female as well as male patriots in the independence period, the insistence that universal suffrage must also mean woman suffrage in the politics of democracy in the post–World War II era, the articulation of a feminist understanding of revolution in the late 1970s—may be seen as accurate indications of whether a true *abertura* has occurred or whether the appearance of political change is in reality but another *parenthése*, a period of disorder, political jockeying, and sporadic violence marking the fall of one leader or party and the rise of another. Such an understanding is not accessible through the examination of the male political experience alone or through an ungendered analysis of events.

The book opens with a discussion of history and the meaning of the creation—and the suppression—of the historical record. Historian Gerda Lerner has written of women and the historical record: "Women's history is indispensable and essential to the emancipation of women."[3] The history of women activists in Latin America, while insisting on the validity of the female experience and the critical importance of retrieving and interpreting that experience, extends Lerner's concept: in the Latin American context, women's history is posited as part of the search for social and political justice for all people.

This introduction opens with a quotation from Colombian historian Carmen de Goméz Méjia: "Our liberation begins with independence. Where will it end? Will peace or war be the means of our liberation?" In Goméz Méjia's phrase, "our liberation" is not limited to women but is inclusive. Conventional historigraphy has subsumed "the Latin American woman" as a nonhistorical actor, rarely depicting her as an agent of change. Examining the history of women activists and the women's movement in Latin America raises the question of what the cost of writing women out of history has been. It suggests that part of the cost of defining the nation-state in exclusively masculine terms, of marginalizing women and others, disestablishes the basis for the very loyalty and commitment necessary to national survival. Redemocratization is, at least in part, an attempt to rethink the state inclusively, in gendered and ethnic terms as well as through class analysis. Knowing the history of a past in which women and others have been written out is a step toward understanding the potential of a future where all people may have a voice.

Latin American Women
and the Search for Social Justice

1. Women, History, and Creating a New Historical Record

Michelle Peña Herrera
Nalvia Rosa Mena Alvarado
Cecilia Castro Salvadores
Ida Amélia Almarza
—Holly Near, *"Hay una mujer desaparecida"* [1]

The names above are those of Chilean women who, among thousands of men, women, and children, were "disappeared," victims of terrorism practiced by the state against the citizenry in Chile, Argentina, Brazil, Uruguay, El Salvador, Honduras, Guatemala. The litany of names, the insistence on the specific naming of the disappeared, reminds us of the need to know our history.

In the twentieth century, Latin American nations have been characterized by international peace and internal violence. With the exception of the contributions of Mexico, Brazil, and Colombia to the Allied cause during World War II and small troop deployments to the UN forces in Korea, the Latin American states have been only peripherally involved in the major conflicts in Europe and Asia. Within the area, the Chaco War (1932–1935) remains an exception; all other international conflicts have been little more than border skirmishes. In contrast, the legacy of internal violence has been bitter as new groups struggled to obtain a political voice, greater economic equity, and social justice within their national polities.

In the late 1960s the response of national elites to the threat of social change, whether reformist or revolutionary, became increasingly uncompromising, and in state after state the military took power "to restore order." Throughout Latin America the military contained units specially trained in counterinsurgency techniques that had been instituted, with the aid of the United States, in the wake of the Cuban Revolution and Cuban-based attempts to export revolution.[2] By 1968 the response of the military regimes in Brazil and Uruguay to the bombings, bank robberies, and attacks on members of the government by revolutionary groups evolved into institutionalized, state-sponsored terrorism: the carrying out of terrorist acts against the citizenry, including kidnappings, torture, the tacit support of death squad activities, illegal imprisonment, and disappearances.

Like their male counterparts, women were visible throughout the political spectrum: victims of political oppression, supporters of incumbent regimes, perpetrators of torture, among the armed resistance, among those who preferred not to know. But the most compelling image to emerge from this era, male or female, is that of *las madres*, the mothers of the disappeared.

The practice of "disappearing" the bodies of victims—through dismemberment, the eradication of identifiable features, burial by bulldozer, dropping the drugged or dying into the sea—was central to creating a "culture of fear." In Chile more than six thousand people were buried in mass graves in the first year of the Pinochet regime. In Guatemala entire villages have been burned over and their inhabitants murdered or dispersed by government troops, and the practice continues. In Argentina, between 1977 and 1983, an estimated thirty thousand citizens were "disappeared." It was in Argentina that the mothers' movement first emerged and where the rituals and the form of protest were developed: women, wearing white head scarves embroidered with the names of disappeared family members and carrying photographs of their disappeared children, meeting weekly in a public place, the Plaza de Mayo.[3]

We have seen pictures of these silent protests by public presence on the television news, images relayed to us by satellite from El Salvador, Chile, Guatemala. It is no accident that we have mental pictures: in the 1980s events are more often brought to us by camera than by print analysis. The original *madres* of Buenos Aires deliberately arrayed themselves to attract the attention not only of passers-by but also of the press.[4] The white head scarves were chosen because "white is the symbol of peace, something which unites all women."[5]

It is important to understand that *las madres* of Buenos Aires are women of the middle sector: private, respectable women who accepted their roles as wives and mothers. It was when their ability to fulfill those roles was threatened that the women were propelled into direct political action, and it is no wonder that the forms that action took drew distinctly on the traditions these women have held dear. For if you believe what you have been raised to believe—that the family is sacred and that the primary role of woman is to nurture that family—then when the family is threatened, your children murdered, your grandchildren kidnapped, your husband-lover "disappeared," you are driven to seek redress. And if you believe what you have been raised to believe—that the state is the protector of society—then you demand that the state be accountable for the situation in which you find yourself. And when you find that the state is in fact the author of the crimes you are protesting, then what? It is at this juncture—the discovery that it was the institutions of the state that were carrying out crimes against the populace—that the ethical convictions of the mothers determined the choice that ultimately made their protest singular in its courage and its efficacy.

Terrified and now knowing, they did not retreat mourning, into their homes; that private space held no more solace, no more life meaning for them. Nor did they go underground to join forces with the armed resistance and seek a violent overthrow of the criminals in office. They chose a yet more perilous path: They went forth into an unknown space, the public space, to demand that the state purge itself of those responsible, to demand that the state respond in accordance with its own claims to being a just and moral entity. Finally, they demanded that the military governments, in order to maintain any claims they once held to being a national conscience, to acting as a moral force, prove their claims by overseeing the installation of new, civilian governments.

Are there historical precedents within the Latin American context for the protests of *las madres*? The meaning of participating in a public demonstration goes beyond the violation of social norms previously accepted. It is literally to expose oneself, to be publicly identified by the forces opposed, a consideration that demands not only the courage to violate social norms but also the courage to face the very real possibility of violent retribution to yourself, to your family, to your friends.

Two precedent examples of public protest involving women of the middle sectors may be drawn from Haiti in 1930 and Mexico in 1968. In each case the women employed traditional feminine activities to make powerful protests against the use of military force by the state against the populace. In different ways each illuminates the meaning and form of female resistance and demonstrates how it may differ from that of men. Both have strong parallels to female resistance to the culture of fear created by certain Latin American military regimes in the 1970s and 1980s.

Haiti, 1930

Within the context of the U.S. military incursions carried out in a dozen of the Caribbean and Central American states and Mexico between the end of the Spanish-American War in 1901 and the Montevideo Conference in 1933, the occupation of Haiti (1915–1934) was particularly long-lasting and bitter. Many Haitian leaders were jailed, and men were forbidden from gathering in groups of more than three. In 1930 the Hoover Commission, headed by William A. White, was dispatched to Haiti by President Hoover to investigate ways of ending the occupation.

Prior to the arrival of the Hoover Commission, a delegation of Haitian women applied to the occupation authorities for permission to hold a public procession, which would be the culmination of a nationwide prayer service calling for an end to the occupation. Despite the support of all five Roman Catholic bishops in Haiti, the authorities refused to grant such a permit on the grounds that the activity "was inspired by anti-American sources in Latin America and might lead to disaster."[6]

On March 2, 1930, Mme Percival Thoby called on the Hoover Commission. Mme Thoby was the wife of the president of the Haitian political party Union Nationale; as part of the ban on political activities by Haitians, her husband was under house arrest. She told the Hoover Commission that the planned demonstration was only to be part of a women's prayer service for the success of President Hoover's Commission. Moved by her plea, Mr. White overruled the local authorities and granted a permit.

The next morning twelve hundred women gathered at the Church of the Sacred Heart in Port-au-Prince. The church filled, and several thousand people crowded the streets outside. Just before the service began, Mme Thoby appeared on the steps of the church and warned the crowd that the service was "exclusively a feminine manifestation" and that in compliance with the women's promise to the gendarmes "men must not participate in nor even follow the procession."[7] The crowd stood for two hours in hushed solemnity; William White arrived just before the climax of the service and was escorted to a seat near the altar.

Led by a clear soprano voice, the congregation joined in an antiphonal prayer for "Our country, its arms broken and its face bruised." "Have pity O God on these erring men who outrage thee and know not what they do" sang the soprano; "God of clemency and power, save Haiti" was the thousand-voice response. At the end of the service the congregation joined the crowds outside and continued the prayer "for the liberation of Haiti" as they paraded from the cathedral past the headquarters of the investigating commission to the Champs du Mars. In that central square, approximately fifteen thousand Haitians waited to witness the end of the procession at the statue of Jean-Jacques Dessalines, hero of the Haitian wars of independence.

The women did what the Haitian men could not do: stage a public demonstration. A women's prayer service for the success of the Hoover Commission's work—what could be more charming? The courtesy extended to Mme Thoby by Mr. White may be understood as an example of racism mitigated by sexism.[8] A gathering of black Haitian men would have been viewed as enormously threatening; a meeting of black, presumably pious Haitian women could be viewed as harmless. But the content of the prayer, delivered as it was in soaring soprano tones, was pure protest: Get the U.S. troops out of Haiti.

Within the traditional guise of feminine piety, the cathedral became the stage, the service became the form, and the hymn was the dramatic means of delivering the message. But what the women had done was far from traditional. They had made a public protest of the military occupation, which had been marked by violence and imprisonment and scarred by the racism of the U.S. Marine Corps officers, who had imported Jim Crow attitudes and segregation practices from their own native states of Mississippi and Alabama.

In addition, the women's prayer meeting culminated in a public march in a country where public gatherings had been outlawed for ten years. Moreover, the thousands who lined the streets and who stood silently outside the church were there, in their own words, "to bear witness to the event." The parade ended under the statue of Dessalines, the first president of independent Haiti, who a century earlier had led Haitian slaves against their masters to "redeem the country from the white man."[9] The Hoover Commission returned to Washington with a strong recommendation to return the reigns of power to Haitians as expeditiously as possible. Withdrawal of the last occupation forces was completed in mid-1934.[10]

Mexico, 1968

In 1968 the Mexican government responded to the student protest movement with stunning and unanticipated violence. The Mexican student movement began to build in July 1968 in the wake of the Soviet invasion of Czechoslovakia. The Olympic Games, scheduled to open in Mexico City on October 12, symbolized to the middle-class students the skewed priorities of the Mexican ruling elite: the expenditure of millions of pesos on sports arenas, publicity, and hotels for foreign athletes while thousands upon thousands of Mexicans had no housing, little food, no health care, no hope for bettering their lives.

Between July and October sporadic clashes between students and riot police served only to unite the students in a nationwide movement and to bring more and more moderate sectors of the population into sympathy with their goals. On October 2 a large rally was called in the Plaza de las Tres Culturas at the center of the huge Tlatelolco housing development in Mexico City. By 5 P.M. six thousand people were in the plaza. At 6:10 P.M. ten thousand armed military troops surrounded the square and opened fire. Tanks moved in, and helicopters dropped flares to aid the sharpshooters.

Hundreds were killed outright, including many who were simply residents of the area. Many others died from their wounds when the military prevented doctors and medics from tending them until they could be interrogated. In the aftermath the student movement was in disarray and was not to recover; the issues it addressed remain unresolved.

In her brilliant and moving book, *Massacre in Mexico: Taking to the Street— the Night of Tlatelolco*, Elena Poniatowska created what she calls a "collage of voices bearing historical witness." Speaking from within that collage are the voices of numerous men and women, members of the student movement, victims of the killing, witnesses of the night of the massacre. And there are the voices of women whose daughters and sons and students were shot down in cold blood.

Perla Velez de Aguilera, who identifies herself only as "mother of a family," told Poniatowska: "We women never in our lives shed as many tears as we have in recent days. It's as though we were trying to wash all of Tlatelolco— all the images, all the walls, all the curbs, all the stone benches stained with blood, all the traces of bodies bleeding to death in the corners—clean with our tears."[11]

Margarita Nolasco, a lecturer in anthropology at the university, whose students were among those killed, related the tale of the women's attempts to schedule a mass in commemoration of the dead: "I went to the Franciscan Brothers of the Tlatelolco parish and told them that I had come as a representative of a group of mothers of youngsters who had been killed and wounded on October 2, and that we would like to have a requiem mass said for them there in Tlateloloco. The reply was, we're sorry, but there aren't any priests available on the day you've requested." Nolasco persisted, pointing out that the mass should be held November 2, a month after the students had died and that it should be held in Tlatelolco "because this is where our children lost their lives, you see." The priests insisted that the schedule was full.[12]

The next day Nolasco returned to the church accompanied by thirty of the women who had lost children in the massacre. The women, who were devout Catholics, pressed the priest to schedule the mass, but they were told that it would not be possible, there was no time available, the candles would make smoke smudges on the ceiling, the four-hundred-year-old walls would be endangered. . . .

"Those of us who had gone to have it out with the priest suddenly shut up and didn't say a word because one of the mothers started to moan in a very strange sort of way, a plaint that started as a kind of quiet lament and ended in a shrill scream that gave us all goose pimples. She said that even the Church was turning its back on them, that it was more than she could bear if they wouldn't say a prayer for her son."

The mothers and families of those killed sent commemoration notices of the deaths to all of the newspapers, asking that they be published on November 2. The notices listed the names of those who had died on October 2 and said that they were remembered with the most profound grief. Not one newspaper published the notices. To hide their brutality, the Mexican government and military refused to acknowledge the names of those who had died in Tlatelolco. The church and press clearly feared to antagonize the government by giving any kind of recognition that a massacre had occurred: there was to be no official record, secular or religious, of the victims, no public acknowledgment of the deaths. But the mothers (and here "mothers" should be understood as a metaphor for the families and friends of the victims) refused to accept this.

Margarita Nolasco continued in her account: "On November 2, a woman with bright blue eyes who's absolutely fearless approached one of the Franciscans of Santiago Tlatelolco and told him that her labor union had given her a wreath in memory of her son, and whether he approved or not, she was going to place it there for him, no matter what. She had no sooner placed it against the wall when people suddenly popped up from all over, and began to light votive candles."

By noon the Plaza de las Tres Culturas was covered with little altars of flowers and candles. People came with armfuls of campazu'shitl flowers, the long-stemmed white lilies that symbolize the hope of rebirth. Others placed cards in memory of the dead: "To the martyrs of Tlatelolco, murdered in cold blood." A cross made of ivy and greens from the Unión de Mujeres bore a card that read: "To our martyrs of October 2"; propped next to it was a large square of bristol board with a drawing of a youngster impaled on a bayonet. Around the edges of the square and throughout the housing unit, fully armed *grenaderos* patrolled, reporting the scene on walkie-talkies.[13]

The women of Tlatelolco sought to commemorate their dead, to record the names of the children. They could not turn to the state, the instrument of death. They could not turn to the church, which refused to perform the commemoration rites. They could not turn to the press, to record the names of the dead children (which, it should be noted, were never publicly recorded). But the mothers insisted on the commemoration—in the very specific meaning of that word, the communal sharing of a memory—and that it be carried out on November 2, a month after the killings, a date with special meaning in the Catholic rituals of mourning. In the public square, the Plaza de las Tres Culturas, the meaning became political, the personal expression of grief in its public manifestation became a defiance of national and religious authority.

In her analysis of the mothers' movements of the 1970s and 1980s, Jean Franco has written: "Resistance to the culture of fear began as family rituals which preserve a relationship with the dead without relegating the dead to the status of non-being. Women and the family are essential to this type of resistance."[14] Franco is referring to the mothers' movements of the 1970s and 1980s, but her analysis illuminates the acts of the Mexican women as well.

The Mexican women acted spontaneously, in response to a specific situation, which might have been viewed as singular, aberrant. However, the loss of their children, who were unarmed when attacked by Mexican troops, the rebuff of their appeals by church and press, the rituals of commemoration they selected, and their insistence that the event not pass unrecorded, unrecognized, denied, links them to the mothers of the disappeared.

Franco writes that "the Mothers' movements involve transforming mothering and transferring it from the private to the public sphere indicates that, from these apparently archaic positions, an ethics of survival has developed." [15] Not *las locas* but *las madres de Plaza de Mayo*: the courageous presence in a public space, marching in front of the Government House of Argentina. Like the Champs du Mars in Port-au-Prince, the Plaza de Mayo in Buenos Aires is a space charged with historical significance. The Plaza de Mayo has been the seat of government in Argentina since the eighteenth century; it was the scene of Evita and Juan Perón's tumultuous rallies; it is associated with the independence movement, with the ideals of liberty and freedom. In Chile women chained themselves to the railings of the closed national legislature; in El Salvador the mothers demonstrated by staging sit-ins in the National Cathedral. As Franco states, "in each case, the space itself conveys meanings that do not need to be spoken." [16]

The majority of the original *madres* were housewives, whose normal sphere was the home: "From washing, ironing, cooking, we came to the street to fight for the life of our children." [17] Although the mothers' movements came to encompass men and women, spouses, fathers, the whole spectrum of relatives and friends of the disappeared, the initial members of the group were mothers. Why was this so? Why women, specifically mothers? An obvious answer is that other family members, particularly fathers, had to continue working to support the household. But beyond that, the women believed that they were less likely to provoke retaliation than men would be, though they found that the "national tradition" that exalts "mothers of families" was formed more from folklore than reality. [18] Women who step out of their socially defined spheres risk losing not only respectability but their claim, as women and mothers, to the protection of society. The tenacity of the mothers' movements—in Argentina, over seven years of terror—drew strength from the women's determination to discover the fate of their disappeared children, their courageous insistence on the accountability of those responsible, and the knowledge of their mutual commitment to these ends.

The movie *The Official Story* portrays the society the *madres* sought to awaken to the horrible crimes being carried out, sanctioned by the state, church, and corporate forces in Argentina. The bourgeois woman at the center of the film does not hear the fiery words of her young history students when they declaim the speeches of the leaders of the Argentine independence movement, who demanded a free press and liberty of thought and action. She dismisses the street demonstrators as subversives who bear no message for her. She is "protected" from knowledge of her husband's activities; as she says repeatedly, "I believe what I am told." For her the institutions of government and church present only a benign aspect—until the truth of the accusations gradually becomes real to her.

The story revolves around one of the particularly heinous crimes against women who disappeared, most of whom were young, between the ages of eighteen and thirty. Many of the young women arrested were pregnant, and it later became apparent that many had been seized *because* they were pregnant, that their alleged subversive political activities were merely a pretense for their capture. Born in prison, the newborn infants were put up for private adoptions, and the mothers were murdered, their bodies buried or dropped from helicopters into the sea.

The woman in the film trails from agency to agency seeking information about the clouded birth of her adopted child; her search and dawning horror parallels the desperate odysseys of the families of the disappeared. It was in their painful journeys to official agencies that the mothers first encountered one another. Hebe de Bonafini, who became the spokeswoman for the Mothers of the Plaza de Mayo after the first leader was herself disappeared, tells of the experience of discovering "when we believed we had a friend in the police, that they are no one's friend. And we began to encounter the same faces. Then, on April 30, 1977, we went for the first time to the Plaza de Mayo."[19] Similarly, in Guatemala the Mutual Support Group for the Appearance, Alive, of our Children, Spouses, Parents, and Brothers and Sisters was formed in June 1984 by several women who had continuously encountered one another at the Guatemala City morgues as they searched for the bodies of their disappeared loved ones.

In an interview with the *New York Times*, one of the mothers told of her search: "My son disappeared six months ago. I went to the government house and they said they couldn't tell me anything. I then went to the police and they said that if he disappeared and I had not heard from him, that meant he was dead. Then, I went to the army and they told me that my son had probably joined the guerrillas and gone underground." Another woman described her confrontation with the officials: "Last April 7, at 4 A.M. several policemen in uniform came to my house and dragged my 18-year-old son away. I immediately told the police and they said they had nothing to do with it. They also did not even try to go out and find those responsible."[20]

In an article entitled "Mother's Day," Argentine writer Ariel Dorfman states: "Everyone knows who is responsible. The very authorities who refuse to acknowledge the arrest of these people. . . . This refusal is as necessary as it is convenient. The government can exploit the terror that comes from its supposedly abiding by the law. Habeas corpus can be rejected, because there is quite plainly, no corpus. No cuerpo. No body. By getting rid of the victim they hope to be rid of the crime. Only the imagination of the relatives, over and over, can suggest what specific and sick forms of the probable have descended. Thus, normality is not only being denied to the victims, it is also denied to those who survive them."[21]

It was this seemingly implacable denial of knowledge and of culpability by the state that the *madres* challenged in their refusal to accept "the official story." When they first began to meet, the Mothers of the Plaza de Mayo were ridiculed, dismissed as *las locas*, "the crazies"; they faced repeated disperse-ment by military police and imprisonment. But they persisted in their demand for news of their lost ones, chanting, "It will end, it will end, this habit of killing will end." Every Thursday at 3 P.M., facing the Government House, they circled the Pyramid of May, a monument to Argentine independence, to stress how betrayed this symbol of freedom and justice had been.

Hebe de Bonafini told of the attempts to disperse the demonstrators: "They often throw us in jail and leave us incommunicado. They forbid us to speak but they can't forbid us to pray. So we start praying at the top of our lungs for others to know that the Mothers are there."[22] Another form of protest developed by the mothers' movement was the representation of the disappeared in empty silhouettes drawn on or pasted to the walls and side-walks and streets of Buenos Aires. More than thirty thousand such silhouettes appeared: men, women, children of all ages, all life size, each bearing a name, age, and date of disappearance. Like the mothers' persistent presence in the Plaza de Mayo, the silhouettes insisted on the reality of the disappeared and on the need to remember their life.

From their personal grief and fear the mothers evolved a communal strength. Their methods of protest—carrying pictures of their loved ones, naming again and again those taken away—emerged directly from forms of grief that would have been, in other circumstances, private: a woman weep-ing over the picture of her lost child, keeping vigil by a window, placing flowers on a grave. But there were no known graves.

It was crucial to the military governments that there be no martyrs in the "dirty war," that there should be no historical memory, no family shrine.[23] Death, which is also the space of immortality, communal memory, connec-tion between the generations, was not to be a form of continuity but an extirpation.[24] That is the full meaning of the disappeared. In Argentina the struggle to retrieve the dead, to give them back their names and identities, became an indictment of the military regime. By refusing to regard their children as terrorists, by reiterating their mothering role and their particular regard for the continuation of human life, the mothers of Argentina, Chile, and El Salvador were able to demonstrate the ethical bankruptcy of the state's position. They ultimately exposed not themselves but the institutions of the state—and in Mexico and Argentina, the church—to public shame.[25]

In 1977 a handful of women went to march in the Plaza de Mayo; on the fourth anniversary of that event, May 1, 1981, in defiance of decrees banning street demonstrations, more than six thousand Argentines joined them. The police stood by. The protestors, who came from all over Argentina, sang the national anthem and carried signs denouncing the continued violation of human rights by the regime. Two years later, the military government, disgraced by the loss of the Falklands War, unable to contain crippling inflation, and held up in the eyes of the world as moral lepers, stepped down from power.

The Mothers of the Plaza de Mayo have become a metaphor for the thousands of Latin Americans who have dared to protest the practice of state terrorism against the populace through nonviolent means. In Brazil a group of men and women, at great personal risk, secretly photocopied the entire court proceedings of the Supreme Military Command, a record that included seven thousand scrupulously detailed cases of torture, illegal kidnappings, and murder. In 1985 they published the material in *Brasil: Nunca Mais*, which became the best-selling book of nonfiction in Brazilian literary history.[26] In Guatemala, the names of over fifty thousand victims of state terror have been recorded and circulated throughout the world by Amnesty International.[27] To see the list of names and ages and dates of death or disappearance is a powerful experience: it is concrete, visible evidence, not only of the existence of the victims but also of the reality of the crime.

Central to each of these examples of protest against the abhorrent abuse of power by the state is the effort to create a historical record that reflects human truth and belies the official story. The effectiveness of the mothers' resistance movements in achieving this end is underscored by the words of Guatemalan chief of state General Oscar Humberto Mejia Victores in a broadcast in March 1985: "To take steps toward the reappearance alive of the disappeared is a subversive act."[28]

There are significant patterns and parallels in the strategies of female protest and resistance in Argentina, Mexico, and Haiti that help to illuminate not only the history of women in these societies but also the broader workings of the societies. In each case the particular dissenting response of the women is rooted in the historical circumstances of her time and place, and in her understanding of her role as a woman, as dissent to the culture of fear in Latin America in the 1980s, to the murderous repression of the Mexican government in 1968, to the brutal military occupation of Haiti in 1930. It is because of this, and not because of any intrinsic sexual characteristic, that the forms of the women's protest, the selected arenas and issues of debate, and the strategies of opposition employed are neither imitative of nor directly analogous to those employed by their male counterparts.

There are parallels in the choice of arenas for the feminine protests and for the demonstrations of resistance, as well as in the use of the imagery of the traditional woman—the mother, the wife, the sister—to legitimize activities in the public arena in ways that are in essence violations of cherished assumptions about women's role in their communities. We see the revered forms turned inside out, the private become public, the protest broadened to a position of ethical prowess.

There are varying degrees of self-consciousness and planning evident and echoes of the reform women's use of the rhetoric of social motherhood to further their causes and of the feminists in the international arena who worked for equal rights and pacifist causes by dusting off the idealism of the independence leaders.

The Haitian women had carefully orchestrated their protest; the leadership in Port-au-Prince included members of the Women's International League for Peace and Freedom and veterans of the Pan-American women's congresses of the 1920s; there is no doubt that they knew exactly what they were about when they set up their "prayer meeting" to help the Hoover Commission succeed.

The most apparently spontaneous response was that of the women of Tlatelolco, but there too lay the knowledge that the acts of commemoration were a defiance: there were armed trucks and military surrounding the plaza, and they walked on stones where their children and other students had died thirty days earlier. The acts of courage and defiance had meaning far beyond the personal, as Elena Poniatowska's account makes clear.

The mothers' movements combine elements of these precedents, in their use of the historically meaningful site, their insistence on bearing witness and on the creation of a historical record that connects to the past and resounds in the present—the opposite of annihilation, of nonbeing, of "the disappeared." There are powerful echoes in the Haitian women's response to foreign occupation, in the attempt to commemorate the slain students in Mexico, and in the strategies employed by the mothers of the disappeared.

Finally, the examination of women, revolution, and reform in Latin America reveals something to us about the nature of history and its critical importance in the search and struggle for human rights and for social, economic, and political justice: we must know the whole record of human achievement and human folly; we are the witnesses. The mothers' movement in Argentina has refused to accept the term "dead" as long as the military is not brought to justice and the disappeared accounted for. Venezuelan poet Teresa de la Parra scorned history with a capital H; but the mothers of the disappeared will not let the generals write the only history: they will write a history that includes "the young, the people, and women."

History is the recorded and interpreted past, the preservation of collective memory.[29] For most of history, women's names have not been inscribed in the record; their unique contributions to the building of communities and nations and to the maintenance of self and family have been lost, "disappeared" from the record of human events. The examination of historical precedents for the mothers' movements underlines the need to write women's names into the historical record, to insist on the importance and reality of the female experience over time, and to see that the analysis of that experience not only enlarges but also transforms our understanding of our past.

2. Precursoras

Sin liberación de la mujer no habrá liberación del hombre.
—Flora Tristán, 1843 [1]

"Without the liberation of woman there can be no liberation of man." So wrote Flora Tristán (1803–1844), the Parisian-born daughter of a French mother and a Peruvian father, in her book *The Workers' Union*, published in 1843. Flora Tristán was one of the first thinkers to argue that the oppression of working-class women was central, not peripheral, to the emancipation of the working class and to the achievement of a harmonious society. [2]

Flora Tristán's intellectual and cultural home was Paris, although she visited Peru in 1833–1834 in an attempt to claim a share of her father's estate. Her importance to Latin American women is as a *precursora*, a female predecessor. Moreover, in her writing and thought, Tristán is a historical predecessor of the socialist feminism that became the predominant strain of feminist thought in Latin America in the twentieth century. In 1944, a century after Tristán's death, Peruvian poet, author, and political activist Magda Portal wrote of her first encounter with Tristán's work and ideas: "In Chile during my four and a half years of exile [from Peru], I was invited by the *Mujeres Socialistas* to their first congress, where they asked me to present a talk for a session titled, 'Flora Tristán, Precursora.'" [3] The Chilean women were familiar with Tristán's life and work but wanted to hear the perspective of a Peruvian woman. Portal writes that in her quest for information on Tristán she went first to biographical dictionaries published in Europe and Latin America but found almost nothing.

Magda Portal did publish an initial essay on Tristán in Chile in 1944. A second edition appeared in Peru after her return there in 1945. Portal's third essay on Tristán was published in Lima in 1983 by the *Editorial la Equidad*, a press dedicated to social and economic justice for all people, in celebration of the UN Decade of the Woman. At that time Portal commented that "Flora's name has been restored [*reconquistado*] to History."[4] To begin this study of Latin American women and the search for social justice with Tristán's words is appropriate in several respects. It emphasizes the importance of recording and understanding women's history, of providing women with their historical antecedents. And it helps to establish the fact that the idea of social justice for women was part of the public debate at the beginning of the nineteenth century.

A Sense of Place

Because the succeeding chapters focus primarily on the recent history of Latin America, a review of events that have served as historiographic landmarks prior to the nineteenth and twentieth centuries, with an eye to the female presence, is in order. These landmarks include the contact period, from 1492 to approximately 1521, when the peoples of the Americas first came into violent contact with seafaring Europeans; the colonial period, when the vast territory of the Western Hemisphere was claimed and administered by Spain, Portugal, France, Holland, and England for nearly three hundred years; and the wars of independence, from approximately 1790 to 1823.

The term Latin America properly belongs to the national period (from 1823 to the present) and refers collectively to the nations that arose from the 9 million square miles of territory previously claimed by the crowns of Spain, Portugal, and France. In North America this includes Mexico and the Central American states of Guatemala, Honduras, Nicaragua, El Salvador, and Panama; in the Caribbean it includes Cuba, the Dominican Republic, and Haiti. In South America it includes Venezuela, positioned on the eastern shoulder of the continent, and the Andean states of Colombia, Ecuador, Peru, Bolivia, and Chile, which lie along the Pacific Coast. In eastern South America, Brazil, Uruguay, and Argentina look to the Atlantic, as does Paraguay, connected to the east coast by the mighty river system that flows into the Rio de la Plata. Because the political and cultural history of the former British territories—Belize in Caribbean Central America; Trinidad and Tobago, Barbados, The Bahamas, and Grenada in the Caribbean; and Guayana in South America—is distinct, they, along with Surinam and various British, French, Dutch, and U.S. dependencies are excluded. Of these, Puerto Rico is the most closely linked to Hispanic Latin America in heritage and culture.

Scholars have long challenged the Euro- and ethnocentrism of periodic designations such as "The Age of Discovery," with its implication that the Americas and the peoples of the Americas did not exist until seen by European eyes, and "The Conquest Period," with its connotation of European superiority and indigenous subjugation.[5] In Latin American historiography the discovery and conquest theses, in addition to being Eurocentric, are also profoundly gendered. The central figures in accounts that describe the contact period in terms of discovery and conquest are male. The Spanish and Portuguese explorers were men led by dreams of glory, given wing by newly developed sailing technology. Their success as discoverers often came as much through chance as by design: Christopher Columbus, sailing under the sponsorship of Queen Isabella of Castile, sought a new route to the spices of Cathay and made landfall in the West Indies in 1492; Pedro Cabrál, headed to the Portuguese colonies in the Orient, was blown far from his intended route around Africa to stake Portugal's claim on the shores of Brazil in 1500. On board their vessels were sailors, soldiers, priests, political and religious dissidents fated to be put ashore, and slaves from the African coast, but as far as has been recorded, none of the sailors, soldiers, priests, dissidents, slaves, or reprobates was female.

If the predominant male figure of the European discoverer of the New World is that of the conquistador, the predominant female figure is that of the Indian woman. In contemporary accounts of the period the indigenous woman was the locus of dreams and terror: "Here we came suddenly upon the excellent land and dominion of the Amazons," Friar Gaspar de Carvajal recorded on June 24, 1542. "We ourselves saw these women, who were there fighting in front of all the Indian men as women captains, and these latter fought so courageously that the Indian men did not dare to turn their backs, and anyone who did turn his back they killed right there before us."[6]

Women of myth: The initial contacts between European explorers and the indigenous population of the Americas were the very stuff of myth; dreams of fabulous treasure, of wealth and land to be had for the taking, of new souls to be won for the glory of Christendom, of hidden empires, of delicious fruits and previously unknown lands had been realized. Why should the awed and frightened friar not take the appearance of the Indian women, fighting side by side—or maybe slightly in front of—their kinsmen, for the incarnation of the legendary Amazons? In the literature of the contact period, in contrast to conventional histories of the colonial and national periods, the presence of the Indian woman is amply recorded but in a one-dimensional role, that of concubine, consort, and mother of a new race. The history of women in Latin America cannot be understood without examining what constituted the lives of real, not mythical, women in the Iberian empires.

The ability of the Spanish and Portuguese colonizers to impose Iberian institutions and cultural values on their vast territorial claims—vividly illustrated in the lasting religious, linguistic, economic, and political forms that persist to the present in the Caribbean and Middle and South America— is one of the most dramatic achievements in human history. What part did women play in this event? Hispanic and Portuguese women are often depicted primarily as "civilizers," indigenous women and girls as "consorts" or "concubines" as well as laborers in field, market, and homes, as are the women of African descent. Colonial society was constructed on distinctions of class, racial heritage, and ethnicity that remain central to an understanding of the history of women in Latin America.[7]

The Contact Period

The societies that existed before the coming of the Europeans were diverse. The people of the Carib linguistic group, those first encountered by Columbus in the islands of the West Indies, were skilled navigators and fierce warriors who, in the century prior to the arrival of the Spanish, had steadily increased their territory in the Antillean island chain at the expense of the more peaceable Arawaks. The resistance of the Caribs to enslavement by the Spaniards was complete: when captured, they committed suicide by whatever method they could devise. Their implacable resistance, combined with their fatal susceptibility to European diseases, a susceptibility shared by hundreds of thousands of the indigenous populations of the Western Hemisphere, ensured that the island Caribs did not survive colonization. Two interesting facts of gender differentiation were recorded by the Spanish: one, that the Caribs generally would kill the captured males of a group, reserving the females for breeding and labor; and two, that in the Antilles, Carib was the ceremonial language of the men, whereas the women communicated among themselves in the Arawak tongue.[8] In other areas of the continent, large settled populations thrived: the Guaraní linguistic groups of modern south central Brazil and Paraguay, the Chibcha of Colombia, the Maya of Guatemala, and most spectacularly, the two great empires of the hemisphere: the empire of the Inca, whose people lived on lands that today constitute the nations of Ecuador, Peru, and Bolivia; and the Aztec Empire, whose stronghold was central Mexico.

The position of women within indigenous societies varied as widely as did the peoples themselves. In her study of Indian women in Peru, Elinor Burkett writes: "The position of women in preconquest Andean society was determined by the forms and culture of that society as a whole. Under Inca rule, Andean peoples were organized into a rigid social order in which positions were assigned by the political aristocracy. There was little escape."[9] Among the Araucanian of Chile and Argentina, Spanish observers—who, it should be noted, were engaged in a prolonged and vicious struggle with the Araucanian for the control of southern South America—recorded that tasks were sharply sex-identified, and they expressed shock at the harsh treatment accorded to Araucanian women and female children. In the highly stratified society of the Aztec Empire, the status and function of women were determined by their social station. High-born young women were educated in

temple schools, as were the young men of their class. Women were priest-
esses, physicians, agricultural laborers, artisans, market vendors, prostitutes,
consorts, and slaves.

Perhaps the best-known Indian woman of the contact era lived in the Aztec
realm as a Tabascan slave: Malinche (1504?–1528), also known as Malintzin or
Marina, played a pivotal role in one of the most dramatic events in human
history, the Spanish overthrow of the Aztec regime in central Mexico. Mod-
erately well born but sold into slavery when still a child, Malinche was among
the slaves given in tribute to Hernán Cortés and his soldiers after their defeat
of the Tabascans. Although her physical beauty was reputedly great, it was
her knowledge of Nahuatl, the language of the Aztecs, and of Maya, known
to one of Cortés's soldiers, that was of critical importance. Allegedly, it was
on the strength of her interpretation that the Spanish and their Indian allies
devastated the village of Cholula in an attack so bloody that it was remarkable
in a record filled with death and devastation.

In modern Mexico, Malinche's name is synonymous with traitor; the noun
malinchista designates a person who disdains the national heritage and prefers
what is foreign. Such an interpretation of the young woman's actions ob-
scures the fact that in many ways Malinche's response to the situation in which
she found herself was not so different from that of others who were caught
up in the turmoil of the Spanish invasion. Her life as a slave of the Tabascans was one of relentless drudgery; the Spanish valued her. She accepted the
faith of the victorious Spaniards and was baptized. She bore Cortés a son
and later was rewarded for her aid to the conquistadors with an *encomienda*, a
guarantee of the income from two native towns for her lifetime. Should she
be judged as a traitor or viewed as an individual who employed her skills to
ensure her own survival? [10]

The Portuguese, reconnoitering the Atlantic coast of Brazil, found neither
empires nor fabulous treasure troves; instead, they encountered peoples living
in extended kinship groups who shared with the seafarers their knowledge
of the fruits and fishes of their regions. Following their practice in coastal
Africa, the Portuguese set up commercial outposts to exploit the valuable
dyewoods that grew near the sea and to solidify their claim to American
territorial rights, but they did not initially commit men and funds to a colonization effort. Portugal's fortune appeared to lie in its holdings in Africa,
India, and Asia.

In the early years of contact it was common for exploratory expeditions
to put ashore individuals—usually political or religious dissidents deported
from the mother country—and abandon them in the hope that if they survived they might later serve as interpreters and guides. One of the most
famous of these castaways was João Ramalho, and the first woman recorded
by name in Brazilian history is Bartira, later Isabel Días, with whom he shared

his life and had many children. Ramalho was put ashore by the Portuguese near the modern port of Santos in the state of São Paulo in approximately 1509; he was taken in by the Guaianazes Indians of the Inhapurambuçú region, of whom Bartira's father, Tabiriça, was a chief. Like Malinche, Bartira is said to have been skilled at languages and interpretation, but it is notable that, in the early stages at least, Ramalho's survival depended on his ability to adapt to her culture and not vice-versa. This is in keeping with the history of the contact period as written by Brazilian historians and especially of the storied origins of the *paulistas,* as those citizens of São Paulo who can trace their paternal lineage to Portuguese males of the colonial period are known. It should be remarked that in Brazil, a society based on racial distinctions, claiming Indian-Portuguese ancestry is most acceptable at a distance of some twenty generations; claiming a Portuguese-African heritage or more recent linkages with Indian peoples would carry no such éclat.

In the 1530s, when permanent colonists and missionaries from Portugal were settling in the São Paulo region, Bartira and her children were baptized. At the request of João Ramalho, in 1553 the Jesuit missionary Manuel de Nóbrega wrote to his order in Portugal asking whether they could determine if the wife Ramalho had left behind forty years earlier was alive or dead, as Ramalho wished to legitimize his union with Bartira. Apparently this did not happen. The words of Adalzira Bittencourt, writing in honor of the four-hundredth anniversary of the founding of São Paulo in 1954, give the flavor of the romantic imagery in which the indigenous woman of the contact period has been cast: "Bartira's name is fixed in the pages of History, engraved in the heroic blood of the *bandierantes* through all the ages."[11] Although the story of Ramalho and Bartira is one of the best known, the genealogical annals of São Paulo are replete with the names and parentage (usually stated as the daughter of the chieftain X) of many indigenous women, their spouses, and the names of their children.

Marriage with an indigenous woman of noble heritage was considered a desirable practice by both the Spanish and Portuguese in the early years of contact. An outstanding example of the use of marriage ties to legitimize Spanish claims to territory and power in the Western Hemisphere comes from sixteenth-century Peru. Beatriz Clara Coya, a pure-blooded Incan princess, granddaughter of Emperor Huáscar, was considered a great marital prize. Born in Cuzco around 1558, Beatriz Clara was heiress to great wealth in land and treasure and possessed of bloodlines that for two hundred years had meant the right to rule in the Andean world; her hand was sought in marriage when she was barely out of infancy. After two early alliances, in 1576 she was given in marriage by order of the viceroy of Peru to Oñez de Loyola as part of his reward for defeating her kinsman, Tupac Amarú. In 1591, Oñez de Loyola was appointed governor of Chile, and Beatriz Clara became *governa-*

dora, or first lady of the realm. The descendants of Beatriz Clara and Oñez de Loyola held positions of the highest status in wealth, power, and social position for generations. Their union provides an example of the way the Spanish sought to continue their traditional practice of seeking advantageous alliances through marriage with the equally hierarchical and blood-conscious Inca elite.

In accounts of the years of contact, it is often the Iberian woman who is invisible, as if she did not appear in the New World until the initial wars were won and towns established. Although it is true that relatively few Spanish and Portuguese women were present in the Americas in the sixteenth century, their absence is more historiographic than real. Both Spanish and Portuguese women were explicitly part of the colonizing project. In 1498, Queen Isabella of Spain issued a decree "permitting thirty Spanish women" to accompany the third voyage of Christopher Columbus, "providing they intend to settle permanently" in the colonies. The intention of the Crown was to use Spanish women "of good birth"—a phrase that in practice meant of Spanish blood— to assist in the imposition of Spanish culture in the colonies and to populate the New World with children of *limpieza pura* (pure blood).[12] It was also hoped that the women would help to instill Spanish morality in the new colonies: Spanish women were to be married and live in "regular unions" in the eyes of state and church.

The women who came as brides for the *conquistadores*, the conquerors who had won undreamed-of wealth and vast lands for the Crown, were literally part of the reward: In their persons they represented the connection of the newly wealthy men to the highest nobility of Spain. Such was the fate of Doña Juana de Zuñiga, daughter of the Count of Aguilar, whose hand in marriage was given to Hernán Cortés by "the very Emperor himself."[13]

A second and equally important function of the Spanish woman was as a vehicle to display the fabulous wealth of her husband. A chronicler relates that "such a gallant courtier was he [Cortés] that the first jewel he lavished upon Doña Juana was an emerald, valued at 40,000 ducados."[14] The writer notes that the voyage to the Indies was often miserably uncomfortable and frightening for the women transported there but that "once established in the Indies, the climate and living requirements would give the fortunate women reason to indulge in ostentation and luxury." Her discomforts and misfortunes would be forgotten when she opened her jewelry chests and garbed herself in "scarlet silk, and plush and velvets."[15] Among the most valuable goods a high-born woman could bring with her were other women of Spanish birth as potential brides for the colonists: "Doña Beatriz de la Cueva, second wife of Pedro de Alvarado [who participated in the conquest of Mexico with Cortés and later conquered Guatemala], brought to Guatemala no less than twenty young ladies of good birth to marry."[16] The writer notes that it was unusual for so many young women to arrive with just one party but that "governors, judges and royal officials set sail from Spain with their own family, plus female cousins and nieces, who were subsequently married to caballeros of superior quality."[17]

The image of the first Spanish women in the Americas that emerges from these chronicles is of a spoiled, pampered creature dressed in heavy brocades and silks, laden with jewels, and elaborately coiffed, burdened with maintaining the stifling standards of the Spanish court in the steamy heat of Havana, circumscribed in her movements, proscribed in her behavior, and closely cloistered during her childbearing years. Such may have been the case for some, but the examination of individual experiences proves otherwise. Many of the young girls imported as brides led short, unhappy lives. Death in childbirth was not unusual, and sudden death from disease and by accident was common. An earthquake in Guatemala claimed the life of one; another bride was killed in an Indian uprising; drownings and loss at sea were frequent as the colonizers probed the seaways and rivers of the continent.

Moreover, although it is in the role of "civilizer" that the Spanish and Portuguese woman has usually been cast by historians—perhaps in the belief that women behaved the way the Crown intended them to—a closer look at the early contact period reveals women whose thirst for adventure and whose drive to find wealth and glory in the Americas was surely equal to that of their male comrades. Not a few of the women who married conquistadores survived to manage properties, govern municipal areas, and mount expeditions of their own.[18] Doña Beatriz de la Cueva outlived her husband to rule over the captaincy of Guatemala (using the device of an "advisory council" to legitimize her regime) and was so popular that "she conjured with her death greater public sentiment than her husband had with his."[19] The wife of Hernando De Soto "governed Cuba with decision," arming expeditions and dispatching provisions: "She was a woman of great knowledge and goodness and of very gentle judgement. . . . Later, she took a squadron to the Philippines with such rigor as has rarely been deployed by men of sea and war."[20]

A number of women also accompanied expeditions that were intended not only for purposes of exploration and conquest but for the purposes of establishing new settlements. Such was the expedition on which Isabel de Guevara and her husband set sail in 1535. Led by Pedro de Mendoza, the expedition was supposed to build a town on the estuary of the Rio de la Plata, thereby strengthening Spain's claims to an area also claimed by the Portuguese Crown. The hardships endured by the colonists were extreme: "The location chosen for Buenos Aires provided little of the necessities for Spanish colonization, least of all a settled Indian population."[21] The settlers were dependent on receiving food from Spain, a chancy and ultimately futile plan.

In her book *Women in Latin American History*, June Hahner quotes from a letter written by Isabel de Guevara asking the Spanish Crown for recompense for her service in saving the expedition from extinction: "So great was the famine that at the end of three months a thousand perished. . . . The men became so weak that the poor women had to do all their work. They had to wash the clothes and care for them when sick, to cook the little food they had; stand sentinel, care for the watch-fires and prepare the cross-bows when the Indians attacked, and even fire the petronels; to give the alarm, crying out with all our strength, to drill and put the soldiers in good order, for at that time we women, as we did not require so much food, had not fallen into the same state of weakness as the men."[22]

The outcome of a similar colonizing and exploratory expedition—in this case sent to reinforce Spain's claim to the Florida peninsula—also attests to the courage and endurance of the early female migrants to the Americas. In 1528, barely seven years after Cortés laid claim to Mexico, ten wives of Spanish soldiers accompanied the expedition of Panfilo de Naváez. On April 4, Naváez and three hundred soldiers went ashore at Tampa Bay, planning to rendezvous with the ships at a harbor farther north. The women, sailors, and one military guard spent the next twelve months reconnoitering the Gulf Coast before abandoning the search for the exploratory force. The ships then proceeded to the Mexican port of Veracruz, where the women, presuming themselves widowed, married the sailors and settled in Mexico.

The records of early European women in the Americas clearly indicate the presence of women whose courage, skills in activities from cooking to combat, spirit of adventure, and adaptability in the face of new, frequently dangerous situations bears little resemblance to the traditional image of the sheltered Spanish lady. That is perhaps an image that developed in later, more settled times. Also, most of the women who came were not "ladies"; they were not of noble birth. They, like the majority of men who came to America, came in search of land and treasure, adventure, and the hope of economic and social advancement to which they could not aspire in the highly structured society of sixteenth-century Iberia. In the Americas they could become *marquesas* and *condessas*; some, including Isabel de Guevara, lived to be social leaders, their less-than-wellborn origins overcome by the respectability conferred by marriage, religious conformity, and economic success—all of which was made possible for them by their Spanish blood, for in America these women joined their male counterparts in constructing and maintaining a social order based on racial distinctions.

The relative invisibility of the Spanish woman is tied up with the depiction of the years of initial contact as a "conquest," the heroes of which are the conquistadores, the male conquerors. The imagery of the "conquest of the Americas" is overwhelmingly sexual: the white Spanish male, in armor, on horseback, shooting firearms in the "virgin territory." The visible woman in these accounts is the Indian woman, beautiful, dark, supine, the fruit of the new Eden. The literal and metaphoric imagery is of rape. It was, in fact, to help combat this lusty and potentially chaotic situation, a situation that threatened to become wholly uncontrollable, that the Spanish Crown dispatched the first women to the colonies. Their purpose was clear and urgent, and it reinforced the mission of the Catholic church. In 1511, less than thirteen years after Columbus's first landfall in the Western Hemisphere, Don Diego Colón (a son of Christopher Columbus) arrived in Cuba "with his wife the Vicereine Maria de Toledo, niece of King Ferdinand, with a cohort of dueñas and daughters of nobles accompanying them" and "transformed in a moment the social life in the nascent island city."[23] It was the arrival of the Spanish women, with their nieces, maids, clothes, customs, that mandated the re-creation of European Spain in America. In Havana, Guatemala City, Caracas, Mexico City, they set up their households and bore their children of *limpieza pura*. They displayed the wealth of their husbands. They attended church and partook of the sacraments. And if some of them were less than conventional in their behavior or background, they were no less participants, whether coerced, unwitting, or enthusiastic, in the overall realization of the imperial project. The cross and the sword are the icons of Spain in America; perhaps the mantilla of the Spanish *doña* should be added.

The presence of the woman of African descent in the early stages of European exploration of the Americas is less remarked than that of either the Indian or Iberian woman. Yet the presence of Africans of both sexes in every region of Spanish and Portuguese America has been recorded: a story of individual men and women, both free and slave, who played a variety of roles in the New World.

The importation of forced immigrants from Africa accelerated rapidly in the sixteenth century as plantations were established in Brazil and Venezuela, eastern Mexico and Central America, and the islands of the Caribbean. The proportion of men to women brought from Africa to the Americas in slavery varied from region to region and over time as economies changed; in the Caribbean, according to some studies, men and women were imported in roughly equal numbers in the earliest years. In Brazil, the Portuguese, who dominated the African slave trade, preferred men as field hands; in the sixteenth and seventeenth centuries only about 10 percent of those imported into Brazil were women. In general, female slaves were found in larger concentrations in urban areas, working in households, or earning money for their owner as street vendors, wet nurses, or craftswomen and through the sale of sexual favors.

In comparison to the Indian woman and the Iberian woman, very little has been written about the African woman in the contact period. Her experience is subsumed in general histories of African slavery, which do not take gender into account. Recent studies, such as Marietta Morrisey's *Slave Women in the New World: Gender Stratification in the Caribbean*, illustrate the extent to which the female experience disappears in such blanket histories; Morrisey makes the point that "although it is clear that bondwomen's place varied in New World slavery, it was also consistently subordinated to that of both whites and male slaves."[24] The lands and nations of origin in Africa changed over time and were as diverse as were those of the Indian populations in America. For example, in the late colonial period the homeland of most of the Africans brought into Rio de Janeiro was West Central Africa. Mary Karasch writes of that region: "For centuries people in Central Africa had dealt with ethnic diversity, developed common religious traditions, and shared cultural forms."[25]

A detailed history of the contact period is outside the scope of the present study, but the salient point is that the economic systems established by European powers in the Americas were based on the forced labor of indigenous and African peoples. The social and political hierarchy that developed in colonial America placed the Iberian-born man and woman, known in Spanish America as *peninsulares* (those born in Portugal or Spain on the Iberian peninsula), at the apex of colonial government and society. Next came those who could claim "pure blood," that is, born in America but of Spanish or Portuguese lineage. Those born of Indian and Spanish heritage were mestizos, meaning of mixed racial heritage, and their social and political rank was usually determined by their economic clout and geographic locale. Similarly, in Brazil light-skinned Brazilians of mixed racial heritage might attain positions of relative economic well-being. The situation of indigenous peoples depended on the degree to which their communities survived or were destroyed by violence and disease, the extent to which they were corralled or coerced into the labor force, and the nature and locus of the work.[26] The vast majority of Africans in the Americas were brought in slavery to work the sugar plantations of the Caribbean and Brazil. Separated from their homelands and cultures, deliberately dispersed over vast areas on arrival, their situation was perilous in the extreme.

This schematic hierarchical social pyramid has been extensively used to describe colonial society in Latin America. It is a highly questionable vehicle of description, serving perhaps more to perpetuate old stereotypes than to shed light on complex human interactions in any given place or time. It does tell us how the Spanish and Portuguese colonists attempted to order and control their world, and it does give an indication of the extent to which perceived racial and ethnic origins reinforced social and political divisions and created a legacy of prejudice and bias. However, as Della Flushe and Eugene Korth state in *Forgotten Females: Women of African and Indian Descent in Colonial*

Chile, 1535–1800: "Throughout society, status depended not only on race but also on such disparate criteria as parentage, lifestyle, religious orthodoxy, freedom and bondage, occupation and income."[27]

The Colonial Period

In Latin American history, the colonial period indicates the three hundred years between the settlement of the Spanish and Portuguese in the Western Hemisphere in the early sixteenth century and the wars of independence in the early nineteenth century. Recent scholarship is revealing a whole new world of individual experience, of resistance and revolt by indigenous people, of the daily lives of a heterogeneous population over three centuries.[28] Here it is possible only to indicate the contours of the period in the broadest outline. One of the outstanding characteristics of the Spanish and Portuguese empires in the Americas was the swiftness with which Iberian institutions were established and forms of government, religion, and commerce adapted to fit the goal of extracting wealth from the land through the labor of the colonized peoples.

Although the substance of this introductory chapter is necessarily limited to introducing general impressions and concepts about colonial heritage of modern Latin America, it must be noted that recent research challenges many long-held preconceptions about the roles women played in colonial society. The image of the cloistered upper-class Iberian woman must be balanced against examples of the upper-class woman who actively participated in the economy by running large estates and overseeing complex familial business affairs. Similarly, the diverse historical experience of women of the lower economic sectors should not be subsumed in blanket assumptions that differentiate her life from that of her male counterpart only through her biology. In the close examination of the history of women in Latin America we can see that women's roles as defined by church and state often deviated from the ideal and that there is great variance from place to place and change over time.

The best-known woman of the colonial era is Sor Juana Inés de la Cruz (1648–1695), who is considered to be one of the greatest lyric poets ever to write in the Spanish language. Because of her status as a great woman, an exception, Sor Juana cannot be used as an "example" of women in colonial Latin America. But perhaps the point is that no single woman can be, whether she was a domestic slave of Afro-Brazilian heritage in Salvador, Brazil, an Aymara woman of the Bolivian Andes whose male kin were taken off by the Spanish to work the silver mines of Potosí, the mestiza wife of a cattle rancher in northern Mexico, or the illegitimate daughter of a Creole mother, as Sor Juana, born Juana Ramírez de Azbaje, was.

Sor Juana lived out her life in Mexico City, which was the intellectual center of Spanish colonial America in the seventeenth century. Mexico City was also the political and religious administrative center of the viceroyalty of New Spain, whose territories stretched from northern California to Central America. It was Sor Juana's fortune that, having shown an exceptional appetite for learning at an early age—she reportedly tagged along to an older sister's lessons and learned to read when she was three—her mother petitioned the viceregal court to take the girl under its protection. Doña Leonora Carreto, wife of the viceroy of New Spain, was delighted with the young prodigy's beauty and intellectual brilliance, and Juana lived under her patronage at the viceregal court from the age of thirteen to seventeen.

In seventeenth-century colonial Mexico there were but two respectable life choices for Creole women, marriage or the convent. Sor Juana clearly saw the difficulties and limitations placed on women within marriage; she also perceived the limitations of a convent life, but she chose the religious life as offering the possibility of more freedom to pursue her scholarship and writing. Of her decision, she wrote: "I became a nun, for although I knew that the religious state imposed obligations . . . most repugnant to my temperament, nevertheless, in view of my total disinclination to marriage, it was the least unbecoming and the most proper condition that I could choose to ensure my salvation."[29] Her first choice, to live alone, was not an alternative.

Sor Juana did encounter painful conflicts and repeated efforts by superiors to suppress her intellectual pursuits; at the same time, it is important to understand that the convents of Mexico City in that day were not necessarily cloistered. In his biography of Sor Juana, Mexican author and poet Octavio Paz writes, "Far from renouncing the world entirely, she convert[ed] her cell into a study filled with books, works of art and scientific instruments and transform[ed] the convent into a literary and intellectual salon. She wrote love poems, verses for songs and dance tunes, profane comedies, sacred poems, an essay in theology, and an autobiographical defense of the right of women to study and cultivate their minds. She became famous, saw her plays performed, her poems published, and her genius applauded in all the Spanish dominions, half the Western world."[30]

Two years before her death at the age of forty-seven, Sor Juana did renounce her intellectual life. She gave up her library, her literature, her worldly contacts, and undertook a course of self-immolation. In a weakened condition due to fasting and scourging, she fell victim to an epidemic while nursing stricken nuns in 1695. The enigma of her life has tantalized scholars. Why did she, at the peak of her intellectual power and fame, renounce the very work that seemed central to her being? What was the nature of her religious vocation? What was the nature of her personal relations with others, male and female, religious and secular? The first biography of Sor Juana was published in 1700 as a preface to a collection of her work. In the twentieth century, interest in her life and work, especially by feminist scholars, has produced fascinating readings of her writings and analyses of her life. For Spanish-American women intellectuals, she has been viewed as a *precursora*, a woman writer whose existence, albeit celebrated and exceptional, gives a gendered face to the historical record of literature in the Americas.[31] In this context, Sor Juana is important not only for her own genius but for representing the possibility that women could be geniuses.

The breadth and quality of Sor Juana's work commands attention in its own right; unlike the expressions of most women of her time it was not lost to posterity. Thus, as Emilie Bergmann has suggested, in Sor Juana's case the issue is not the rediscovery of her work or the restoration of reputation; it is to understand the conditions of her prestige and the ways in which she may be read.[32] The conditions of her prestige remind us of those, male and female, who might have possessed intellectual potential but who were not born where they could receive even a modicum of schooling, who did not secure royal patronage—even if that patronage meant being treated like an unusual pet (Bergmann uses the term "freak"). And it reminds us that women's lives were especially circumscribed by gender roles, which demanded that they commit themselves at an early age to the confines of marriage and childbearing or life in the church. The goal for women was self-effacement, not self-affirmation.

Despite her widespread fame during her lifetime, it is fortunate that any of Sor Juana's work is extant: she herself gave away her library and papers; what now exists was further reduced by the closure and reduction of religious institutions, including convents, during the Mexican reforms of the 1850s. As Paz puts it: "What survived the carelessness and venality of men fell victim to the mice." Among the known losses of Sor Juana's writings were a play, a treatise on morality, miscellaneous papers, and much of her correspondence.[33] Again, the precarious nature of the survival of the written record, which has served as the primary resource for historians attempting to understand how previous generations thought about themselves and their world, emphasizes the historical invisibility of those whose words and thoughts and deeds were not preserved or whose existence was recorded mainly by others. The rediscovery of these lost histories remains a moving force in women's history.

The history of women in colonial Latin America is a growing area of research that is contributing theoretical insights as well as new data to the understanding of the era. The central institutions of the colonial period were state, church, and family. The importance of the church in the lives of all women, especially white and middle-class mestiza women, cannot be overestimated. The Catholic church was the only institution that reached to every outpost of the colonial empires of Portugal and Spain and France. Its activities touched all classes: through conversion and in the rituals of life, through baptism, confirmation, marriage, burial. The church determined social mores and wielded enormous economic and political power.

However, when the history of the Catholic church in Latin America is ad-

dressed with women at the center of the question, the usual focus on the hierarchy of archbishops, bishops, Jesuits, Dominicans, lay brotherhoods, priests,
and friars shifts toward female congregants, nuns, *beatas*, convents, church-
sponsored beneficent societies, and the social control the church exerted over
many women's lives from birth to grave. The question of religion, asked with
the experience of the Latin America woman in mind, also gives rise to the
need to discuss dissident belief systems where women do hold power, from
the pre-Columbian Maya to the spiritist practices rooted in the African and
indigenous heritage of many Brazilians, Haitians, and Cubans. Much of this
research is only now being undertaken.

Additionally, church records have served as a major repository of information on the lives of colonial peoples. The essays in two pathbreaking collections on the history of colonial women, *Latin American Women: Historical
Perspectives* and *Sexuality and Marriage in Colonial Latin America*, both edited
by Asunción Lavrin, draw on the records of parishes and ecclesiastical courts,
as does Silvia Arrom's *The History of Women in Mexico City, 1790–1857*.[34] Arrom's
pioneering research, carried out in the 1970s, is a good example of using the
archival record to dispel stereotypes through the retrieval of concrete information about real women's lives. For example, she writes: "The most easily
refutable aspect of the stereotype of the traditional Latin American woman is
her isolation from economic activities."[35]

The examination of female occupations in colonial Latin America reveals
not only the broader economic patterns of different regions and communities but the importance of class, race, and gender in determining how people
lived their daily lives. With few exceptions, the work performed by women of
the upper classes during the colonial period was carried out within the home
or convent. Although the lives of some of the most economically privileged
women may have been largely idle, aside from their role in reproducing the
next generation, most women played an active part in the managing of their
households. Brazilian *donas de casa*, for instance, took pride in their ability to
manufacture elaborate sweetmeats with their own hands, as a cookbook published in Rio de Janeiro in 1832 attests. Housewives oversaw the production
of food and clothing and the purchase of household goods, as well as the care
and training of their children, particularly their daughters.

There is a long record of female entrepreneurs active in family businesses
as artisans and merchants in the administrative and commercial centers of the
colonies. Widows in particular carried out legal transactions and ran small
shops and businesses. In areas where settled agricultural populations had
thrived prior to the appearance of the Europeans, such as in the viceroyalties of Mexico and Peru, indigenous women were the main provisioners of
foodstuffs for the towns.

Throughout society, occupation was sharply determined by class, racial heritage, and geographic locus; however, within each economic level the kinds of jobs performed were often delineated by gender. Thus, in urban centers the overwhelming number of lower-class women, free or slave, were in domestic service or in occupations that paralleled those of housewives: seamstresses, laundresses, preparers and vendors of foods, midwives, and *curanderas*. In rural areas gender was also often a factor in determining the kinds of manual and field labor performed. In Brazil and Cuba, where the enslavement of Africans and their American descendants persisted well into the nineteenth century, men and women alike were harshly exploited; but men were preferred for heavy field labor, whereas women performed the tedious if less brutal tasks of hulling cotton, shelling nutmeg, hauling water, and sorting dross from ore.

Female work and occupation have attracted the attention of many scholars in the past decade. Though the colonial period is outside the purview of the present study, this brief overview may indicate the extent to which the once static-appearing colonial era is being brought to life by the new social history to provide an ever more accurate understanding of the ways in which our historical predecessors, female and male, lived out their lives in that time and place.

The Wars of Independence

Beginning with Haiti in 1804, Argentina in 1810, Colombia in 1819, Mexico, Peru, and Chile in 1821, and Brazil in 1822, the transition from colonial status to independence was marked by armed conflict and by political and economic turmoil. In retrospect the results of the wars were far from "revolutionary" for the vast majority of the population. An American-born ruling elite replaced the French, Spanish, and Portuguese elites in power, with little change in the welfare of those who worked the mines and fields and labored in the towns and villages. However, for those whose lives were played out in this transitional era (for example, a person born in central Mexico or Gran Colombia in 1790 and who died in 1830, a not unlikely life span for the time) the social and economic dislocation that resulted from the wars clearly had significance.

The wars of independence also represented a confrontation of political ideas. Two predominant strains of thought, which may be roughly characterized as conservative and liberal, dominated political debate. Conservatives defended the corporatist values of hierarchy, order, religious orthodoxy, and collective obligations to church and Crown, substituting the newly independent nation-state for the deposed imperial crown. Liberal leaders generally saw their own countries as backward in comparison to European states, and they looked to the political thought of the U.S. and French revolutions and the economic success of Great Britain as models. Political liberalism emphasized individual rights, anticlericalism, and Enlightenment values. In most of Latin America, the first half of the nineteenth century was marked by bitter civil discord, which often broke into open warfare over the issues of what group or man could claim legitimate authority to govern and whether that authority should rest in a strongly centralized government or a federal system wherein power was shared by state and local authorities. National boundaries among the newly emergent nations, only vaguely defined as divisions between imperial territories, viceroyalties, and captaincies in the colonial period, were also in dispute.

The hope for new forms of government necessitated the repudiation of the "detested emblems of colonialism"[36] by proponents of liberalism and conservatism alike. The place of women in the debates surrounding the formation of the new nations must be examined from two different points: the voices of individual women in the period and the documents that attempted to define woman's role in the national scheme. Women's allegiance was claimed by all: the church, the formative national governments, the federalists, the centralists.

The Wars of Independence had their heroes, from Toussaint L'Ouverture in Haiti and Simón Bolívar and José de San Martín in Spanish South America to Father Hidalgo in Mexico and Dom Pedro in Brazil, as numerous statues and portraits attest. But they also had their *heroinas*, who were immensely popular figures and whose exploits and courage have been immortalized in folktales as well as national histories. Often these women were martyrs, their stories told to inspire patriotism. Policarpa Salavarrieta (1795–1817) was publicly executed by the Spanish in 1817 for her role in the revolutionary cause in Gran Colombia. Nicknamed "La Pola," the tale of her bravery and the calumny of the Spanish in killing the young woman resulted in a successful uprising against the Spanish official who gave the orders for her death.[37]

Leopoldina, the wife of Dom Pedro I, played a central part in the design of the Brazilian separation from Portugal, an independence movement notable for its relative bloodlessness. Leopoldina may be more aptly described as a true hero than as a *heroina*, for though she was a well-known and well-liked figure, her influence over policy places her among the leadership in the revolutionary period.[38]

Heroinas generally emerged from the popular classes, and in addition to such figures as La Pola, whose martyrdom was given particular weight because of her femininity, there were also women who donned men's clothing in order to take up arms. The best-known such heroine in Brazil was Maria Quiteira de Jesus. Born in the interior of the state of Bahia on a small cattle and cotton-raising ranch, she was trained from childhood in the use of firearms as well as in the intricacies of weaving and spinning. She described her decision to join the patriot armies to Maria Graham.[39] At the beginning of the wars an emissary seeking recruits visited their ranch and told of "the greatness and the riches of Brazil, and the happiness to which it might attain if independent. He set forth the long and oppressive history of Portugal; and the meanness of submitting to be ruled by so poor and degraded a country."[40] Maria Quiteira told Maria Graham, "I felt my heart burning in my breast."[41] Maria Quiteira's father declared that he was too old to go to war, that he had no sons to send, and that he would not send a slave in his place, "For what interest had a slave to fight for the independence of Brazil?"[42] Maria Quiteira, however, took matters into her own hands and fled to the home of a married sister. Her sister helped her disguise herself as a young man, and she succeeded in joining the troops. She distinguished herself in battle, and in 1823 she was decorated by the new emperor of Brazil. A portrait of Maria Quiteira shows her in the full uniform of one of the emperor's battalions, cockaded hat on her head, medal on her chest, musket resting in her hands, with a kilt secured around her waist. She explained to Maria Graham that she had adopted the kilt from a picture of a highlander, as "the most feminine military dress."[43]

In every country, women combatants were noted. Simón Bolívar, who is known as "The Liberator of South America," lauded the "Amazons" of Gran Colombia in 1813. In Haiti bondswomen took part in the initial revolt of 1791; Marie Jeanne a-la-Crete-a-Pierrot and Victoria, who commanded troops and was known as "Toya," are two women whose names have survived. In the decade of fighting that ensued, women were omnipresent. Henriette St. Marc was among the rebels executed by the French in 1802 when they retook the island.[44] Tales of women's heroism and patriotism were used to inspire support for the patriot cause. A typical story of female patriotism was told of a nun in Bahia, Brazil, who sheltered rebel troops in the convent by placing herself at the threshold and declaring that the loyalist troops must kill her before they could enter the consecrated grounds. According to the story, the loyalist troops were abashed and turned away.

Although the tales of women warriors and spies, of women who tore up their ball gowns to make tricolored flags to carry into battle,[45] had an immediate contemporary purpose, it is also significant that such stories have been used by women over time to make the point that women fought on the right side of events in the wars of independence: against the colonial powers of France, Portugal, and Spain and for the right to national self-government. Recovery and reiteration of the distinct forms of women's participation in the wars of independence has held particular meaning for women active in the women's movements from the late nineteenth century to the present. The information on the participation of women in the Haitian revolution is taken from an essay written in 1984 for the volume *Sisterhood Is Global* to demonstrate the female presence in the anticolonial struggles of Haiti. The iconography of women participating in the wars of independence is a means of inscribing women in history as actors and precursors of latter-day female political activists. For example, the statue built to commemorate the role of Josefa Ortíz de Dominguez in the Mexican revolution of 1810, which stands in the Plaza de Santo Domingo in Mexico City, became an icon for women claiming their right to full citizenship in the 1950s. If women had fought for independence, they deserved the right to vote and to be elected.

Such an argument was in fact made at the time of independence. A petition written in 1824 to the government of Zacatecas, Mexico, states: "Women also wish to have the title of citizen . . . to see themselves counted in the census as 'La ciudadana H . . . La ciudadana N.'"[46] Mexican historian Elias Amador further records that in the immediate postindependence period "the people [*las poblaciones*] asked for assistance, supported with pledges from the townships, to break up the detested emblems of colonial domination, placing power [literally, *el fusil*, the gun] in the hands of the worker and the campesino in order to make them into soldiers of the patria and the State, and hasten our daring footsteps along the path of progress. No one wishes to be last in this important and sweeping advance. Even the woman, that angel of the hearth, that blessed benefactress of the family, who has been forgotten, vilified, proscribed from the temple of knowledge by regressive and freedom-killing [*liberticides*] tendencies, does not wish to be without some part in the great feast of a people redeemed."[47]

Amador has infused his retelling of the desire of women—and campesinos and workers—to be counted as citizens with the sensibilities and rhetoric of the Mexican Revolution of 1910. But the original petitions to the government of Zacatecas in the immediate postindependence period more closely echoed the ideals of the French Revolution, including the image of the citizen-soldier. In Flora Tristán's words: "Then came the Revolution of 1789 . . . serfs and peasants are to be called citizens. Finally they proclaimed the rights of man in full national assembly. What happened to the proletariat is a good omen for women when their '1789' rings out."[48]

The exuberant expectations expressed in the Zacatecas petitions and elsewhere faded quickly. The political openings created by the wars of independence closed down as power struggles became localized. The constitutions of the new states primarily ensured that the control of resources and governmental power would pass to an American-born elite: the Rights of Man pertained to men of property. Women's legal status would continue to be determined through her relationship to the male head of household, her de facto status defined through her social and economic locus, marital status, ethnic heritage, and place of residence, among other factors. Mention of women in the new constitutions was mainly referential, reflecting their dependent role.

The constitution of Bolivia, written in 1826 under the guidance of Simón

Bolívar, may serve as an example. Bolivians are "all who are born in the territory of the republic."[49] Closer examination of the constitution reveals that the generic "all" (in Spanish the generic is indicated by the masculine plural form, *todos*) includes women when referring to whom laws apply but excludes them when defining who may exercise the rights of a free citizen. Women are envisioned as the mothers and wives of Bolivian citizens but are not themselves citizen-voters; citizenship may be claimed by those born to Bolivian women and foreigners married to Bolivian women. As was true in the other Spanish-American republics, the publication of the new constitution marked the legal end of slavery; in theory, the category of citizen included all former slaves. However, indirect elections, literacy requirements, and specifications of employment ("excepting those subject to another in the capacity of a domestic servant") effectively limited the electorate to white and mestizo males. These requirements, though not couched in terms of gender or ethnicity, excluded virtually the entire indigenous population as well as women of all social and economic backgrounds.

The final constitutional clause defining Bolivian citizenship stated: "Citizens are, first, the liberators of the republic."[50] This was the basis on which women staked their claim to inclusion in the national project in the immediate postindependence period. The numerous tales of female patriotism, written during the wars with an eye to rousing enthusiasm for the cause of independence, were used in the early nineteenth century as evidence that women should be citizens. And it should be noted that such claims were not limited to women of the political elite.

For some women, as for many men, the circumstances of war and disruption of the prevailing order offered opportunities for greater personal freedom. The story of Manuela Saénz offers one example of a woman who seized the opportunity of the wars to cast aside social conventions and seek adventure and romance. Inscribed in history as "La Libertadora del Libertador" (Liberator of the Liberator), Saénz was a mistress of Simón Bolívar, and it is because of her liaison with him that her story was preserved. Moreover, because she was the illegitimate daughter of a mestiza mother and a Spanish father, her life story was construed by patriotic writers to illustrate the resentments and frustrations felt by the American-born against the haughty *peninsulares*. A biographer writes of an early escapade in her life, when she ran away from her convent school with a Spaniard: "This love, which would have seemed everything to the young Manuelita, did not last long; like her mother, she was abandoned by the Spaniard, by the hated member of the dominant race, who found it so easy in America to leap the barriers which in Spain protected the honor and dignity of peninsular women."[51]

The Wars of Independence were particularly bloody and hard-fought in northern South America as Spain sought to retain control of the viceroyalty of

New Granada, which included the present nations of Venezuela, Colombia, and Ecuador. As Evelyn Cherpak points out in her article, "The Participation of Women in the Independence Movement in Gran Colombia, 1730–1830,"[52] women participated in the struggle as combatants, spies, and nurses, through donations of jewelry and funds and supplies of every kind, and through commitment to the cause. In Caracas and the other urban centers, women hosted and attended salons where "ideas of independence and revolution were discussed."[53] It was at such an event that Manuela Saeñz, who had gained a measure of respectability through marriage to a British doctor, met Simón Bolívar.[54] Their subsequent liaison lasted throughout the battles, as their letters, preserved as part of Bolívar's voluminous correspondence, attest.

In subsequent patriotic histories, Manuela Saeñz's bold commitment to Bolívar, her public flaunting of their adulterous affair, and her defiance of the social conventions of her station in life are excused because of her equally passionate commitment to the revolutionary cause: "Because Manuela Saeñz was above all an American, innocent but enslaved, then in her blood, in her history and in her memory, lies the drama of an America whose time had come. She was one of those who rose, vital and energetic and powerful, on the horizon of the American Continent."[55]

As was apparent in the constitution of Bolivia cited above, Simón Bolívar's appreciation of female support during the wars of independence did not extend to envisioning women as full citizens in the newly independent nations. Cherpak cites a letter from Bolívar to his favorite sister, Maria Antonia, written after the close of the wars in 1826, as an example of his attitude: "I warn you not to mix in political business nor adhere to or oppose any party. Let opinion and things go along although you believe them contrary to your way of thinking. A woman ought to be neutral in public business. Her family and her domestic duties are her first obligations."[56] Bolívar's attitude is emblematic of that of men of his time and class. At the close of the wars of independence, when American-born patriots took political power, it is clear that some women did aspire to fuller participation in the affairs of the new nations for which they had fought and sacrificed. What happened is that upper- and middle-class women especially were encoded into the polity as mothers of future citizens of the republic. To ensure that women could properly fulfill this mission, the emergent nations turned their attention to the idea of educating them.

3. Women and Education in Latin America

The examination of the education of women in a given time and place provides a vivid indicator of what women's proper roles in the larger society are perceived to be and of how those roles—economic, intellectual, cultural, social, political—differ from or coincide with those of the women's male peers. First, to properly measure who in a society was educated and who was not, we must understand what was meant by education in a particular time and place. Then we may ask how access to special kinds of education differed for socioeconomic groups and for women and men within those matrices.

Female teachers, who are overwhelmingly the teachers of young women in Latin America, come from two distinct traditions: that of the *normalista* (the woman trained in normal, or teaching, schools) and nuns and lay members of Catholic female teaching orders. In each country the history of public female education is intimately linked with attempts to secularize, or modernize, the state. Thus, in midnineteenth-century Mexico, Benito Juárez's government, which sought to weaken the church, passed legislation providing for public secondary schools for girls; in Argentina, Domingo Sarmiento and the Liberals placed the training of female teachers near the top of their national agenda—a move that incited furious opposition from Catholic female teaching and nursing orders, who regarded education and health care as their domain.

In addition, there is a strong correlation between the advent of public female education, the appearance of *normalistas*, and the rise of feminism in certain Latin American nations. At the end of the nineteenth century in Argentina, Uruguay, Chile, Brazil, Mexico, and Cuba

. . . it was the female school teachers who formed the nucleus of the first women's groups to articulate what may be defined as a feminist critique of society. Two factors are of great importance: First, the teachers represented a new group in Latin American society, the educated middle sector, which included skilled workers, clerks, and government employees, as well as educators, and they were well aware of their precarious social, economic and legal status; second, these women were in touch with one another through their training institutions and through a number of *congresos femininos* which took place in this era from Mérida in the Yucatán to Buenos Aires in Argentina.[1]

The story of the education of women in Latin America consists of three interwoven strands: first, the history of the idea of educating females; second, the debate over what the content of that education should be; and third, the establishment of educational institutions that admitted females.

The nature of a society's attitude toward the education of its women tells us much about what women's proper roles in that society are perceived to be. In colonial Iberian America, girls of the upper classes were destined for marriage; intellectual attainment was deemed irrelevant if not antithetical to the achievement and fulfillment of that destiny. However, in practice, a number of factors served to ameliorate this situation. Equally as important a component of the image of the ideal woman was her piety, which required that she receive at least a modicum of religious instruction. The quality and extent of that instruction varied: Was it by rote, or was literacy a component? Was instruction given in the home by tutor, in which case the quality of education was dependent on the qualifications of the individual tutor, or was it received in a convent or private school?

A second ameliorating factor was the perception of a young girl's family as to what her role as an adult would truly be, not just what it would ideally be. Many colonial brides were also destined to become widows, and the ability to read and write contracts, to make wills, to figure and plan the allocation of property and resources, to oversee the education of their children, as well as to run their households, was critical to the survival, not to mention the enhancement, of the family fortunes.

Before considering what educational opportunities were available to women, a brief overview of the general state of education in the colonies is in order. Intellectual patterns in the Iberian colonies were closely attuned to those in the Catholic countries of Europe, and most people, male or female, did not receive any formal education. Churchmen and churchwomen made up the largest educated class, and it was the religious orders that provided teachers and supported educational institutions. In colonial Latin America, the great male teaching orders—first the Dominican and later the Jesuit—were instrumental in the founding of institutions for the education of the sons of the Creole elite. In the early colonial period, schools were also established for sons of Indian leaders, with the intention of promoting religious conversion among the indigenous population. By the end of the colonial period, partly as a consequence of the expulsion of the Jesuit order from the colonies and partly in response to the ideas of the Enlightenment, religious influence on education lessened.

Spanish concern with education is reflected in the early establishment of institutions of higher education: The first university in the Americas was founded in 1538 on the island of Santo Domingo; in 1551 universities were established in Mexico City and Lima. The university consisted of faculties of arts, law, medicine, and theology, and curricula in the liberal arts included the study of mathematics, Latin, logic, rhetoric, physics, and metaphysics; in some institutions the leading indigenous languages were taught. By the end of the colonial period twenty institutions of higher learning and numerous *colegios*, or preparatory schools, existed in Spanish America for young men.

The situation in Portuguese America was somewhat different. Between 1550 and 1700 the Jesuits were successful in establishing over a dozen *colegios* in Brazil, but the intellectual center of the Portuguese empire was the University of Coimbra, situated some two hundred miles from Lisbon, in Portugal itself. Coimbra was founded in 1209 and revitalized in the sixteenth century by the flow of wealth from Portugal's holdings in Africa, India, Asia, and the Americas, and it was there that the ruling families of Brazil sent their sons. The practice of sending young men to the metropolis to be educated ensured a cohesiveness and cosmopolitanism among the Brazilian elites; it also effectively restricted education to a handful of privileged males.

To pose Virginia Woolf's question, "What if Shakespeare had a sister?"[2] in an Iberian colonial context, we could take two siblings, perhaps born to a wealthy sugar baron in the capital city of Salvador de Bahia, of equal social and economic background and equal intellectual potential. The children would first be tutored at home, which confers rudimentary literacy. At age ten, the brother begins to attend the *colegio*; the sister's formal education ends. At age fifteen or sixteen the brother goes to Coimbra to complete his studies and travels to Lisbon, Paris, and London before returning home. At age fifteen the sister is married; at age sixteen she is a mother. For the next twenty years her energies will be consumed in childbirth, her sphere of action limited to her household.

In Woolf's parable the disparity of opportunity between the siblings is complete, the stifling of any potential female Shakespeare vividly illustrated. However, the fact that women did not have access to institutions of higher education should not be used to imply a blanket indifference on the part of Iberian society to the training and instruction of its women.

New research, notably by Luis Martín in his book on women in colonial Peru, *Daughters of the Conquistadores*, has shown that as early as the midsixteenth century public concern about the education of young women existed: what it should consist of, who should impart it, who should receive it. Feminine religious orders arrived early in New Spain and Peru, and the first convents were established in Mexico and Lima by the midsixteenth century. Soon thereafter special papal dispensations were sought and granted to bring female teaching orders, such as the French Order of St. Anne's, to the colonies. Martín writes, "In colonial Peru, there was a widespread interest in, and at times an almost obsessive concern with, the training and education of young women. Kings, viceroys, governors, city fathers, families, and public and private agencies showed that interest and concern at one time or another during the three hundred years of colonial rule." The evidence amassed by Martín in support of this conclusion presents a fascinating picture of "the existence and nature of female education in the Spanish viceroyalty."[3]

Ideas concerning what should constitute female education evolved considerably between the sixteenth and eighteenth centuries. The education of young Isabella of Castille in preparation for her role as queen had excited lively discussion in fifteenth-century Spain; in the sixteenth, the medieval cult of Mary, or marianism, prescribed the feminine ideal: pious, chaste, protected. These values were germane to two treatises on the education and training of women in the period, *De Instrucione feminae Christianae* by Luis Vives and *La perfecta casada* by Fray Luis de Leon, which offered prescriptive formulas for the education of the Christian woman and defined the sphere of the virtuous wife, respectively.[4] Education, for both men and women of the period, was intended to instill aesthetic and moral values; it was not designed with professional specialization or the mastery of a specific body of facts in mind.

In colonial Lima, high-ranking colonial officials and well-to-do landowners with residences in the capital city enrolled their daughters in convent schools. These young ladies received religious instruction, which usually imparted literacy, and studied music (for which the Conventos Grandes were renowned), French, embroidery, and perhaps the rudiments of mathematics. Schooling ended for most at about the age of thirteen, when the daughters of the elite were considered marriageable. If the young woman chose a religious vocation, she might, depending on the order she entered, continue to expand her intellectual horizons. Members of the female religious orders, like their male counterparts, constituted the most highly educated sector of colonial society.

Throughout the colonial period, in all of the viceregal capitals and larger centers of population, there were also schools dedicated to the instruction of the children of the poor. These too were under the auspices of the Catholic church, and girls were taught by nuns or laywomen attached to a female religious order. In educational character the charitable schools for girls reflected a more "practical" version of the education offered to the young ladies: moral and religious instruction, often imparted by rote rather than through reading and writing, and training in various domestic skills, such as sewing, cooking, and personal hygiene.

The purpose of the instruction of women, of whatever class, was to prepare them for their future roles in society: the well-born as wives and mothers or nuns and the poor as properly trained servants. In this, female education paralleled that of males. Literacy and intellectual attainment were not requisites for material or spiritual success in colonial society for either sex; for most of the population any kind of education other than the instruction that might occur as part of religious conversion was deemed irrelevant.

The difference in access to formal education for female citizens of Spanish America and of Portuguese America reflects the contrast in opportunity for their male counterparts, with the caveat that the dearth of institutions outside the family that were available for the education of young Brazilian women was even greater than that for the Brazilian man. Female religious orders, which provided a nucleus of literate women and schools for girls in the viceregal capitals of Spanish America, were prohibited in Brazil until the eighteenth century. The reason for the royal prohibition of convents underlines the officially desired role for white women in Portuguese America: marriage and childbearing. It was not so much the fear of educating women—conventual instruction was designed to produce proper and pious women, not intellectual rebels—it was the fear that upper-class white women, who were scarce, might choose a life of seclusion, thus depriving the colony of their persons, as well as of the monies and properties that made up their doweries.[5]

The patterns for female education established in the colonial period, that of the private, usually Catholic, education of the daughters of the privileged classes and the moral and vocational instruction of the daughters of the poor, usually provided by Catholic charitable societies, persisted in nearly all areas of Latin America throughout the nineteenth century. The private education of the elite woman continues today in many countries; the vocational instruction of the lower-class woman is more apt to be under the auspices of the state.

The intellectual ferment that marked the period of the wars of independence included the discussion of the "rights of man," and Latin American women intellectuals joined their North American, British, and French sisters in expanding the debate to the rights of women. The passion for republican ideals and the increased secularization of the institutions of society, including schools and universities, raised the level of debate on the merits of female education to the national level in Argentina, Chile, Brazil, Uruguay, and Mexico. However, little was done to implement reform in the first half of the nineteenth century.

The wars of independence had a significant intellectual dimension, fostered in the secret meetings of the Freemasons and in the discussions of newly founded scientific societies. Although women were generally barred from these masculine enclaves, they did participate in the discussion of ideas and current politics in the salons of Mexico City, Lima, Caracas, and Rio de Janeiro. In the aftermath of the independence movements some changes occurred in formal education. The first was the decline in clerical control of education, a trend begun with the expulsion of the Jesuit teaching order in the 1760s and intensified in the secular climate of the wars of independence, a struggle in which the hierarchy of the colonial church sided with the mother country. Female teaching orders were not expelled from the colonies, but their political sympathies in general had also allied them with the Spanish and Portuguese loyalists; at the dawn of the national period, patriots looked to private dame schools rather than convents for the instruction of their daughters.

A second trend was the establishment of national universities, a move in keeping with the ideals set forth in the constitutions of the new Spanish American republics. The universities at Buenos Aires (1821), Montevideo (1833), Santiago de Chile (1842), and those of El Salvador, Costa Rica, and Honduras date from this postrevolutionary period, as do the faculties of medicine and law in Brazil. In Mexico, which already possessed a central university, a number of state institutions, most of which offered a bachelor of law degree, were inaugurated. Women were excluded from these formal institutions of learning, which were intended as training grounds for the American-born male elite; however, the result of the broadening of the educated public, even though relatively slight, created a climate in which the subject of educating women could be broached.

Many of the constitutions of the newly independent countries contained articles that proclaimed the state's responsibility to create and support public education at all levels, as did Chile's (1833), which provided that "education is one of the subjects of primary importance of the states." The Brazilian constitution, drafted in 1822, declared the commitment of the nation to the education of children of both sexes, although this clause was deleted from the constitution imposed by the Emperor Dom Pedro in 1823. In Mexico the constitution of 1822 declared elementary education free, and a nascent public education system for the children of the poor was instituted, employing the "Lancastrian" method, where more advanced pupils taught younger students.[6]

However, as has often been noted, these constitutions were more statements of the aspirations of the national leadership than programs that could be immediately put into practice. Even the long-established educational institutions struggled to survive in the political turmoil and economic disruption of the postwar period, which absorbed the attention of the leaders and the scarce resources of the societies.

The Brazilian independence movement differed in many important respects from that of its Spanish, French, and British neighbors in the Americas, and so did the intellectual environment that evolved in the former Portuguese colony. In 1808, as the troops of Napoleon entered Lisbon, the royal family of Portugal, the Braganças, fled to Brazil. From 1808 to 1821, Rio de Janeiro was the seat of the Portuguese empire, an occurrence unique in the history of the Americas. Prior to the arrival of the court Brazil had been regarded, not unjustly, as an intellectual backwater. The court introduced the first printing press to the colony, an instrument long available in the Spanish colonial capitals of Mexico, Havana, and Lima. The Portuguese regent, Dom João VI, opened his considerable library to the Brazilians; experimental botanical gardens were established, and, most important, the ports of Brazil were opened for the first time to non-Portuguese ships. The diplomatic envoys, explorers, and travelers who came included artists, scientists, and writers from all over the Western world.[7]

Brazilian women—and men—had a highly visible model of a well-educated woman in their midst: the Empress Leopoldina, daughter of Francis I of Austria and wife of Dom Pedro, heir to the Portuguese throne. As a young woman in the Hapsburg court, Leopoldina (1797–1826) was "fascinated by the natural sciences, mathematics, history, and travel literature; she collected coins and medals, studied insects, plants and animals, read widely, and learned to converse in ten languages. Leopoldina's Vienna was the Vienna of Haydn, Beethoven and Mozart and [she] absorbed a love of music from the air she breathed."[8]

Leopoldina arrived in Brazil in 1817, and in 1822, working closely with José Bonifácio de Andrade y Silva, "The Architect of Brazilian Independence," was instrumental in persuading her husband to place himself at the head of the Brazilian independence movement. Leadership of the Brazilian independence movement by a scion of the royal house of Bragança ensured that Brazil, in contrast to its Spanish-American neighbors, would choose a more conservative political structure; in 1823, Brazil became a constitutional monarchy, ruled by Dom Pedro I. Leopoldina, already widely popular with Brazilians, was hailed as a heroine of the independence movement.

Leopoldina died of puerperal fever in 1826. Though her death was a consequence of afterbirth infections, which killed many women, it was perceived by the public to be a consequence of the ill-treatment accorded her by her husband, who had flaunted his amorous adventures and illegitimate offspring at court. Leopoldina did not live to oversee the education of her children, but her son Pedro de Alcantara, who reigned as emperor of Brazil from 1840 to 1889, inherited her love of learning.

The spirit of patriotism and the need to educate a new generation of American-born citizens for leadership of the independent states, whether republics or constitutional monarchies, inspired the establishment of the national universities noted above. The institutions may have restricted entry to the sons of the new political elites, but the spread of revolutionary ideals was not so restricted. In the United States, women were using the rhetoric of "liberty, equality and the rights of man" to call for the education of "the daughters of the republic."[9]

That similar challenges were being raised in the Latin American states is illustrated in the writings of Nisia Floresta Brasileira Augusta. Born in Rio Grande do Sul in 1810, she assumed her patriotic pseudonym (which translates to Nisia of the Majestic Brazilian Forest) at the age of twenty. Her well-to-do family encouraged Nisia to study with the tutors provided for her brothers in their home and in 1832 subsidized the publication of her translation into Portuguese of Mary Wollstonecraft's *Rights of Women*. The reception of the work was such that a second edition was put out a year later by a press in Pernambuco.

Nisia married but continued her activities as a writer and also instructed young girls in her home. Her articles on the education of women include "Advice to My Daughter" (1842), "The Complete Young Woman" (1847), and a collection of articles published in the journal *O Liberal*. Dona Nisia's concern with women's education was shared by other Brazilian women, and a number of articles devoted to the topic appeared between 1840 and 1850: "A Voyage to Parnassus: Education of the Woman" by Anna Barboza de Lossio e Silbitz; "The Education of Girls" (1849) by Anna Eugenia Lopes de Cadaval, and the *Jornal das Senhoras*, edited by Anna Edeltrudes de Menezes, which published works by women as well as works about women. In this period many women also established private seminaries for young women; their efforts bore fruit in the next generation. In the 1840s, in Brazil as in Mexico, the call was not for higher education for women but for the establishment of primary schools.

The prolonged political struggle that plagued the republics of the Rio de la Plata in the early national period had profound consequences for the education of women. In 1810, Buenos Aires was an increasingly prosperous commercial center with close ties to the capitals of Europe, circumstances that created an economic and intellectual climate receptive to the ideas of the Enlightenment. Liberal reformer Bernardino Rivadavia raised the issue of women's status in society and, as minister of government in 1823, established the Society of Beneficence, which was charged with the establishment and administration of a public elementary school system for girls.[10]

Whether or not this initial step toward quasi-public (funding was to be privately provided) education for women would have resulted in a broader commitment to that goal became a moot point in the ensuing years of internecine warfare. Argentina's famous "Generation of 1837," whose members spent the years of Juan Manuel Rosas's regime (1838–1852) in exile, returned to Argentina after 1852 fired with enthusiasm for creating a public educational system that would include both men and women.

Domingo F. Sarmiento, who later became Argentina's most outstanding educational reformer, was among the exiles. Settling first in Chile, he eked out a living as a schoolmaster and in 1842 was appointed director of a newly established teacher-training institution in Santiago, the first of its kind in South America. In 1845 the Chilean government sent him on a mission to study educational practices in Europe and the United States, a three-year sojourn during which he established a close relationship with Horace and Mary Mann, the parents of American public education. From his contact with the Manns and their colleagues, Sarmiento became convinced that governmentally supported free public schools would transform Argentina into a prosperous, civilized nation. During his tenure as president of Argentina (1868–1874) Sarmiento put his ideas into practice.

The early years of independence in Mexico were as strife-torn as in Argentina, and not until the 1840s did school enrollments actually exceed those of the late colonial period. Silvia Arrom writes that in 1838, 3,280 girls were registered in eighty-two convent, parish, municipal, and private institutions in Mexico City. But in the 1840s and 1850s primary school enrollment doubled, with girls and boys attending in roughly equal numbers. Arrom also traced a rise in female literacy in this period by examining the number of women who were able to sign their names to legal documents versus the number of men able to do so (Table 1). Although this survey was perforce limited to propertied members of society, this was also the group most likely to have had access to education in this era.[11]

At midcentury several patterns are visible in female education in the larger Latin American states. First, as had been true during the colonial era, most formal education had a significant religious content. Young women of the upper classes might be tutored at home or might attend a convent school, where the course of instruction was likely to stress accomplishment in the *belles artes*, such as an acquaintance with French, a little musical training in voice or piano, sketching, fine needlework, and religious instruction.

In addition, female charitable societies sponsored schools for female orphans and children of the poor. In Argentina all public education for girls was under the auspices of the Society of Beneficence. In Brazil in 1870, the Society for the Propagation of Instruction of the Working Classes celebrated the opening of a new school in Rio de Janeiro with premises spacious enough to allow separate classrooms for boys and for "the other sex," as girls are consistently referred to in the records. The school was free, and another charitable organization, Protectoresses of the Children of the Poor, provided uniforms and school materials. Similar societies, many with church affiliations, carried on comparable activities in Mexico, Colombia, Venezuela, and Peru. As was true in the colonial period, the charitable schools for girls emphasized training in household skills that would prepare them for domestic service.

The impetus for dramatic reform in the content, availability, and quality of female education—an impetus that in the twentieth century became the drive

Table 1. *Illiteracy Among Mexico City Will-Makers, 1802–1855*

	Females		Males	
Period	No. in sample	No. illiterate	No. in sample	No. illiterate
1802–03	100	20	100	0
1825–27	100	17	100	1
1853–55	100	13	100	1

Source: Silvia Marina Arrom, *The Women of Mexico City, 1790–1857* (Stanford, Calif.: Stanford University Press, 1985) 22.

for universal education—came not from the socially elite women nor from the charitable schools they established but from the women of the emergent middle sectors. These reform-minded women were urban and tended to be the wives and daughters of professional men: lawyers, doctors, magistrates, professors. Their appearance in Buenos Aires, Santiago, Rio de Janeiro, and Mexico in the 1860s and 1870s is directly proportionate to the degree of political stability and economic expansion attained by these societies by the late nineteenth century. Conversely, in the societies in which small oligarchies continued to exercise exclusive economic and political power and in areas where political instability was the norm, such as Bolivia, Ecuador, and the Central American states, there was little interest in educational reform.

The medium of expression for social criticism was the periodical. In Brazil, for example, as abolitionist and republican sentiments reached a crescendo in the 1870s, there were some 250 papers and journals in print, and though most of them issued from the major urban centers, no region was without its own. The numerous articles written by women represented the whole spectrum of Brazilian political thought, from monarchist to republican, and ranged in subject matter from romantic poetry to advice on childbirth; however, one theme was common to the women's articles: the commitment to education for women. Education is presented as the sine qua non, the road to greater control over their lives, in both domestic and political spheres.

An excellent example of the spirit of the women's writings is evident in the following passage from *O Sexo Feminino*, which was published intermittently in Rio de Janeiro between 1873 and 1889. It was dedicated to the principles of education for women and to the elimination of all forms of slavery in Brazil: "It is to you [*Os Senhores*, the masculine form] that is owed our inadequacy; we have intelligence equal to yours, and if your pride has triumphed it is because our intelligence has been left unused. From this day we wish to improve our minds; and for better or worse we will transmit our ideas in the press, and to this end we have *O Sexo Feminino*; a journal absolutely dedicated to our sex and written only by us. *Avante, minhas patricias!* The pen will be our weapon."[12]

A brief profile of the editor of *O Sexo Feminino*, Dona Francisca Senhorinha da Motta Diniz, gives an idea of the social and economic background of these literate women. She was married to a lawyer and widowed at a young age; in 1873 she became the directress of a school for girls in the province of Minas Gerais, where she inaugurated her journal. In 1874 she moved to Rio de Janeiro, continued publishing *O Sexo Feminino*, and became headmistress of a secondary school for young women. Motta Diniz had numerous counterparts in Cuba, Mexico, Argentina, Chile, and Uruguay.

The efforts of these early reformers resulted in the establishment of a number of primary schools and a few secondary schools for young women, but the effect for most women in most places of Latin America was negligible. By and large, education remained within the domain of the church and was restricted to a small sector of the population, the majority of whom were male. The more important contribution of these *precursoras* was in creating a more receptive atmosphere toward the idea of educating women.

It was the introduction of the government-supported normal school that broadened and strengthened the move to educate a larger sector of the population, male and female. From their inception normal schools were overwhelmingly female institutions, although a few should be noted as being among the first coeducational institutions in Latin America. Many were reserved solely for women students (who were identified from the first as "natural teachers") so that girls from good families would be attracted to them. Normal school students were drawn from the newly emergent middle classes; in the societies of the Southern Cone many of them were the children of European immigrants. Teacher training schools were also open to men, but young men of this emergent middle class had job opportunities in industry, commerce, banking, government, the military, higher education—realms from which young women were excluded. The normal schools offered girls a chance to acquire an education for themselves and a respectable, if poorly remunerated, profession teaching primary school children. In nations where this emergent class did not exist, such as Peru, normal school programs had few advocates and no constituency. The presence or absence of educational opportunities for women in a society provides a valid litmus test of the extent of social change that society has experienced.

Several factors combined to favor these new secular institutions in societies where education had traditionally been under the auspices of the Catholic church. One was the exemplary pace of economic growth and industrialization being enjoyed by the United States, where public education was widespread. A second factor was the gradual change in public opinion about the value of an educated society, male and female. Less tangible but significant was the belief that the New World experiments in political democracy, whatever their present imperfections, offered the opportunity to build better societies than had previously existed and that an educated citizenry was essential to the realization of this ideal.

Although there were parallel movements in Chile, Uruguay, Brazil, and

Mexico, the most famous normal school program was carried out in Argentina. In 1870, President Domingo Sarmiento founded Argentina's first public, coeducational normal school at Paraná. Sarmiento's enthusiasm for educational reform influenced the development of public education, not only in Argentina but throughout Spanish America. His program was modeled on what he had observed in the United States. The school system was to encompass kindergarten through secondary school, and the curriculum, which was entirely secular, would emphasize physical fitness, responsible citizenship, vocational instruction, and skills in reading, writing, and arithmetic. The teaching staff would be drawn from the newly established normal schools, which he envisioned as the keystone of the projected public system. In a singular effort to assure a strong beginning for the system, Sarmiento recruited young women schoolteachers from the midwestern United States, and between 1869 and 1886 some sixty-five graduates of normal schools in Minnesota and upstate New York went to teach in Argentina. Their dedication to and influence on the fledgling system was considerable; through their efforts and the efforts of those they trained, Argentina's literacy rate rose from less than one-third of the population in 1869 to more than two-thirds in 1914.[13]

The Argentine schools also served students from neighboring Paraguay. Paraguayan coffers were bare in the wake of the War of the Triple Alliance (1865–1870), and the factors that had inspired the educational reform movements in neighboring Uruguay and Argentina were absent. Rosa Pena, known as "the Mother of Paraguayan Education," was educated at the School of Orphans of Mercy (Colegio de Huerfanos de la Merced) in Buenos Aires. From 1864 to 1869 she studied under the direction of Domingo Sarmiento and returned to Asunción to open her own school for girls in 1870. Later, two of her students, Adela and Celsa Speratti, received their teacher training at Concepción de Uruguay in Argentina, and in 1890 the Speratti sisters founded the first normal school in Paraguay.[14]

In Brazil, Emperor Dom Pedro II supported the establishment of normal schools, and at his opening speech to the gathered dignitaries at the U.S. Centennial celebration in Philadelphia in 1876 he proudly announced that Brazil had established teacher training. The ambitious program, which sought to open coeducational normal schools to train primary school teachers in all of Brazil's twenty-two provinces, foundered in the face of poor administration, lack of funding, and the indifference of most Brazilians to the scheme. Not until two decades later, in response to the effects of intense industrialization and urbanization in São Paulo and Rio de Janeiro, did a sustained effort at public education succeed.[15] In the meantime, female education by and large remained in the hands of private schools, such as that of Motta Diniz, and the Catholic church, where instruction for females was limited to about six years. One influential exception was the establishment of the Protestant, coeducational American School in São Paulo in 1871, which later became Mackenzie College. Female graduates of the American School were in the vanguard of a number of newly visible educated, upper-middle-class Brazilian women.

In Mexico, the Liberal government of Benito Juárez passed legislation in 1868 calling for the establishment of a public educational system for both sexes, but it was not until the era of Porfirio Díaz (1876–1911) that government-supported schools, including normal schools, were widely established. The first secondary schools, one for boys and one for girls, were opened in 1869; in 1878 the Escuela Secondaria was converted into the Escuela Normal de Profesoras to meet the rising demand for teachers, and in 1880 an academic preparatory course was appended to the school. In 1887 the Escuela Normal de Profesoras began the instruction of secondary teachers. The influence of the *científicos* was apparent in 1890 in the inauguration of the pedagogical institute, where professors for the teachers colleges were to be trained. The institute promised "to create a scientific professoriate of both sexes, with the goal of establishing a sound basis from which to propagate popular education."

When teacher instruction was first formalized in Mexico, more young men than women attended the teachers colleges. For example, the normal school in Jalapa opened in 1886, but the first woman did not enter until 1891; the normal school in Jalisco graduated three women out of a class of sixty in 1894. In practice, however, most schoolteachers were in fact young women without credentials; in education as in other fields men were the higher-paid professionals; women, the lower-paid practitioners. The initial predominance of men over women in the Mexican normal schools also suggests that employment opportunities and social attitudes differed from those in the Southern Cone; in nineteenth-century Mexico coeducation was not regarded as entirely respectable.

As was true elsewhere, female educators established their own private schools for girls.[16] The distribution of schools and evidence of a literate population in Mexico was distinctly regional. Schools were concentrated in the Federal District; in the central states, including Morelos; and in the north, where prosperous mining, ranching, and commercial activities supported the establishment of schools. Justo Sierra, minister of state and a leader of the positivists during the Porfiriato, believed in the need to educate citizens of both sexes to build a better Mexico, but he wanted to make the purpose of feminine education very clear: "The educated woman will be truly one for the home: she will be the companion and collaborator of man in the formation of the family. You [f.] are called upon to form souls, to sustain the soul of your husband; for this reason, we educate you . . . to continue the perpetual creation of the nation. *Niña querida*, do not turn feminist in our midst."[17] Sierra's qualms proved to be well founded: the early secondary schools and normal schools produced a group of educated women who aligned with the forces of change in the prerevolutionary years.

Two points should be noted. First, the most successful normal school programs were those instituted in the Southern Cone societies of Argentina, Uruguay, and Chile, nations that were not only economically prosperous but that had relatively homogeneous populations compared to societies such as Brazil and Cuba, where Negro slavery persisted until the 1880s, or to countries such as Mexico, Guatemala, Ecuador, or Bolivia, where the majority of the populace lived in harsh peonage and near-universal illiteracy. For most of the rural population of indigenous descent in these nations, Spanish was not the first language if it was spoken at all: Quechua and Aymara prevailed in the Andean regions, and in Mexico and Guatemala more than fifty different language groups persisted.

A second point to note is that the normal school programs were instituted and promoted by the central government: we have mentioned the president of Argentina, the emperor of Brazil, the minister of Mexico and their support for these nascent public education programs, which were seen as a means to building a modern, industrialized state. One result of the initial impetus issuing from the federal level has been the extreme centralization of educational systems in Latin American states, where decision-making power frequently resides not only in the national ministry but in the hands of one individual.

The importance of normal schools for the education of women cannot be overestimated. Women could not attend the universities, and secondary schools for women were scarce in most societies, nonexistent in others. The normal schools offered women an opportunity to extend their education beyond the primary level for the first time, in institutions with standard curricula that stressed the importance of literacy and analytic skills. Although there is ample evidence that young women and their female teachers were quick to take advantage of the opportunity to expand their educations through the normal schools, this was a limited channel of opportunity. Normal-school graduates completed their certificates at the age of seventeen or eighteen, and they were barred from entry to universities, as their preparation was considered inferior to that of secondary, or preparatory, school students.

Access to university education for Latin American women came first in Chile.[18] On April 11, 1881, Eloísa Díaz Inzunza received her bachelor's degree in philosophy and humanities. Eloísa went on to study at the College of Medicine, from which she received her medical degree in 1886; a year later Chilean president Balmaceda conferred upon her a diploma of medical surgery, commending her as the first Chilean woman to obtain a professional title. It is significant that, although she was attached to the medical staff of the Hospital

San Borja, most of her career was carried out in public health, first as a medical professor and inspector of hygiene at the Escuela Normal de Preceptoras del Sur and later as medical inspector of primary schools in Santiago. By 1901 she was a leading figure in the inter-American scientific congresses, where she presented numerous scientific papers on the need to improve health care for women and infants, and she was an outspoken advocate of women's rights.

In 1882, Ernestina Pérez Barahona became the second woman to receive a B.A.; she also chose to pursue a career in medicine. After completing her medical studies in Chile, she went to Europe to study gynecology and was the first South American, male or female, to be elected to the prestigious Academy of Medicine in Berlin. She too was active in the inter-American conferences, where her work on tuberculosis, infectious disease, and antialcohol education was noteworthy. A committed feminist, she served as the first president of the Chilean *Consejo Nacional de Mujeres* in 1919.

Mexico was the second Latin American country in which women earned professional degrees. On February 1, 1887, Margarita Chorne y Salazar became the first Mexican woman to earn a professional title with a degree in dentistry from the Faculty of Medicine. She was followed by Matilde P. Montoya, who earned her title of medical surgeon in 1888, and Maria Sandóval de Zarco (law) in 1889. However, in comparison to Chile, these Mexican women were exceptional within their society. In 1910 one hundred young Mexican women received teaching certificates, but only nine completed university degrees: five doctors, two dentists, one lawyer, and one chemist. As elsewhere, most young women who continued their education beyond primary school attended normal schools.

What is striking about the Chilean case is not that we can identify one or two women who matriculated at the university and who received professional degrees but that a number of women were able to do so at a time when the doors of higher education remained firmly closed against women, not only in other Latin American states but also in most of Europe and all of Asia and Africa. By the 1920s, 49 Chilean women had earned medical degrees, 115 women held degrees in dentistry, and 130 were pharmacy graduates. The law school at the Universidad de Chile proved more resistant to female applicants: In 1892, Matilde Throup Sepulveda received a law degree, but it was another six years before a second woman, Matilde Brandau, did so. Brandau's thesis was titled "Los Derechos Civiles de la Mujer" (The Civil Rights of Woman).

Why were women first successful in achieving access to higher education in Chile? A number of factors combined to make it possible. The intellectual groundwork of the pioneers was certainly a factor; as elsewhere, women's journals calling for female education had been published throughout the nineteenth century. Moreover, Domingo Sarmiento, in exile from Argentina during the Rosas regime, had begun his normal-school work in Chile in 1842. But the prerequisite step was the establishment of secondary schools for young women that would prepare them for the university entry exams.

On February 5, 1877, Aníbal Pinto, president of the republic, and Miguel Luis Amunátegui, minister of public instruction, signed into law a decree declaring that "women ought to be admitted to examinations which would confer professional status with the same qualifications required for men." Pressure for the creation of governmentally recognized secondary schools for young women came first not from the capital city of Santiago but from the frontier mining town of Copiapó in Atacama, the bustling port city of Valparaiso, and the city of Concepción, known as a center of liberal ideas. Within a month of the February decree, the Liceo de Niñas, supported by the Association of Fathers of Families opened its doors in Copiapó. Similar *liceos* were opened in Valparaiso and Concepción the following year, and by 1880, in Santiago, the Liceo Santa Teresa and the Isabel Brun de Pinochet School were receiving fiscal subsidies from the government in support of their secondary school programs. In addition, numerous girls' schools run by Catholic religious orders began to offer secondary curricula. The Colegio Santiago was founded by Methodist missionaries in 1881. Under the direction of Adelaide Whitfield de la Fetra, it became known as the most progressive and best-endowed secondary institution for young women in Chile; its students were "the daughters of the best liberal families."[19] The demand for female education in Chile directly reflects the power that advocates of liberal ideas enjoyed in the country in that period; it is no coincidence that the first generation of educated women in Chile were the daughters of Freemasons.

A number of factors distinguish Chile from its neighbors in this period. It had a small, relatively homogeneous population and a prosperous economy based on mining revenues and agriculture. Ambitious Spanish, Italian, and German immigrants sought better opportunities for themselves and their children. But the most important factor for the advancement of women in Chile was the entry of women into numerous public occupations previously designated for men during the War of the Pacific (1879–1883). The work done by women—from trolley-car conductor to office clerk—was praised as a patriotic contribution to the Chilean cause.[20] In the aftermath of Chile's decisive victory over Peru and Bolivia, Chile enjoyed an economic boom in which many new jobs were created, a situation that meant the women were not forced out of their positions when the men came home. It was in this climate that the first female professionals began their careers.

Social and economic change, produced in the Chilean instance by war and immigration, created the space where women could move into new arenas in society, and the identification of women with patriotism and with the concept of nation building proved highly effective in promoting the cause of female education in a number of countries. The case of Cuba is particularly interesting. At the end of the nineteenth century the education of women in Cuba paralleled the situation in Mexico and Brazil, with private dame or church schools for the upper-class women, charitable and vocational schools for the daughters of the poor, and a normal-school program that had yet to reach any substantial portion of the population.

From the beginning of the independence struggle, Cuban feminists were strong supporters of the patriot cause. In the years of civil war that preceded Cuban independence in 1902, a number of private, secular girls' schools were established. One of the most famous was that headed by Maria Luisa Dolz, who in a commencement speech in 1894 called for an end to discrimination against women and extolled the benefits of offering young women a full curricula, including the study of science and physical education, so that women might "participate in all acts of civil life in the family and in the State."[21]

Cuban women emerged from the War of Independence (1895–1898; under U.S. occupation, 1898–1902) with claims to full partnership in building the new Cuba. The Cuban Constitution of 1901, which was perforce modeled on the U.S. Constitution, declared public schools to be under the control of the state and therefore secular and open to all Cuban children. Cuban women thereby became the first women in Latin America with full access to all levels of education in coeducational institutions. (In Chile, primary, normal, and secondary schools were segregated by sex, and nearly all secondary institutions were privately sponsored, which limited higher education to those who could afford tuition and fees.) This singular advantage did not change the female role in society, for young Cuban women, like their North American contemporaries, were channeled into occupations that were in effect extensions of their feminine role: elementary school teaching, health care, the arts, and social work. However, by 1930 female literacy and attendance at institutions of higher learning in Cuba (mainly in Havana) was nearly equal to that of their male counterparts.[22]

Teaching could be seen as a public extension of woman's traditional mothering role. The need to educate young women was stated as the need to educate them for their roles as the mothers of the new generation of citizens. Moreover, the issue of female education gained support from the reform parties that sought to separate church and state: secular, state-supported education for women was seen as a means of weakening women's traditional loyalty to the church.

One of the characteristics of the Progressive Era throughout the Western world was the lively exchange of ideas that took place at international conclaves. Educators were prominent participants at these meetings, and Latin American scholars were no exception. The influence of North American and European pedagogy on the modernizing sectors of Latin America was considerable. We have mentioned the importation of U.S.-trained school teachers to Argentina; German educators were also widely admired and influential in establishing normal schools in Mexico, Brazil, and Chile. In preparation for the opening of the new Cuban educational system in 1901, one thousand Cuban teachers, male and female, attended a summer session at Harvard University to improve their skills. The *Escolas de Verano* became institutionalized as refresher courses in Cuba, with a cadre of teachers also traveling to Cambridge each year.[23] Many leading Latin American scholars and educators, including Amanda Labarca of Chile, Paulina Luisi of Uruguay, and Elena Torres of Mexico, who were leading socialist as well as feminist thinkers, attended Columbia University Teachers College in New York City in the pre–World War I era.

The importance that women intellectuals attached to improving the accessibility and quality of female education in their respective countries is visible in the records of the Latin American scientific congresses held in Buenos Aires, Montevideo, Santiago, and Rio de Janeiro between 1898 and 1909.[24] The women scientists and educators meeting at the scientific congresses formed the nucleus of women who organized the *Congreso Femenino* held in Buenos Aires in 1910. The *Congreso Femenino* was concerned with a broad spectrum of women's issues (which are discussed more fully in the next chapter), and "Education: Arts, Letters and Industry" was one of the four principal categories under consideration. Organizational sponsors of the *congreso* included the *Escuela Normal de Maestras de Tucumán*, the *Asociación Nacional del Profesorado*, the *Sociedad Nacional de Kindergarden*, and the *Asociación Educacional de Chile*; among the topics addressed were improved curricula for girls' schools, coeducation, scholarships for orphans, night schools for working women, methods to combat adult illiteracy, and teacher preparation. A major concern in the Southern Cone nations in this era was the integration of hundreds of thousands of European immigrants into the social order, and public primary school programs in Argentina, Brazil, and Uruguay were imbued with materials intended to inspire patriotism and loyalty to the state. Interestingly, one of the Argentine teachers, who was herself the daughter of Italian immigrants, gave a speech at the *congreso* in which she asked that "Argentineness" not be stressed to the point where the immigrant children became ashamed of their own heritage.[25]

The results of the efforts of these early female reformers and their male colleagues are visible in the educational surveys undertaken in the 1920s. Typically, the surveys were undertaken and published by the national ministries of education, and they carefully denoted figures for both girls and boys. The optimism of the Chilean surveyors is conveyed in the following quote from the Chilean yearbook of education, published in 1925: "A strong patriotic feeling is keeping alive the desire to secure greater educational progress, which will make possible the more complete utilization of the powers of all individuals in the country, insure the predominance of social justice, and promote the growth of economic prosperity."[26]

Maximiliano Salas Marchan, director of a normal school in Santiago, noted that although a compulsory education law requiring six years of primary schooling for all children had been passed in 1920, "owing to the lack of buildings, equipment, supplies, and teachers, compulsion only extends to four years." The statistics for Chile, despite its long history of support for public education, reveal that education continued to be more accessible to children of the upper and middle classes who lived in or could afford to board in towns and cities; only rudimentary primary schooling was available in rural areas. However, in 1924, in the 3,357 public elementary schools, girls actually outnumbered boys, with 225,692 girls and only 213,089 boys enrolled. The margin of girls over boys attending primary school reflects the fact that boys were more likely to apprentice in a trade or to enter the work force at an earlier age. In the private schools, which served a more elite population, young men outnumbered girls two to one; marriage, not education, was the desired goal for daughters of the elite.

Three different educational paths were available beyond the primary sequence: vocational schools, normal schools, and secondary schools. The vocational school had come into vogue in the United States and Latin America in the nineteenth century and was envisioned as a training ground for children of the lower classes. The schools were strongly gender-differentiated, with boys in machine workshops and girls in sewing classes. In Mexico in the 1880s, vocational schools for girls were explicitly touted as providing an alternative to prostitution. In fact, the young women who attended were usually the daughters of artisans and factory workers; the very poor remained entirely outside the formal educational system.

In 1925 the Chilean vocational program included ten central schools for "manual work," with an enrollment of 1,206 men and 1,786 women; at this level, girls were trained primarily for domestic service. The next level, first opened in 1849, was exclusively male and was designed to produce skilled workmen, foremen, and heads of shops. The agricultural institutes were similarly exclusive. In 1888 the School of Arts and Crafts for Women was founded; by 1925 there were 27 such institutions, offering four types of courses: "Commercial, Women's Work, Household Arts, and Domestic Economy."

It was in the teaching profession that women predominated. In Chile young women students had outnumbered men from the first in the normal schools that trained primary teachers. By the 1920s women had also moved into more prestigious and better-paid positions in secondary education and into administrative positions that had formerly been the province of male educators. The change is clearly documented: Between 1889 and 1919, 60 per-

Table 2. Graduates of University Schools in 1927

	Men	Women	Percentage of Women
Medical School	751	62	8
School of Pharmacy	155	214	58
Dental School	157	55	26
Law Schools			
Univ. Chile	557	69	11
Valparaiso	58	10	15
Univ. Católico	283	16	5
School of Engineering	167	1	—
School of Architecture	100	11	10
Institute of Agronomy	95	—	—
Institute of Education	127	291	70
Institute of Physical Education	57	99	63

Source: Amanda Labarca, "Educación secundaria," in Actividades femeninas en Chile, (Santiago de Chile: Imprenta y Litografía la Ilustracion, Santo Domingo, 1928) 431.

cent of the graduates of the Instituto Pedagógico, which trained secondary teachers, were men; 40 percent were women. Between 1919 and 1927, the figures were nearly reversed: men constituted 42 percent of the graduates; women, 58 percent. The first woman to hold a university professorship was Amanda Labarca in 1922, at the Instituto Pedagógico (Institute of Education). Labarca was among the students who had attended the International Teaching Institute at Columbia University in New York in 1909 and had devoted her career to the advancement of women.

Chile had an unusually high proportion of young women enrolled in secondary schools. With an estimated national population of 3,754,800 in 1925, 13,306 boys and 11,241 girls were attending secondary schools. At the university level, records from 1927 show the gains Chilean women had made in access to education, the fields they entered, and the proportion of male to female graduates in each field (see Table 2).

Women constituted 25 percent of those receiving university degrees in Chile in 1927. By comparison, in the United States, women comprised 36 percent of the university population; in Cuba, 23 percent, in Argentina, 15 percent. Sara Guerin de Elgueta, who was herself a graduate of the University of Santiago with a secondary teaching degree in mathematics and physics, compiled the information on women in the Chilean universities. She also calculated the percentage of women holding licenses to practice medicine, dentistry, and pharmacy (Table 3).

Chile, with its record as the first Latin American nation to offer women entry to higher education, presents a contrast to the situation in other countries. However, the general patterns we can observe for the fields that were first opened to women in Chile hold true for the other Latin American states with advanced educational programs. Despite the continued difficulties in

Table 3. *Percentage of Licensed Doctors, Dentists, and Pharmacists Who Were Women, Chile, 1927*

	Santiago	Valparaiso
Doctors	3	4
Dentists	11	9
Pharmacists	55	31

Source: Amanda Labarca, "Education secundaria," in *Actividades femeninas en Chile* (Santiago de Chile: Imprenta y Litografia la Ilustracion, Santo Domingo, 1928).

providing education to broad sectors of the population, as well as the strong class bias that persisted, the Chilean record of education is admirable; within Latin America, only Argentina, Uruguay, and Cuba could be favorably compared to it prior to World War II.

Ernesto Nelson, who was the husband of Ernestina Lopez de Nelson, a leading advocate of female education, reported in his 1925 survey of Argentina that primary schools were reaching "a balanced number of boys and girls." The population of Argentina at the time the survey was taken was 9,548,092. As was true in Chile, schools were segregated by sex. Enrollment in secondary schools, which were used solely as preparation for entry to the university, had increased from 3,200 students in 1900 to 24,250 in 1925; 86 percent of secondary students were boys. The first institution to offer a university preparatory course to girls, the National Girls' High School, opened in Buenos Aires in 1907. Nearly half of the students were the daughters of immigrants; the director of the school noted that "foreign women study those subjects that would open the road to higher culture."[27] As we observed in the Chilean case, girls of the upper class did not pursue a higher education; their schooling was intended to impart polish and social grace, and it was carried on in exclusive private schools. Only a handful of Argentine women received university degrees prior to 1916; in that year thirty-eight matriculated in medicine, and others were entering law, pharmacy, and education.

The majority of young women who continued their education beyond the primary level entered normal schools. Commercial schools were also important, training young women in stenography, business, arithmetic, and economics. Despite their improved education, laws and custom continued to restrict young women to the lower echelons of the wage-paying market, whether as primary school teachers or as secretaries and clerks.[28]

In 1925, Uruguay had a population of 1,640,214, one-fourth of whom lived in the capital city of Montevideo. Eduardo Monteverde wrote in his educational survey that "politically Uruguay is one of the most progressive countries in America and has during the past 20 years introduced extensive measures of social legislation which would elsewhere be regarded as radical.

Education has kept step with the social progress of this period."[29] Monteverde undertook a literacy survey that illustrates a dramatic division between the cosmopolitan and the rural populations. Illiteracy had been reduced to less than 30 percent in the country as a whole, ranging from 10 percent in Montevideo to over 50 percent in the rural province of Rivera. All training beyond primary school was concentrated in Montevideo, and Monteverde noted that "great difficulty is found in securing teachers for rural schools." The problem of rural schooling was ubiquitous in Latin America, but the situation was exacerbated in Uruguay, where no sizable population centers existed outside Montevideo. In Chile, as we have seen, Valparaiso, Concepción, and Copiapó led the way in female education; in Argentina, the first normal school was established at Paraná, not in Buenos Aires, and the federal university was at Córdoba.

The University of Montevideo was the only university in the country, and the central secondary school was attached to it; girls were specifically excluded on the grounds that it was "dangerous" to allow young men and young women to mingle. Not until the establishment of the Colegio de Mujeres in 1917, which provided preparatory schooling as well as teacher training for girls, did young women enter the university in any numbers. In 1916 women constituted but 6.5 percent of the student body; by 1929, 43 percent of the students were women. The percentage of women students is somewhat exaggerated, as girls enrolled in the normal school attached to the university were included in the count. The pattern of female preponderance in the teaching profession is echoed in Uruguay, where public elementary schools employed 2,552 women and 275 men.

In Brazil, which had a population of 30,635,605 in 1920, educational reform comparable to what had occurred in the Southern Cone countries was not undertaken until the 1930s, as the paucity of educational opportunities available to women demonstrates. Faculties of law and medicine had been established in the nineteenth century; the first university was organized in Rio de Janeiro in 1920. It should be noted that universities in Latin America in this period were European in structure and consisted of a number of separate faculties located in different areas of a city. By 1924 a total of 7,046 students was enrolled: 6,855 men and 191 women. Educational institutions were concentrated in the states of Rio de Janeiro, São Paulo, Minas Gerais, and Rio Grande do Sul. Outside of metropolitan Rio de Janeiro and São Paulo, vocational schools were nonexistent. In the strong states' rights atmosphere that characterized Brazilian politics in this period, no national educational system existed. By mandate, each of the twenty states was to maintain a secondary school and a normal school for both sexes in its capital; but the quality of the education offered varied widely from one place to another, and whenever resources could support only one school, girls were excluded.

In 1924, Minister of Education Carneiro Leão lamented the current situation: "The extent of the educational problem is shown by the high percentage of illiteracy. This ranged in 1920 from thirty-nine percent in the Federal District to eighty-eight percent in Piauhy. Of the twenty states the percentage of illiteracy in 1920 was between sixty and sixty-nine percent in two states; between seventy and seventy-nine in ten; and over eighty percent in eight. At the same time, these figures represent a considerable improvement over those of 1900." He noted that whereas only slightly more than half of the children living in the Federal District of Rio de Janeiro in 1907 had attended two years of primary school, nearly 75 percent had done so in 1920. Part of this improvement was attributed to programs established by private agencies, which, although primarily designed to bring health care and food to poor children, also provided some instruction in letters and numbers.[30]

In contrast to Chile, Argentina, and Uruguay, where the national governments instituted far-reaching public education programs, in Brazil the private sector continued to be the main provider of education. The Catholic church maintained its dominance of male secondary and preparatory education, charitable organizations ran schools for the poor, and girls from well-to-do families attended convent schools or private dame schools. In some places coeducational Protestant schools offered an alternative for young women; Mackenzie College in São Paulo, mentioned earlier, was one.

The result was a dual educational system, sharply divided along lines of class, race, and privilege. The newly established public primary schools, normal schools, and vocational schools served the children of the urban middle and working classes. Secondary education was designed to prepare the sons of the elite for attendance at the law school or the school of medicine and for further education in Europe.[31] It was rare for a young Brazilian woman to receive any higher education; Bertha Lutz, who studied at the Sorbonne and ultimately received her doctorate from the Pasteur Institute in Paris, was an exception.

There were indications of a growing enthusiasm for public education. Carneiro Leão wrote that despite a 100 percent increase in spending on educational programs between 1920 and 1925, "the demand for public education has outstripped the economic resources." In the wake of the 1930 revolution, decrees that restructured secondary and higher education were passed. Brazilian scholar Heleith Saffiotti describes the effect for women: "The reforms were a distinct boon for women. Besides extending the term of schooling for women [which had formerly rested at seven years] it put off the choice of professional specialization from age 12 to age 17."[32] The content and duration of training in the normal schools was also improved. Still, a normal school certificate was not considered equivalent to a secondary-school degree, which effectively barred students at the teaching institutes, who were mainly female, from continuing their studies at the university level.

The history of female education in Mexico presents parallels to the patterns we have observed elsewhere. Educator Manuel Barranco wrote of the years of the revolution: "In spite of the turmoil and war that is raging over the country, still the work of education is going on and some faithful still keep the sacred fire burning."[33] The trends visible in female education during the years prior to the revolution continued, with girls of the upper classes in private, usually Catholic, girls' schools and educational institutions concentrated in the northern and central states and Mexico City.[34]

In 1920, Mexico had a population of approximately 14 million, nearly two-thirds of which was illiterate. In the years prior to 1910, a number of normal-school graduates demonstrated a strong sympathy for critics of the Díaz government, a sympathy they communicated to their students.[35] The commitment of many women teachers to social change was apparent at the two *congresos femeninos* held in Mérida in 1916, which produced a platform demanding that rights for women be included in the deliberations of the constituent assembly then meeting in Queretaro.[36]

Thus, it is not surprising that women schoolteachers were the heart and soul of the literacy campaign instituted by the Mexican government in 1921. The campaign was unprecedented in its scope. Under the leadership of Minister of Education José Vasconcelos from 1921 to 1924, the ambitious program aimed not only to bring education to rural children but also to attack the great problem of adult illiteracy. Elena Torres, who had received her master's degree at Columbia University, was a prime organizer of the project to improve teacher preparation, insisting that the adult literacy program contain political education as well as the three R's. A contemporary educator described the program:

The basic program used to bring education to the countryside involved the establishment of missions. A Congress of Missioners met for the first time in September, 1922, in Mexico City to discuss the problem of bringing education to remote rural areas where it was practically nonexistent. Elena Torres, after working with the rationalist educational program in Yucatán and heading the free breakfast program for 12,000 children in Mexico City, became Chief of the Bureau of Cultural Missions. The main purpose of the missions was to improve culturally and professionally the primary school teacher. Rural teachers were also instructed in socialism under this method. Under Torres six missions served more than 2,000 rural teachers in 1926. In the next decade, the number grew to eighteen missions serving more than 4,000 teachers.[37]

The Mexican program attracted the interest of educators throughout the hemisphere. At Vasconcelos's invitation, Chilean poet and teacher Gabriela Mistral came to Mexico in 1922. In the next two years she helped to establish a series of practical schools for women, known as the Escuelas-Hogar (Homemaker's Schools). She assisted in organizing programs in rural areas and oversaw the introduction of the new mobile libraries. In an effort to make readings of quality available to those enrolled in the literacy classes, she edited an anthology of poetry and prose that included many of her own pieces. Entitled *Readings for Women*, the volume was published by the Mexican government in 1923. Mistral concentrated on female education, and it should be noted that her emphasis was to better prepare women to fulfill their traditional roles as mothers and homemakers, not to seek new roles.

The Mexican program is also important as a precursor of subsequent state-sponsored drives to eradicate adult illiteracy and impart the rudiments of socialist political analysis, notably in Cuba in the mid-1960s, Chile in the 1970s, and Nicaragua in the 1980s. The Mexican literacy drive was a significant part of the government's effort to disestablish the Catholic church; here, as elsewhere, secularization of education was critical to the success of that effort. During the Cristero rebellion that wracked western Mexico from 1926 to 1929, a number of rural teachers were victims of the fury of church loyalists.

The patterns we can observe in women's education hold true throughout the continent. It was in the 1920s that the first generation of urban, literate women appeared—in Buenos Aires, in São Paulo and Rio de Janeiro, in Santiago, Montevideo, Mexico City, and Havana. In the early decades of the twentieth century the expansion of female education meshed with the drive to modernize and the perceived need for an educated citizenry. For the first time, women entered new fields of study, and secondary preparatory schools and universities were opened to them. In states such as Peru, Ecuador, Bolivia, and the small Central American states, where no true middle class emerged until after World War II and where conservative regimes held sway, female education was little valued, and education in general was restricted to the Spanish-speaking upper classes.

At the end of the 1920s most Latin American women who attended school went to all-female institutions, public or private, secular or religious. Women continued to receive different, and less, education than men. However, many barriers had fallen. Hundreds of elementary schools had been established, and women were the teachers. Women were no longer excluded from higher education, though it was more accessible to urban women in Mexico, Cuba, Brazil, and the Southern Cone nations than elsewhere. Not until after World War II did this situation change substantially.

The trend toward greater access to education for women, haltingly begun in the period between 1910 and 1940, and apparent only in some places in some countries, was strengthened after 1945. Female education in Latin America became a particular focus of international agencies: The *Comision Interamericana de Mujeres* (CIM) founded in 1947 at the Organization of American States (OAS) meeting in Bogotá, has the following statements in its mandate: "The economic and social development of our countries calls for the effective participation of scientifically or technically trained women at all levels of endeavor," and "The Inter-American Commission of Women has the duty to provide women with the information most of them lack with regard to their rights in family legislation, labor codes, and in public education."[38]

Since 1950 UNESCO has set up educational programs and collected extensive data on education, always with an eye for the proportion of women present—as teachers and as students. In reading these figures it should be kept in mind that they often represent only percentages of those students actually enrolled in educational programs, which in many countries means only a small percentage of the school-age population. Another difficulty in assessing data on education is that enrollment and attendance figures do not reflect the high rate of attrition that affects nearly every area of the educational systems. In 1963, CHEAR (Council on Higher Education in the Americas), calculated that out of every thousand Latin American students who began primary school, thirty would finish secondary school and only one would complete six years at a university. This calculation masks great variations between regions but does dramatize the scope of the problem. Despite the need for caution in interpreting statistics on education, the data give us a broad statistical profile of female education from 1950 to the present.

In the immediate postwar period, the emphasis in education was on the expansion of opportunity. Monies from national and state budgets were supplemented by USAID, among other programs, and the results, in gross terms, were remarkable: In 1950 there were 16 million students enrolled at primary, secondary, and higher levels of education in all of Latin America; in 1980 there were 85.9 million. Primary education more than quadrupled, from 14.2 million to 64.5 million; secondary education increased more than ten times, from 1.5 million to 16.5 million; and higher education increased nearly twentyfold, from 265,818 to 4,893,000.[39]

At the national level, legislation to improve the content of programs was implemented; in Brazil, for example, a 1946 decree revamped the course of study for teachers so that normal school graduates could be admitted into arts and science college courses; as 86 percent of Brazilian normal school students were female in this era, the change was directly beneficial to young women seeking higher education.[40] In 1947, Colombia opened the doors of the National University law school to women.

However, in the 1950s the enormous expansion of the educational system did not substantially alter the trends we have observed in the prewar period. The expansion was numerical, a response to the needs of the expanding urban middle classes and to the pressures of internal rural-to-urban migration and rapidly accelerating birthrates. Indigenous peoples, who did not speak Spanish (or in Brazil, Portuguese) were effectively excluded from the system, as were rural children and the poor. Little beyond primary schooling was available to anyone outside the cities; for instance, in the agricultural Cajamarca region of Peru, which was much more closely linked to Lima than most of rural Peru and which had a Spanish-speaking mestizo population, "schools were virtually non-existent on the haciendas up through the 1950s."[41]

The educational profile in the 1950s shows continued discrepancies between male and female students. As was true in the 1920s, Cuba showed a high percentage of female students, with girls comprising 51 percent of primary students, 41 percent of secondary students, 94 percent of normal-school students, and 46 percent of those enrolled in higher education, which included vocational and technical schools as well as university training. Many countries were approaching gender parity at the primary level; and in every country, between 60 and 90 percent of normal-school students were girls (and primary school teachers earned less than taxi drivers). At the secondary level the Dominican Republic, Panama, and Chile reported that 50 percent of the students were female. The greatest difference shows up in higher education: In Cuba, 46 percent of postsecondary students were female; in Argentina, Uruguay, Paraguay, and Chile, approximately 27 percent; in Brazil, 22 percent; in Mexico, Colombia, Venezuela, Ecuador, and Peru, 17 percent; in Guatemala, Honduras, and Haiti, around 7 percent.[42]

In the 1960s there was a push to change the traditional content of post-primary-school programs. The intention was to make education more relevant to industrial, technical, and commercial development plans; the traditional education that emphasized Latin and rhetoric did not promise to produce students outfitted for response to the post-Sputnik era. In addition, vocational schools and normal schools were to include more academic work, which would enable their students to pursue higher education.

In many cases the work-oriented programs were funded by a combination of private industry, government monies, and international agencies. In 1969 the Colombian government, in collaboration with the World Bank and UNESCO, introduced a program known as INEM (*Instituto Nacional de Educación Media Diversificada*). By 1970 the program already involved nearly one hundred thousand students in nineteen different schools; students could specialize in academic, commercial, industrial, agricultural, or social services programs. In 1978 a survey of the effects of the program concluded that "the earnings differences between [graduates of] INEMs and traditional schools are not very large. As far as men are concerned, the differences seem to be due largely to the effect of self-employment, and concerning women, graduates from traditional schools seem to do somewhat better than those from INEMs." Second, "the INEMs have not altered to any great extent the employment pattern of young people as compared with the structure of the traditional school system. If anything, the data suggest that INEMs, particularly in the case of males, have accentuated the propensity of high school graduates for higher education." And finally, "INEMs do not show a differential effect on the number of people who end up enrolled in the best universities of the country, nor as regards the number of graduates who end up unemployed."[43]

What is apparent is that the INEMs did not take into account the importance of the class background of the students, a factor that is implicit in the differences between the results for women and men: Girls who attended the traditional (in Colombia, mainly private) schools came from a sector of society that enjoyed financial and social advantages. The INEMs attracted girls whose families could not afford private schooling for them; the advantage of the girls from the traditional schools in the job market clearly reflects these factors. The young male graduates of the INEMs gained an advantage through setting up their own businesses, which would have been a daunting prospect for young women in the conservative milieu of Colombia. The propensity of young men given a "boost up" by these new programs to pursue higher education again emphasizes the class origin of the INEM students, where going for specialized secondary education was a novel idea for young women, and the idea of the university was not an aspiration. It also underlines the difficulty women have in transcending their class origin through education and employment. (For further discussion, see chapter 6.)

Similar programs were inaugurated in a number of other countries, including Costa Rica, Brazil, and Venezuela. Within the programs offered, women tended to enroll in greater numbers than men in the commercial and service courses, whereas men outnumbered women in the industrial and agricultural courses.[44]

The impetus to expand educational systems and inaugurate new curricula throughout Latin America in the 1960s should also be understood as part of the hemispheric response to the Cuban Revolution: Educational programs were central to the Alliance for Progress plans. And educational programs were seen as central to the success of the revolutionary program in Cuba. At the time of the revolution (1959), Cuba boasted one of the highest literacy rates in Latin America, as well as a high percentage of school-age children enrolled in schools, and we have noted the exceptional proportion of girls at all levels of education. What we do not see in this picture are the deep divisions that existed, divisions between those who could afford private schooling, those who could afford public schooling, and those who could afford nothing; between Cubans of predominately Spanish blood and Cubans of predominately African blood; and between Cubans who lived in Havana or in a provincial city and those who worked the land and lived in the countryside. In each sector women were more likely to be educationally disadvantaged than men; in rural Cuba women were twice as likely as men to be illiterate.

The educational program of the Cuban revolution was two-pronged: First, it meant to disassemble the existing educational structure, banning all private (especially private religious) instruction and creating a free public educational system open to all in which advancement was based on merit and students were directed into careers that corresponded to the needs of the economy. Second, it attacked the problem of adult illiteracy. Vilma Espín, leader of the Federation of Cuban Women (FMC) spoke to the issue of female education in 1972:

> Another important achievement has been in education, in educating adult women . . . today [it is possible for] the woman to study any career she wants. In this sense, the FMC is making a gigantic effort, creating special adult courses, directing specific plans for the training of organizational cadres, opening technical courses according to the needs of production. . . .
> During 1961, in addition to taking part in the literacy campaign, the FMC had the responsibility of creating massive educational courses. The first thousand attendants for the nursery schools were trained in that year, as well as 17,000 peasant girls who learned to sew and received a general primary education. Thousands of women who had been servants in the homes of the bourgeoisie who had left the country took courses preparing them for administrative work. Later different courses were organized by the FMC in coordination with organizations that needed skilled labor. We also worked hard to help out the primary and secondary schools.[45]

As Espín indicates, women played a central role both as teachers and as beneficiaries in the massive literacy campaign undertaken by the Cuban government in 1961, in which illiteracy was reduced from 23.6 percent of the population to 3.9 percent. Women also benefited from the innovative "schools in the country," in which study, work, and recreation are combined, and from equal access to the elite polytechnical high schools: "In some of these institutions, a majority of the rigorously screened entering students are females."[46]

The efforts of the Cuban government in education and the emphasis on science, engineering, and agriculture at the university level have placed Cuba in the forefront of education in Latin America. However, as can be seen in Table 4, the pattern of female education in Cuba from 1960 to 1985 closely parallels that in Costa Rica, Argentina, Chile, and Uruguay, nations that share with Cuba a historical commitment to higher education for women. The critical difference for young women in Cuba may be that young women are more likely to pursue studies in the hard sciences and technology.

The history of female education in Peru presents a contrast to the history of female education in nations where women successfully pushed for equal access to educational institutions. Of first importance is the fact that instruction for both boys and girls has remained by and large under the auspices of the Catholic church. Church domination of instruction did not mean that females did not receive education, nor even that education was restricted to an elite class, but that the content of that education was designed to preserve the social status quo, not to modernize or change it. It also meant that educational institutions were effectively restricted to urban, coastal Peru, where Spanish-speaking Catholics primarily resided. As we have seen, private Catholic schools continue to constitute a significant proportion of educational institutions throughout most of Latin America, but in most countries these exist in conjunction with government-supported public schools with a secular curriculum. In contrast, the church in Peru retained its primacy in education almost to the exclusion of public schools well into the midtwentieth century. Education continued to be sex-segregated and mainly accessible to Limeños who could afford to pay for it.

In the years following World War II, Peru participated in the educational development programs designed to promote democratic reform. These reforms did not reach beyond the urban centers; it was not until the Velasco coup in 1968 that serious attention was given to the education of the rural population. Ironically, the domination of female education by the church, which was diminished in the post–World War II period with the wider establishment of state schools, has increased in recent years. The penetrating educational reforms instituted by the Velasco government in the 1970s brought significant numbers of the poorest sectors of society into the public schools. One effect of this change is that by 1987 families of the middle and better-paid working classes were sending their children, especially their daughters, to private schools: "Girls' education for the middle classes is still carried on almost exclusively in institutions run by nuns or in expensive private schools under secular auspices that offer a traditional 'genteel' education . . . as more children of the lower-middle and working classes have moved into the public schools, private schools in Peru have proliferated."[47] Thus, the educational system continues to buttress the existent social divisions of gender, race, and class: the white blouses of the public school children are associated with lower-class origin and non-Hispanic ethnic heritage. Nor is the trend toward increased enrollment in private institutions in the 1980s limited to Peru: "While higher education has grown faster than primary or secondary education, and its growth rate in Latin America is the highest for any region of the world (approximately twelve percent annually between 1965 and 1980), it is the private sector that has registered the most dramatic gains. In the 1970s, approximately five percent of higher education students were enrolled in private institutions; in the 1980s over thirty percent attended private universities and colleges."[48]

The history of female education in Peru and in Cuba presents strong contrasts, between a country where no significant middle class appeared until the 1970s and one where a substantial middle class emerged by the end of the nineteenth century; between a country where the power of the traditional ruling elite remained unbroken until the late 1960s and a country that underwent radical social change in the late 1950s; between a country with a large, unassimilated indigenous rural population and a country with a small, more closely intermingled population; between a country where the Catholic church retained its influence in the face of secular challenges and one in which secularism triumphed. The history of female education in most of Latin America lies between these extremes. Elements of both the Cuban and the Peruvian experience are apparent in Mexico, Venezuela, Colombia, and Brazil, where a mixture of private, religious, international and government-sponsored programs work to keep pace with unprecedented population growth, to attack rural–urban discrepancies, and to diminish the high attrition rate of students from impoverished backgrounds.

In every country particular attention has been paid to the special needs of women. The recognition of women's disadvantaged position vis-à-vis men in education, which was first articulated in Latin America in the eighteenth century, was a central focus of the International Decade for Women, 1976–1985. Table 4 illustrates the success of the effort to win access to higher education for women and the great gains Latin American women have made in education in that twenty-five-year period.

Women in several countries have achieved parity with men in higher education, and the projected curves promise similar achievement in the future for the majority of Latin American countries. These curves sharply differentiate Latin America as a region from other areas of the developing world, especially from Africa and South Asia; the pattern of female education in many Latin American nations parallels that of Western nations and compares favorably with southern European nations. The figures also illustrate the perils of trying to discuss Latin America as if it were an entity: the historical development of female education reveals marked differences between nations and between regions within a nation, as well as striking disparities in educational opportunity for rural and urban children, for children of the elite, the middle sectors, and the poor. However, in the past, no matter what the country, region, locus, or socioeconomic status of the individual, men have had greater access to education than women have had. In the latter twentieth century that is no longer true: what the implications are for the larger society must be sought in how women's greater access to education translates into economic and political power.

The figures for the increased participation of women in higher education in the area are even more impressive when considered within the context of the population growth that has marked these same decades. In Brazil the population in 1960 was 71 million; in 1985 it was 131 million; in Mexico, the population in 1960 was 36 million; in 1985 it was estimated at 78 million: the sheer number of people, female or male, enrolled in educational programs in the hemisphere has increased at a pace unmatched anywhere in the world. One of the results of this increase is that although women are now propor-

Table 4. Enrollment in Higher Education by Gender 1960–1985

	1960		1985		Ratio of Women to Men (Men = 100)	
Country	% Women	% Men	% Women	% Men	1960	1985
North America	23	38	59	54	59	107
Canada	10	17	41	56	61	107
United States	24	41	61	39	59	104
Latin America	2	4	17	20	41	82
Argentina	7	14	25	24	49	103
Bolivia	2	7	9	19	29	50
Brazil	1	2	18	15	39	116
Chile	3	5	13	18	58	72
Colombia	1	3	13	16	22	77
Costa Rica	4	5	25	29	81	82
Cuba	3	4	28	31	76	85
Dominican Republic	1	2	15	16	36	92
Equador	1	4	37	58	22	64
El Salvador	—	2	9	15	26	59
Guatemala	—	3	6	17	11	37
Haiti	—	1	1	3	17	43
Honduras	—	2	13	19	21	69
Mexico	—	4	13	23	21	53
Nicaragua	—	2	11	19	27	58
Panama	4	5	28	22	74	120
Paraguay	2	3	9	11	48	80
Peru	2	6	15	28	42	54
Uruguay	6	9	20	17	70	113
Venezuela	3	6	23	25	45	91

Source: Ruth Leger Sivard, ed., Women . . . A World Survey (Washington, D.C.: World Priorities, 1985).

tionately better represented at all levels of formal education vis-à-vis men, in several countries the *absolute number* of women illiterates has remained the same or increased in recent decades.[49] The data on illiteracy are a reminder that the poorer countries—and the poorer sectors within individual countries—are still far from the goal of basic education for all.

The link between education and literacy is not as direct as it was once believed to be; recent research has shown that even students with a number of years of schooling may be functionally illiterate. In the rural areas and in the *favelas* and *barriadas* of urban areas, few girls attend more than a year or two of school. Studies have repeatedly shown that female adults are more likely to be illiterate than are male adults, and women have been a special concern of literacy campaigns, from Mexico in the 1920s and Cuba in the 1960s to Nicaragua in the 1980s. The Nicaraguan case is unique: more than half of the adult population, which numbered approximately 2 million in 1981, was described as illiterate; within nine months the Sandinista literacy campaign, carried on under the duress of war, reduced that figure to 15 percent of those over ten years of age.

The Nicaraguan campaign against illiteracy incorporated the principles of Brazilian educator Paulo Freire. Freire's "pedagogy of the oppressed" describes the adult literacy process as "cultural action for freedom." At the center of Freire's pedagogy are *circulos de cultura*. The circles are predicated on dialogue between teachers (as facilitators) and illiterate adults; the learning process involves the development of teaching materials that focus on the most pressing social problems of the particular community. Literacy is acquired in the process of "naming the world" and participating in efforts to change it.

In the late 1980s belief in the need for female education is undiminished, as the following quote from a study by the UN International Decade for Women attests: "Ignorance was and still is a factor in the subservence of women. From their earliest years, they tend to be kept in ignorance of schooling possibilities. Later they are kept in ignorance of their matrimonial, social and legal rights. . . . Information is the only guarantee of freedom."[50] The mutual self-help committees of *feminismo popular*, which we will explore in chapter 7, are based on this premise. Deriving their methodology and practice from the Catholic *comunidades de base* and Paulo Freire's pedagogy of the oppressed, their politics from a feminist perspective of society, and, often, funding from international agencies, these local women's centers are visible in the *pueblos jovenes* of Callao, the factory districts of São Paulo, the rural villages of Guatemala.

Education is often assessed as a tool of the state or church to subjugate or pacify the working classes, to "mold" a particular kind of society, to mobilize the population in a particular cause. And this is the genesis of public funding programs, of education whose aim is religious or political conversion. But ideas cannot be so carefully controlled: To teach an individual to think critically, not just to learn a certain body of material, is indeed potentially revolutionary. What we can observe in studying the history of female education is that access to education for women has created its own dynamic in Latin American societies. From the first *normalistas* who raised the issue of gender discrimination, from the dame school directoresses who preached the principles of a sound body in a sound mind and equal rights for women, to the *feminismo popular* of the 1980s, where poor women have come together to learn to read and stayed together to demand better living conditions, to protest the abuse of their sisters and daughters, and to articulate a gender-conscious critique of the state and the traditional opposition as well, the education of women carries the potential of broad social and political change.

4. Feminism and Social Motherhood, 1890-1938

The struggle of women is much broader and more encompassing than that of men. Women are moving not only toward winning a more human existence with greater dignity in economic matters, but they are moving also along the roads of social struggle in which they aspire to win the right to develop their own personality, aspirations which have been marginalized by prejudice and lack of understanding.
—Magda Portal, *Hacia la mujer nueva* [1]

This chapter examines the effect of the rapidly changing social, political, and economic environment through the years 1890–1938 on the status of women in Latin America.[2] The emergence of women novelists, poets, journalists, and political activists and the development of a shared feminist consciousness in the early twentieth century in certain nations of Latin America are directly linked to the presence in those countries of trends that combined to produce a process of modernization. Women intellectuals first found their voice—and their audience—in Argentina, Uruguay, Chile, and Brazil, states that received hundreds of thousands of European immigrants, whose urban centers became true cities, and where social and political reform movements were mounted; and in Mexico and Cuba, where major social upheavals took place.

The rise of a feminist consciousness in Latin American societies is often obscured by historiographic assumptions about the nature and extent of feminist thought in Latin America. The development of a feminist critique of the traditional social order was most vocal in the Southern Cone nations of Uruguay, Argentina, and Chile, where the combination of relatively advanced public education systems open to both sexes and the influx of European immigrants seeking better lives combined to produce a new class of educated, articulate women whose reformist ideals intersected with those of their male counterparts on issues of health care, social welfare, and general political reform but diverged on issues of equal female rights in marriage, to jobs, to higher education, and to political power.

By the latter half of the nineteenth century there were numerous individuals raising the issue of women's rights, especially in regard to civil status. In Latin America the typical forum was the political journal, not the public podium, and the arguments for women's equality were cast in terms of progressivism and the hope of a better life in the New World.[3] *O Sexo Feminino*, discussed briefly in chapter 3, was one such journal. The first issue, "dedicated to the emancipation of women," appeared in Campanha, Minas Gerais, on September 7, 1873. September 7 commemorates the date on which Brazil's "Grito de Independencia" (Cry of Independence) was given in 1822. Motta Diniz writes: "It will be seen that America will give the cry of independence for women, showing the Old World what it means to be civilized, that women are as apt for education as young men."[4]

The 1870s was a decade of great political turmoil in Brazil. The central institutions of the empire were under attack from republicans, and the movement to abolish slavery was gaining momentum. Motta Diniz often invoked the national pride of the Brazilian politicians to whom her journal was addressed: "Our Empire of Brazil must not be a submissive imitator of Europe and the United States in progress," and she suggests that if Brazil will pass legislation allowing women to be educated in the sciences, it will show its stature as a world leader. Interestingly, Motta Diniz saw the issue of women's equality as an issue of moral justice rather than as a political one. When the editor of *O Colombo*, a periodical that advocated the establishment of a republic, attacked Motta Diniz for publishing a poem dedicated to Emperor Dom Pedro II on his birthday, she responded hotly: "We do not know in what great republic or small republic woman has ceased to be a slave, and has political rights, such as the power to vote and to be elected. What is inarguable is that in all the world, barbarous or civilized, woman is a slave, whether she lives in a monarchy, or under unrestrained despotism!"[6]

In the 1880s the journal ceased publication, but in the wake of the signing of the Emancipation Act of 1888, which freed all slaves, and the establishment of the Republic of Brazil in 1889, it reappeared, renamed *O Quinze de Novembro do Sexo Feminino* in honor of the new republic: "[Our journal] . . . rises again on the immense ocean of freedom of ideas . . . once more we [women] ask equal rights, freedom of action, and autonomy in the home." The fact that the Emancipation Act had been signed by a woman, Princess Isabel, was not missed: "[This heroine's act] is an excellent testimony to the energy and capacity of woman." The editions of 1889 were edited by Motta Diniz's daughter, and the voice of a new generation is apparent in her admonitions that "modern society does not educate women exclusively as an ornament of the salons, but that she may be useful to herself and to humanity. . . . In our century, woman accompanies step by step the intellectual progress of man, but has many times over proved her superiority in the world of morality and intuition."[6]

O Sexo Feminino was but one of many journals advocating woman's rights published in the latter half of the nineteenth century in Brazil, and there were similar publications in many other areas of Latin America.[7] *La Mujer*, published in the 1890s in Chile, was committed to the idea "that woman is the basis of universal progress" and was aimed at an audience of "the American community of writers who speak Spanish." In Mexico the tradition of journals published by women and dedicated to women dates back to the eighteenth and early nineteenth centuries; *El Aguila Mexicana*, which began publication in 1823, the year of Mexican independence, called for the rights of man—and woman.

The linkage of the ideas of independence, the emancipation of slaves, and the drive for political and economic modernity are also evident in the speeches and writings of early Cuban feminists. Lynn Stoner writes:

The initial demand for equal rights for women came during the Ten Years War, 1868–1878. On April 10, 1869, at the Constitutional Congress in Guaimaro, a woman, substituting for her ailing husband, rose to speak to the revolutionary government. Ana Betancourt de Mora, herself a republican patriot and a member of a landholding family, stood before the male representative body and demanded that Cuban democracy include women. . . . She pointed out that Cuban independence meant the rejection of slavery, political bondage to Spain, and discrimination against blacks. She insisted that the Assembly look to the question of female subjugation, an unexcusable condition, as women had shown their valor beside male nationalists. She challenged the Assembly to do away with all forms of slavery including that of women:

"Citizens: The Cuban woman, from the dark and tranquil corner of her home, has waited patiently and with resignation for this sublime hour in which a just revolution will break her yoke, will untie her wings. Everyone was a slave in Cuba: the Family, Race, and Sex. You wish to destroy racial slavery, fighting until death if necessary. Racial slavery no longer exists, you have emancipated men of servitude. When the moment arrives to liberate women, the Cuban male, who has been thrown between family and racial slavery, will also dedicate his generous soul to women's rights, for women, who today in wartime are his sisters of charity while being denied their rights, tomorrow will be his exemplary companions." Despite this courageous and forceful speech, the Assembly did not consider women's rights in their "Bases de la Revolucion." In 1869 the notion of granting full constitutional rights to women was unprecedented.[8]

As we saw in chapter 3, these early Latin American feminists, whether in Cuba or Mexico, Argentina or Chile, were unanimous in their call for equal educational opportunity for both sexes. Brazilian Motta Diniz wrote in 1890, "Women's emancipation through education is the bright torch which can dispel the darkness and bring us to the august temple of science." In 1878, *La Internacional*, a socialist journal published in Mexico, included in its platform a clause advocating "the emancipation, rehabilitation, and integral education of women." An Argentine journal, *La Ondina del Plata*, which appeared in Buenos Aires in the 1870s, carried articles by María Eugenia Echenique ("The

Needs of Argentinian Women" and "The Emancipation of Women") in which Echenique called for the right of women to control their own destinies, to work, and to participate fully in society.[9]

The reiterated concept of emancipation and the identification of woman's state with the condition of slavery may seem an overdramatization of the female condition, but women were in fact the legal chattels of male heads of household. Married women had no control over their own lives and possessed no legal rights over the destinies of their children. Individual efforts to publish journals, start schools to educate a new generation of women, and influence politicians did not translate into legislation designed to change the women's situation. Even the association of female emancipation with the drive for progress and modernization and the appeals to national pride, which were effective in winning the support of some national leaders, brought little change in women's legal status prior to the twentieth century.

Latin American intellectuals, male and female, were well aware of the women's movement in Europe and the United States. The international exchange of ideas was particularly important for the earliest proponents of women's rights in Latin America. However, the acknowledgment of the influence of international intellectual currents should not be allowed to obscure the fact that a feminist critique of society arose from the experience of the women themselves.

Whereas many of the early proponents of women's rights in Latin America were upper-class women, speaking out as individuals, it was female schoolteachers who formed the nucleus of the first women's groups to articulate what may be defined as a feminist critique of society, that is, to protest against the pervasive inequality of the sexes in legal status, access to education, and political and economic power. Two factors are of great importance: First, the teachers were the first generation of educated middle-sector women, and they were well aware of their precarious social, economic, and legal status; and second, they were in touch with one another through their institutions of learning and through professional associations, forums in which they could share their common experiences.

These young women lived and were educated in the growing urban centers of Latin America, where they were exposed not only to local issues and ideas but to national and international political discourse. For example, in 1870 the Mexican poet and educator Rita Cetina Gutierrez called a meeting of a group of primary teachers in Mérida to form La Siemprevivia, a female society dedicated to overcoming women's unequal status in society and to combating "social problems" by improving hygiene and by educating mothers in nutrition and child care. The women published a newspaper and founded a secondary school for girls, and from 1886 to 1902 Gutierrez oversaw the education of "a generation of female teachers who taught in the capital, in the major towns, and on the few haciendas that provided primary schools for the children of peons."[10]

Mérida, a wealthy port city on Mexico's Yucatan Peninsula, offered a propitious environment for the women teachers: In the late nineteenth century it had grown into a cosmopolitan center by virtue of its direct trade with Europe and the United States, and its prosperous and progressive government placed great importance on education for both sexes. In their decision to found a newspaper to espouse their ideas and to open schools to train a new generation of female teachers and students, the members of La Siemprevivia employed tactics used by the earlier advocates of women's rights. The critical change was that these women spoke for a new group within society, the middle sectors, and that their activities were collective, not individual.

The emergence of a collective female critique of discriminatory practices based on gender is well illustrated in the discussions of the series of scientific congresses held in the Southern Cone between 1898 and 1909. In 1898, in honor of its silver jubilee, the Sociedad Científica Argentina inaugurated a series of Latin American scientific congresses. As we saw in chapter 3, the majority of the women scientists and educators who attended the meetings in Montevideo in 1901, in Rio de Janeiro in 1905–1906, and in Santiago in 1908–1909 came from Argentina, Chile, Brazil, and Uruguay, a reflection not just of geographical proximity but of the entrance of women into the professions in those countries. They presented papers on health care, hygiene, child care, nutrition, mother welfare, and botanical and biological research, as well as the divisive issue of equal education.[11]

The debate over female education began in a discussion of what kinds of education were suitable for women. The women delegates were indignant that the debate should be cast in these terms, insisting on the need for equal facilities for all. The debate gradually broadened into a wide-ranging attack on the pervasive inequality of the sexes within society.

At the Latin American scientific congresses women delegates were full participants. The Third Latin American Scientific Congress was held in Rio de Janeiro in 1905 and was seen by the women scientists and educators as particularly important for two reasons: first, for the emphasis placed on social issues, and second, for the part taken in it by women. Selected as honorary president of the congress was Dr. Constança Barbosa Rodrigues, who was cited in the program as the "wife and collaborator of the director of the Jardim Botanico of Rio de Janeiro." Her selection as honorary president was greeted with great applause, and the chairman congratulated the congress "for having broken down a social prejudice."

The fourth congress, held in Santiago, Chile, in December and January 1908–1909, was expanded to become the first Pan-American Scientific Congress. The preceding congresses had attracted approximately eight hundred participants; the Santiago meeting brought two thousand delegates from throughout the hemisphere. Special notice was taken of the attendance of women; Eduardo Poirier, president of the congress, reported that women comprised 6 percent of the total membership of the conference. U.S. delegate W. R. Shepherd of Columbia University wrote: "Women school teachers constituted a large part of the audience . . . and it must be said that they express their opinions, as well as their difference in opinion from those held by the other sex, with a freedom and frankness quite surprising to anyone who might fancy that no phase of the feminist movement has yet reached Latin America."[12]

The outspoken presence of Latin American women in these scientific congresses established a precedent of female participation in an inter-American meeting that was to be of great importance in the years to come. However, the discussion of the disparity between the men and women teachers' attitudes toward female education was appropriate to the forum of the scientific congresses and does not represent the breadth of the feminist social critique that existed in the Southern Cone republics at the turn of the century.

On May 10, 1910, the date of the centennial celebration of Argentine independence, the first *Congreso Femenino Internacional* convened in Buenos Aires, with more than two hundred women from Argentina, Uruguay, Peru, Paraguay, and Chile in attendance. Dr. Cecilia Grierson presided. Grierson had attended the Second International Council of Women (I.C.W.) meeting in London in 1899 and had returned to Argentina intending to found an Argentine branch of the I.C.W. The initial meeting took place in 1900, with representatives from female beneficent societies, religious groups, and female auxiliaries, many of whom were associated with foreigners resident in Argentina. Drawing as it did only women from the more traditional sectors of Argentine society, the I.C.W. conference represented only one facet of women's organized activity in the country. In 1910 the International Feminist Congress, which was organized by the University Women of Argentina (Universitarias Argentinas), included among its sponsoring groups the National Argentine Association against the White Slave Trade, the Socialist Women's Center, the Association of Normal School Teachers, the Women's Union and Labor Group, and the National League of Women Freethinkers.

That the International Feminist Congress should be held in Buenos Aires was entirely appropriate: In 1910, Buenos Aires was the most cosmopolitan city in South America, a wealthy port open to the world's commerce, boasting a splendid commercial and cultural center and a population that had grown from 300,000 in 1880 to 1,500,000 in 1914. European immigrants, many of whom were skilled workers from the Mediterranean countries, had transformed the political and social complexion of the city. The metropolitan atmosphere, combined with a relatively advanced public education system, provided the background from which new social groups emerged, and the aspirations of these middle-sector women are reflected in the issues raised at the International Feminist Congress.

In this atmosphere, the wide differences in the political orientation of the women who attended the International Feminist Congress, evident in the sponsoring groups, were viewed not as a potential obstacle to consensus but as a reflection of the enormous political diversity evident in Buenos Aires and to a lesser extent in Montevideo, São Paulo, Santiago, and Lima in the period. Many of the reformist women belonged to the Socialist party; others rejected the Socialist political platform for being too concerned with class and labor and aligned themselves instead with the Anarchists, whose platform held the promise of a comlete reform of the bourgeois household.[13] The loyalties of others lay with the Argentine Radical party, which represented a more traditional brand of political opposition.

The congress brought together representatives of women's groups that had formed in very different ways, ways in which their class interests were directly reflected: telephone operators and factory workers whose interests lay with the trade union movement; teachers and professors and lawyers, who sought the right of entry into professional fields; and volunteer workers whose charitable activities were directed at alleviating the conditions of poverty. The women were not insensitive to these divisions of class but believed that the overwhelming discrimination against all women gave them common ground. In her speech on divorce, Carolina Muzzilli put it thus: "The aristocratic women and the proletarian women are equally victims. . . . It is time that the Argentine woman recognizes that she is not inferior to men and even if she has a different mission, her civil and natural rights must be restored."[14]

The belief in woman's "different mission" lies at the heart of feminist movements in Latin America and differentiates them from the predominant form of feminism that developed in England and the United States, where equality with men was the goal, and gender differences were denied or at least played down. In the Latin American context, the feminine is cherished, the womanly—the ability to bear and raise children, to nurture a family—is celebrated. Rather than reject their socially defined role as mothers, as wives, Latin American feminists may be understood as women acting to protest laws and conditions which threaten their ability to fulfill that role. Moreover, there is an explicit spiritual or moral content to the declarations of Latin American feminists which has strong parallels with feminist thought as it developed in Catholic Europe.[15]

The topics addressed at the International Feminist Congress ranged from international law, particularly as it related to the rights of married women to retain their citizenship, to health care and the problems of the married working woman. It reflected the participants' conversance with the international reformist and feminist dialogue of the day. Resolutions were passed commending the government of Uruguay for the passage of a Bill of Divorce and one demanding equal pay for equal work: "The work of women should not be less well remunerated than that of the man." The congress formulated a proposed modification to the Argentine Civil Code that would protect women from losing all civil rights and control of their properties upon marriage; the proposition was unanimously approved by the delegates.[16]

The debate that ensued over the acceptance of the platform of the Socialist Women's Center of Buenos Aires demonstrates some of the differences among the delegates. The platform included eight propositions: (1) universal suffrage for both sexes; (2) absolute divorce; (3) an eight-hour work day for adults and a six-hour day for children under sixteen years of age; (4) provision of a place to sit down for women workers in stores, workshops, and factories; (5) thirty-four days of leave before and after birth with full pay; (6) compulsory secular education for children of both sexes to the age of fourteen; (7) regular inspections to ensure compliance with the laws governing female and child labor; and (8) establishment of commercial schools for women, improvement of sanitary and health conditions, and promotion of the aesthetic education of the woman worker.

The congress approved the platform in general, but the proposals calling for special consideration for women workers were challenged. The debate between those who sought special protection for women workers and those who sought equality before the law for all adults was a watershed in the women's movement throughout the Western world. In Argentina in 1910, the proponents of equal rights prevailed over the protectionists, and the propositions of the Socialist Women's Center were modified accordingly before the platform was approved by the assembly.

Approval by the International Feminist Congress did not mean that any of the resolutions had the force of law; the women had no means of enacting their platform. What they were able to do was to present their program to the legislators and politicians of their respective countries and to act as an organized pressure group. They were also able to publicize their position in the hope of enlisting supporters and educating the public. There were new political alignments pushing for political reform in Argentina at the time, one result of which was the passage of the Saenz Pena Law, which granted universal male suffrage in 1912. No mention was made of the possibility of female suffrage.

The International Feminist Congress, convened by women, addressed the issues they deemed to be of collective importance to women. It was in this forum that a broad-based feminist critique of Argentine society (and by extension of Spanish South American society) was formulated. It is significant in the context of the development of feminism in Latin America that these women did not reject their feminine role—mother, wife, sister—in their formulation of a gender-based critique of the status quo in their societies. Also, the discussions, platforms, and resolutions of the congress demonstrated a blending of the concerns that had emerged in response to local circumstances and the ideas generated at the international level by the woman's movement and the labor movement.

In 1916 two feminist congresses were held in Mérida. The Mexican feminist congresses were unlike the International Feminist Congress held in Buenos Aires in 1910 in several fundamental ways. First, the instigation to hold a woman's conference came from Salvador Alvarado, Socialist governor of the state of Yucatán, who "unlike many Mexican revolutionaries, considered women's emancipation an integral part of Mexico's overall revolutionary goals of elevating oppressed peoples."[17] Second, although Alvarado's proposal was accepted with alacrity and carried through by women teachers in the Yucatán, the agenda was drawn up by Alvarado. Third, the congress was conceived within the Mexican national picture rather than in the international mold, a position in keeping with the ardent nationalism that fired the revolutionary spirit of the period. The discussions were cast in terms of *la mujer mexicana*, the Mexican woman, not universal womanhood.

The First Feminist Congress was held in January 1916; more than seven hundred women, mostly teachers, attended. Alvarado's agenda outlined themes for discussion, which included encouraging women to greater participation in public life, the importance of primary education for girls, and ways to "free women from their traditional yokes."[18] The opening paper, written by Hermila Galindo, very nearly ended the conference. Her advocacy of sex education and her belief that women were the sexual as well as the intellectual equals of men shocked the assembled teachers. One delegate demanded that the paper be burned on the spot.

The women, as well as Governor Alvarado, were well aware of the preparations underway for a national constitutional convention, to be called in Querétaro in December 1916. The purpose of the Constitutional Convention was to attempt to transform into law the disparate ideals in whose name the Mexican Revolution had been waged. Mexican feminists saw this as an opportune moment to bring the question of women's rights to the forefront of public debate.

What the First Feminist Congress revealed was that even among these women of similar social and economic background there were passionate divisions on what women's roles in society should be. The Catholic conservatives fought all proposals they considered threatening to the maintaining of women in their traditional roles as wives and mothers. Even education came under attack: "Women teachers don't marry!" warned Francisca García Ortiz in her speech. "Encyclopedic knowledge is an obstacle to happiness!" At the other end of the spectrum were the radicals, who insisted on the equality of woman to man, supported woman suffrage and the right of women to run for office, and looked to the government for the redress of discriminatory injustice. The centrists supported nonreligious education for women, often on the grounds that education would better prepare women for motherhood; but they were cautious on the issue of the vote, for which they felt most Mexican women were unprepared. They concurred with the radicals on the need to reform the 1884 Civil Code, which denied women, married and single, the right to act independently of the male head of household in nearly all matters, including child guardianship and inheritance.[19]

In contrast to the International Feminist Congress in Buenos Aires, where proposals for broad social and legal reform dominated the proceedings, in Mérida woman suffrage was at the center of the discussion. There are several reasons why this was so: First, a primary motive for calling the convention was Alvarado's desire to broaden the base of political support for his Socialist government in Yucatán; second, the rhetoric of the Mexican Revolution promised political participation for all citizens; and third, in 1916 women reformers throughout the world were closely watching the battle being waged for woman suffrage in the United States and England.

The argument that women needed the vote to bring about social and legal reform proved effective at Mérida, and after a prolonged and heated debate the First Feminist Congress unanimously passed a resolution calling for the state government of Yucatán to assume leadership in altering the national constitution to allow women to vote in all municipal elections and for the state of Yucatán to immediately grant women local suffrage and the right to run for office.

The Second Feminist Congress met in November 1916, with about half the number of participants that had attended the January meeting. The discussion topics paralleled those of the first congress, including primary school education, marriage, rights of divorced parents and their children, and woman suffrage and office-holding.[20] The tone of the November meeting was far more restrained, but the divisions of opinion among the women were equally as sharp. The final resolutions were cautious, with the delegates approving woman suffrage on the municipal level but rejecting the right of women to seek election.

The Mexican Constitutional Convention met at Querétaro in December 1916 and in ten months produced the Mexican Constitution of 1917, hailed as the most advanced social and political document of its day. Political rights, including the right to vote, were granted to all Mexican citizens; women were excluded from the category of citizen.

Despite this defeat, the impact of the Mexican feminist congresses was apparent in President Venustiano Carranza's Law of Family Relations, also passed in 1917, which "guaranteed the rights of married women (1) draw up contracts, (2) take part in legal suits, (3) act as guardians, (4) have the same rights as men to the custody of their children, and (5) have equal authority to spend family funds. It also permitted paternity suits and gave parents the right to acknowledge illegitimate children."[21] The Mexican Civil Code of 1884, which the Carranza law amended, was based on the Spanish Civil Code, which endowed the husband, as male head of household, with legal authority over his wife's property, her activities, and their children.

Similar reforms of the civil codes that governed family relations were undertaken in many of the Latin American states in the period. In Uruguay a variety of social and political reforms were introduced under the regime of José Batlle y Ordóñez (1905–1929), including the Bill of Divorce mentioned above. The right of Uruguayan women to a university education was incorporated in the constitution of 1918.

In Cuba, which gained independence from Spain in 1901, the old Spanish Civil Code was attacked in the Senate in 1916 on the grounds that it conflicted with the new constitution, which was based on that of the United States. The desire to be part of the progressive, modern nations of the world helped to dislodge old prejudices; and in Cuba, as in the Southern Cone nations and in Mexico, new groups were exercising political power. The arguments put forth by one senator, a nephew of the feminist educator María Luisa Dolz, illustrate a new aspect of the reformist approach to women's issues:

Senator Dolz acknowledged the historical momentum of the international feminist movement and admonished the senators for not taking it seriously enough to pass more general laws of equality between the sexes. He warned against locking up such a movement and granting it only grudging conditions. Women should have their rights because the movement was worldwide, it was just and moderate, and the women had not asked to dominate men. Resisting the woman's movement would encourage female activists to become socialists and fulfill everyone's greatest fear: If women were denied political participation, they might become socialist; if the divorce bill were turned down, women, the guardians of Cuban morality, would choose to live in unions of free love.[22]

On the issue of revising the Civil Code, the Cuban reformers found themselves in alliance with the upper-class conservative members of the senate, who wished to protect their family properties from falling under the control of potentially unworthy sons-in-law. After a two-year debate, the all-male senate approved a new family law on May 18, 1917. It began: "The married woman of majority will have the free administration and disposal of her paraphernalia property and her dowry, without the permission of her husband." It is noteworthy that the arguments put forth by both the progressive and conservative senators in favor of revising the Civil Code rested on the idea that, without revision of the family code, women might do something that would endanger the interests of men: In the one case, women might be forced into the arms of the Socialist party; in the other, a flighty daughter might marry an upstart and lose the family inheritance.

The drive to revise the civil codes should be distinguished from the extension of political rights to new groups in society. The civil codes governed interfamilial relationships, and the movement to reform them was part of the move toward secularization and away from the influence of the Catholic church. In many areas of Latin America where individual voices were raised in support of social and political reform, broadly based movements that included the advocacy of women's rights did not materialize. In Central America and in the Andean nations, small family oligarchies and a conservative church hierarchy maintained their traditional social, economic, and political control.

The history of feminism in Peru offers an example of the woman's movement in a country where a strong middle class did not develop in the early twentieth century and secularization of the schools did not occur. Although the development of public, secular education was clearly critical in the formation of feminist movements as they emerged elsewhere, the lack of the little red schoolhouse should not lead us to assume ignorance or indifference to the status of women but to ask what forms of feminist consciousness did exist and how these were made manifest. Women born and educated in Peru did become feminist thinkers. We know from Luís Martín's *Daughters of the Conquistadors* that the viceroyalty of Peru was concerned with the education of women by the late sixteenth century, when Chile, the Rio de la Plata, and Plymouth Rock were as yet untenanted by Europeans. In the eighteenth century, male and female intellectuals alike called for women's rights and debated the merits of scientific education for both sexes in the salons of Lima.

In the late nineteenth century, Clorinda Matto de Turner and Mercedes Cabello de Carbonero wrote and spoke on women's rights. Their forum was the private literary salon; their medium, the novel. As Elsa Chaney points out, "In Peru, the precursors of [female] emancipation were, with few exceptions, novelists and poets, whereas in Chile women's emancipation from its beginnings in the 1870's was tied to the entrance of women into higher education and the professions. . . . The sharp differences between women's early activity in Peru and Chile may account, at least in part, for the significantly greater progress Chilean women later made in public life."[23]

María Jesús Alvarado Rivera is credited with opening public discussion of "the woman question" in Peru in a speech at the prestigious Geographic Society of Lima in 1911. Alvarado had studied with feminist thinker and author Elvira García y García at her private secondary school for girls. Alvarado, whose political activities included underground activity against the dictator Augusto B. Leguía on behalf of workers and students and who championed the cause of justice for the indigenous population, later discounted any intellectual debt to García y García, whom she dismissed as too narrow in her views.[24]

A number of Peruvian women were involved in the transnational conferences held in South America in this era. Seventeen of them, including Alvarado, attended the *Primero Congreso Feminino* in Buenos Aires in 1910: the *Nomina de Adherentes al Congreso Femenino Internacional* records the presence of María Jesús Alvarado, María Camacho y Bueno, J. E. Corvalan, J. J. del Pino, Julia Rosa B. Delaney, Juana A. de Dammert, Dra. Esther Festini, Elvira García y García, Rosa Gómez, E. Gutierrez de Quintanilla, Felicia Manuela Gomez, Clorinda Calero de Hernández, Adelaida Hintschel, Dora Mayer, Prado y Ugarteche, M., Drs. Elvira Rodriguez Lorente, Dorotea J. Ros Georges. Dra. María Camacho y Bueno spoke on "A Single Moral Standard for Both Sexes." María Jesús Alvarado Rivera spoke on *femenismo*, enumerating reforms in education, remuneration for work, the legal system, and "in the moral order where it is necessary to combat the belief that practicing religion has the virtue of relieving one of the responsibility for great evils."[25]

In 1914, Alvarado founded *Evolución Femenina*, a women's society, in Peru. Much of the inspiration and support to do so came from her attendance at the Argentine Congreso; the core group of members included the women named above, all of whom were Limeñas. One of the key differences between these pioneer Peruvian feminists and their sisters in Argentina, Brazil, Chile, Mexico, and Cuba is that they had a comparatively narrow audience for their ideas. Some liberal, reform-minded male politicians offered support, but there was no receptive group of educated women entering the workforce. On the contrary, in the Peruvian context, feminist ideas appeared wildly radical. The majority of convent-educated women were vehemently hostile to the principles espoused by *Evolución Femenina*: the opposition of the *Unión Católica* (Catholic Women's League) to Alvarado's work led directly to her imprisonment and eventual exile in 1925.

Moreover, the Peruvian feminists were not immune to the sharp divisions of race and caste that marked the larger society, a fact that prevented alliances not only between women of the middle sectors and the lower classes, as was true elsewhere, but also prevented the formation of supportive coalitions between upper-middle-class intellectuals and educated middle-sector women. In Peru there were few claims to the sisterhood of all women.

In 1923, Carrie Chapman Catt went to Peru in her capacity as president of the Pan-American Woman Suffrage Alliance. In a candid letter to a friend, Catt wrote, "We had heard much about conditions in Peru before our arrival. Everyone predicted failure. The organizing difficulty was a wholly new one.

[Women of the upper middle classes] will not associate. All the university women, doctors, etc. are not only middle class but mostly of decidedly mixed blood. The pure castillian woman would die before she moved equally herself with those of color: Every man had done his best to populate Peru and has had no hesitancy about miscegenation, but the castillian woman imagines herself as keeping the race pure."[26]

Catt also noted that the sessions at the university were monitored by unfriendly male clerical emissaries, who intimidated some of the would-be speakers, and concluded that "after my trip I'm inclined to the opinion that the chief asset of the Catholic Church is its 'sisters.'"

Alvarado, who was Catt's chief contact in 1923, became secretary of the Peruvian National Women's Council. In Chile, Uruguay, Argentina, and Mexico the national women's councils, most of which were established between 1918 and 1920, were made up of representatives of women's organizations; in Peru the impetus to form a "national" council came in response to the need to organize a committee to host the Second Pan-American Women's Conference, which was scheduled to meet in Lima in 1924. The members of the committee included wives of foreign ministers; the focus was on suffrage to the exclusion of broader issues of social reform: "Not all the members agreed that women ought to work for any rights beyond the vote; when María Alvarado asked the council, on behalf of *Evolución Femenina*, if she might present a project to reform the civil code and give women equality before the law, there was an uproar."[27]

The conservatism of the Peruvian polity is illustrated in the nine-year campaign undertaken by *Evolución Femenina* to secure the right of women to serve as directors of the *Sociedades de Beneficencia Pública* (Public Welfare Societies). In her study of women in Peruvian politics, Elsa Chaney comments, "With vast properties at their disposal, a seat on the directing committee often meant more than a seat in congress. The law permitting women to serve was significant because until then women were excluded even from charitable enterprises whenever these involved large sums of money or political power."[28] A bill was passed in 1922 that allowed women access to this previously all-male domain.

That the drive for female equality should be articulated as a campaign for appointment to charity boards indicates a number of things about Peruvian society in this era. First, it reinforces the fact that the Leguía government was primarily a caretaker institution acting on behalf of oligarchic interests. The women of *Evolución Femenina* did not want to enter the political arena per se: they wanted access to where the real power lay. Second, it illustrates the class origins of the membership of *Evolución Femenina*: they sought equality with the elite males of their own class. Third, it emphasizes the degree to which even these privileged women had been excluded from public spheres of action: the large private charitable organizations had been the province of women in Argentina, Brazil, Mexico, Cuba, Chile, and Uruguay for a hundred years and more. As was true elsewhere, women's voices were raised in Peru on behalf of women's estate in the early twentieth century, but the forum within Peru was limited to a small number of people who lived in the capital city, who, by virtue of their Hispanic background, their education, and their geographic locale, were set apart from the vast majority of women in their own country. The political climate was particularly intolerant of dissident thinking, whether reformist or revolutionary; in the 1920s several outspoken Peruvian feminists, including Alvarado, were forced into exile.

The evidence suggests that the transnational arena held a particular appeal for Latin American feminists. There are a number of reasons for this: First, within their national communities, they were disenfranchised; and as elsewhere, the national social and political arenas were characterized by androcacy. Second, Latin American female intellectuals were particularly alienated from politics as practiced within their countries, excluded from leadership positions not only by the status quo but by the forces of opposition. By the 1920s and 1930's, the international forums seemed to offer activist women the opportunity to effect reform through the passage of resolutions that would oblige signatory governments to raise the issues within their domestic arena.

The ideas brought forth in the early feminist congresses in Latin America did influence the legislators who revised the civil codes to end the legal inequality of married women, and they were effective in bringing social issues to the attention of the educated public. Moreover, the presence of Argentine, Uruguayan, Chilean, and Brazilian women at the scientific congresses held between 1898 and 1910 established a tradition of female participation in inter-American meetings. The importance of this precedent and the leadership of the Latin American women was demonstrated at the Second Pan-American Scientific Congress, held in Washington, D.C., in 1915–1916.

The Washington congress took on far more significance within the context of inter-American relations than the previous scientific congresses had done. At the time of the Washington congress, Europe was at war and Mexico was in the throes of revolution. The U.S. Department of State, aware that the audience of the scientific congress would include the diplomatic representatives of the states of the Western Hemisphere resident in Washington, took the opportunity to put forth its interpretation of hemispheric security and the need to build up defensive power. Thus, the character of the meeting was altered from the collegial exchange of professionals to the facsimile of a full-dress inter-American diplomatic conference. One of the consequences was that, unlike the South American congresses, the Washington congress did not include women among the "savants, scientists, and publicists" invited. The women were relegated to the balconies.

Thus began a second phase in women's efforts to focus attention at the international level on issues of their special concern. In response to their disbarment from the official Washington meetings, a number of Latin American women educators, professionals, and diplomats' wives—including Flora de Oliveira Lima, wife of the Brazilian minister to Washington; Amanda Labarca, a Chilean educator who had participated in the 1909 Santiago scientific congress and had attended the International Feminist Congress in Buenos Aires in 1910; and Mme Charles Dubé, wife of the Haitian minister— met with Eleanor Foster Lansing, wife of U.S. Secretary of State Robert Lansing, and laid plans for the "First Pan-American Women's Auxiliary Conference." In the minutes of their first meeting, the Latin American women's previous involvement in the scientific congresses was recognized for bringing legitimacy to the project.[29]

Forming an auxiliary was very much in the mainstream of women's organizational efforts in the period and was not regarded as especially remarkable. The *Pan-American Union Bulletin* reported the women's activities thus: "So many delegates came to Washington accompanied by their wives and other ladies of their families that an auxiliary was suggested."[30] The *Bulletin* missed the point: The women's plans were in place before the congress began and were not a response to a numerous female presence for which tea parties and expeditions needed to be arranged.

The women took themselves seriously, and they had a clear sense of the historical importance of their venture. In fact, the meeting of the auxiliary was so successful that the participants overflowed the small room to which the women had originally been assigned, and the meeting was moved to the ballroom of the Mayflower Hotel. In these early phases of women's involvement at the international level, the women participants were of the same social and economic background as their male counterparts. However, the women had a different agenda. On issues of social welfare their program often intersected with that of reform-minded men; the split came when women sought to have equality of rights for their own sex, such as equal access to education and to the ballot box and within marriage. It is also significant that the women acting at the international level at this time were not, as the men were, professional diplomats, paid commercial agents, or subsidized scholars. The women were involved because they had issues on which they could agree despite great diversity in background and personal political orientation.

The agenda drawn up at the Mayflower Hotel in 1916 stated that the purpose of the meeting was not only to "exchange views on the subjects of special interest to women," which included "the education of women, training of children and social welfare," but also to discuss "subjects of Pan Americanism." In her keynote speech to the auxiliary, Eleanor Foster Lansing underlined the theme of Pan-Americanism: "In every way and through every channel of association, we the women of North and South America, which possess similar conceptions of individual rights and constitutional government . . . possess a common duty to mankind which we must not ignore." The most important result of the "First Pan American Women's Auxiliary Conference" was the decision, voted on by more than three hundred women, "to start an organization of a Pan American Union of women."[31] Each republic was to have a national committee, the headquarters were to be in Washington, and it would meet in conjunction with future scientific congresses. Notable too is the fact that this was the first inter-American meeting attended by a significant number of women from the United States.

In the 1920s the early efforts of the women bore fruit. The members of the Pan-American Women's International Committee were in close touch with the powerful new trends in international thought and in particular in the great women's international organizations. Nearly all of the women active in the Pan-American arena were members of the council founded in Norway in 1920 to urge the inclusion of women and women's issues on the League of Nations. Of the American states, only Uruguay included a woman in its delegation to the First Assembly of the League of Nations, Dr. Paulina Luisi. Many of the Pan-American women also belonged to the Women's International League for Peace and Freedom (WILPF), which supported both feminism and pacifism.

The idea of effecting change through international treaty and the belief in the efficacy of moral suasion at the international level were hallmarks of the era. For the women of the western hemisphere, the effort to obtain their goals through the League of Nations was not a viable strategy: the United States was not a member, and the Latin American nations that belonged felt relatively powerless compared to the European members.

What was the meaning of women's involvement at the international level for feminists and reformers in various countries in Latin America? An interesting example of the cross-fertilization of local, national, and international reformist and feminist movements can be observed in the career of Brazilian Bertha Lutz, whose activities on behalf of women's economic, social, and political rights began during her studies in biology in Paris in 1917 and continued throughout her life. In 1975, the year before her death, she represented Brazil at the United Nations Conference on Women in Mexico City.

Lutz's international orientation was in a sense a birthright. Her father, Adolpho Lutz, who did pioneering work in tropical medicine, had emigrated to Brazil from Switzerland; and her mother, Amy Fowler, was a trained nurse who had been born in England. Bertha Lutz was born in São Paulo in 1894; she earned a degree from the Law School in Rio de Janeiro and in biology from the Science Faculty of the University of Paris. On her return to Brazil in 1918, she published a call to Brazilian women: "I am proposing the establishment of a league of Brazilian women. I am not proposing an association of 'suffragettes' who would break windows along the street, but, rather, of Brazilians who understand that a woman ought not to live parasitically based on her sex, taking advantage of man's animal instincts, but, rather, be useful, educate herself and her children, and become capable of performing those political responsibilities which the future cannot fail to allot her."[32]

Lutz was instrumental in founding the League for Female Intellectual Emancipation (*Liga para a Emancipação Intelectual Feminina*) in Rio de Janeiro in 1920. It focused on female education, employment, and suffrage, and it publicized its program through articles in the popular press, the circulation of petitions, and the issuance of proclamations. The leadership of Bertha Lutz gave the league special access to governmental agencies: in 1919 Lutz had won the job of secretary to the National Museum, thereby becoming the second woman in Brazil to hold a high civil service post. The strategies employed by the league reflect the influence she was able to wield within the highly personal world of Brazilian politics. She appealed directly to the minister of education to provide secondary education of a high quality for women, which would enable them to prepare for university entrance examinations and be competitive with men in securing paid employment. In 1922 women were admitted to the prestigious Rio de Janeiro preparatory school, Colegio Dom Pedro II.[33]

Lutz believed that the emancipation of women lay in wage work: "Work is the most powerful instrument in the hand of a woman. . . . I consider that in Brazil the true 'leaders' of feminism, correctly understood, are the innumerable young women who work in industry, in commerce, in teaching, and in other spheres of human activity."[34] She saw woman suffrage as a recognition of women's worth and as a means of ensuring women's future material and moral welfare.

Her family and her own employment provided Lutz with the means to travel, and she took the opportunity to represent Brazilian women at numerous international conclaves. In turn, her attendance at meetings in Washington, Paris, and Geneva enhanced her personal prestige and authority at home. In 1919 she was chosen as Brazil's official delegate to the International Labor Organization's conference on the conditions of working women.

In April 1922, Lutz was one of the Brazilian women who traveled to Baltimore to attend the first Pan-American Conference of Women, which was sponsored by the League of Women Voters of the United States, working with the Pan-American Women's International Committee. Suffrage had been won by U.S. women in 1920, eighty-two years after it was first proposed at Seneca Falls, and the Baltimore conference was called with the intention of furthering woman suffrage in the Americas. With more than two thousand women in attendance, the meeting was far larger than any previous inter-American meeting of women. A broad spectrum of women's groups from the United States was represented, and nearly one hundred Canadian women attended. Present in the Latin American delegations were most of the women who would provide leadership in hemispheric affairs in the next two decades, including Bertha Lutz of Brazil; Elena Torres, Luz Vera, and Clara Gonzá-les of Mexico; Sara Casal de Quiros of Costa Rica; Ester Niero de Calva of Panama; Mme. Charles Dubé of Haiti; and Emma Lopez Seña de Garrdio of Cuba.[35]

Woman suffrage had not been a central concern of Latin American feminists for a variety of reasons. First, most Latin American women lived in countries where there was no history of effective male suffrage and no legacy of reform achieved at the ballot box. Social and economic concerns dominated the discussions of the various women's congresses; the issue of women's right to vote was generally introduced to the agenda as part of the Socialist women's platform, which called for universal suffrage for both sexes.

Second, Latin American feminists by no means agreed on the value of the vote to their cause. Some, like Julieta Lanteri-Renshaw—who, though unable to vote, ran for congress in Argentina in 1919—equated the denial of the vote to the denial of full adulthood to women. Many, like Bertha Lutz, promoted the right to vote as a means to enable passage of reformist legislation. Others, like many of the teachers who attended the Mexican feminist congresses, viewed woman suffrage with suspicion, believing that women should abstain from such a corrupt, masculine realm. And still others saw the woman's vote as potentially dangerous to the causes of feminism and reform, believing that the female vote would be essentially conservative, supportive of the status quo, and under the influence of the clergy.

By 1922, with the example of the North American women's success and in the wake of the war to "make the world safe for democracy," the movement to promote woman suffrage throughout the hemisphere was acclaimed by the delegates to the Baltimore conference. One immediate result was the organization of women's societies in a number of Latin American nations that were linked together through the newly formed Pan-American Association for the Advancement of Women, which included suffrage as a goal. It is significant that the association was founded at the instigation of the Latin American delegates to Baltimore; it was proposed by Celia Paladino de Vitale of Uruguay and strongly supported by Flora de Oliveria Lima of Brazil and Amanda Labarca of Chile, both veterans of the Latin American and Pan-

American Scientific Congresses. Elena Torres, a well-known Mexican activist who had sided with the radical Hermila Galindo at the feminist congresses held in Yucatán, was elected the Pan-American Association's vice-president for North America.

The breadth of the women's concerns were undiminished by the decision to work for woman suffrage, and the final document of the Baltimore convention directly reflected the issues to which Latin American feminists had given priority over the years, as well as the influence of the international peace movement and woman's movement. It called for international peace through arbitration, abolition of the white slave trade, access to public education at all levels, and the right of married women to control their own property and earnings and to secure equal child guardianship; it encouraged organization, discussion, and public speaking among women and freedom of opportunity for women to cultivate and use their talents; it pressed for political rights and promoted friendliness and understanding among all Pan-American countries, with the aim of maintaining perpetual peace in the hemisphere.

The immediate goal was to organize national umbrella groups of women's organizations in each country to work toward the goals agreed on in Baltimore. North American suffragist Carrie Chapman Catt was elected president, and she undertook a South American tour to lend her organizational skills and prestige to the establishment of the associations.[36] Bertha Lutz was elected vice-president of the Pan-American Association for South America and upon her return to Brazil used the network of the League for Female Intellectual Emancipation to establish a new organization, the Brazilian Federation for the Advancement of Women (*Federação Brasileira pelo Progresso Feminino* [FBPF]), which, unlike the league, was national in scope, with representatives from all twenty Brazilian states, women's professional organizations, and social action and charity groups. The goals of the FBPF paralleled those outlined at the Baltimore conference.

In December 1922 the FBPF attained national prominence by staging a five-day international convention. The timing of the event was propitious; in 1922 Brazil was celebrating the centennial of its independence from Portugal, and a powerful nativist intellectual movement was in bloom. Educated Brazilians wanted to be seen as progressive, as leaders of artistic, intellectual, and political movements, rather than as imitators of the Old World. Lutz and her fellow workers were able to invoke national pride in the inauguration of the FBPF. The international convention was attended by numerous congressmen and government officials as well as by female delegates from all over Brazil. Carrie Chapman Catt inaugurated her tour of South America at the convention. The international woman's movement also was represented by Ana de Castro Osorio from Portugal and Rosa Manus from Holland. Edward Morgan, U.S. ambassador to Brazil, gave a luncheon honoring Bertha Lutz that brought together the leaders of the Brazilian feminist movement and the vice-president of Brazil, the minister of foreign relations, the director of public education, and various congressmen. Although few if any of the Brazilian officials or Ambassador Morgan could be described as entirely sympathetic to the women's movement, the FBPF began operations in an aura of respectability unmatched in feminist annals.[37]

Despite the clearly upper-class origins of the leadership of the FBPF, the membership encompassed women from many walks of life. At the December meeting representatives of the Teacher's League, the Rio de Janeiro Union of Employees in Commerce, and the Bureau of Employees of the Young Women's Christian Association spoke on the problems faced by working women, citing poor transportation, excessive hours, low pay, sexual harrassment, unhealthy workplaces, and lack of legal protection. The FBPF endorsed the recommendations made by the International Labor Organization in 1919, which called for legal regulation and protection of female employment, and passed the following resolution: "Considering the urgency of insuring legal protection for female labor, which has been subject to inhuman exploitation, reducing women to an inferior position in the competition for industrial and agricultural salaries, as well as in other activities of modern life, it has become necessary to call to the attention of political leaders the need to incorporate protective measures for women into our social legislation."[38]

The FBPF established commissions to address various aspects of women's estate; problems faced by women in the workplace were given high priority, as was the issue of female education. The Brazilian Female Suffrage Alliance (*Aliança Brasileira pelo Sufragio Feminino*) was established; its officers were the wives of leading political figures. Within the year woman suffrage associations had been founded in São Paulo, Bahia, and Pernambuco. The focus of the FBPF was women's rights, and the issues of suffrage, equal education, and legal reform dominated the platform; more controversial social issues, such as divorce and sexual equality, were avoided. Although members of the FBPF professed to speak on behalf of all working women, they in fact addressed the problems of the new professional women—teachers, government employees, clerks.[39] The vast majority of Brazilian women were untouched by and unaware of the activities of these upper- and middle-class political activists.

The impact of the Pan-American Federation for the Advancement of Women was visible in other areas of the hemisphere as well, as was the move to form nationwide "umbrella" organizations. In Cuba meetings of the National Women's Congress were held in Havana in 1923 and 1925.[40] Like the Brazilian women, the Cubans disavowed the militant political tactics of British and North American suffragists. In the 1920s general political violence was rife in Cuba, and the women's strategy was to link their role as the national keepers of morality with the claim that the female vote would put an end to public violence and stabilize an unsteady democratic system.

A number of Cuban women had been present at the founding of the Pan-American League for the Advancement of Women in Baltimore in 1922, and it was not a coincidence that woman suffrage became a central issue of the National Women's Congress held in 1923, at which thirty-one women's organizations were represented.[41] María Luisa Dolz and Domitila García de Coronado gave the keynote address, "The Social Mission of Women," which emphasized the value of woman's separate political ideals. The two women had been active in Cuban politics since the 1880s; they not only represented an earlier generation of Cuban feminists but, because of their ardent support of the Cuban cause during the wars of independence, symbolized the patriotism of Cuban women.

Fourteen resolutions were agreed on at the First National Women's Congress in Havana in 1923:

1. That all women wage a campaign for suffrage for all women. (The repeated insistence on "all women" was meant to emphasize that the conferees would not restrict the vote on grounds of property ownership, marital status, class background, or race, the latter being a particularly divisive issue in the Cuban context.)

2. To work for general educational reform, including special schools, and give attention to homogeneous grouping within grades.

3. To work for reform of civil and penal law with the intent of equalizing the rights and responsibilities of men and women.

4. To work for the passage of protective legislation for children and to ensure its enforcement.

5. To pay special attention to reformatories and to establish juvenile courts.

6. To intensify the love of plants and animals.

7. To work for the beautification of the city.

8. To create popular state schools as a means of intensifying nationalism.

9. To intensify the fight against drugs, prostitution, and the white slave trade.

10. To participate in the high echelons of organization and inspection of the education system.

11. To influence penitentiary reform.

12. To consider the rights of illegitimate children.

13. To revise legislation on adultery.

14. To work intensely and efficiently, with all of the legal tools available and without compromise, to obtain suffrage.

The content of the resolutions raises a number of points about the national Cuban women's alliance. First, in ranging from suffrage to urban beautification to adultery legislation, the resolutions illustrate the diverse backgrounds of the conference participants and reflect the priorities of both progressive and conservative political constituencies within the country. Cuban women, no less than Cuban men, had participated in the fight for independence from Spain, won in 1901; and in the 1920s the women joined the struggle to establish democracy, with universal suffrage and justice for all. The national political crisis aroused common feelings of patriotism and national pride that temporarily obscured social and political differences among the women. Second, it should be noted that the Cuban women were asking for reforms within the educational system, not just for access to higher education, as the Brazilian women had done: the principle of equal education for both sexes from the primary level through the university was embodied in the Cuban Constitution of 1901.

At the Second National Women's Congress in 1925, the resolutions were fewer, but women were unyieldingly firm in the call for social as well as political reform:

1. Social equality between men and women.
2. Protection of the child.
3. Equal pay for equal work.
4. Equality of the claims of illegitimate children.
5. Elimination of prostitution.
6. Prohibition of the unequal treatment of women.

In her study of the Cuban women's movement, K. Lynn Stoner states that "no literate Cuban could have been unaware of the women's campaigns"[42] and that by the mid-1920s woman suffrage was a popular political issue in the country. In this respect more than any other, the situation in Cuba presents a contrast to that in Brazil or Mexico or Argentina, where strong women's movements were also gaining momentum in the period but where enormous problems of communication existed. Although the particular historical circumstances and political configuration that existed in each nation provided the matrix from which the women's movements emerged, more obvious but often overlooked factors were also critical. In contrasting the Cuban situation with that of Brazil or Mexico or Argentina, the relative size of the country and of its national elite should be kept in mind. In 1925, Cuba, whose national territory encompasses 45,397 square miles, had a population of approximately 3.5 million people and one major city, Havana. In contrast, Brazil, the fifth largest nation on earth, with a territory of 3,286,344 square miles, had a population of more than 30 million; in the 1920s it was markedly regional, as was Argentina, with a population of some 11 million and an area of 1,072,745 square miles. Mexico, with 767,919 square miles, counted a population of 16.5 million people in the mid-1920s and had a number of major urban centers in addition to the federal capital district. The logistics of communication in these enormous nations, combined with problems of illiteracy and regionalism, obviated the possibility of national awareness of any issue.

The situation in Mexico provides contrasts to the Cuban and Brazilian experiences. Whereas both Cuban and Brazilian feminists were able to attract the support of members of the national political elite, the revolutionary government in Mexico paid scant attention to the petitions of women working for women's rights. In 1920 the political situation in Mexico, although not as violent as in the preceding decades, remained volatile, marked by revolts and assassination. The struggle between church and state was bitter and bloody, and the leaders of the revolutionary government believed most women to be in sympathy with the church. Those Mexican women who had made some small gains toward political and civil reform, and in industrial employment in the period between 1890 and 1920, found themselves under siege. As men returned to the work force, women were pushed out of their jobs; workers' unions, far from protecting women, proved to be bastions of male supremacy. Virulent antifeminist cartoons appeared regularly in the national press; a typical example published in *Excelsior* in 1925 depicted a Gertrude Stein–like figure seated in what obviously had been Papa's easy chair, smoking a cigar and reading a feminist newspaper while her ragged, weeping children pulled at her skirts, begging for food and attention, and her husband, evidently unmanned at the transformation "feminism" had made in his wife, cowered in the kitchen.

The most vociferous opponents of feminism were members of the Confederation of Catholic Associations of Mexico, founded in 1920 to combine Catholic youth, worker, journalist, and women's groups. The Union of Catholic Women of Mexico "asserted that woman's place was in the home, and equated socialism with free love and feminism."[43] The government, determined to wrest away the power and wealth of the church, began to enforce the articles of the Constitution of 1917, which divested the church of its schools, property rights, and jurisdiction over ceremonies such as marriage. In 1926 the Cristero Rebellion against the government broke out in full force; women were deeply involved on both sides of the conflict.[44] Ironically, by the early 1930s, when the rebellion had been quelled, the women who had supported the government's struggle against the church still were unable to realize their political program. Most government leaders continued to view all women as potentially conservative and thus dangerous to their cause. Such distinctions did not seem so difficult to make among men, who had also fought on both sides of the conflict.

Despite the hostility toward feminism and the indifference of the government to women's issues, women played a central role in the campaigns to consolidate the revolution. Women teachers and health care workers were recruited in great numbers in the government's massive campaign against illiteracy and poverty, particularly in the rural areas of Mexico. Prior to the Revolution of 1910, education and social welfare were primarily under the aegis of the Catholic church. As was noted earlier, the literacy and health care campaigns of the 1920s were secular in content and thus presented a direct challenge to church authority. Elena Torres, teacher, feminist, and admirer of Leon Trotsky, was named chief of the Bureau of Cultural Missions. The female educators who filled the ranks of mission instructors were poorly paid, often receiving as little as one or two pesos per day,[45] but they were inspired by the vision of building a truly revolutionary society, where ignorance and poverty were vanquished. Female health care workers and educators were equally vital to the efforts of the government to improve sanitary conditions and disseminate information. "Sanitary brigades" went into the countryside, and prenatal clinics were established in urban centers. Smallpox vaccinations, lectures on child and maternal health care, and information on tropical and venereal disease were offered. In 1925 one clinic in Mexico City distributed thousands of copies of Margaret Sanger's pamphlet on family limitation.

The involvement of Mexican feminists in the international arena had a direct effect on the establishment and direction of both the educational and health care programs in Mexico. In 1918, Elisa Acuña y Rossetti, a school-teacher and journalist who, with Juana B. Gutierrez de Mendoza, edited the feminist journal *Vesper*, joined Elena Torres and Luz Vera to found the National Council of Mexican Women (*Consejo Nacional de Mujeres*) in Mexico City. Luz Vera, a teacher and writer, served as secretary and, together with Torres, represented the council in 1922 in Baltimore. In May 1923 the Mexican branch of the Pan-American Association for the Advancement of Women held its first national convention in Mexico City with one hundred women in attendance.[46] The women addressed the need for education and woman suffrage and presented research papers showing that Mexican women had lost ground, particularly in employment, since the revolution.[47] Women speakers pointed out that prostitution and alcoholism were on the rise, with especially pernicious effects for poor women and children.

The question of divorce was an issue of profound disagreement among Mexican feminists. The more radical women, like Socialist schoolteacher Ines Malvaez, believed that Carranza's Law of Domestic Relations, passed in 1917, should be amended to permit divorce at the will of only one spouse in a marriage. Sofia Villa de Buentello, who was a lawyer and an advocate of equal civil rights for men and women, "feared that lenient divorce laws, in the context of Mexican society, would benefit men and leave women with even less legal protection."[48] Many other women believed that divorce was immoral and should not be discussed. To faithful Catholic women and men, divorce threatened home, family, and church.

The meeting of the Mexican branch of the Pan-American Association was but one of numerous women's conferences convened in the 1920s.[49] Mexican feminists had strong ties to the international socialism movement and international feminist associations, as well as a heritage of grass-roots women's organizations, including teachers and workers associations and workers unions. The proliferation of conferences and congresses in the 1920s in Mexico showed a breadth of concerns and opinion, as well as demonstrating that an impressive number of women were involved in organizing to discuss and gain support for their programs. Although there are clear ties between the founding of some of the Mexican national associations and the international women's movement—the International Congress of Women in 1918, the Pan-American Association in 1923, and the Socialist Congress in 1925—Mexican women always exhibited a strong sense of the native origins of their movement, and even political moderates were careful to distance themselves from the North American feminist movement.

Between December 1924 and July 1925, Sofia Villa de Buentello organized a Congreso de Mujeres de la Raza. Sponsored by the Liga de Mujeres Ibericas e Hispanoamericanas and the Unión Cooperativa, the meeting opened in Mexico City on July 5, with more than two hundred representatives from Mexico, Latin America, and Spain in attendance. The ideologic splits that were to characterize the women's movement in the hemisphere in the following decades were manifest at the *congreso*. Irreconcilable divisions emerged between the Socialist left, led by Elvia Carrillo Puerto and Cuca García, which insisted on the economic basis of women's problems, and conservatives and moderates, led by Sofia Villa, who believed female inequality to be rooted in social and moral conditions. Questions of class loyalties and the continuing struggle between the church and the Mexican state further exacerbated the proceedings.

By July 10, Sofia Villa had increasing difficulty in maintaining any semblance of order, and many delegates left. Villa cried out, "This is an international congress, not a socialist or worker Congress; the foreign delegates have abandoned us and now there is no Congress." Elvia responded, "If it is to be said that this Congress, to be international, is for people of class, why have you invited us, the workers? The heart, the very fiber of the country, protests against the parasites that suck the lifeblood from it."[50] Even more outrageous to many of the Mexican delegates was the attack of the women of the left on the revolution itself. The radicals denounced the presence of "reactionaries" in government, particularly in the Department of Education. To the assembled women, many if not most of whom were teachers and a number of whom were leaders in the education programs, the proposal struck at their lifework as well as their political beliefs.

Ultimately, fewer than half of the original delegates remained, representing an uneasy collection of women of the left and right wings: the foreign delegates and the moderates who were the original organizers of the congress had departed by July 15. The problems of the congress were seized on by a press already inclined to be hostile to women's political activities. The Mexico City daily, *El Universal*, ran an editorial titled "A Defeat of Feminism," which stated that if this were an example of women's participation in public life, it was a fraud . . . a scandalous caricature of the National Congress . . . run by women trying to behave like men."[51]

Prior to this time, in Mexico as elsewhere, there existed a generally accepted assumption among politically active women that their common interests as women—in gaining the vote, in health care, in education—cut across class backgrounds and ideological orientations. This assumption of a cross-class, supraideological "women's cause" (an assumption that would reemerge in the sisterhood movements of the 1960s and early 1970s) characterized the early *congresos* and the political platforms agreed on by feminists in Cuba, Mexico, Brazil, and Argentina, even though the political allegiances of the conferees were often disparate. The breakdown of this coalition based on gender, illustrated at the 1925 *congreso* in Mexico City, was apparent throughout the hemisphere by the 1930s.

In the 1920s women in Mexico, Brazil, Argentina, and Cuba continued their organizational efforts at the local and national level, but they also took the opportunity to carry their platform to the inter-American meetings, which had not convened since 1910. Both North and South American feminists hoped that if they could win support for their cause at the diplomatic tables they could bring pressure on their national governments to consider reform at home.

The first evidence of the direct impact of the women's efforts on the International Conferences of American States came at the Santiago meeting in 1923. Chile, with its sizable community of activist women, provided a favorable setting for introducing the women's issues. Moreover, the Chilean meeting was in many respects a departure from pre–World War I conferences. The old emphasis on commercial exchange had given way to heated political discussions that challenged the growing dominance of the United States in hemispheric affairs. The early Pan-American meetings, convened between 1881 and 1910, had been primarily devoted to establishing conventions that would enhance inter-American commercial opportunities. They exhibited little of the fiery idealism expressed by Simón Bolívar, who had dreamed that "the assembling of a Congress of American nations will form a new epoch in human affairs."

The invocation of the ideals of Pan-Americanism by the feminists added a new dimension to the inter-American conferences. The International Conference of American States held in Santiago in 1923, the first since the onset of

World War I, took place in an atmosphere of controversy. The desire of the women to insert feminist issues and matters of broad social reform into the program coincided with the widespread desire of many in both North and South America, male and female, to use the conferences to challenge U.S. imperialist activities in Central America and the Caribbean.

A sizable number of "unofficial" female delegates attended the Santiago meeting. At their instigation, Maximo Soto Hall, a member of the Argentine delegation, introduced a motion pertaining to the rights of women in the hemisphere. It included the recommendation that the member states appoint women to their official delegations and suggested that the individual nations undertake a study of their laws with the intent of abolishing the inequality of the sexes. The motion passed but was advisory rather than binding.

The next International Conference of American States met in Havana in 1928; there were no official women delegates. But women from throughout the hemisphere foregathered in Havana for the inter-American conference. Their organizational efforts were evident in the diverse constituencies they represented: They spoke for the Consejo Feminista Mexicana, the WILPF, the National Woman's Party of the United States, the Club de Madres of Buenos Aires, and many others. They were hosted by the Alianza Femenina Cubana and the Club Femenino de Cuba.

By the end of the conference the women had secured an audience before a plenary session, presented an Equal Rights Treaty for the consideration of the governments of the hemisphere,[52] and successfully lobbied for the creation of an officially designated body, the Inter-American Commission of Women (IACW), which was charged with the investigation of the legal status of women in the twenty-one member states. The IACW was "the first governmental organization in the world to be founded for the express purpose of working for the rights of women."[53]

The choice of the Pan-American meetings as a forum for the discussion of women's and feminist issues proved politically astute. Whereas many of the women found little support from their national governments for their programs in the 1920s, their success at the inter-American meetings gave them political leverage back home. The Latin American women provided the precedent of using inter-American congresses as a forum for the debate of feminist issues with the scientific congresses at the turn of the century; their leadership is also evident in the insistent inclusion of issues of social justice in the Pan-American women's platforms. Moreover, although the hope of effecting reform at the transnational level was a characteristic of the period, the transnational arena held particular appeal for Latin American feminists, who had historically identified with the forces of change in their own societies.[54] The inter-American conferences provided the opportunity for a different strategy, demonstrated by the presentation of the Equal Rights Treaty to the assembled diplomats in Cuba in 1928. Had the treaty been agreed on, it would have been introduced to the national governments of each member state for ratification; the political opponents of equal rights could no longer prevent the issue from being considered.

The first task undertaken by the IACW was the investigation of the legal status of women in all countries of the hemisphere. Their work drew attention to the legal inequities suffered by women, and as the symbolic representative of numerous women's organizations in the Americas, the IACW was able to lend support to women's efforts within their national communities by providing information and acting as a communications center—the support was never financial. A rare instance of direct action occurred in Havana in 1928, when the women attending the Sixth International Conference of American States took the opportunity to parade in support of the Cuban woman suffrage movement.[55]

It was in this period that full suffrage was first granted to women in a number of Latin American nations. Three time periods are discernible: the earliest, 1929–1934, during which the governments of Ecuador, Brazil, Uruguay, and Cuba granted woman suffrage; the middle, 1939–1945, when El Salvador, the Dominican Republic, Guatemala, and Panama did likewise; and the postwar period, 1947–1961, when the remaining nations conformed. The following chart gives the dates when woman suffrage was enacted in each state:

Pre–World War II	Post–World War II
Ecuador, 1929	Venezuela, 1947
Brazil, 1932	Argentina, 1947
Uruguay, 1932	Chile, 1949
Cuba, 1934	Costa Rica, 1949
	Haiti, 1950
	Bolivia, 1952
	Mexico, 1953
World War II	Honduras, 1955
El Salvador, 1939	Nicaragua, 1955
Dominican Republic, 1942	Peru, 1955
Panama, 1945	Colombia, 1957
Guatemala, 1945	Paraguay, 1961

The enactment of female suffrage should not be interpreted as a signpost that the women's program had triumphed in a particular time and place. The meaning of the vote and the reasons woman suffrage was enacted in a particular nation at a particular time vary greatly. Moreover, irregular transitions in power and the suspension of civil liberties, including elections, characterized the political scene in many Latin American nations during the 1930s. Effective universal suffrage, male and female, did not exist anywhere until after World War II.

Examining the ways in which women gained suffrage underscores the political diversity of the hemisphere. In the earliest period there was no consistent pattern of achievement of the franchise; woman suffrage was enacted by reform administrations, by one-party systems that sought to further consolidate their power through incorporating the female vote, and by conservative governments. In each country women had to work within the national political context to gain their ends. But if the means to the end was not consistent, the program was: In Latin America woman suffrage was almost universally portrayed by its advocates as the means to a more moral society, with a platform that emphasized social motherhood issues and peace more than gender equity.[56]

The fact that woman suffrage had been passed in the United States in 1920 provided impetus to the woman suffrage movement in Latin America; it also demonstrated that the female vote was far from revolutionary in its impact. Female suffrage could be viewed as a step toward democracy, and a safe one, particularly if women were indebted to the incumbent government for their enfranchisement and if the vote was restricted to those who could fulfill certain literacy and property requirements.

In 1929, Ecuador became the first nation in Latin America to grant woman suffrage. The political coalition in power that promulgated the female vote was deeply conservative and sought to broaden its political base in the event of a renewed threat from the group of young Socialist officers who had staged a successful military coup in 1925. The Ecuadorean establishment saw women as congenitally conservative, loyal to the Catholic church, and politically maleable; certainly, few feminist voices had been raised in Quito or Guayaquil to challenge this view.

In contrast, in Brazil, Uruguay, and Cuba the enactment of woman suffrage was the result of years of hard work and carefully planned campaigns; the women were prepared to act when an advantageous political situation arose. In Brazil the revolution of October 1930 brought to power men who had promised to enact a reform agenda. The *Federação Brasileira pelo Progresso Feminino*, well-organized and with a nationwide network, immediately took steps to ensure that their platform would be part of those reforms. Their first victory came in the electoral reform decree of February 24, 1932, which granted woman suffrage. Bertha Lutz, appointed to the government commission charged with drafting a new national constitution, and Carlota Pereira de Queiroz, elected to the Constituent Assembly from São Paulo, ably represented the women's program.

Working with other members of the FBFP, Lutz prepared the Thirteen Principles, which included woman suffrage and equality before the law; the right of married women to retain their nationality; equal pay for equal work; paid maternity leaves; the right of women, whether married, single, or widowed to hold all public positions; the appointment of qualified women to administer welfare programs that dealt with maternity, child care, female labor, and homemaking. The FBFP's Principles also reflected their long commitment to legislation that would protect female workers by incorporating the central tenets of the labor platform: minimum salary, the eight-hour day, paid vacations, and compensation for illness, injury, disability, and retirement.[57] The efforts of the Brazilian women were successful; the Thirteen Principles were incorporated into the constitution of 1934. One year later, María Luiza Bittencourt wrote to the IACW to report that she had been elected to the state legislature of Bahia, and that "eighteen of the twenty states in Brazil have elected women to their legislatures, and the new president of the State of Rio de Janeiro has appointed women to the portfolios of Labor and Education in his cabinet."[58] The political opening in Brazil proved short-lived; in 1937 President Getúlio Vargas proclaimed the *Estado Novo*, and neither Brazilian women nor Brazilian men participated in open elections again until 1946.

Uruguay was, in theory, the first of all Western Hemisphere nations to recognize female suffrage: the constitution of 1917 stated that women had the right to vote and hold office at local and national levels. However, the principle of woman suffrage required a two-thirds majority in each of the legislative houses to become law. By 1932 popular pressure for reform, including reform of the electoral process, was acute: A rapidly expanding population, which included thousands of European immigrants, a strong and articulate labor movement, and liberal politicians, joined in demanding an opening up of the political process. The Uruguayan economy, which depended almost exclusively on the export of its range products for revenues, was reeling in the aftermath of the Great Depression. A decree of December 16, 1932, provided for women's participation in the elections scheduled for 1934; those elections were not held, but the new constitution of 1934 stated that "national citizens are all men and women born within the nation . . . and every citizen is as such a voter and qualified to hold office." The reluctance of the government to grant political rights to immigrant male workers, who were the most numerous—and potentially most disruptive—group of residents, is reflected in the stipulation that "foreign men and women, when married, and of good repute, have the right to vote, if they are employed in a profession or hold property and have resided in the Republic for fifteen years." In short, when the government in Uruguay could perceive the female vote not as an opening for feminists, many of whom had traditionally aligned themselves with the Socialist or Anarchist parties in Uruguay, but as the incorporation into the political process of native-born Uruguayan women who would buttress the class interests of the ruling elite, female suffrage became law.

In Cuba the configuration of events surrounding the passage of woman suffrage in 1934 presents both contrasts and parallels to the situations in Uruguay and Brazil. As was true in those countries, the Cuban woman's movement was well-organized, with long roots, but Cuban women also laid claim to a history of direct political participation for their role in the Cuban independence movement. Historian K. Lynn Stoner writes:

In 1934 Cuba became the fourth Latin American country to extend the franchise to women. Cuba's rapid passage of women's suffrage coincided with a crisis in the Cuban democratic system which President Gerardo Machado's government, stricken by economic decline during the Great Depression, guilty of repressive action against the population, and suspected of becoming a dictatorship, created. Suffragists gained influence during this period because of the turmoil and because of their importance as a legitimizing force. . . . Cuban suffragists could not play one established party off against another, as United States and British suffragists had done, nor could they treat the franchise as an issue separate from a national crisis. . . . The overthrow of Gerardo Machado was for Cuban women what World War I was for British and American women: the crisis that forced respect for female political and national action.[59]

Since the national women's congresses of 1923 and 1925, numerous women's associations in Cuba had worked for suffrage. The *Alianza Nacional Feminista*, the *Partido Nacional Sufragista*, and the *Partido Democrata* were joined by women attending the International Conference of American States in Havana in 1928 in a parade calling for the government to grant woman suffrage. In 1930 Cuban women and their supporters received further support from the members of the IACW, which held its first meeting in Havana in that year. In the increasingly violent political situation in the early 1930s, politically active Cuban women threw their support behind the opposition. Recognition of the potential legitimizing value of women's support was apparent in the attempts of successive administrations to establish woman suffrage between 1928 and 1934; the formal extension of the franchise to women was incorporated in the provisional constitution of February 3, 1934. In the first elections in which women participated, in 1936, six women were elected to the House of Representatives, and several others took office as mayors and members of municipal councils.

In other countries partial suffrage was enacted. The Peruvian Constitution of 1933 allowed women to vote in municipal elections but retained the definition of "citizen" to mean propertied males; in Chile in 1934, a law opened local elections to women and "male and female foreigners who had resided in a district more than five years." In Argentina, which boasted one of the strongest women's movements in Latin America, a bill to grant the vote to women passed the Chamber of Deputies in 1932 but failed to pass the Senate and never became law. The Argentine province of San Juan passed a local female suffrage law, and in 1934 Dr. Ema Costa became the first Argentine woman elected to a provincial legislature. San Juan's proximity to Chile and its distance from the federal government in Buenos Aires was a factor in this achievement.

In its 1936 survey of woman suffrage the IACW reported that the constitutions of the Dominican Republic, Colombia, and Guatemala "definitely limit the suffrage to male nationals." The report noted that "in the Dominican Republic, however, Dominican women were allowed by a decree of November 22, 1933 to go to the polls at the 1934 election and indicate whether or not they wished the suffrage. Over 90,000 women took advantage of this privilege and only 9 voted no; but so far no action has been taken on this plebiscite."[60]

In Mexico, women continued their campaign for the extension of political rights to women. The Mexican Constitution of 1917 granted voting rights to all citizens, which the constitution defined thus: "All Mexicans are citizens of the Republic who fulfill the following requisites: Are eighteen years old if married, twenty-one if not, and have an honorable means of livelihood." From the time of the *congresos femininos* in the Yucatán to the meetings of the 1920s, Mexican women had tried to insist that this constitutional definition of citizen did not exclude them. Although their earlier efforts on behalf of woman suffrage and a feminist agenda had met with resistance from the federal government, the election of Lázaro Cárdenas as president in 1934 was greeted with enthusiasm by women activists. Cárdenas had spoken out on his commitment to fulfilling the promise of the revolution through incorporating peasants, indigenous peoples, urban workers, and women into the national agenda. He stated: "A sound basis for social revolution will not be achieved until the constitution is reformed to grant equal rights."[61]

Soon after taking office, Cárdenas appointed Palma Guillen as minister of Mexico to Colombia, making her the first Mexican woman to hold a high diplomatic appointment. Apropos of this appointment, Margarita Robles de Mendoza, who was president of the *Consejo de Mujeres* and represented Mexican women on the IACW, challenged Cárdenas with the need to extend citizenship to all Mexican women. The question was referred to the Department of Government, which, in 1935, responded that there were no reasons to deny Mexican women citizenship in the republic. In his address to Congress later that year, Cárdenas said, "A necessary consequence of this plan to unify the working masses has been the recognition by the National Revolutionary Party that the working woman has the right to take part in the elections, since the constitution puts her on an equal footing with man."[62] A constitutional amendment giving women the vote was drafted; with strong support from Cárdenas; in 1938 it was passed by the Senate and the House and referred to the states for ratification. Ratification was not forthcoming, and it was to be another fifteen years before Mexican women won full suffrage.

It is evident that there was no one road to woman suffrage in Latin America, and it is apparent that woman suffrage carried different meanings in each country. The class interests of those in power are clearly reflected in the ways in which female suffrage was defined or limited. Cárdenas wanted to bring working women into the electorate to broaden the constituency of the National Revolutionary party. The Uruguayan government wished to use the vote of native-born Hispanic women to increase its mandate and simultaneously to weaken any threat from foreign-born radicals. In Brazil suffrage was won by a coalition of upper- and middle-class women who used their personal connections to the incumbent government to gain their ends; property and literacy requirements were such for both male and female voters that only 5 percent of the Brazilian populace was in effect enfranchised prior to 1946.[63]

It would seem that the women's movement in Latin America would have found a powerful ally in the labor movement. The first major political party to include universal suffrage for men and women in its platform was the Socialist party, and, as we have seen, many of the early women activists were members of the Socialist or Anarchist parties. By 1900 much of the labor platform had been incorporated into the agenda of Latin American feminists. The political crises in Brazil in 1932 and in Cuba and Uruguay in 1934, which gave women the opportunity to enact their program, were in fact partly created by the push by labor for the extension of political rights to broader sectors of the national populace. However, the attitude of the revolutionary party in Mexico, which espoused the principle of social justice and yet remained hostile to woman suffrage, is emblematic of the attitude of the Latin American political left toward the woman's movement.

The political left, like the political right, tended to view women as highly conservative, politically malleable, and subject to the influence of the church, despite eloquent evidence to the contrary. Peruvian poet Magda Portal was a founding member and the first secretary general of Peru's *Alianza Popular Revolucionaria Americana* (APRA). In 1924 a group of young Peruvians, including Portal, who were living in exile in Mexico, outlined the APRA program. Revolutionary in intent in the 1920s and 1930s, APRA sought to integrate the Indian into Peru's social and economic structure and to end the monopoly of political power by landowners, the clergy, and foreign corporations. APRA also had a significant international dimension, with supporters throughout Spanish America, especially among university students in Argentina, Bolivia, and Chile. Portal summarized the APRA program as "anti-imperialist, for the unity of the peoples of America, and for the realization of social justice." Though Magda Portal's attitude toward gender discrimination changed over time and through her own experience, in 1933 her alienation from *feministas* was explicit: "But the *aprista* woman, who professes our ideology, does not want to conquer her rights through an open fight against men, as 'feministas' do, but to collaborate with him as her companion."[64]

Portal exemplified the attitude of the political left toward woman suffrage in her essay written in 1933, *El aprismo y la mujer*: "What class of women ought to have the right to vote? The cultural level of the Peruvian woman, her prejudices, her unquestioning dependence on masculine influence, and often, on clerical influence, makes the female vote a measure to better support conservative ideas than revolutionary ones. . . . Consequently, the woman *aprista*—the woman worker, the woman of conscience—believes that the female vote must be qualified."[65]

Portal's alienation from feminism (she labeled feminists *las damas patrioticas civilistas*) and her tutelary attitude toward working-class women who needed to be educated in the principles of *aprismo* in order to vote did little to endear her or her ideas to either working class women or other intellectual women in Peru: Women need tutoring; men don't. Portal was not an original political thinker, and her assessment of the probable effect of woman suffrage was part of the received political wisdom in Latin American in the 1930s. Her unflattering attitude toward her own sex reflects a conflict that many politically active women felt.

In contrast, Portal's antifeminism was not shared by all women active in the political left. Alicia Moreau de Justo was one of Argentina's most prominent feminists and, with her husband, Juan Bautista Justo, was a leading member of the Argentine Socialist party. In her pamphlet *El socialismo y la mujer*, published in 1931 in Buenos Aires by *La Vanguardia*, the Socialist press founded by the Justos, Moreau de Justo declared: "Women suffrage is true democracy: Approximately one-half of the population is female—how can the governments and parliaments call themselves representative of the people when half of these people cannot vote and express their opinion?" Moreau de Justo denounced the idea of the qualified vote, which limited the vote to the propertied classes, stating heatedly: "We would prefer not to have the vote than to have it qualified!"[66]

Moreau de Justo and Portal were in agreement that the practice of restricting the vote to propertied and literate women was wrong, but Moreau de Justo rejected all limitations. She wished to open the vote to all people, a position that showed considerably more confidence in the potential electorate than did Portal's. The contrasting political positions of the two women reflect the political milieus in which they were acting. Argentina had a large, articulate middle sector with a history of vibrant political discourse that ranged across a broad ideological spectrum in which both men and women participated; Portal's audience in Peru was limited to a narrow segment of the population. Peru had no self-conscious middle-sector population comparable to Argentina's; the circumstances conducive to the development of a broad-based woman reform movement did not exist. In fact, Portal's dislike of *feministas* stemmed from the upper-class origin of many Peruvian feminists.

Furthermore, the political atmosphere in Peru was extremely hostile to political dissent; Portal herself was repeatedly imprisoned and forced into exile.

The persecution Portal suffered for her participation in revolutionary politics was compounded by the fact that she was female; adult women who advocate the violent overthrow of the state are often viewed as acting "against nature";[67] they are subject to social ostracism and particularly harsh punishment. But within the context of international revolutionary politics in the 1930s, Portal conformed to the dominant belief that when the revolution came, all people in society, including women, would have social and economic justice. Women activists who sought to introduce women's issues into the agenda of the Latin American left found themselves isolated; the revolution was to change class and property relationships, not gender roles. Women were subordinate within the organizations; women's issues were subordinate on the party agenda, and were, in fact, considered threatening to the party's agenda and "public image."

The experience of Brazilian Patricia Galvão, who was known by the nickname Pagú, illustrates the problems faced by radical women who had the temerity to suggest that women's issues demanded special attention within the revolution. After her graduation from the Escolas Normais do Bras e da Praça da Republica, she became involved with the circle of cultural revolutionaries known as the *antropofagistas*, and in 1930 she joined the *Partido Comunista Brasileira* (PCB). Pagú shared Magda Portal's scorn for "bourgeois feminists," whom she characterized as "bleating for sexual liberation, conscientious motherhood, the right to vote for cultured women" when "the economic and social problems of life are still to be resolved."[68]

But Pagú had her own feminist vision. She recognized that female workers faced problems that male workers did not, and she posited an ideal woman who would be "a pioneer of the new era." In 1933, writing under the pseudonym Mara Lobo, she published the novel *Parque Industrial*. The book was orthodox enough in its Marxist analysis, its call for the Socialist revolution, and its support of the Brazilian Communist party as the proper vehicle to bring about the revolution. But the book was original in that Pagú "took her point of reference from the female—rather than the male—proletariat."[69] Moreover, the female proletariat in urban Brazil was largely composed of women of color, and Pagú not only raised issues of sexual inequality and harassment but of racism within the workplace. ,

The leadership of the Brazilian Communist party was outraged by the sexually explicit descriptions in the book and even more so by her daring to raise the taboo subject of race; the party demanded that the book be suppressed. Men of the Brazilian left were no more enlightened on the subject of female sexuality and women's issues than were their male counterparts throughout society; in addition, in the 1930s they tended to incorporate the prudishness characteristic of Stalinist communism. Not only did the men fail to share Pagú's conviction that the exploitation of female workers was an urgent political issue for the left, but the leadership of the PCB believed that Pagú's radicalism as a woman was threatening to their public image, that it would damage their grass-roots support and wreak havoc on their internal discipline. Within a year of publication, *Parque Industrial* was withdrawn from the market, and unsold copies were destroyed.[70]

Pagú's trials with the male orthodoxy of the Brazilian Communist party pale in comparison to the ostracism suffered by her compatriot, María Lacerda de Moura, who was sympathetic to the goals of international socialism, but rejected all political affiliation. María Lacerda's book *Amai e . . . não vos multipliqueis*, published in Rio de Janeiro in 1932, was an outcry against politics as practiced by men of whatever political stripe or ideological orientation:

Up until now, which has been the party or program that presented a solution for the problem of female happiness? Who remembered to liberate women? [The woman] eternally tutored, doubly enslaved, in the name of reclaiming her rights, in the name of female emancipation, under so many banners, so many idols . . . fatherland, home, society, religion, morality, good manners, civil and political rights, communism, fascism, every other ism, revolutions, and barricades . . . continues to be the slave, an instrument skillfully manipulated by men for their sectarian, power-hungry, economic, religious, political, or social causes. . . . Within all [parties], with the most varied platforms, I know those who are interested only in their own freedom and the victory of their own party, without the slightest concern for women, and without the least understanding of women's rights and needs. They are libertarians and their legal family is very bourgeois. . . . Every [reformer] absolutely every one seeks to stifle the true inner necessities of women.[71]

María Lacerda's disillusion with traditional political approaches to social injustice echoes the words of her Brazilian predecessor, Francisca Senhorina de Motta Diniz, written half a century earlier.

By the mid-1930s the political openings that had accompanied the economic dislocations of the early Depression had disappeared; both liberal reformists and leftist revolutionary groups were under harsh attack in many areas of Latin America. In Brazil, the Woman's Union, which had been founded in 1934 by intellectual and working women and was affiliated with the left-wing National Alliance for Liberation, survived less than a year before it was outlawed and its leaders arrested or forced into exile. In Peru, Portal, along with many other *apristas*, was again imprisoned. In Argentina, Chile, Uruguay, Brazil, and Peru, a significant sector of the political and military elites openly admired the impressive economic recovery made by the Fascist governments of Adolf Hitler in Germany and Benito Mussolini in Italy. Within this political atmosphere neither the reform agenda of the feminists nor the revolutionary platform of the radical women fared well. Suffrage, whether universal or limited to the propertied and educated, became a moot point in states where political liberties were suspended and government was carried on by decree.

The exigencies of the international situation were directly reflected at the inter-American conference tables in the 1930s. In addition to working to fulfill their domestic agenda, the women active at the inter-American congresses took strong stands on international issues, supporting the principles of nonintervention and the resolution of conflict through arbitration, and the rights of small nations.

Many of the North and South American women who met for the formation of the Inter-American Commission of Women at the Sixth International Conference of American States in Havana in 1928 were members of the WILPF, and the positions they took in hemispheric politics directly reflected the political platform of the WILPF.[72] At the Sixth Conference, the women demonstrated against the U.S. occupation of Nicaragua and protested the dismissal of representatives of the Haitian government-in-exile.[73]

In the decade between 1928 and 1938 the IACW operated as an autonomous body within the inter-American organization. The themes of equal rights and peace, both of which were believed to be within the special province of women, mark their efforts. In the words of Nelly Marino Carvallo, who edited the international woman's journal *Mujeres de America* in Buenos Aires from 1930 to 1935, "from its inception, *Mujeres de America* has been dedicated to peace. Yes: it is through women that peace will be secured in the world."[74] The idea that women have a special role as peacemakers is persistent, despite evidence that men have in fact been the diplomats who have arbitrated peace agreements and sought international concord. Certainly, the male representatives to the International Conferences of American States saw themselves as working toward peace in the hemisphere. But there are a number of factors that differentiate the attitudes and expressions of men and women in the transnational discourse of the period. First, the male diplomatic community recognized force as a legitimate diplomatic tool; they were not pacifists. Second, the male diplomats and representatives to the inter-American conference tables were speaking for their governments, not from their personal convictions.

By the spring of 1928, in conformance with the resolution adopted at the February 18, 1928, plenary session of the Sixth Pan-American Conference that charged it to prepare information "of a legal and other nature" that it might consider useful for the study of "civil and political equality in the continent," the IACW had undertaken the task of collecting material on the legal status of women from every country in the hemisphere.[75]

The first meeting of the IACW was held in Havana, February 17–24, 1930.

The members of the first commission were Flora de Oliveira Lima (Brazil), Aida Parada (Chile), Alicia Ricode de Herrera (Colombia), Lydia Fernández (Costa Rica), Elena Mederos de González (Cuba), Gloria Moya de Jiménez (Dominican Republic), Irene de Peyre (Guatemala), Mme Fernand Dennis (Alice Garoute?) (Haiti), Margarita Robles de Mendoza (Mexico), Juanita Molina de Fromen (Nicaragua), Clara Gonzáles (Panama), Teresa Obrogoso de Prevost (Peru), and Cedilia Herrera de Olavarria (Venezuela). Doris Stevens (United States) was chairman. The commission drafted a resolution to establish equality in nationality for presentation to the World Conference for the Codification of International Law, to be held at The Hague in March 1930. The resolution stated: "The contracting parties agree that from the going into effect of this treaty there shall be no distinction based on sex in their law and practice relating to nationality."[76]

Other resolutions requested the American governments to appoint the IACW commissioners plenipotentiaries to the conference, asked financial support for their work, and thanked the Carnegie Endowment for International Peace for its initial grant of $5,000.

The women, who had little secretarial help and who had secured a small office in the Pan-American Union building in Washington only after dealing with numerous harassment tactics (when they arrived at their office space in the first few months of their existence, they often found that their two desks had been "borrowed" or that all of the chairs were missing), nevertheless succeeded in gathering a substantial amount of legal information from throughout the hemisphere, all of which was carefully collated, hand-labeled, and placed in black leather three-ring notebooks.[77] The intention was to be able to select the information pertinent to particular issues as they arose. The first of these was the issue of the nationality of married women.

The commission drew up a two-part Resolution on the Nationality of Women, which asked signatory governments to (1) introduce into their law the principle of the equality of the sexes in matters of nationality, taking particularly into consideration the interests of children, and (2) affirm that in principle the nationality of the wife should henceforth not be affected without her consent either by the mere fact of marriage or by any change in the nationality of the husband. The first opportunity to bring the resolution before an international body came at the meeting of the Council of the League of Nations in 1931. The resolution was introduced by the American members of the council—Matos of Guatemala, Barreto of Peru, and César Zumeta of Venezuela—and was adopted on January 24, 1931. James Brown Scott, editor of *The International Conferences of American States 1889–1928*, commented on their achievement: "In the interest of historical accuracy, it is necessary to record that the initiative of the Council's action came from the IACW. The League's Commission of Women, when created, will concern itself with, and report to, the 1931 Assembly upon a single point: nationality and the status of women."[78]

The Seventh International Conference of American States, held in Montevideo in 1933, was the first meeting at which women had an official presence, both within the IACW and as members of national delegations. At that meeting, the Convention on the Nationality of Women was presented to the conference by the IACW. It was signed by twenty American countries, becoming the first treaty in the history of the world to extend equality to women. Doris Stevens commented, "It is not accidental that it has happened in the New World. What the Hague conference rejected in 1930 and what the League of Nations refused to remedy has been done by you."[79] The IACW had been successful in creating an officially recognized commission and in passing a convention which included the principle of the equality of the sexes. Though the League of Nations did not adopt this convention, the work of the IACW contributed to the establishment of a committee on the legal status of women in the League in 1937.

The women's work for gender equity did not diminish their commitment to the cause of international peace. Of central concern to the women in southern South America in this period was the conflagration in the Gran Chaco. The dispute between Bolivia and Paraguay over the vast territory of the Chaco, which stretches from the eastern slopes of the Andes to the Paraguay River, began with isolated armed skirmishes in the late 1920s. The conflict flared into a bloody war that ultimately took nearly one hundred thousand lives and bankrupted the treasuries of the participants before a truce was reached in 1935.

During the war nationalist passions were high; in this unsympathetic atmosphere *Mujeres de America* ran a petition initiated by the Circulo Argentino "Pro Paz"[80] calling for arbitration and denouncing the participants in the war as tools of international capitalist interests. But most telling of the sentiments of the publication and its audience was the dedication of the July–August 1933 issue to the women of Bolivia and Peru, "reviving the spirit of the glorious days of Independence (when the two nations were one)."

The editorial began, "In the unhappy tragedy which has shaken the solitudes of the Chaco, . . . *Mujeres de America* aspires to form a new concept of nation ('patria') that is progressive; 'patria' that is peace, 'patria' that is undivided. Women of Bolivia, we are one. We work together with faith, with love, so that someday we may have *la patria grande*, a nation without frontiers, a nation founded in our highest ideals."[81]

The conflict in the Chaco proved resistant to the arbitration efforts of the inter-American community; the desperate fighting continued until 1935. The major diplomatic success of the Montevideo meeting was the agreement on nonintervention, which stated that no nation has the right to intervene in the internal or external affairs of another. The nonintervention resolution is regarded as a major watershed in inter-American relations, signifying the end of U.S. military interventions in Central America and the Caribbean, an end to which the IACW had given its full support.

In the late 1930s, as the inter-American community became increasingly concerned with the outbreak of war in Europe and Asia, the feminist and pacifist platform of the first generation of IACW leaders was dismissed as less than urgent and potentially divisive. The Eighth International Conference of American States met in Lima in 1938. The main business of the conference was the effort, led by the United States, to unite the hemisphere in the event of war. In the Declaration of Lima, the American republics reaffirmed their continental solidarity and "determination to defend themselves against all foreign intervention."[82] The IACW did succeed in putting forth the resolution that "women have the right to the enjoyment of equal civil status," but the Lima Conference was also the scene of the disestablishment of the IACW as an autonomous entity.

The IACW had never enjoyed the support of the U.S. diplomatic corps, and under the Roosevelt regime it became a particular target of Eleanor Roosevelt. Mrs. Roosevelt's antipathy toward the IACW was trifold. First, she was a strong supporter of protectionist legislation for women workers and viewed the equal rights agenda of the IACW as elitist and threatening to protectionism. Second, the IACW had come into being during the administration of Herbert Hoover, and the women delegates from the United States were Republicans. Finally, Eleanor Roosevelt had a strong personal dislike of Doris Stevens, who was a founding member of the National Woman's party, an advocate of equal rights, and a Republican; Stevens had been chair of the IACW since its inception.[83]

At the Lima meeting in 1938, Stevens resigned the chairmanship, fearing that the IACW would be entirely dismantled if she attempted to stay on. Ana Rosa S. de Martinez Guerrero of Argentina was selected in her stead. The IACW was recast as a subsidiary commission of the inter-American organization and was advised to turn its efforts to the defense of democracy.

Though the women's platform at the international conference tables may have been subsumed in the face of the coming crisis in 1938, and though authoritarian regimes prevailed in the Latin American nations in the period, what is evident is that, from the first feminist congresses in Mérida in 1873, in Buenos Aires in 1910, in Lima and Havana and Mexico City in the 1920s to the passage of the resolution affirming the right of women to equal civil status with men in Lima in 1938, Latin American women were deeply involved in trying to achieve broad-based political reform within their nations and no nation was completely untouched by their work. A history of activism existed, an activism that bore the special stamp of feminism as it developed in

Latin America, with insistence on issues of social justice and the preservation of the feminine.

Finally, it is apparent that the nature and extent of feminist thought in Latin America was far greater than has heretofore been understood. Though the number of women involved in local, national, and international congresses and conferences was small in proportion to the total population of women in the hemisphere, their numbers had grown impressively since the first lone voices calling for female education were raised in the midnineteenth century.

5. Democracy and the Search for Social Justice, 1938-1958

We the people of the United Nations Determined to save succeeding generations from the scourge of war, which twice in our lifetime has brought untold suffering to mankind, and to reaffirm faith in fundamental human rights, in the dignity and worth of the human person, in the equal rights of men and women . . .
—Charter of the United Nations 1

In the study of feminism as the story of the emergence of a collective critique of discriminatory practices based on gender, the assumption has persisted that there is a generational break between "first wave" feminists, whose efforts appeared to culminate in the suffrage campaigns of the early twentieth century, and "second wave" feminists, whose efforts to date have been most visible in the UN Decade for Women 1976–1985. Within the Latin American context, where the existence of a widespread first wave of feminism has only recently been documented,[2] the assumption continues that women's activities on behalf of improving the status of women—in education, in the job market, in the political sphere—were virtually nonexistent prior to the stimulation of the international women's movement of the 1970s. Closer examination of the activities of certain groups of Latin American women in the 1940s and 1950s belies these preconceptions and challenges the first-wave, second-wave periodization and the implication that feminism in Latin America is derivative.

One of the crucial differences between the Latin American women's movement and that in the United States is that the campaigns to secure woman suffrage and more equitable contractual rights for women in marriage and employment had not, with few exceptions, resulted in success in Latin American nations prior to World War II. Thus, whereas the focus of the woman's movement in the United States became diffuse in the aftermath of the passage of the Nineteenth Amendment in 1920 and was subsumed to the war effort by 1940, the campaigns in Latin America continued, as did the interest in using the inter-American conference tables to promote the feminist program.[3]

In Lima in 1938, it was the Mexican delegation to the Inter-American Commission of Women (IACW) that proposed the Declaration in Favor of Women's Rights. The Mexican women were inspired to do so by the pending triumph of woman suffrage in Mexico, as state after state ratified an amendment to Article 34 of the constitution of 1917 that would redefine "citizen" to include women as well as men. From its inception, the presidency of Lázaro Cárdenas (1934–1940) seemed to promise success for the Mexican woman suffrage movement. In 1933 women organized in support of Cárdenas's campaign; the Feminist Revolutionary party, founded by Edelmira R. Escudero, is but one example. The Partido Nacional Revolucionario (PNR) published pamphlets that declared, "the incorporation of women into the economic life of the country will make good revolutionaries of them . . . the National Revolutionary Party has recognized that working women have the right to participate in electoral struggles."[4]

In 1935 the United Front for Women's Rights (*Frenté Único pro Derechos de la Mujer*), led by Communist Refúgio García, adopted a platform that called for the right of women to vote and to be candidates for all elective offices, modification of the Civil Code to give women the same political rights as men, modification of the Agrarian Code to permit women to receive grants of land from the government under the same conditions as men, incorporation of indigenous women into the social and political life of the nation, and establishment of work centers for unemployed women. Cárdenas and the PNR responded by creating a Feminine Action section of the party. However, in spite of the fact that the most visible and vocal leaders of the women's movement in Mexico were women of the left and center, who supported the revolutionary and reform programs of the government but who wished to see women as full participants in the design of those programs, the cause of female suffrage in Mexico continued to suffer from the apprehension of government leaders that the female vote would be conservative.

The kind of response that the idea of women suffrage all too often evoked is clear in this exclamation from a member of the Chamber of Deputies: "Twenty-five thousand women coming before the Chamber to ask for the vote for women! How horrible! It means that, if they obtain their object, we shall have a Bishop for President!"[5]

The momentum gained by the feminists in the early stages of the Cárdenas administration was lost in the political fracas that erupted as Cárdenas sought to dethrone labor boss Luís Morones and consolidate his own power base in the PNR. A further blow to the cause of woman suffrage was the undeniably conservative nature of the first elections in which women participated in Spain, where the female vote seriously undermined the delicate coalition of Socialist and centrist parties that formed the basis of support for the republic. Opponents to woman suffrage spread the rumor that "in some places [Spanish women] marched directly from the Church to the polling places."[6]

Still, the Mexican women continued to pressure the government, and Cárdenas proposed an amendment to Article 34 that consisted of the insertion of the phrase "and women" so that it would read: "All those men *and women* are citizens of the Republic, who, having the quality of Mexicans, possess also the following requisities: One, Are 18 years of age or over if married and 21 if not, and Two, Have an honest means of livelihood." The redefinition of "citizen" to include women would also guarantee women the vote, as all Mexican citizens had that right. By the end of 1938 every Mexican state had ratified the amendment, and it remained only for Congress to declare it law. Ward Morton writes: "The jubilant feminist organizations urged the Mexican delegation to the Eighth Pan American Conference to take advantage of Mexico's progress toward women's rights by submitting a declaration on the subject."[7]

The subsequent fate of the Mexican movement for equal rights raises several points that have parallels elsewhere during the years 1938–1945. On the one hand, after 1938 women's issues were regarded as secondary to the war effort. On the other hand, women themselves were now recognized as a significant political force, and both governments in power and opposition parties and groups sought to organize them. The usual strategy was to create a "women's section" of a party, a tactic that at once mobilized women on its behalf and marginalized them from leadership and policymaking power, which remained in the hands of the male political hierarchy. This was true across the political spectrum, from the left-wing APRA in Peru, which charged Magda Portal with organizing a "women's section" in 1945, to the right-wing National Action Party (PAN) in Mexico.

In the Mexican case both the ruling party and the opposition vied to organize female support—without giving women themselves political rights. The passage of Article 34, which seemed imminent in 1938, stalled and was later buried in Congress, a casualty of the political struggle that preceded the elections of 1940. The problem arose from the success of the conservative opposition, which in 1939 was uniting behind PAN and presidential candidate Juan Andreu Almazán, in rallying feminine support. Known as the Feminine Idealist party, the pro-Almazán forces were proclerical and sympathetic to the pro-Fascist Falange and Sinarquistas. The PAN women also proved to be highly skilled fundraisers and political organizers: by the end of 1939 they claimed a national network of Feminine Idealist centers. To the government, it did not seem a propitious time to grant women the vote.

The presidential nominee of the government party, the *Partido Revolucionario Mexicano* (PRM), was General Manuel Ávila Camacho. Camacho was cautious on the issue of women's rights but did not entirely ignore the topic. Speaking at a major political rally at the Mexico City bull ring in April 1939, with his wife by his side and "with no apparent thought to the irony of the location," Camacho declared that "as an act of justice of the Revolution we must train women, elevating them to their full rights."[8] The idea that women must somehow be "trained" before they gained the right to vote and the un-voiced but concomitant notion that men need not be "trained" was shared by politicians of all political perspectives, emphasizing again that the women's vote was wanted only if it could be used to bolster a particular person or party; it was not seen as a just right in itself.

Historian Lillian Estelle Fisher described the meaning of the vote for Mexican women: "Without every member of their sex having the right to vote, Mexican women realize that they cannot obtain all that is needed rela-tive to social legislation, as they do not have a legal weapon. Frequently Mexican husbands are Marxists outside and feudalists within their homes."[9] The failure to secure suffrage before the elections of 1940 was a bitter blow to Mexican feminists; their response demonstrates the continuing intensity of the Mexican women's movement. In 1942 the United Front for Women's Rights, riding the wave of feminist anger that followed the elections and buoyed by the pro-Russian sympathy that characterized the early years of the war, reached its peak of power, claiming eight hundred affiliated organiza-tions and more than fifty thousand members.[10] The women's sections of the CTM, CNOP, and CNC joined together in the *Alianza Naciónal Femenina*: their ten-point platform included a call for solidarity among women, full equal rights, better educational opportunities, equal access to government positions, and support for rural women.[11]

Women did gain suffrage in the small Spanish-speaking nations of El Sal-vador (1939) and the Dominican Republic (1942) during the war years. The situation in the Dominican Republic stands in contrast to the atmosphere of intense political debate that characterized Mexican politics in the 1930s and early 1940s. By 1933 "the Great Benefactor," Raphael Leonidas Trujillo Molina, had strangled political opposition and consolidated support for his ruthless dictatorship. Although the United States had temporarily abandoned direct military intervention in Central America and the Caribbean during the era of the Good Neighbor Policy and World War II, strong American eco-nomic and political involvement in the area continued. The priorities of the Roosevelt administration in the region were stability, loyalty, and the mainte-nance of order, and the dictatorships of Trujillo in the Dominican Republic, Maximiliano Hernández Martínez in El Salvador, Anastasio García Somoza in Nicaragua, and Jorge Ubico in Guatemala filled the bill on all counts.

The nascent feminist movement in the Dominican Republic had in 1931 organized a Dominican Feminist Action party; by the mid-1930s the tone of their program, like all other political voices that were allowed to be heard in the Dominican Republic, was clearly shaped by their need to conform. Membership was drawn from the upper middle class, and their program was couched in highly conservative terms. Founding member Lara Fernández de-scribed their purposes thus: "Women must be prepared to sustain the moral and material equilibrium of the home. We must not forget that the equilibrium of the home means the equilibrium of the nation."[12] The vote would bring the "moral fibre" of women into the public sphere, in support of the state. It should be noted that the idea that women have special qualities that they will bring to the political sphere is persistent and pervasive across time and cultures, but it is more characteristic of the arguments of liberal, reformist, and conservative women than of women of the political left, who have historically rejected the notion of gender difference as detrimental to the class solidarity necessary to build the revolution.

Despite the Dominican women's clear recognition that any hope for the success of their program to secure suffrage and improved rights lay in their ability to play politics with Trujillo, who monopolized all power within the country, and despite the compliant tone of their agenda, which was but a pale echo of the comprehensive demands of the Mexican feminists, the women made little headway in the first decade of the dictatorship. But by the early 1940s the Trujillo regime had become a political embarrassment to a Washington that was publicly committed to the defense of democracy. The war years also initiated considerable economic and demographic change in the Dominican Republic, as manufacturing industries brought more and more people into the cities and a nascent urban proletariat emerged. Women, particularly women committed to the unthreatening concept of the "equilibrium of home and state," seemed to offer a valuable new base of political support, and woman suffrage seemed a safe way to demonstrate the regime's newfound commitment to democratic reform.[13] Thus, in 1942, Dominican women won the right to vote—for Trujillo.

The idea of woman suffrage legitimizing a regime was clearly articulated in the Cuban suffrage movement, and a number of the same elements are visible in the Dominican case. In each instance there were organized women's groups acting with support from the international women's movement—representatives from the IACW visited the Dominican Republic in support of the efforts of the Alianza Femenina Dominica in 1938[14]—and women activists realized and used the political bargaining chips they had within their national political context. However, in the Cuban case the political pressures that brought the government to support woman suffrage were domestic. Although domestic considerations played a role in the Dominican Republic, the more compelling need was the improvement of the Trujillo regime's international image and the gratification of its North American patron.[15] What should not be overlooked is that in both cases women's organizations played a role; women acted on their own behalf within the available political space.

Elsewhere, suffrage and women's rights campaigns stalled during the war years, but a continuum of women's work on behalf of women is visible in the organizations formed to implement the Declaration in Favor of Women's

Rights set forth at Lima in 1938. At Lima, the IACW was charged with organizing the women of the hemisphere "in defense of democracy." Women's Action (*Acción Femenina*) groups with ties to the IACW were formed in a number of countries. Though nominally national in scope, they were in fact established through the preexisting women's organizations and thus were centered in the major cities. At first glance, the *Alianza Femenina Peruana*, the *Alianza Naciónal Femenina* in Mexico, and the *Aliança Brasileira* appear to be little more than ladies-aid societies. But two factors suggest that these organizations were not limited to knitting socks and rolling bandages. First, the membership brought together the women who had participated in taking the feminist agenda to the inter-American conference tables—Amanda Labarca in Chile, Amália Ledón in Mexico, for example—with a newly emergent social group: the urban, middle-sector working woman. The older women had invoked the ideals of independence to call for liberty and equality for women as well as for men; the young women believed that the ideals of democracy should apply equally to both sexes. The feminine alliances were indeed "dedicated to the defense of democracy," and the women explicitly intended that democracy should include them.[16]

The membership of the *Acción Femenina Peruana*, for example, included teachers, office employees, nurses, writers, and members of the Women's Section of the Trade Union Federation. University students were also active. In 1942 a member of the Arequipa section of *Acción Femenina* described the immediate purpose of the group to be the defense of democracy and the organization of women in Red Cross–type activities but stressed that the long-term plan of work was "justice for women." Not surprisingly, these young women were also concerned with improving conditions for wage-earning women.[17]

The interests of the members of the *acción femeninas* overlapped with those of other women's groups, such as the *Liga de Empleadas Católicas* (LEC), an organization sponsored by the Catholic church. The LEC was founded in the 1920s as a specific counter to the secularism of the emergent women's movement. Like the *acción femeninas*, LEC had sections throughout Latin America that sought to serve the needs of the rising ranks of young working women while keeping them within the Catholic fold. But if the organizations drew on similar constituencies of young working women, the political purposes of the two were often antithetical. Not only did the church oppose the agenda of the women's movement, but in the late 1930s and early 1940s the political sympathies of many members of the hierarchy of the Latin Catholic church lay with Fascist Italy and Spain. In contrast, the international concerns of the *acción femeninas* are apparent in this quotation from a letter sent by the Arequipa section to the IACW in Washington in 1943: "All the Women of the Continent are interested in the solidarity of our peoples for the victory of the United Nations, and we believe that the Atlantic Charter will give us the necessary means of contributing with firm will and conviction to the establishment of justice and liberty throughout the world."[18]

On March 8, 1945, the Chapultepec Conference on the Problems of War and Peace met in Mexico City. The resolutions included commitment to social and economic justice, which was the foremost issue for the Latin American delegates, male and female. Six months later, in San Francisco in October 1945, a delegation of women from the IACW that included Bertha Lutz of Brazil, Minerva Bernardino of the Dominican Republic, and Amália Caballero de Castillo Ledón, chairwoman of the IACW and delegate from Mexico, led the move to insert the phrase "the equal rights of men and women" into the Charter of the United Nations.[19] They pointed out that a precedent had been established in international law by the resolution agreed on at the Eighth International Conference of American States at Lima in 1938 on the equal civil rights of men and women. The motion was adopted; all adherents to the UN Charter were committed in principle to the equality of the sexes before the law.

All twenty of the Latin American republics were signatories of the Declaration of the United Nations, and, with the exception of Argentina, had aligned with the Allied cause during World War II. By 1944, as it became clear that the Allies would prevail, the ideals of democracy were in ascendance. In state after state in Latin America, dictatorships that had lasted through the war years found their credibility eroded, their claims to legitimacy challenged by restless and articulate members of the growing urban middle class.

Such was the case in Guatemala, where, in June 1944, students, teachers, labor leaders, professionals, and businessmen united in a general strike calling for the end of the regime of Jorge Ubico, who had perpetuated himself in the presidency since 1931. Free elections were held for the first time in Guatemalan history, and a reform administration was inaugurated. The Guatemalan Constitution of 1945 reformed the electoral laws to include women "over eighteen who can read and write." The literacy requirement appears quite straightforward, but it should be noted that the ability to read and write meant literacy in Spanish, which effectively excluded nearly 50 percent of the Guatemalan female population. There was no equivalent literacy requirement for men.[20] The new Guatemalan constitution opened government employment to men and women "on the same terms." In Venezuela a similar political coalition of the urban middle sector formed an effective opposition party, *Acción Democrática* (AD), and joined with reformist military officers in a coup d'etat that placed Rómulo Betancourt in the provisional presidency. Hubert Herring wrote of this event: "The victory of AD was exhilarating to the people of Venezuela."[21] The new leaders were civilians, democratic in conviction, who incorporated their principles in a new constitution that provided for moderate social reform. Women voted for the first time in the

December 1947 election of AD candidate Rómulo Gallegos, a famous novelist and popular hero.[22]

In Cuba the election of Grau San Martín in 1944 temporarily ended the domination of politics by Fulgencio Batista, with promises (albeit unfulfilled) to adhere to the liberal constitution of 1940. In Brazil the military withdrew its support from Getúlio Vargas, who had held power since 1930 and in 1946 oversaw the election of Eurico Dutra and the promulgation of a new constitution based on that of the United States.[23] On February 24, 1946, Argentines elected Juan Perón, signaling the growing political power of labor and the urban working class in that country. The revolution of 1948 in Costa Rica brought about a period of rapid reform, including the abolition of the armed forces, a broad social security program, nationalization of banks and utilities, and woman suffrage. In preparation for the election of a constituent assembly, women were granted suffrage in Panama in 1945.

In each of these cases there was widespread belief that the practice of political democracy would lead to increased social and economic justice. The immediate postwar political atmosphere supported the aspirations of increasingly broader sectors of the populace; women throughout the hemisphere participated in the politics of democratic reform.

The changing political winds of the period are reflected in the metamorphosis that Mexican women's political organizations underwent during and immediately after the war, as the women sought to adapt their political structure and nomenclature to identify themselves with the prevailing political trend. In 1942, when Mexico entered the war on the side of the Allies, the *Frenté Único pro Derechos de la Mujer*, the largest of the Mexican women's rights organizations, became the Women's Coordinating Committee for the Defense of the Country (Patria). At the end of the war in 1945, it became the *Bloque Naciónal de Mujeres* and during the election campaign of 1946, the *Unión Democrática de Mujeres Mexicanas*.

Unlike many of the feminist movements in Latin America in this period, the Mexican women's movement has a distinctly nationalist tone to it.[24] Though contemporary historians generally agree that the revolutionary phase of the Mexican Revolution ended with the administration of Cárdenas in 1940 and label the revolution as "moribund" by 1946, Mexican women were still struggling to be full participants in national politics. And they identified with the inclusive rhetoric of the revolution, with the concept of *la raza cósmica*, the idea of Mexicanness. Adela Formoso de Obregón Santacilia, in her prowoman suffrage treatise, *La Mujer Mexicana en la Organización Social del País* (1939), invoked the goddess Malinalxochitl, who was present at the creation of *la raza* and who was stronger than her brother Huitzilpochtli (as Formoso de Obregón believed that women were spiritually stronger than men and would vote accordingly). Malinalxochitl "ordered that arms be laid down and the bodies buried and dedicated herself to solving the problems of the living, but she was undermined by the conspiracy of the priests, who envied her power and conspired against her with Huitzilpochtli."[25] The myth of the strong, intelligent goddess whose first concern was "the people" and whom the priests feared was a powerful one in the Mexican political context; it was intended to align the women's movement with the accepted concept of what it meant to be "Mexican."

The redirection of women's political energies apparent in the metamorphosis of the Mexican women's patriotic associations into women's associations that carried on the prewar women's agenda of peace, equal civil and political rights, and social activism has parallels in Brazil. Brazil, like Mexico, contributed troops to the conflict.[26] Following the directive of the Lima Conference in 1938, Brazilian women established an umbrella organization, the Women's Division of the League for National Defense. Their focus was on the war effort, and there was little opportunity for the discussion of women's issues within the national polity in the early 1940s. However, women organized at the neighborhood level to combat high food prices and to deal with problems specific to their families' immediate needs. In this period, continued support of the prewar women's agenda is most visible at the inter-American conference tables.

By the end of the war numerous women's committees and neighborhood associations were established, involving both middle- and working-class Brazilian women. Helieth Saffiotti describes the evolution of these loosely knit groups into a nationwide organization: "When hostilities ceased, leaders of various women's and feminist organizations and a number of nonaffiliated women held a round-table discussion that lasted three days. In attendance were women of the middle classes, as well as from the hills and the shanty towns, whose life experiences instilled the discussions with an air of realism and immediacy. The need for social equality between the sexes and for breaking down old prejudices about women was only one of the problems considered. The need for a nationwide organization to unify the women's movement was stressed over and over again."[27]

As was true elsewhere, the Allied victory brought with it a resurgence of political activity marked by a call for democracy and broader popular political participation. In Brazil, women of the political left organized a Woman's Committee for Amnesty; in 1945 amnesty was granted to numerous political prisoners. For the first time since 1935, labor leaders, Socialists, and members of the Brazilian Communist party (*Partido Comunista Brasileira*) were able to organize openly. The reemergence of the political left was apparent in the women's organizational meetings and manifest in heated debates about the proper mandate of a national women's organization.

The principal division was between the members of the Communist International and women whose political allegiances lay with labor, Socialist, and reformist platforms, a reflection of the bitter international struggles as the Communist International sought to assert dominance in Eastern Europe and the Balkans. In December 1945 a number of Brazilian women attended the First International Congress of Women (*Congrés International des Femmes*) in Paris, sponsored by the Women's International Democratic Federation (WIDF).[28] WIDF received its funding and direction from Moscow;[29] pro-Soviet feeling was high in the immediate postwar period. In 1945 the Brazilian Communist party was at the height of its power: In the presidential elections it polled over half a million votes, the best showing of any minority party.[30] Two years later, the president of the *Federação de Mulheres do Brasil* (Brazilian Women's Federation [BWF]) represented Brazilian women at the WIDF council meeting in Prague, and in 1947 the BWF officially joined the WIDF.[31] In an effort to make the BWF truly national, branches were established in every state. The emphasis of the BWF was on antifascism, peace, and bread-and-butter issues. The organizational strategy paralleled that of contemporary populist movements: a nationwide network with representatives from each state, construction of a constituency among working-class women, and the extension of neighborhood associations focused on alleviating the problems of daily living—adequate food, clean water, housing.

In 1949 the BWF held its first national meeting, attended by members from all states. It was also successful in aligning itself with other women's organizations, such as the Trade Union's Women's Division, and held several congresses, including a well-attended all-Latin American conference. The Federal District Women's Association, located in Rio de Janeiro with a membership of approximately a thousand women, was an affiliate of the BWF and worked vigorously on behalf of the BWF agenda. The Women's Committee for Amnesty, having succeeded in its campaign, became the Women's Committee for Democracy, "which over a five-year period devoted itself to the struggle for women's rights and to broadening women's cultural and political horizons."[32]

The neighborhood associations were the primary unit of organization for the BWF and its affiliates, and they proved highly effective in combating rising food costs and solving specific problems. There were broad gains, primarily for middle-sector women, in this period. Access to education was expanding rapidly, and some juridical gains were made: the Alfonso Afranio Law of 1951 empowered the government to penalize abuses of the equal rights provisions of the constitution. At the same time, the leadership of the BWF, suspect for its ties to the Communist International, was subject to various harassment tactics; in 1952 members of the BWF delegation who planned to attend the WIDF congress in Moscow were unable to secure visas. In 1956 the activities of a number of women's organizations, including the Federal

District Women's Federation and the BWF, were first suspended and then prohibited by law. It is interesting that the women's organizations were apparently granted greater leeway than the male-dominated central party; all political activity by the Brazilian Communist party was banned in May 1947.

The political situation in postwar Peru resembled that in Brazil in that political liberties were restored, amnesty was granted to political prisoners and exiles, and a broad array of new political parties appeared. APRA, which had been formally outlawed since 1935, emerged as the *Partido del Pueblo* and, in an attempt to legitimize itself and exert a broader popular influence, formed a coalition with more centrist parties; liberal candidate Luís Bustamante was elected president. Magda Portal described the political opening of 1945 thus: "The entire world lives in a type of democratic euphoria, especially those countries which in one way or another have participated in the triumph over totalitarianism. As the date of the election approaches in Peru, it would be absurd to suppose that the dictatorship of Prado would not offer the country the necessary guarantees to allow events to unfold along normal lines."[33]

But Peru, unlike Brazil, did not possess the essential political matrix of urban, educated, middle-class women and men that nourished the impulse toward democratic reform, including the reformist women's movement, in Argentina, Uruguay, Chile, Cuba, and Mexico as well as in Brazil during this era. In the late 1940s, Peru was primarily an agricultural society with a weak and fragmented urban middle sector that exhibited little sense of class identification and constituted less than 4 percent of the population. Furthermore, the upper and upper-middle classes were ethnically Hispanic; Lima was the center of their world. Their separation from the overwhelming majority of the populace, which was rural and ethnically Indo-American, was distinct. Economic power remained firmly in the hands of a small national elite in conjunction with North American and European financial concerns. In this respect Peru resembled its Andean neighbors, and as the Bolivian Revolution would do little for Bolivian women, the electoral victory of APRA did little to improve the lot of Peruvian women. The women warriors who fought to end the dictatorship of Prado (1939–1945), who endured imprisonment and exile and remained loyal to the revolutionary principles of APRA, found themselves discounted within the party councils, valued only for their ability to mobilize women, who remained disenfranchised.[34]

Magda Portal's experience is emblematic. As was noted in chapter 4, Portal was a founding member of APRA and served as secretary-general of the party, a position of considerable prestige and influence. Although she did not consider herself a feminist because of her disdain for the "bourgeois" orientation of most Peruvian feminist organizations, she wrote eloquently of the plight of the working woman. In 1945 she returned from exile and organized a nationwide meeting, the *Convención de Mujeres*, in Lima: "For the first time, married women, with children, with husbands, came to a convention which lasted eight days. Mothers of families, Indian women, teachers came." The APRA women's organizational units established at the convention were called *comandos femeninos*.[35]

APRA had long since adopted a platform proposed by the *Sección Femenina* in 1931 that included equal civil and political rights for men and women and equal pay for equal work, but despite the organizational success of the *Convención de Mujeres*, the women's agenda was set aside by the party leadership. Portal, disgusted by the politics of compromise, which she felt betrayed the original commitment of the *apristas*, wrote: "In effect, the new features of the brand-new *Partido del Pueblo* depart in great part from the doctrine which inspired the Aprista party, whose principles were built on anti-imperialist action and the revindication of the rights of the people in the realization of a new democracy with liberty and social justice."[36]

Many other *apristas* shared Portal's disillusionment and left the party in this period, but Magda Portal's break with APRA was particularly painful. Ironically, Portal, who had undertaken the organization of a "women's sector" of the party with great reluctance, insisting that the party was one for men and women alike and disdaining as she did the separatist politics of feminism, ultimately was confronted by the specific ways in which, despite her loyalty, her lifelong service to *aprista* ideals, her imprisonment and exile, she was discounted by the male leadership because she was a woman. The Second Congress of the Party (*II Congreso del Partido*) met in Lima from March 27 to June 3, 1948. Portal described her experience thus: "Women are not active members of the Party, they are only compañeras, because they do not have the quality of citizenship. And what does it signify that we have fought during twenty long years, when after all the victories were exclusively for men? Whenever I would point this out . . . , they would tell me that 'There is nothing to discuss.' Then I got up and left."[37] In her absence, she was stripped of her secretary-generalship and demoted to the position of second subsecretary, with no powers whatsoever. Her office, "where all the women had met," was no longer hers.[38]

Very few *aprista* women joined Portal's protest at the convention. APRA had been the first political party to attempt to involve women directly in national affairs "and did so by creating a very specific ambiance."[39] APRA, and specifically the *comando femenino*, set up a whole system of supports through a youth corps, counseling services, and community cafeterias and made legal, medical, and dental services available to members at reduced rates. Female party members were not expected to relinquish their traditional roles or to compromise their femininity; the APRA leadership remained masculine and patriarchal.

Portal was isolated and suffered further from attempts to discredit her through sexual innuendo. She expressed her rage and sense of betrayal in a declaration "To all of the Apristas of Peru" titled *"¿Quiénes traicionaron al pueblo?"* (Who Has Betrayed the People?) (1950) and in her novel *La Trampa* (The Trap) (1957). Portal's break with the party did not spare her from the harsh persecution suffered by *apristas* in the aftermath of the military coup d'etat that placed General Manuel Odría in the presidency on October 3, 1948; both of her publications were suppressed.

Of the South American nations, only Argentina resisted joining the Allies during the war years. Diplomatic antipathy toward the United States, an immigrant population with strong ties to the motherlands of Italy, Germany, and Spain, and the presence of Fascist sympathizers in the military and the church hierarchy muted the "democratic euphoria" noted by Portal in Peru and apparent elsewhere in hemisphere politics. By 1945, Juan Domingo Perón was forging the political coalition that would make his name synonymous with contemporary Argentine politics.

Nowhere is the practice of bringing women into the political arena to support a particular regime clearer than in Perónist Argentina (1945–1955). In his drive to break the political clout of the old Argentine elites who had dominated politics and shared in the economic wealth of the international investors, Juan Perón built his power base in the junior military and male working class. His wife, Eva María Duarte de Perón, is perhaps the best-known Latin American woman in history. Her beauty, her youth, and the undeniable power she derived through her association with Perón and built into a formidable power base of her own all contributed to the myth of "Evita." She was critical to Perón's crusade to enlist the support of middle- and working-class women.

In 1947 the Argentine legislature passed a bill of woman suffrage. Eva Perón is frequently credited with this "victory" for women's rights.[40] This is a distortion of the truth, an excellent example of the way the Peróns created and used Eva's popular image and of the ways in which the myth of Evita continues to obscure the woman Eva Perón. First, it should be remembered that by 1947 the woman suffrage movement in Argentina had been active for more than half a century, involving the efforts of hundreds of women and men. Second, by 1947 woman suffrage laws had been passed in most of the European nations and in nine of the Western Hemisphere nations, and the commitment to equal political rights for men and women was part of the Declaration of Lima (1938) and of the Charter of the United Nations, to both of which Argentina was a signatory.[41] Third, there were no fewer than six bills proposing woman suffrage before the legislature at the time it passed: woman suffrage was an idea whose time had come (at last) in Argentina.[42]

Eva Perón became so closely associated with woman suffrage in Argentina not through her rather tepid support of the idea but because of her highly successful efforts to rally the newly enfranchised middle-class and working women on Perón's behalf. In their study *Eva Perón*, Nicholas Fraser and Marysa Navarro describe the opening act of this campaign: "At the ceremony celebrating the passage of the bill, Perón signed the law, making it public; and then he handed it to Evita, making it hers, along with this substantial new constituency of women voters."[43]

Two years later, on July 20, 1949, Eva Perón led the women attending a Perónist political rally out of the Luna Park Stadium to the nearby Cervantes Theater, where she proposed the establishment of a Perónist Women's Party, over which she would preside: "To be a Perónist is, for a woman, to be loyal and to have blind confidence in Perón."[44] The Perónist women rewrote the words to the song "The Perónist Boys" to describe their commitment:

> *Las muchachas Perónistas*
> *Con Evita triunfaremos*
> *Y con ella brindaremos*
> *Nuestra vida por Perón.*
>
> The Perónista girls
> With Evita we will triumph
> And with her we will dedicate
> Our life to Perón.[45]

Eva Perón had little or no interest in or understanding of women's rights, and she expressed disdain for feminists as "women who did not know how to be women." What she did care about was empowering Juan Perón; she worked indefatigably to re-create herself as the symbolic embodiment of the Argentine working class, male and (now that they had the vote) female. As Fraser and Navarro point out, "Evita's effect on the condition of women in Argentina and on their political life was decisive. She created an entire generation of loyal women Perónists."[46] Increasingly skilled in the populist politics that characterized the Perónist regime, Evita was effective in bringing large numbers of women "who cared little about women's rights and were indifferent to the concerns of upper and middle-class feminists" into the political sphere. The power of Evita's Perónist Women's Party was evident in the elections of 1951. With 500,000 members and 3,600 offices across the nation, the results of the women's efforts were apparent: in the presidential election, 63 percent of the female electorate gave Perón their vote.[47]

The Eva Perón Foundation, which commanded enormous revenues through donations from all sectors of society and the economy, is emblematic of her style and her success. Established in 1947, it grew into an enormously wealthy charitable foundation from which Eva personally dispensed monies and aid of every kind to the supplicants who flocked to her office. Blood banks, hospitals, and clinics were funded by the foundation, and the first effective campaigns against tuberculosis and malaria in Argentina were carried out under its auspices. Whether the foundation was begun "as the simplest response to the poverty she encountered" as her supporters aver or as an attempt to humiliate and disestablish the wealthy matrons who refused her entrée to the Sociedad de Beneficia, which had been Argentina's premier charitable association since 1823, there is no denying the benefits dispensed or the formidable political power exercised by Eva Perón. Idolized by the working class, depicted as a madonna-like figure in the Perónist press, Eva remained a potent political force for Perón even after her premature death from ovarian cancer in 1952.

Nineteen forty-seven was a watershed year in international politics. It marked the end of the postwar detente with the Soviet Union and the opening of the cold war, the turning point for Mao in China, the independence of India, the end of the U.S. occupation of Japan. In the Western Hemisphere, in many instances, the political openings that appeared in the postwar enthusiasm for democracy proved brief: democracy became secondary to anticommunism. Indeed, all reformist efforts, such as that of the Arévalo government in Guatemala, were suspect. The change in the political climate was clear at the Special Meeting of the Foreign Ministers of the American States in 1947. Called by the Latin American governments, which did not wish to be left defenseless in the event of another global conflict, the Rio Conference met to debate issues of security. Its purpose was to continue the defense of the hemisphere, but now the perceived common enemy was not fascism but communism. In Europe, Communists responsive to Moscow's direction were consolidating their control of the East European governments, expelling and imprisoning non-Communists. The "iron curtain" was descending and would be confirmed with the coup d'etat and sovietization of Czechoslovakia in 1948. This was the international political climate in which the Rio Conference was called.

Part of the impetus for the conference should also be understood as the desire of the weapons industry to continue its profits in the postwar era. Latin American states were a likely market, as they had not been fully armed during the war and, unlike Germany and Japan, were not under disarmament strictures following the war. This factor, combined with the desire of national militaries to build up their power, contributed to the creation of the "need" to arm the hemisphere against possible Soviet penetration. The shift in the attention of the inter-American diplomatic community from social and economic reform to a focus on anticommunism was a position embraced by most Latin American governments. The extraordinary meeting of American foreign ministers and heads of state convened at the Interamerican Conference for the Maintenance of Continental Peace and Security, in Petropolis, near Rio de Janeiro, from August 15 to September 2, 1947.[48] The delegates drew up the Treaty of Reciprocal Assistance, known as the Rio Pact, which put into effect the principle that an attack on one American state would be considered an attack on all. The emphasis on arming the nation-states of the Western Hemisphere, which has formed the bulk of inter-American assistance in postwar history, dates from this agreement. The Rio Pact also served as the model for the North Atlantic Treaty Organization (NATO), which was signed in 1949.[49]

The term "extraordinary" has a specific meaning in diplomatic parlance: it denotes the appointment of a special ambassador or the convocation of a special meeting outside the normal schedule of events. In this sense the meeting of foreign ministers at Petropolis was extraordinary. But a meeting that was perhaps even more exceptional was held simultaneously in Guatemala City from August 21 to August 27, 1947.

In the earlier examination of women's activities at the inter-American conference tables, the emphasis was on their efforts to effect equal rights for women. But international peace had been an important part of the women's agenda since the inception of the inter-American women's network in 1915: It was a central consideration of the Latin American women in Montevideo in 1933, and the desire for peace was expressed in the UN Charter. As the lines of opposition were drawn in the opening months of the cold war, the Women's International League for Peace and Freedom (WILPF) called together the *Primer Congreso Interamericano de Mujeres*.[50]

Women from nineteen American nations attended.[51] They came not as representatives of their governments but as delegates from women's clubs throughout the hemisphere: Zonta International, Sociedad Cívica Femenina de Santos, Brasil; Unión Femenina de Colombia; Movimiento Pro Emancipación de las Mujeres de Chile; Asociación Puertorriquena de Esposas de Masones; La Cruz Blanca de la Paz (Cuba); Federación Argentina de Mujeres Universitarias; Atenéo Femenino (Bolivia); Asociación de Mujeres Tituladas del Uruguay; Alianza Femenina Colombiana; Comités Populares Femeninos de Guayaquil; Sociedad Unión de Costureras (El Salvador); Ligua Feminine d'Action Sociale (Haiti); Unión Democrática Femenina Hondureña; Atenéo Mexicano de Mujeres; Sección Femenil del Sindicato Naciónal de Trabajadores de la Educación (Mexico); Cruzada de Mujeres Nicaragüenses; Asociación Continental de Intelectuales de America (Panama). Most of the representatives from the United States, who hailed from Minneapolis and San Francisco to Boston and Brooklyn, were members of the WILPF, as were the Canadian women.[52]

The importance of the WILPF, which was founded in 1915 and had its headquarters in Geneva,[53] in the Latin American context may be seen in the fact that nearly all of the Latin American women who attended the Fifth International Conference of American States in Santiago in 1923 and the North and South American women who converged on the Sixth Inter-American Congress in Havana in 1928, as well as the women in attendance at Guatemala in 1947, were members. The positions the WILPF took in matters of hemisphere politics are discussed in report of the *Comité de las Americas de la Liga Internaciónal de Mujeres de la Paz y Libertad* published in 1947: "The [American] Section has worked for many years against North American imperialism, and has cooperated with favorable results on the following goals: (1) The Declaration of the Government of the United States not to intervene in foreign nations to protect North American property; (2) the retirement of United States Marines from Haiti, Nicaragua, and the Dominican Republic; (3) the annulment of the Platt Amendment in the Cuban Constitution. Since 1926, the Section has contributed to the improvement of relations between the United States and Mexico. It has tried to expose and lessen the exploitation of workers in Cuba, Bolivia, Chile and other countries."[54]

As is apparent in the nature of their affiliations—wives of Masons from Puerto Rico, service organizations such as the Atheneum and Pilot Clubs, professors and teachers—these were not politically radical women within their national communities. But they were women who believed strongly in the need for women to speak out on issues of social and political equality, human welfare, and peace. Their first press release stated: "The First Inter-American Congress of Women meeting in Guatemala, representing mothers, wives, daughters of our Continent, has resolved in a plenary session to denounce the hemispheric armament plan under discussion at the Rio Conference, asking that the cost of the arms program be used to support industry, agriculture, health and education for our people." The women declared their right to speak on international issues: "We consider that inter-American political problems deserve particular attention on the part of women of the Continent. . . . We resolve to ask the Pan American Union and all Pan American associations to enact the following resolutions in the inter-American conference." Their first concern was that the "American governments meeting in conference in Rio de Janeiro comply in good faith with the Final Act of Chapultepec, which is an instrument of peace, and not give it a militaristic interpretation."[55]

The newly formed *Unión de Mujeres Democráticas* of Guatemala hosted the conference. Gumersinda Paéz of Panama presided, and Elisa Martínez de Arévalo, wife of Guatemalan president Juan José Arévalo, was honorary president. Funding for the conference came mainly from North American sources, including the U.S. WILPF Section, Zonta International, the People's Mandate Committee, the Pan-American League of Miami, the National Council of Negro Women, and the National Federation of Business and Professional Women's Clubs. The Guatemalan government was particularly pleased to welcome the women in celebration of the recent overthrow of the Ubico dictatorship and the establishment of civil liberties, including freedom of speech and woman suffrage, under the Arévalo administration. Señora Arévalo made the point in her welcoming talk: "In my role as wife of the Constitutional President of Guatemala, I am greatly pleased to welcome the Primer Congreso Interamericano de Mujeres. . . . Since the Guatemalan Revolution of October 20, 1944, which now is seen as a shining example [*movimiento ejemplar*] to the other countries of America, the doors of Guatemala are open to the free discussion of ideas guaranteed under the generous precepts of our Constitution. And also since the Revolution, the Guatemalan woman has been invested with citizenship. . . . Women of America: We meet in a land of free men and women." [56]

An additional, but unspoken, point was being made: that freedom of discussion might be more open at this time in Guatemala than it was in the United States. The organizing committee in Washington had been severely harassed and made the object of rumors in the press. In the words of Gumersinda Paéz, "Hidden forces worked to disrupt the realization of this Congress." [57] In Guatemala the opposition press also criticized the congress, accusing the members of pro-Communist leanings.

In scope and tone the conference was an interesting blend of the democratic rhetoric of the postwar period and an elaboration of themes put forth at the prewar women's conferences. The insistence that women's voices should be heeded at the international conference tables, for example, has a long history in the Western Hemisphere, but the Guatemala conference displayed a deeper understanding of the need to include broader sectors of the population in the debate of foreign affairs, a decidedly new idea but a logical outgrowth of the thrust of the women's movement to open up the political process to women. Also new was the predominance of working women among those in attendance: representatives of trade unions, teachers, businesswomen, and professionals.

One of the most intriguing questions about the *primer congreso* is that it happened at all: Women had, after all, succeeded in incorporating their agenda into the Charter of the United Nations, and a few women had been appointed to government delegations. It would seem that in the postwar era a separatist, explicitly feminist pacifist strategy was no longer necessary. In theory, women could take issues directly to the diplomatic council tables. In practice, however, very few women held diplomatic appointments, and those who did were spokespersons for their governments, not for their own conscience or a feminist constituency. And in 1947 the governments of the Western Hemisphere were not interested in disarmament.

The women who came to the Guatemala conference were well aware that they were setting up a counterdiscourse to the official story put forth by the Interamerican Conference for the Maintenance of Continental Peace and Security. Many of them were members of the IACW and familiar with the transnational women's network and its history of success. Of the Latin American women present, Gumersinda Paéz, Amália de Castilla Ledón, Isabel Sanchez de Urdaneta (Venezuela's first woman consul to New York), and Olga Nuñez Abaunza de Saballos (a lawyer from Nicaragua) had participated in the Chapultepec Conference in 1945 and were delegates to the IACW. But there were no women among the American foreign ministers and heads of state meeting in Petropolis, and the issues the women deemed of primary importance were not under consideration there.

The attitude of the *congreso* was strongly prodemocratic but diverged from the prevailing mentality of the Rio Conference in its commitment to the belief "that the expansion of communism will be contained not by force of arms (*que despierta alarma*) but through the improvement of the living conditions of the people."[58] The congress established committees to address six principal themes. First was women's responsibility in "the face of the terrible consequences of the use of the Atomic Bomb"; the congress members called on their governments to appoint women to posts of importance in the United Nations that "we may help in the establishment of an effective world system which will ensure the peaceful use of nuclear power."[59] The second principle concerned the means by which to promote true democracy in the Americas. The proposals for realizing this goal included the commitment to fight against all antidemocratic systems; the delegates sent a telegram to Raoul Fernández, president of the conference in Rio de Janeiro asking "the American Republics to break relations with Trujillo [Dominican Republic], Somoza [Nicaragua], and Carias [Honduras], whose regimes are shameful to democratic peoples."[60] Additionally, the women asked that military power be subordinated to civil power, that universal disarmament be enacted, and that the problems of minorities receive particular attention. A third theme was the struggle for human rights. The eradication of illiteracy, improved health care, economic security, and freedom of expression were seen as central concerns in this section.

A fourth committee addressed "Problems of Inter-American Politics." It was chaired by María del Carmen Vargas of Guatemala and Matilde Elena Lopez of El Salvador. The principal recommendation of the committee was for the governments of the hemisphere to adhere to the Act of Chapultepec, "to maintain peace in the Continent and in the world, to support industrialization in the Latin American countries, to raise the standard of living for all people, to guarantee essential rights to the American man and woman, to abolish non-democratic regimes and to extinguish the tinder-boxes of war which exist in our America."[61] Although the overriding philosophic basis of the conference was a commitment to an effective world system, and most of the resolutions are articulated in transnational terms, in the report of the fourth committee the positions of individual women on issues of political importance within their national communities was apparent. For instance, the Puerto Rican women called for recognition of the right of national self-determination "as guaranteed in the Atlantic Charter." The Bolivian delegation asked for recognition of Bolivia's right to a Pacific port. The Guatemalan women called for support of "the justice of Guatemala's claims against Great Britain with respect to Belize." The women also called for support from throughout the Americas for a Central American Union; the abolition of the use of passports in the hemisphere and creation of a union in which only tourist cards would be needed to travel from country to country, greater cultural exchange, and an inter-American fair to show off the industrial, artistic, and folkloric products of the American countries. The government of the United States was critized on a number of issues. It was pointed out that the Taft-Hartley Act violated the rights of workers as established in the Act of Chapultepec. The Department of State was asked to assure that North American corporations operating in the Caribbean and elsewhere be strictly apolitical. The need for schools and agricultural banks in rural areas was another point in the discussion of potential "tinder-boxes" in inter-American politics.

In short, the women at the *Primer Congreso* wanted to carry out the promises of the Atlantic Charter, the Act of Chapultepec, and the fledgling United Nations. They had a history of effective participation in the inter-American arena, and when they saw the threat posed by the anti-Communist rearmament drum-beating, they organized and spoke out. The women were right: the carefully laid plans for a peaceful and more just world, drawn up over the years by men and women of goodwill, were destined to be jettisoned, relegated to the back burner at the official international council tables as the cold war loomed. The Latin American women clearly recognized the potential for the use of weapons not for international defense but by the state against the populace; the tinderboxes they identified proved to be exactly that. And the failure of the Department of State to curb the political activities of North American companies resident in Latin America would be vividly and cruelly apparent in Guatemala itself in the very near future.

The focus of the fifth committee was on European immigration, refugees, and victims of war; however, a Honduran woman, Paca Navas de Miralda, expanded the debate to include the topic of political prisoners and political exiles in Latin America: "During the fourteen years of the present regime, hundreds of Hondurans have been forced to migrate to Mexico, Cuba, and other American countries. . . . I urge this meeting of women [*organismo femenino*] . . . to send a cable to the Conference of Ministers in Rio de Janeiro asking their intercession on behalf of political prisoners in Honduras and that a general amnesty be declared so that all Honduran emigrés may return to their country." Paca Navas sought guarantees of protection for returning political exiles and concluded: "The same problem exists in Nicaragua in Central America and in the Dominican Republic in the Antilles."[62] Paca Navas's plea underlines again the importance of the inter-American conference tables for Latin American women: she could speak out on issues of political repression, exile, and refugees in an American context, using this forum to press for domestic reform.

Similar pressure for domestic political reform was central to the work of the sixth committee, whose theme was "The Civil and Political Rights of Woman, and Her Access to Posts of Responsibility"; the commission was chaired by Mexican suffragist Amália de Castilla Ledón, who was also vice-president of the IACW. The governments of the hemisphere "who had not already complied" with the declaration of the equal political rights of men and women were called on to do so immediately. Additionally, the women were deeply concerned that their right to fill important national and international positions be observed; it was clear to them that until that was the case their voices would be neither heard nor heeded.

The women at this conference believed that it was necessary for women to continue a separatist political strategy, at both domestic and international levels. One of the resolutions stated: "We support the formation of associations of women, not to fight against men, but as a method of unity and with the aim of winning better representation in the legislatures."[63] To that end, they called for the formation of a *Federación Inter-Americana de Mujeres* to continue their work and "the collaboration of women of the Americas to secure peace."[64]

The women who attended the conference were women who were active outside the home in their respective communities; they were involved in volunteer work and/or employed in both white- and blue-collar occupations (e.g., lawyers, teachers, professors, and representatives of various women's unions). This was a rapidly growing population group, and it was not by any means directly analogous to the male diplomatic community gathered in Rio de Janeiro. Male diplomats, drawn from the national elites, were not nearly as diverse in their social, economic, and political backgrounds as were the women assembled in Guatemala. However, it should not be forgotten that these women were far from typical within their national communities; they differed from the majority of their countrywomen in their education, economic resources, and engagement in international politics.

At the conclusion of the conference, six cables were sent. The first was addressed to George Marshall, U.S. secretary of state and Raoul Fernández, president of the Rio Conference: "The *Primer Congreso Interamericano Mujeres* meeting in Guatemala, representing mothers, wives, daughters of our Continent, resolved in plenary session to denounce the universal armament plan under discussion at the Rio conference, asking that the cost of the program be used for industry, agriculture and the health of our people."

Three cables went to individuals: to Eleanor Roosevelt "in profound appreciation for her work for peace and international understanding"; to Paulina Luisi, "rendering homage to the great leader in the fight for women's rights [*rendirle homenaje gran luchadora*]"; and to Henry Wallace, "saluting the defender of peace and great friend of Latin America."[65]

One cable asked the American republics to break relations with dictators in the Americas, and another recommended "the repudiation of the Spanish dictator Franco by the republics of America." Ironically, the one notable woman who attended the Rio Conference was Argentine first lady Eva Perón, who made a ceremonial call at the conference on her way home from her controversial European tour, during which she had accepted lavish hospitality from Generalissimo Franco. Unlike Eva Perón's tour, the work of the *Primer Congreso Interamericano de Mujeres* received little press coverage. The *New York Times*, which gave daily page-one coverage to the meeting of the inter-American ministers and heads of state, published a brief notice of the women's meeting on August 19, on page 21 in the Women's Section, under "Food."

There is no evidence that the proposed women's federation was indeed launched, but the congress had an immediate legacy in the formation of the *Comision Inter-Americano de Mujeres* (CIM) in Caracas in 1949; though under the auspices of the Organization of American States, the women's mandate is drawn almost verbatim from the resolutions of the Guatemalan conference.[66] There were connections through personnel as well: Amália Castilla de Ledón was the first chairwoman of CIM. The importance of the work of these women extended well beyond the hemisphere; Castilla de Ledón, Minerva Bernardino, Bertha Lutz,[67] and members of CIM were crucial in founding the United Nations Commission on the Status of Women and served as officers of that body. The IACW served as a model for the League of Nations committee on women; in the postwar period it served as a model for the UN commission. And at the twenty-third session of the UN Commission on the Status of Women, held in Geneva, Switzerland, in 1970, a resolution recommended "the establishment of a commission similar to CIM in the Arab League."[68] Subsequently, in the mid-1970s, similar commissions of women were founded in Asia and sub-Saharan Africa.

Though the women attending the Guatemala Conference in 1947 were not successful in halting the arming of the Americas, or even in gaining coverage of their proceedings, their legacy is clear. The issues they addressed and the debates survived in CIM and the United Nations, and the central themes of their work came to the fore once more in the Decade for Women (1976–1985).

The optimism and pride with which the Guatemalan government greeted the delegates to the women's conference reflected the hopes of the new regime. President Arévalo (1945–1951) and his supporters visualized a restructuring of their society to afford greater economic opportunity and social justice for all citizens. Educational reforms, a labor code, and health and sanitation projects were enacted, and a climate of political freedom prevailed. Arévalo's political tolerance and idealism, which he described as spiritual socialism,[69] were regarded with deep suspicion by the military, conservatives, and the international business community, most visibly represented in Guatemala by the United Fruit Company. Arévalo survived, but his successor, Jacobo Arbénz Guzmán, did not. Arbénz's close association with leaders of the Communist movement within Guatemala[70] and his attempt to enact agrarian reform provided the catalyst that cemented an alliance among large landholders, reactionary elements in the military, international business interests, and the anti-Communist agenda of the Eisenhower administration. Arbénz was overthrown in a CIA-backed coup d'etat in 1954.[71]

Women played a highly visible and important role in the political shift from the democratic socialism of the Arévalo presidency to Arbénz's increasing reliance on the support and advice of leaders of the Guatemalan Communist party, which held its first national Congress in 1949. The women who hosted the *Primer Congreso Interamericano de Mujeres* in 1947 and who formed the *Unión de Mujeres Democráticas* of Guatemala were educated, upper-middle- and middle-class women who supported the democratic reforms of the Arévalo regime; these women were conspicuously absent from the delegation of Guatemalan women who attended the WIDF-sponsored *Congrés des Femmes* in Paris in 1947 and returned home to form a WIDF affiliate, *Alianza Femenina Guatemalteca* (AFG). The women most closely associated with the AFG were, by and large, the wives of the Central Committee of the Communist party as it emerged in 1950: Irma Chávez de Alvarado, wife of Bernardo Alvarado Monzón, who served as minister of the economy under Arévalo and secretary general of the Communist party; Elsa Casteñeda de Guerra Borges, wife of Alfredo Guerra Borges; María Jeréz de Fortuny, wife of José Manuel Fortuny Araña, the first secretary-general of the Guatemalan Communist party. Concepción Castro de Mencos was an effective organizer among textile workers and one of two women members of the Central Committee of the Communist party (the other was Irma de Alvarado).[72] These men and women were in general younger than the members of the Arévalo administration and tended to be the first generation in their families to secure a university education and aspire to professional status.

In November 1953 the AFG, which was centered in Guatemala City, held its first national congress as part of an effort to attract members from other geographic and social locales, particularly women agricultural and textile workers. The extent to which the AFG was identified with the Communist movement by 1953 is apparent in the composition of the board of the *Comision Femenina* of the Communist party, which was chaired by Irma de Alvarado and included Elsa Casteñada, María Jeréz de Fortuny, and Concepción Castro de Mencos. Bernardo Alvarado Monzón described the work of the AFG as an "important fighting front," which had to be made into the "united front of women" and was the best tool for winning the women of Guatemala away from their "traditional conservatism."[73] In a circular distributed to all committees of the Guatemalan Labor party in 1953, he wrote: "In our party we ought to give every type of aid to this organization of women and to its Congress."[74]

Interestingly, the wives of presidents Arévalo and Arbénz were also active on the political stage, which (with the vivid exception of Eva Perón) is a highly unusual phenomenon in the context of Latin American politics wherein political wives may be seen but not heard. Elisa Martínez de Arévalo participated in the 1947 inter-American congress and worked to support her husband's programs. María Vilanova de Arbénz, who married Juan Jacobo Arbénz against the wishes of her wealthy Salvadoran family, was an active member of the AFG; her friendship with exiled Chilean Communist Virginia Bravo Letelier[75] and with María Jeréz de Fortuny, who served as her secretary, were later used to support allegations that she influenced her husband to legitimize the Communist party and to appoint party members to his government; María Jeréz de Fortuny, for example, was named to the National Agrarian Department. It should be noted that the allegations were drawn from "evidence" compiled post facto by the Guatemalan National Committee for Defense against Communism to justify the armed overthrow of President Arbénz in 1954.[76]

The prominence of women in Guatemalan postwar politics suggests an intriguing story. It is not remarkable that women should have been so highly visible in the Communist ranks; women, youth, and workers were of primary concern to party organizers throughout the hemisphere, and numerous strategies were undertaken to attach their loyalties. In Brazil, Uruguay, and Argentina, where the participation of women in politics was more acceptable than elsewhere, women were often candidates for office on the party ticket, though even there women comprised but a small proportion of party members, 10 to 15 percent. But by the late 1940s in most of Latin America, the Communist party was illegal, its members in exile or forced underground. In contrast, the movement flourished in Guatemala. Poppino writes: "Only in Guatemala, where the party sought to identify itself with a popular revolution and received the backing of a friendly government, were the Communists temporarily able to build a position of strength and influence during the postwar decade."[77] The high profile taken by Guatemalan women in the movement is an indicator of its extraordinary success.

Under both Arévalo and Arbénz, the Guatemalan government sought change through the enactment of reform legislation. In 1945 the Guatemalan government wrote a new constitution, promising improved social and economic justice for its citizens, including women, in compliance with the resolutions of Chapultepec and the Charter of the United Nations. Guatemalan women supportive of Arévalo-style socialist democracy were represented at the inter-American conferences and proud to welcome the *Primer Congreso Interamericano de Mujeres* in 1947. Guatemalan women who believed that international communism promised a surer path to social, economic, and political equity attended the *Congrés des Femmes* in Paris in that same year. Both groups of women, though of slightly different generations and class origin, were articulate and effective critics of politics as traditionally practiced in Guatemala and advocates for women.[78]

In the climate of the cold war, work on behalf of women was highly suspect and became part of the "case" against the elected governments of Arévalo and Arbénz put forth by their domestic enemies and the government of the United States. With the coup d'etat in 1954, the impulse toward a more open political and economic structure, from which urban, Spanish-speaking Guatemalan women made significant de jure gains, was shut down and did not resurface in the ensuing authoritarian military regimes.

In postwar Mexico, Brazil, Venezuela, and Guatemala, a combination of intellectual leadership, autonomous women's organizations with feminist or reformist agendas, neighborhood groups, international connections with the IACW, the WIDF, the Socialist International and the ILO, and female sectors of political parties sustained the impulses of the prewar women's movement and continued to press for inclusionary reforms in education, employment, and political practice. Yet in Bolivia, which had experienced the most prolonged social revolution of the era, recognition of women's issues appears to have been almost entirely lacking.

The roots of the Bolivian Revolution of 1952 lay in the Chaco War (1932–1935), in the wake of which the economic, social, and political fabric of Bolivia was near disintegration. From the late 1930s to the 1940s, opposition to the traditional leadership increased, and numerous opposition parties formed. In 1941 the Movimiento Naciónalista Revolucionaria (MNR) was founded. Profoundly nationalist in orientation and committed to diminishing the stranglehold of the "Big Three" tin mining companies in the country, the MNR gained its first political strength by championing the tin miners in their struggle to organize labor unions. MNR members of the House of Deputies defended the tin miners who were prosecuted by the government in the aftermath of the Catavi massacre of December 21, 1942, in which government troops fired on and killed hundreds of unarmed men, women, and children who had joined together to protest the conditions in which they were forced to work and live. In 1943 the MNR supported the coup d'etat that brought the reformist government of Gualberto Villarroel to power.

The murder of Villarroel in 1946 inaugurated the period known as the *sexenio*, the six-year interval between the overthrow of the Villarroel government and the success of the revolutionary movement that brought the MNR to power in 1952. Women were vital in sustaining the resistance throughout the *sexenio*, staging street demonstrations and hunger strikes aimed at winning amnesty for political prisoners, acting as clandestine messengers and arms transporters, nursing the sick and sheltering political refugees. One of the best-known female leaders, Lydia Gueiler Tejada, held the post of commander of the MNR armed militias. Yet according to historian Gloria Ardaya Salinas, "There is not one single political or ideological document belonging to the MNR that addresses or proposes the matter of women's struggles."[79] Evidently, the Bolivian women, in contrast to the Mexican women during Cárdenas's presidency or the Argentine women under Perón (both of which regimes employed populist tactics similar to those of the MNR) were unable to bargain for improvements in women's status.

The MNR did recognize the political value of female support for the revolution, and to this end it organized a women's sector of the party known as the "Female Command." The most visible women within the Female Command of the MNR were the Barzolas, named after María Barzola, a woman miner and labor rights activist who lost her life in the Catavi massacre. The function of the Barzolas, for which they became notorious, was described by MNR leader Victor Paz Estenssoro as "a sort of women's secret police."[80] A witness later said of these female shock troops: "The MNR's Barzolas gave of themselves to serve the party's interests, and instead helped repress the people. In La Paz, for example, when a sector of the working class demanded something, the Barzolas would jump in front of them, brandishing razors, penknives, and whips, attacking the demonstrators . . . in Parliament, too, the Barzolas would shout down and throw tomatoes at anyone who spoke against the MNR."[81] It was also well known that the Female Command of the MNR exercised a virtual monopoly over women's traditional activities in the informal market, such as the sale of food and drink in public places.[82]

In 1952 the women won the right to vote as part of the revolutionary government's promulgation of a bill of universal suffrage, an act that expanded the electorate tenfold. In her book *La mujer y la revolucion*, published in 1959, Lydia Gueiler criticized the ways in which the MNR incorporated masses of women and manipulated them in the party's interests without considering the legal, economic, and political limitations under which most Bolivian women struggled: "As a central theme in its messages to the female sector, women were repeatedly reminded that it had been the MNR that had granted women political rights through universal suffrage."[83]

In 1954, faced with the disaffection of labor, the collapse of the international tin market, and a disintegrating economy, the revolutionary regime called on the National Female Command of the MNR to rally the women's vote. Gueiler writes that "the party needed a total mobilization of its forces to shore up its political position against the opposition in what were to be the most democratic elections ever held in the country. For this, naturally, they remembered the women."[84] The elections of 1956, the first in which Bolivian women voted, were a triumph for the MNR. They were also notable for the almost total absence of women among those running for office or elected to office.[85]

In the 1920s and 1930s, upper- and middle-class Bolivian women participated in the international woman's movement, and during the Chaco War, they joined with Argentine and Uruguayan women in calling for peace. At various women's congresses and in the pages of *Mujeres de America*, Bolivian feminists wrote eloquently of indigenous women, denouncing the double burdens of racism and sexism. Individual women such as Emiliana Cortez Villanueva wrote articles promoting education for rural children and founded the *Primer Centro Ferroviario Femenino* to raise money for food, books, and clothes for the schoolchildren. She later represented Bolivia on the IACW and chaired the *Comisión de Derechos de la Mujer* at the CIM meeting in Rio de Janeiro in 1952. In addition to her work on behalf of education and organizing charitable activities, she wrote about issues of feminism. This work, which invoked the sisterhood of Spanish American women, was published in her column "Union America" in the Uruguayan journal *Iris*. Her book *Manantial* was published under the auspices of the Mexican legation in La Paz in 1939.[86] Two things are apparent in Cortez Villanueva's career. First, there are strong parallels to the situation of Peruvian feminists in the prewar era, when women who espoused feminist ideas and held reformist values looked to private organizations rather than to the government to implement their programs. Second, the importance of the international women's arena for continuity and as a forum for the debate of feminist issues and publication of feminist writing when almost none existed within the national community.

Lydia Gueiler, who might have expected some political reward for her leadership during the revolution, also found it necessary to forge her role in the international community. Despite her criticism of the MNR's manipulation of women cited above, Gueiler was passionately committed to the nationalist cause and dedicated to serving the MNR. She believed that the full realization of the revolution must include "the free association of women in legitimate defense of her interests, without distinction of class, race, creed or even political ideas, independent of her membership in syndicates or political parties which pursue broader and more general ends."[87] She advocated that women take advantage of the political opportunity presented by the suffrage act: "Women have recently obtained, at least at the legal level, the chance to intervene actively in the politics of the nation. . . . [N]ow we must fight to have women elected to office."[88] Her most radical vision was that women must take the fight for their interests into their own hands—and she saw that those interests were far broader than political rights—that the ideals of the revolution, carried to their true extent by women in their daily lives, at all levels and through all means, would be the realization of the revolution.

Gueiler's own experiences at the time the MNR took power did not diminish her enthusiasm or loyalty, but they are indicative of the disregard of the male leadership for women with minds of their own. Gueiler, the only woman to head a battalion during the revolution, was first appointed secretary of a small municipal electoral board, a position far from the center of national power, and then posted to Hamburg, Germany, as a "functionary" of the Bolivian consulate in that city. She writes of the assignment: "On the 19th of April 1953 my political life took a drastic change. By the decision of the Government of the National Revolution I was sent to the Old World. At the news that I would be separated from my country and the revolutionary experiment, I became terribly depressed. I did not wish to abandon the place [*el puesto de lucha*] which I had earned through years of sacrifice by my presence in the revolutionary actions. The duty assigned to me was not very important. Nevertheless, I used it to prove my tenacity as a political fighter and my faith in the destiny of the Revolution."[89]

Gueiler did not remain in an unimportant role for long. Shortly after her arrival she moved from the Hamburg consulate to Bonn, and when that mission was upgraded to the status of embassy, she became the first female chargé d'affaires in Germany. Gueiler commented on her reception: "I attended a function with the fifty-six heads of diplomatic missions accredited to this country. There was a good deal of comment and approval of the appointment of a woman by the Government of Bolivia to their diplomatic delegation. In this way, the National Revolution was able to show, across great distance, its profound progressive sentiments."[90]

Gueiler made the best of her circumstances and throughout gave credit to the national revolution. In fact, it appears that this great progress was pretty much unknown in La Paz, which confirmed her appointment only after the German government had recognized her in the capacity of chargé.[91] At home in Bolivia in the 1950s, women received little attention except as their votes were desired. Gueiler was ardent in her support of the Bolivian Revolution;

she was equally ardent in her advocacy of feminism. She writes that she found "renewed enthusiasm and support" for her views at the CIM meeting in Mexico City in 1954.[92]

The lack of interest in, even the lack of awareness of, women's issues on the part of the Bolivian revolutionary government stands in contrast to the response of the revolutionary government in Guatemala and in fact is unusual in the context of revolutionary and reformist governments from Mexico in 1910 and Uruguay in 1916 to Cuba in 1959 and Nicaragua in 1979 in that in each case the new regimes tended to incorporate the most advanced social thinking of their era into new constitutions. What may be concluded is that the Bolivian revolution, while intensely nationalist, did not envision a more equitable society; rather, it aimed at enlisting miners, railroad workers, peasants, and urban workers in the service of a corporate state. Enfranchised women were just another sector of the population to be incorporated into the MNR political apparatus.

The experiences of Lydia Gueiler in Bolivia and Magda Portal in Peru illustrate the difficulty that even the most valiant women faced in attempting to claim a voice in policymaking once their parties came to power. Having accepted the concept that the revolution was for all people, they found that it was for all men: women remained in subordinate positions, support positions, formed into women's units. When Portal and Gueiler had the temerity to raise women's issues, they found themselves under attack by their former comrades in arms.

It was characteristic of women's organizations in the 1950s that, no matter what their ideological perspective, they were nontransformational; the thrust was toward including women in a particular vision of politics, not on altering the relationship between men and women or revising the traditional family unit. The themes of reformist feminists, the appointment of women to policymaking bodies, the election of women to high office, equal access to education and jobs, equal pay for equal work—were kept alive in the Brazilian, Cuban, Mexican, Uruguayan, Chilean, and Argentinian women's associations and, at the international level, through the efforts of the UN Commission on the Status of Women and CIM. National governments and major political parties could be persuaded to implement or support such reforms in return for the expansion of their constituencies; the search for political legitimacy led women in different national settings to take on the trappings that seemed most likely to attain that end.

It is critical to distinguish between the mobilization of women—for a cause, a regime, a party, a man—and the improvement in the status of women, much less the liberation of women. In Argentina, Juan and Eva Perón mobilized women on behalf of Perónism; in Bolivia, the MNR mobilized women in support of the governing party; in the Dominican Republic, Trujillo hoped to increase the base of his support through woman suffrage. In Guatemala, women made juridical gains in the postwar enthusiasm for democracy; in the early 1950s women and men dedicated to the Communist movement sought to enlist enfranchised women in support of their cause.

In Brazil and Mexico, where there already existed strong autonomous women's organizations with the historical experience of success in their campaigns for suffrage, equal nationality, and access to education, women, particularly women of the middle classes, made significant gains in the 1950s. Heleieth Saffiotti describes this phase of the women's movement in Brazil as the struggle to move from de jure to de facto equity. The Alfonso Afranio Law, mentioned above, is an excellent example of the efforts of women to implement rights that had been written into law. In contrast, in those matrices where only a fragile tradition of feminist reformist activity existed and where the linkages of feminists to women of the popular classes was mainly tutorial or charitable in nature—as was true in both Bolivia and Peru—women were unsuccessful in pressuring either the revolutionary MNR or the reformist APRA regime into paying attention to women's issues. Women were involved but had little or no say in decision making; their access to paid work and public employment remained limited; the issues or regimes for which their support was solicited sought to reinforce rather than change women's traditional role. Concerns with the social motherhood issues—mother and child care, clean water, adequate food and housing, access to schooling—which had long been predominant among Latin American feminists and in the women's movement, persisted in charitable organizations, church and secular aid societies, and, increasingly, in development programs.

An example of the extent to which a gendered understanding of society persisted, faintly, in the 1950s among urban upper-middle-class women may be seen in Adalzira Bittencourt's *A mulher Paulista na história* (*Women of São Paulo in History*) published in 1954.[93] Bittencourt held a law degree and published on women and the law (1925), children and the law (1926), and health care (1942) and also produced anthologies of women's literature. *A Mulher Paulista* was compiled as a contribution to the celebration of the four-hundredth anniversary of the founding of the city of São Paulo; it consists of four hundred pages of laudatory biographical sketches of women participants in the settling of São Paulo and of contemporary lawyers, teachers, and artists, concluding with two sections on "The First Ladies of São Paulo." The emphasis is on charitable work and artistic accomplishment, highly respectable occupations for women of the upper social strata. Women's rights' pioneers such as Bertha Lutz, Carlota Pereira de Queiroz, and a handful of women who held political office are pointed to with pride.

The work is similar in style and content to the numerous biographical dictionaries that focus on the achievements of Brazilian men: patriotic in tone and intent, a celebration of regional rather than nationalist values (the *patria* in question is São Paulo, not Brazil). Although the work is not analytic, Bittencourt was determined to make a statement about the importance of women's activities, and the biographical data she includes is impressive and carefully documented. She is also well aware that women's achievements are overlooked in traditional histories; for example, she writes of pioneer Francisca Roiz ("of gypsy descent") that Roiz secured the first commercial license—to establish a store to sell food—in São Paulo in 1603. Bittencourt comments, "The history of commerce in São Paulo, which is today the primary commercial center of Brazil, begins with a woman, whose name is almost forgotten!" Bittencourt footnotes this with the source and the exclamation "Our warm applause to Francisca Roiz! [*Nossas calorosos aplausos!*]."[94] The work fits in the Brazilian tradition of laudatory biography; the emphasis on society matrons reflects the era in which it was written and the anticipated audience; the comments and the production of a book that recalled São Paulo's female precursors reflect the sensibilities of an individual author. In the mid-1950s women's collective activities on behalf of women's issues were muted.

In Guatemala, the *arevalista* women were reformist with a feminist understanding, and the Communist women worked to engage women in the larger campaign for the redistribution of wealth and power; both impulses were shut down in the coup d'etat of 1954. Yet even as the Guatemalan social experiment was crushed, the first salvo in the revolution that came to define the politics of a generation was fired. Haydée Santamaria was one of the two women to participate in the attack, led by Fidel Castro, on the Moncada garrison near Santiago, Cuba, on July 26, 1953. The Moncada assault was triggered by the March 10, 1953, coup d'etat of Fulgencio Batista that aborted the elections of 1952. Batista had dominated Cuban politics since 1933; his regime was notoriously corrupt and brutal. One writer has observed that in Cuba in the 1950s "students were revolutionaries almost by definition."[95] Haydée Santamaria expressed it thus: "Like much of the youth of that time, I believe, we belonged to various distinct political groups. But on that March 10 we were ready to fight alongside any group, because the most important thing was not to accept what had been imposed on us [the Batista coup d'etat]. And organizing was one way of fighting it, although we may not have been in agreement concerning all that had gone before. This was our position until we found Fidel."[96]

Moncada was the base of the Maceo Regiment of some 1,500 troops; during the annual carnival no more than 500 were expected to be in their barracks. The immediate objective was the armory and its store of military weapons and ammunition. The plan was to arm the people of the surrounding area of Santiago, and when they could no longer hold out there, to head for the mountains of the Sierra Maestra. The assault group of approximately 165 fighters traveled by car from Havana; as a result of various problems, only about half of them ultimately reached Moncada. Haydée Santamaria and Melba Hernández were part of a contingent of twenty who provided support for the fighting and the wounded from the hospital. The women were the only members of their group to survive the night; most of the others were killed in cold blood after the fighting had ended. Both Haydée's brother Abel and her fiancee, Boris Luís Santa Coloma, were tortured and murdered after they were taken prisoner. Haydée was forced to hear their screams and to listen to the details of their gruesome deaths during her own interrogation.[97]

Roberto Fernández Retamar writes: "But Moncada was not only a military battle: it was also a legal battle and, above all, a political battle. As a military battle—followed by an atrocious slaughter—Moncada was a terrible defeat for the attackers."[98] As a legal and political battle, it was a success: the courtroom became the stage from which the testimony of the revolutionaries inflamed the charged Cuban political atmosphere. It was from the prisoner's dock that Fidel gave the speech that became the basis for "History Will Absolve Me." Haydée Santamaria's testimony, an eyewitness account of the atrocities committed by the guards under the direction of Colonel Alberto del Río, was an indictment of Batista-style politics-as-usual, all the more telling for being related in a woman's voice. And the assault gave the cause a name: *Movimiento Revolucionario 26 de Julio* (The Twenty-sixth of July Revolutionary Movement).[99]

Speaking before an audience of students at the School of Political Science of the University of Havana in 1967, Haydée discussed the meaning of Moncada to the revolutionaries:

Like all Cubans, we who went to Moncada have lived through many things, some greater, some smaller, all with very deep feeling. And I have wondered why, if we survived Moncada and the Sierra Maestra and before the Sierra the underground, if we survived the battles of 1959, and later Grión [the Bay of Pigs], enormous things, why then was Moncada different from all the others?

The explanation came to me, very clearly, when my son Abel was born. When my son was born there were difficult moments, the pain was terrible, pain enough to tear out one's insides, yet there was also the strength to keep from crying . . . and why? Because a child was coming. That was Moncada.[100]

Haydée Santamaria and Melba Hernández were sentenced to seven months in prison. On their release they continued the clandestine publication and circulation of revolutionary materials that Abel and Haydée had engaged in before Moncada.[101] The women's first postprison release was *Mensaje al Cuba que sufre* (Message to Suffering Cuba), a manifesto written by Fidel describing the massacre that followed Moncada; perhaps their most significant task was the editing and distribution of the text of *La história me absolvera*, which was smuggled from Castro's prison cell to them page by page. Haydée recounts: "After Moncada, we saw clearly that the problem was not to change a man—Batista: it was to change a system."[102]

Haydée Santamaria and Melba Hernández were spared summary execution because they were female; Haydée's testimony was the more potent because she was a woman speaking of unspeakable crimes committed on human beings who were her loved ones, a woman speaking of the terrible violation of the sanctity of human life. And Haydée Santamaria employed the primary female metaphor, childbirth, to describe the meaning of Moncada to the revolution. Yet Santamaria and her generation of revolutionary women did not see the world in gendered terms. They saw themselves as one with the male revolutionaries and did not identify with women as a group. They adopted Marxist-Leninism as the analysis that best explained the coruscating social and economic disparities they saw around them and that offered a path to radical change. For this generation, the experiences of Magda Portal, publishing her novel of betrayal in Peru (1957), and Lydia Gueiler, writing of her experiences in Bonn (1958)—women who had participated in revolutionary movements but who also had an understanding of the particular struggle of women—went unheard. The voices of the old feminists, critics of the establishment all, held no meaning for those engaged in the life-and-death struggle of the revolution.

Two major themes emerge from the examination of women and politics in Latin America between 1938 and 1958: first, the recognition of women as a potentially significant political force within national arenas; second, the attempts to enlist that support and incorporate women into existing political parties. In this effort, the political left was slower to support equal political rights for women, partly because of lingering perceptions of women's "inherent" conservatism and partly because of the ideological rejection of gender inequity as a valid concern of revolutionary politics. Women activists themselves worked on behalf of women within the political space available. In Mexico the most patriotic of the Latin American women's movements worked to expand the meaning of the national revolution to include women as well as men; in Venezuela, Brazil, and Guatemala postwar democratic openings supported broad reform movements within which women as well as men expanded their political rights.

Since the late nineteenth century the main strand of feminism in Latin America had been closely associated with the rise of secular liberalism, and this impulse remained the predominant influence until the late 1950s, when the prescriptions of democratic liberalism seemed increasingly inadequate to address the glaring social, political, and economic problems of the region.

The development programs for education, vocational training, and promotion of domestic industry that characterized the postwar period foundered in the face of traditional landholding patterns, exploitative labor practices, and rigid class barriers buttressed by racial and ethnic prejudices. Rapidly changing demographics—geometric increases in population, rising internal migration from rural to urban areas—further confounded the effectiveness of traditional reformist approaches to problems.

By the mid-1950s the democratic forces that had gained power in the immediate postwar period in Guatemala, Venezuela, Cuba, and Peru were crushed by harsh military dictatorships; and in states where electoral politics were sustained, such as Brazil, Chile, and Mexico, the political center was authoritarian and conservative. For example, the decision of Brazilian president Juscelino Kubitschek to suppress the Brazilian Federation of Women in 1956 was undertaken in response to pressure from right-wing members of the national oligarchy. Acceptable women's activities—charitable associations, working women's leagues, political auxiliaries—continued; by 1957, when elections were held, women as well as men could vote in every Latin American country but Paraguay, where female suffrage was not enacted until 1961. When elections were not held, the support of women for the reigning regime was solicited. Women of the urban middle classes had greater access to public educational institutions than ever before and to jobs as secretaries, clerks, and teachers. But by the late 1950s the fiery zeal of the early feminists was no longer apparent: The "first wave" of feminism in Latin America was at ebb tide. The older generation of feminists were dying or dead; the causes around which they had rallied were no longer in the political foreground. New groups, male and female, demanded a political voice. The vision of political, social, and economic transformation that came to the fore in the revolutionary politics of the 1950s was no more gendered than the political understanding of reform-minded women of the same era.

The extent to which the political climate had changed in the hemisphere was made startlingly clear during the near-disastrous "goodwill" trip of U.S. vice-president Richard M. Nixon to eight South American nations in 1958. The diplomatic mission, set up to celebrate the inauguration of Arturo Frondizi as president of Argentina, became a focus for the deep economic stress felt by out-of-work meatpackers in Uruguay, striking miners and railroad workers in Bolivia, and Peruvians whose salaries were reduced to a pittance by steep inflation. The frustration and rage that erupted in demonstrations as Nixon proceeded through Montevideo, La Paz, Lima, Bogotá, and Caracas were shocking: it was the first time that a representative of the United States was publicly attacked in such a way.[103] The demonstrations were attributed to Communist agitators.

In Cuba men and women of various political persuasions denounced the blatant excess of Batista regime. A large segment of the urban population, articulate and politically sophisticated, united around one theme: the removal of Fulgencio Batista from office. Women were involved at all levels: they were leaders within the Student Directorate and active in the underground movement. Carmen Castro Porta was a key organizer on behalf of Fidel Castro while he was in exile in Mexico; Haydée Santamaria is described as an "organizer, instigator, fund raiser, terrorist tactician, and a national coordinator of the underground."[104]

On January 1, 1959, Batista fled the country, and eight days later Fidel Castro and Camilo Cienfuegos entered the city of Havana in triumph. A participant, who designates herself only as "La Silenciada," writes of the time: "Early in 1959 we all went and signed the Declaration of Havana. We thought we had gained, conquered, reconquered, won our paradise. Women wanted to share in the triumph we had so courageously fought for, both in the mountains and in the underground."[105] The story of women and the revolution is examined in the next chapter; what was certain in 1959 was that politics for Latin American women, as well as for men, was permanently altered.

Brazilian schoolgirls, Belo Horizante, Minas Gerais, 1941. Courtesy of the Library of Congress.

Business session of the Inter-American Commission of Women at the Seventh International Conference of American States, Montevideo, December 1933. Courtesy of the *Comisión Interamericana de Mujeres* (CIM).

(*opposite*) Poster promoting hemispheric solidarity prior to World War II. Courtesy of the Library of Congress.

AMERICA UNIDA
ES LA PAZ DEL MUNDO

Feminist journals from Latin America, 1976–1991.

Flyers and small journals from feminist collectives and information centers in Uruguay, Brazil, Paraguay, and Chile.

Grafitti ("Stop the Violence") with shirt from the feminist center and journal *Mujer y Sociedad*, Lima, Peru, 1991.

6. Revolution and Counterrevolution, 1959-1973

I went to the shoemaker to collect paper. He asked me if my book was communistic. I
replied that it was realistic. He cautioned me that it was not wise to write of reality.
—Carolina María de Jesus, *Child of the Dark* [1]

Inspired by the success of the Cuban revolutionary movement, urged on by Fidel Castro, and encouraged by Moscow,[2] in the early 1960s guerrilla movements formed in nearly every country in Latin America. The most notable rural guerrilla movements took place in Guatemala, Venezuela, Peru, Colombia, and Bolivia;[3] only in the Colombian case was there any specific political statement about women. The *Platform for a United Popular Movement*, drafted by Camilo Torres, was published in May 1965. It concluded with a description of ten objectives: agrarian reform, urban reform, planning, tax reform, nationalization, international relations, social security and public health, family policy (protection of women and children guaranteed by law), armed forces (women obliged to undertake a term of civil service after they reach eighteen years of age), and rights of women: "On a basis of equality with men, women will take part in the economic, political, and social activities of the country."[4]

A draft of the platform circulated to various rebel groups toward the end of February 1965 did not include the clause on the rights of women; the tenth clause was the only significant change in the draft document before the final version was made public.[5] It is interesting to speculate that Torres's mother, Isabel Restrepo Gaviria, known as "a feminist who often took to the streets to demonstrate against her sex's inequalities,"[6] who was Torres's close confidante, may have influenced her son to remember women as a particularly disadvantaged group.

The role that Colombian Camilo Torres Restrepo envisioned for women in the revolution is more clearly seen in a quotation from his "Message to Women," published in his newspaper, *Frenté Único* in October 1965: "The Colombian woman is readying herself for the revolution. She has been and will be the support of the revolutionary man. She has to be the heart of the revolution. If every revolutionary has a home with a wife who supports, understands, and helps him, we will have many more men deciding to fight. After the revolution, the wife will know that equality of rights and duties will not remain merely a dead letter."[7] Torres, scion of a wealthy Colombian family, left the priesthood to join the revolutionary movement: "I took off my cassock to be more truly a priest." He was killed in a guerrilla action on February 15, 1966.[8]

Torres's vision of the woman—more specifically, the wife—as the support of "the revolutionary man" succeeds in bringing the woman into the imagery of the revolution, making her a vital part of the struggle while simultaneously preserving her in her traditional role: mother, wife, helpmeet. Despite the heroics of Celia Sanchez, Haydée Santamaria, and Vilma Espín, all of whom fought in the Sierra Maestra, the image of the rural guerrilla fighter in the mid-1960s was a bearded male wearing a beret and jungle fatigues and carrying an M-1 semiautomatic rifle. This was the visage of the defrocked Torres, of the towering Fidel Castro, and of the best known *guerrillero* of them all, Ché Guevara. The very term *guerrillero*, Spanish for guerrilla fighter,[9] was given only as "noun, masculine" in dictionaries.[10]

In *Guerrilla Warfare*, the book that became the bible of Latin American rural revolutionary movements, Ché Guevara described the role of the woman: "The part that the woman can play in the development of a revolutionary process is of extraordinary importance. It is well to emphasize this, since in all our countries, with their colonial mentality, there is a certain underestimation of the woman which becomes a real discrimination against her."[11] Guevara, drawing on his experience in the Cuban Revolution, wrote that "the woman is capable of performing the most difficult tasks, of fighting beside the men."[12] But having made this pronouncement, he proceeds to make it clear that her primary role is support for the male fighter: As a fighter, she could, on certain occasions "perform a relief role" but "indispensable physical characteristics" mean that "combatant women are naturally a minority."[13] Her principal revolutionary tasks are in communications, on the assumption that a female inspires less fear of danger in the enemy; transporting ammunition; teaching literacy and revolutionary theory ("women arouse more enthusiasm among children"); and as a nurse or doctor ("with a gentleness infinitely superior to that of her rude companion in arms").[14]

Ché had a sincere appreciation of traditional feminine skills, as this heartfelt paragraph in the guerrilla handbook demonstrates: "The woman can also perform her habitual tasks of peacetime; it is very pleasing to a soldier subjected to the extremely hard conditions of this life to be able to look forward to a seasoned meal which tastes like something. One of the great tortures of the [Cuban] war was eating a cold, sticky, tasteless mess. Furthermore, it is easier to keep her in these domestic tasks; one of the problems in guerrilla bands is that they [masc.] are constantly trying to get out of these tasks."[15]

Torres's statement about women was part of the revolutionary platform, a blueprint for the ordering of society once the revolution was achieved; Ché's was a prescription for women's participation in bringing about the revolution. And revolutions, no less than other military actions, were masculine; the soldiers were men, "tiene los cojones," they were macho. Besides, as Ché's ingenuous comment shows, trying to get (male) members of guerrilla bands to carry out domestic work was problematic.

Moreover, the women who accompanied Ché to the Sierra Maestra and who fought alongside their male companions elsewhere could be explained as exceptional, unusual, unlike most women, and welcome, especially if they did not partake in decision making and performed unglamorous daily chores. Also, it was true that many of the women who were part of guerrilla bands were the sexual partners of men in the groups[16] and could thus be viewed as being there because of a man, for a commitment to him rather than for a commitment to the revolution. The reverse was not true: men were not seen as joining up to be with "their" women.

The thoughts of Ernesto Ché Guevara and Camilo Torres Restrepo on the woman's role are, in fact, what one would expect of men of their cultural background and political beliefs and perhaps could be shrugged off as but two more men prescribing roles for women, no less than the good friars had done centuries earlier. But these were not just two men; they were the heroes of a generation of youth who wanted to change the world. Their words were read and quoted in English, Spanish, Portuguese, and French and distributed around the globe. With their subsequent deaths under fire, they became martyrs, their faces blazing from posters in universities and ghettos alike.

Were the young women who joined the revolutionary movements—the most highly educated generation of young women in history—to content themselves in consort roles? We know the answer to that: in Latin America it was this generation of women who became the fiery feminists of the 1970s, giving up not a whit of their commitment to radical social change but adding to it a new brand of feminism.

The rise of a militant left that caught the popular imagination in an unprecedented way in the early 1960s was but one response to ever-broadening perceptions of the seemingly implacable disparities between rich and poor, not only within national communities but also between nations. The development model, used for the reconstruction of postwar Europe and Japan, was prescribed for Latin America by policymakers whose main motivation was often their anticommunism rather than the alleviation of poverty as a goal per se.

By the late 1950s, and especially after the Cuban Revolution aligned itself with the USSR in 1961, Latin American leaders joined with North American politicians and strategists in supporting multilateral development schemes that included large-scale sales and transfers of military supplies as well as plans for building schools and health clinics and providing loans for small businesses. The plans were formalized in the Alliance for Progress, inaugurated at Punta del Este, Uruguay, at the Special Meeting of the Inter-American Economic and Social Council in 1961.[17] Cuba was the only Latin American nation denied participation in the Alliance; Ché Guevara, in his capacity as Cuban minister of industry, went to Uruguay and used the occasion to denounce North American imperialist designs. On that occasion Ché was outshone by the presence of the equally youthful and charismatic John F. Kennedy.

The Alliance for Progress signaled an acceptance by the U.S. government of the argument long put forth by its Latin American peers: that revolution, or the spread of communism, was not an extrahemispheric threat that could be prevented by the military isolation of the hemisphere but an internal response to poverty, disease, and hopelessness. The United States did not abandon its original position that there was a real external threat; the social reforms and economic assistance that made up the Alliance program were in addition to the commitment to defense against external intervention. UN secretary-general U Thant declared the 1960s "the Decade of Development."

Disillusion with the development programs set in quickly among Latin American analysts, who became convinced that "any development that took place would be dependent development."[18] They saw that the impact of the programs was uneven and inequitable, in many cases exacerbating the existing situation. As one analyst wrote, "They predicted that the poor would get poorer. And they were right."[19]

A third response to the increasing political, economic, and social turbulence of the time came from the Roman Catholic church. Catholicism was overwhelmingly the major religion of Latin Americans, but the hold of the church had been greatly weakened in many areas by the rise of the secular state, the identification of the church hierarchy with national elites, a foreign-born clergy, and numerous other factors.[20] Women had always been the principal churchgoers; in the 1950s the female Catholic congregation was also decreasing. In 1955 in Rio de Janeiro, the Latin American Episcopal Council, known by its Spanish acronym CELAM, was formed. It was the first time that the hierarchy of the Latin American Catholic church had gathered in Latin America. This in itself was not revolutionary; what developed in the next decade, however, was. The stage was set at Vatican II, called by Pope John XXIII in 1962. Dominican scholar Edward Cleary writes: "Vatican II was the most important experience of the Latin American Church in almost five hundred years of existence. . . . The council brought Latin Americans into daily contact with church leaders from all over the world and it forced submerged issues to the surface. It set in motion or reinforced a whole series of properly Latin American initiatives: the emergence of a Latin American theology, grass roots movements, new authority relationships, and critical stands on social issues."[21] One of the first results of Vatican II was that the service could now be said in Spanish or Portuguese: the Latin-Americanization of the Latin American Catholic church, the largest in the world, was underway.

In South America leadership and direction in turning the attention of the church toward issues of social justice came from the hierarchies of the Brazilian and Chilean churches. The ideas of Catholic activist and theologian Paulo Freire, expressed in his book *Pedagogy of the Oppressed* (1958), were formed from his work in the impoverished northeast of Brazil. At the core of Freire's work lay the concept of conscientization: that "it is necessary for repressed peoples to reflect on their own cultural, economic and social situation to begin to become masters of their own lives."[22] Another central concept came from his work in adult literacy programs: that the "students" must not be viewed as objects to be filled with learning (and thereby, in his view, molded into their place in the system) but as subjects who learn by examining and coming to understand their own reality, a transformation that will empower them to change that reality. So threatening did the Brazilian government find Freire's ideas that adult literacy campaigns were abandoned after the military coup d'etat of 1964.

The winds of revolution, the search for effective reform through nonviolent means, the response of the institutions of government and church and international agencies to change marked the decade. Where were the voices of women? The politics of revolution, of the national and international development agencies, of the church and the military were expressed primarily in male voices. The allegiance of women was sought by all; but women, as a group, were objects in the Freirian sense: to be organized, to be catechized, to be enlisted in the support of the cause or program.

The publication in Rio de Janiero in 1960 of Carolina María de Jesus' *Cuarto de despejo* (literally, "garbage dump," translated into English as *Child of the Dark*) is symbolic of the shift in public consciousness that was taking place. Carolina lived in a shack, built with her own hands from lumber pilfered from a church construction site, in the *favela* Caninde in the city of São Paulo. Black-skinned, the mother of three children, she lived by collecting paper, rags, and bottles from the street and more affluent residential neighborhoods and selling them to a junk dealer. Her diary, discovered and published by Audálio Dantas, a reporter for the São Paulo weekly *O Cruzeiro*, told in eloquent detail the struggle of each day to secure money to buy food and care for her children: "It's raining and I can't go looking for paper. On a rainy day I am a beggar. I wear the uniform of the unfortunate. At the slaughterhouse I got some bones. They'll do to make soup. At least the stomach won't remain empty. . . . [T]oday he who lives till the hour of his death is a hero. Because he who is not strong gives in."[23] Carolina was acutely suspicious of politicians, who courted those who lived in the *favelas* before elections and forgot them afterward, and of the "famous Social Service": "It was there that I saw the tears slipping from the eyes of the poor. The coldness in which they treat the poor. The only things they want to know about them is their name and address."[24]

As a child in the interior state of Minas Gerais, Carolina's mother had seen to it that her daughter attended school. The young girl was able to do so for just two years, but unlike many others, she not only learned to read and write but retained her skills as she grew older. The reporter Dantas first encountered her at the inauguration of a playground near Caninde. He recounts: "When the politicians had made their speeches and gone away, the grown men of the favela began fighting with the children for a place on the teeter-totters and swings. Carolina, standing in the crowd, shouted furiously, 'If you continue mistreating these children, I'm going to put all your names in my book!'"[25] Struck by this unusual threat and intrigued as to what the book of this tall, handsome, poor woman might be, Dantas introduced himself to her. At first Carolina María de Jesus would have nothing to do with him. Then she refused to let him see her diary, saying that "it was full of ugly things." She wanted him to publish her fantasy stories of princesses and dragons. After nearly a year's negotiations, the material, which Carolina had written on scraps of paper over a period of three years and saved in the drawers of her one bureau, was readied for publication. It proved to be a literary phenomenon: "In three days the first printing of 10,000 copies was sold out in São Paulo alone. In less than six months 90,000 copies were sold in Brazil . . . having sold more than any other Brazilian book in history. Never had a book such an impact on Brazil."[26]

Why? Why should the story of a poor black woman strike such a chord of response in the national consciousness? The prestigious law school of São Paulo gave her the title "Honorary Member," the first such person so honored who did not have a university education. Jean-Paul Sartre was originally designated to receive the honor that year, but the students deemed Carolina "far worthier in the fight for freedom" than the French philosopher. Carolina's diary spelled out in concrete images the consequences of the grandiose national development programs—enormous hydroelectric dams, highway networks, construction of a new capital city—for the poorest 50 percent of the Brazilian population. President Juscelino Kubitshek's ambitious "Fifty Years in Five" program was financed with paper money. Inflation pinched the middle classes, but it was devastating to Carolina: "I started to add up how much I would spend on the streetcar to take the children into the city. Three kids and I, twenty-four cruzieros coming and going. I thought of rice at 30 cruzieros a kilo. Because of the raise in transportation fares the police were in the streets in case of riots. . . . They spend in the elections and afterward raise everything. It is the people who pay the election expenses!"[27]

Hunger and survival are the central themes of *Child of the Dark*, but what makes the book memorable is Carolina María de Jesus' strong sense of self. She has few illusions about politicians and politics, but she identifies herself as a Brazilian and asserts her love for Brazil. Similarly, she sees the racial discrimination all around her and is proud of her racial heritage: "They told me: 'It's a shame you're black.' They were forgetting that I adore my black skin and my kinky hair. If reincarnation exists I want to come back black."[28] "The white man says he is superior. But what superiority does he show?"[29]

And she is proud to be a mother. For Carolina, the diary is the story of her struggle to provide for her children, to keep them safe in a hostile environment, to protect them from disease in a slum town built on a swamp, to feed them something every day, to find clothes for them, to get them to school. Most *favela* households consisted of a single mother with children, and many of Carolina's neighbors had six, seven, eight children to feed and sometimes an unemployed male companion to care for as well. On Mother's Day she observes, "The sky is blue and white. It seems that even nature wants to pay homage to the mothers who feel unhappy because they can't realize the desires of their children."[30] But on Father's Day she writes: "Fathers' Day! What a ridiculous day!"[31]

Carolina's description of the daily life of poor Brazilians, and specifically poor women, is a graphic indictment of the failure of the national development programs to address the problems of the neediest citizens. The theory of the Kubitshek development plan was that the creation of a solid infrastructure would enable Brazil to reach a "take-off" point where the economy would profit everyone. But by the early 1960s inflation had reached such a pitch that it jeopardized Brazil's political and social institutions.[32] The elections of 1960 were bitterly controversial and marked by ultranationalist rhetoric. Jânio Quadros, who ran as a reform candidate, was elected president but left office after seven months. His vice-president, João Goulart, a labor-leftist, was feared as too radical by many Brazilians, and his succession to the presidential office was qualified by congressional limitations on his power. The new administration inaugurated a three-year social and economic plan that was both politically and economically feasible but promised no immediate redress in two key areas: the soaring cost of living in the urban areas and the lack of land available to the small-holder in rural areas. Both engendered radical grass-roots movements in which women played critical roles.

Part of the Quadros-Goulart campaign platform promised an independent foreign policy. In essence this meant two things: one, less reliance on the United States as a trading partner, and two, reestablishment of relations with the Communist bloc, primarily the USSR and Cuba, and rapprochement with the People's Republic of China. One of the domestic repercussions of this policy was the creation of a political opening for groups that had been banned for their ties with the international Communist movement. On April 16, 1960, women staged a major demonstration in front of the Brazilian Press Association in Rio de Janeiro in honor of the tenth anniversary of the death of the founding president of the Brazilian Women's Federation (BWF), which had been outlawed since 1956. They formed a new organization, the Women's League of the State of Guanabara,[33] which shared the goals of the old BWF. Focusing its organizational efforts in working-class neighborhoods, the league established children's libraries; set up courses in tailoring and sewing, reading and writing, gymnastics, and housekeeping; and sponsored puppet plays for children, as well as lectures and political discussions for adults.[34]

The most spectacular work of the Women's League was its campaign against the high cost of living. The women organized street demonstrations, made radio and television appearances, and attended plenary sessions of the national price regulatory commission to protest the high price of food. Through coordination of effort on a variety of levels, they succeeded in bringing their cause to national attention. Saffioti describes it: "Together with economists and technical workers of the Ministry of Agriculture, the league carried out studies to determine the causes of the exorbitant prices demanded for items such as milk, meat, grains, and vegetable products, and made its findings public. The results of its research in hand, it presided over the organization of a movement against the rising cost of living in other states, and arranged a caravan, joined by more than 200 women, to Brasília (a nineteen-hour trip by car) where it sent a petition with 100,000 signatures to President João Goulart proposing ways to combat the high cost of living."[35]

The political climate also proved propitious for the reform of the Brazilian Civil Code.[36] Initially written by feminist lawyer Romy Medeiros de Fonseca in 1952[37] and sponsored by the National Congress of Brazilian Women, a women's rights association formed in the 1950s, the reform passed in 1962, part of the Goulart administration's effort to win the support of all possible constituencies. The reformed code mainly affected married women, who previously had been considered permanent minors. The 1962 law gave the married woman control over her own earnings and property gained before marriage, the right to administer common goods, and the right to receive one-half of her husband's estate. The reform also forbade discrimination against married women in employment.[38]

The impulses of reformist feminism were faint in the political climate of the early 1960s, however. The women who worked in the league were engaged in the ideology of class struggle and, despite the fact that their organizational work was mainly with women in working-class neighborhoods, did not privilege women in their analysis, a position that was augmented by the spread of Marxist analysis among young women intellectuals. Danda Prado, who was a student at the University of Brazil in Rio de Janeiro at the time, has described the response of her contemporaries to Simone de Beauvoir's visit to Brazil in 1960: "Her book *The Second Sex* had been published in Portuguese in 1949 and served as a major consciousness-raiser for generations of Brazilians. I experienced her impact personally at the university, and I vividly remember our impassioned discussions about her condemnation of male privilege. At that point, however, de Beauvoir still believed that socialist regimes would solve the problems between the sexes. Her words were, 'Women should fight alongside men to reorganize the world's productive forces and for social justice, not to uphold the equality of the sexes but rather the parity of men and women.'"[39]

Prado records that "many Brazilian women were beginning to question the extreme socioeconomic injustice in our country, and some had found a solution through a Marxist analysis. Thus, while part of de Beauvoir's book excited us by verbalizing the oppression we felt as women, our combativeness in that very direction was diverted by the other part and by her speeches, in which she pointed to class struggle as the priority."[40] At that time, Prado herself rejected feminism as irrelevant, but she believed that de Beauvoir's ideas helped to inspire an editor of *Claudia*, the most widely read women's magazine in Brazil, to inaugurate a section called "The Art of Being a Woman" in 1963. Despite its unprepossessing title, the column, as written by Carmen de Silva, became a forum for ideas that were "revolutionary for those days,"[41] denouncing the inferior status of married women—the so-called queens of the hearth (*rainhas do lar*)—and proposing a broader life for women. Though Prado is undoubtedly correct that the primary influence on feminist thought in Brazil at this time was de Beauvoir, the *Claudia* column, with its focus on middle-class married women, sounds as if it may also have been influenced by Betty Friedan's *The Feminine Mystique*, published in the United States in 1963.[42]

In 1963 the cost of living spiraled to 80 percent.[43] The populist politics of the Goulart administration offered no clear line of leadership. The government was denounced by nationalists of the political left and the political right, and conservatives in the church and military hierarchy were gathering increasing support. On April 1, 1964, the government of President João Goulart was overthrown by coup d'etat. The First Institutional Act, on April 9, established government by decree; Marshal Humberto Castello Branco was elected president by congress. It was the first time the Brazilian military had taken power in its own right in the twentieth century; they were not to step down for twenty years.

Women played a crucial role in the conservative revolutionary movement. The radical political strategies of the Women's League, rooted in the politics of the political left, promoted no effective response from the government. Ironically, the tactics of the League—public demonstrations by women protesting the high cost of living—were successfully adopted by the right wing. Beginning in 1962, with the founding of the Campanha de Mulher pela Democracia (Women's Campaign for Democracy), including the Movimento de Arregimentação Feminina (Feminine Movement for Regimentation) and the *União Cívica Feminina* (Feminine Civic Union), women from the upper and middle classes mobilized around the call to protect "the Family, with God, for Liberty."[44] Pocketbook concerns were presumed to be those of every housewife; to this was added fear of the Communist menace and of destruction of family life and of the moral fabric of society.[45] The women's demonstrations reached a crescendo in the weeks preceding the coup d'etat and lent legitimacy to the action: the highly visible participation of "respectable" women blessed the coup d'etat with the aura of having come to the rescue of the family.[46]

Most of the many thousands of women involved in the "marches of the pots and pans" were undoubtedly responding to what Temma Kaplan has called their gender-related interests. These women accepted their traditional roles as wives, mothers, and homemakers; and when they believed those roles to be threatened, they were moved to take action.[47] However, the women's marches were perhaps the most successful part of a campaign against the spread of communism in Brazil, orchestrated to a large degree by the U.S. government in concert with members of the Brazilian military, conservative politicians, and the international business establishment.[48] The right-wing women's organizations received monies and organizational support from the CIA through several front groups, including the *Instituto Brasileiro de Ação Democrática*, which was established in 1959 especially as a conduit for CIA funds into anti-Communist activities.[49]

It was expected by those who supported the coup that the military, having deposed the Goulart administration, would return power to the civilian sector as it had done in the past; the rationale of the intervention was to protect the constitution. The military leaders, however, feared a return to popular politics. Drastic measures were set in motion, ostensibly as a campaign against corruption and demagoguery but truly aimed at the political left. More than seven thousand people were arrested, and nine thousand were removed from office in the weeks following the coup; among the groups suppressed was the Women's League, whose leaders were arrested and detained for questioning.[50]

In 1960, Carolina de Jesus wrote in her diary, "Today I went to the shoemaker to collect paper. He asked me if my book was communistic. I replied that it was realistic. He cautioned me that it was not wise to write of reality."[51] By 1964, Carolina herself had escaped from the *favela*, but writing of the reality of the poor had become truly dangerous.

With the success of the Cuban Revolution and the promulgation of revolution throughout the hemisphere by the Cuban leadership, the political atmosphere in the Americas became ever more highly charged. In Washington the Kennedy and Johnson administrations were committed to fighting communism on a global scale. Kennedy in particular was responsible for the development and application in Latin America of counterinsurgency tactics in response to and ultimately in anticipation of guerrilla activities. Robert Wesson, an analyst for the Hoover Institution, writes: "Counterinsurgency was developed under a theory of total conflict in the cold war between good and evil, in which the nation was at stake and its whole forces were to be guided. [In Brazil] the intellectual basis for this approach was furnished by the Superior War College [*Escola Superior de Guerra*], a remarkable institution important for the formation of higher officers before 1964 and subsequently for the ideological direction of the military government."[52] One of the most pernicious results of the counterinsurgency strategy was the "erasure of the boundary between civilian and military affairs."[53] At the core of counterinsurgency warfare is the assumption that the enemy may be anywhere around you. In many Latin American countries in the 1960s and 1970s, the theory of total conflict repeatedly meant the suspension of civil liberties and of freedom of speech and of the press, the arrest and detention of persons without recourse to legal proceedings, and the imposition of military-authoritarian regimes. Directed at first against guerrilla movements and Communist organizers, targets of repression quickly came to include anyone associated with grass roots organizational work.

In Bolivia the MNR, which had been in power since the 1952 revolution, struggled to maintain itself and to stimulate the economy. Nationalization of the tin mines, the principal source of Bolivian foreign exchange, had not, for a variety of reasons, brought in the anticipated revenues. In 1961, in an effort to revitalize the industry, President Victor Paz Estenssoro entered into an agreement with the International Monetary Fund and the governments of the United States and West Germany that stipulated, among other things, a decrease in the number of mine workers, the freezing of wages, and the suppression of worker control by management veto.[54] Though the plan was ultimately successful in making the mines profitable,[55] it was carried forth at great cost in human dislocation and misery.

Domitila Barrios de Chungara was born in the Bolivian highlands on May 7, 1937, and in the early 1960s lived with her husband and children in the mining center Siglo XX. In her oral history *Let Me Speak!*, she tells of the conditions that resulted from the imposition of the plan: "They decreed a 'monetary stabilization,' all to their advantage. Well, the workers criticized the situation we were in. When all the steps were taken against the people, there was fighting in the mines, and protests and demonstrations. They cracked down hard on us: they didn't send groceries, they didn't send wages, they even cut off our medical supplies. And they put the leaders in jail."[56] The lack of medicines was particularly harsh, as dysentery was endemic and a constant threat to the lives of the children. During the crisis a group of performers, sponsored by the international "Moral Rearmament" crusade arrived to put on shows (in Domitila's phrase, "anti-Communist type shows") for the miners. Furious that the government would send them entertainers but deny their families medicine, the mine leaders announced that they would take the performers hostage until medicines were delivered and the hospital reopened: "All day long those foreigners waited for the train to come. And they'd ask, 'What's happened?' And we'd tell them that the rain had washed out part of the tracks and they were being repaired. But the problem was that the rails had been taken away by the workers."[57] Ultimately, the medicine was delivered, and the bewildered hostages were sent on their way.

Domitila describes the origins of women's organizing in the mining community: "At the beginning, we had the mentality they'd taught us, that women are made for the home, to take care of the children and to cook, and that they aren't capable of assimilating other things, of a social, union, or political nature. But necessity made us organize."[58] The women had a model for organization: the miners' unions had a long and turbulent history and had played a key role in the *sexenio* and the MNR revolution in 1952. In protest against the ever-worsening conditions in their area, in 1961 the miners organized a march to La Paz—some 335 kilometers away across treacherous roads—and women and children were included in the protest. The march was halted by government troops, and the male leaders were arrested and taken to prison in La Paz: "So one by one their *compañeras* went to find out about their husbands. But in La Paz the women were treated badly and they even tried to put them in jail and abuse them. Each one of the women would return completely demoralized. In the union hall they met with us and began telling angrily about what had happened to them. And that's when an idea came up: 'If instead of going like that, each one on her own, we all got together and went to claim our rights in La Paz, what would happen? Maybe we could all take care of each other and get better results.'"[59]

Though not sure exactly what tactic to take, a number of women decided to go to La Paz, where a meeting between government ministers and representatives from the mine workers was scheduled to take place. They demonstrated at the meeting, shouting, "Freedom, freedom for our husbands!" The women were attacked and dispersed by a unit of *barzolas*.[60] Undaunted, the women returned to the meeting site and declared a hunger strike: "That night San Roman came, the terrible San Roman whom nobody wanted to meet.[61] And something happened there. One of the *compañeras* stood in front of him and said, 'San Roman, you know very well that we don't have arms to defend ourselves from your hangmen. But if anything happens, we'll all blow up together, at this very minute. We and you will blow up, because all we've got here is dynamite.' And she took something out of her pocket and asked for a match. But while the *compañeras* were looking for a match, San Roman and his group went running out."[62]

The women were joined in their hunger strike by factory workers, university students, and women who came in from other mines to offer their support. After ten days, in the face of widening sympathy for the hunger strikers, the government gave in. The imprisoned miners were released, the back wages were paid, and food was shipped to the stores in the mining areas. On returning home, the women who had carried out the strike decided that in these hard times they needed a continuing organization. The Housewives' Committee of Siglo XX was formed with about seventy women. Domitila relates: "Of course at the beginning it wasn't easy. For example, in the first demonstration in Siglo XX after they came back from La Paz, the *compañeras* went up on the balcony of the union hall to speak. The men weren't used to hearing the women speak on the same platform as them. So they shouted: "Go back home! Back to the kitchen! Back to the washing! Back to your housework!"

The women paid no heed. Emboldened by their success in La Paz, they "got hold of a typewriter" and began a newsletter, sent numerous letters to the president and ministers presenting the miners' point of view, and broadcast on the miner-controlled radio stations. Within the community they acted as an oversight committee to try to ensure that the grocery store did not cheat the customers, that the schools gave children the breakfasts they were supposed to, that the sick were properly cared for in the hospitals. Though Domitila reiterates that all of the women worked hard, and each did as much as she could, she tells that one of the hardest workers, and most inspiring, was Norberta de Aguilar: "They told me at the beginning that a doctor's wife named Vilma de Garrett was organizing. But it was Norberta, wife of an old mine company worker, who really made the committee go."[63] The two-tiered battle the women were forced to fight, against the government-owned mine management and the prejudices against them as women, are evident in Domitila's account.

Domitila did not begin to participate in the Housewives' Committee until 1963. The work the women did was increasingly dangerous as they staged more hunger strikes in support of the miners protests and aided the men in trying to guard miners' union property—their meeting hall, the radio station, the library—which were subject to sabotage. Many women suffered miscarriages as a result of the hunger strikes, and in 1964, in the wake of the military coup d'etat that overthrew the elected MNR government, the Housewives' Committee became a target of direct government repression: "When General Barrientos came to power in 1964, he immediately saw the danger in women's organizations." The first step taken against the committee was the deportation of the husbands of the female leadership to Argentina: "You're an honorable and hardworking man . . . but we aren't satisfied that you allow your wife to lend herself to foreign interests."[64] The women and children were then evicted from the company-owned house and cut off from the resources of the mining community.

The accusation that the Housewives' Committee was controlled by "foreign interests" referred to the belief that all organizational activity not supportive of state interests was directed from Moscow or Havana. There were, in fact, many "outside" or international groups in Bolivia working among the miners, peasants, and urban workers, and there had been for years. Among the ones Domitila mentions were Jehovah's Witnesses and women from the Christian Family Movement. Workers' unions had many factions; one of the largest in Siglo XX were Trotskyites, with roots that dated to the 1920s. The Catholic church was seen by the miners as allied with government and management interests, a view reinforced in 1961 when the bishop of La Paz excommunicated the miners and their families, calling them heretics and Communists.

The labeling of protest movements as "Communist inspired" allowed the authorities to act with impunity. The fear of "another Cuba" in the hemisphere became the rationale, in this era, for the brutal repression of organized resistance and protest. The proclamations from Havana lent credence to the actions and apprehensions of the anti-Communist response. From Havana, Castro called for a continent-wide revolution; from Havana, Guevara was writing that "the armed victory of the Cuban people over the Batista dictatorship is not only the triumph of heroism as reported by the newspapers of the world: It showed plainly the capacity of the people to free themselves by means of guerrilla warfare from a government that oppresses them."[65]

The enlistment of women throughout the hemisphere in support of the revolutionary cause was given serious attention. In Havana in 1963, the Cuban Federation of Women (FMC) cosponsored with WIDF the Second Congress of Latin American Women, calling for the participation of women in the revolutionary effort. Reports published in the *World Marxist Review* (*WMR*) testify repeatedly to the inspiration of the Cuban revolutionary success among women as well as men. Amador Adaya, reporting from Honduras in October 1962, wrote "Ten years ago there was not a single woman Communist in our country. Today there are many, despite the difficulties of illegal work. . . . We have the example of the socialist countries and the Cuban revolution to inspire us in this struggle."[66] In a report titled "Party Work among Women: The Experience of the Women's Movement in Argentina," Fanny Edelman opens with the assertion that "one of the major tasks of the Communist Party in Argentina in its efforts to build a national democratic front is to organize women and draw them into the emancipation movement."[67] She notes that the Argentine Women's League, founded in 1947, continued its efforts among women workers in the textile, food, and clothing industries. The league published a newsletter, *Nuestras Mujeres*, and like its Brazilian counterpart, "organized housewives' committees and street marches and petitions" protesting the high cost of living. Though the Argentine league suffered harassment from authorities at times, it was not forced to disband as the Brazilian league had been forced to do in 1956.

The attempted invasion of Cuba by U.S.-trained anti-Castro troops[68] in April 1961 aroused intense sympathy for the Cuban people, as well as intense anti-Americanism, among many Latin Americans. Argentine Rosa Pantaleon wrote: "A sign of the growing political awakening of women generally is their participation in the campaign to support Cuba. With money collected peso by peso they bought and sent to Cuba an airplane and a tractor. And now, despite hounding by the authorities and the high cost of living, women are campaigning for funds to build a school in Cuba."[69] Another report from Argentina stated: "Special mention should be made of the activity in promoting solidarity with Cuba. Our women collected hundreds of thousands of pesos for the purchase of surgical instruments for a maternity home in Cuba. Members of the League made articles for sale at bazaars, collect gifts, conducted first-aid classes to train a thousand young people who volunteered to go to Cuba in the event of an invasion, hold bake sales, raffles, and so on. The significance of the Cuban revolution is widely discussed. At the time of the invasion of Cuba, our women, despite police persecution, demonstrated their solidarity with Cuba."[70] The activities of the women members of the Communist party of Argentina in support of the Cuban Revolution sound remarkably like the activities of women trying to raise money for a charity anywhere in the hemisphere.

Despite these efforts and the optimism expressed in the reports of the WMR, women constituted a very small percentage of the formal Communist parties in Latin America.[71] Women were, however, increasingly active in a wide variety of grass roots activities that became, like the Housewives' Committee of Siglo XX, ever more analytically radical and politically militant. As was true in Cuba, women elsewhere in Latin America made up the corps of teachers in literacy campaigns. In El Salvador, for example, Rosa Ochoa, who had long worked to organize women against discrimination at home and in the work place, helped to establish the Sisterhood of Salvadoran Women. In the early 1960s the sisterhood was successful in a two-pronged campaign to foster literacy among rural women and to promote the social reforms promised in the new constitution. As the hope of significant social and economic reforms faded, many women from the Sisterhood of Salvadoran Women became pioneers in the trade-union movement of teachers and food workers that evolved into ANDES, a militant teachers' union with 85 percent female membership.[72]

As the attempt by the United States to overthrow the Castro government through a surprise invasion backfired to become a means of creating solidarity domestically and garnering sympathy for the revolution internationally, so too did the attempt by Cuba to give direct support to revolutionary forces in Venezuela in 1963 backfire. As was noted in chapter 5, Venezuelan women won the vote in the brief political opening that followed World War II and participated in electing a democratic slate that was overthrown by a military coup d'etat in 1948. The *Agrupación Cultural Femenina* was suppressed during the dictatorship of Peréz Jiménez from 1948 to 1958. Giovanna Merola writes of this period: "Women in the underground fought alongside men against the authoritarian government. These years saw the founding of the *Unión de Muchachas Venezolanas* [Union of Venezuelan Girls] by the *Juventad Comunista* [Communist Youth], while the *Organización de Mujeres Comunistas* continued to function and the Democratic Action party founded, clandestinely, the *Asociación Juvenil Femenina de AD*."[73] All of these organizations were either underground or semiclandestine; their goal was "the return of democracy to Venezuela."[74] On January 23, 1958, Peréz Jiménez was removed from office.

Merola reports that immediately after the fall of Jiménez a broad spectrum of women's groups emerged and put together the *Primer Mitín Femenino* (First Women's Meeting) in Caracas: "Women from the Venezuelan Communist Party, the Democratic Republican Union, and the AD were among the participants. The group issued a call to the entire nation to work for their newly won freedom."[75] On December 7, 1958, Democratic Socialist Rómulo Betancourt, the AD candidate, was elected to the presidency.

Dissatisfaction with fiscal austerity programs and the slow pace of reform led to increasing unrest among students and workers, and by 1962 two guerrilla movements formed, the Armed Forces of National Liberation (FALN) and a splinter group from the AD. The immediate goal of the revolutionary movement was the disruption of the presidential elections in 1963. In the face of terrorist actions and right-wing threats to abort the election, AD candidate Raúl Leoni was chosen; he took office on March 11, 1964, the first time in 134 years of independent history that one elected president succeeded another.[76] Between the elections and the inauguration tensions mounted; with the discovery of a cache of Cuban arms and subsequent evidence that Cuba had supplied substantial military aid to Venezuelan guerrillas, the OAS and the United States moved to isolate Cuba diplomatically within the hemisphere. Only Mexico maintained relations with Havana.

Giovanna Merola observes that the women's coalition that formed around the common goals of removing Peréz Jiménez from office and instituting democratic practices broke down in the divisive atmosphere of the early 1960s: "Women divided along class lines. Class struggle and each party's desire to win control of the country became priorities, and women's demands once again gave way to other issues, although women were active on a variety of political fronts, as guerrillas—both in rural and urban areas—or as members of women's organizations of traditional parliamentary parties."[77]

The subsumption of women's issues to the political exigencies of the period is not surprising. The Cuban model brought women into political and economic service to the state; likewise, reformist and development plans were based on the assumption that women would benefit to the same degree as their male counterparts and did not differentiate need on the basis of gender, excepting always the needs of the woman as mother. Woman suffrage, which had served as a rallying point for many of the middle-class women's movements in Latin America, as it had done earlier in the United States, was (as of the 1961 suffrage amendment in Paraguay) on the books in every country in the hemisphere. Women had greater access to education than ever before. At the international level, CIM (which instituted a number of innovative projects focused on rural women in the 1950s and over the years sustained the echo of the early feminists' social concerns and political perspectives), did not convene a full meeting between 1959 and 1967.[78] The Thirteenth Assembly was held at the Pan-American Union, Washington, D.C., in 1959; the Fourteenth convened in Montevideo, Uruguay, in 1967. In the interim, Special Assemblies were held in Washington in 1961, 1963, and 1966. The thrust of these meetings was to make plans that would supplement the work of the Alliance for Progress. The main program that emerged was the Inter-American Program for Training Women Leaders. It set up seminars in various national capitals and provided fellowships for participants; it was an obvious extension of the North American emphasis on women's political rights and of dubious relevance in the face of escalating tensions between counterinsurgency forces and the militant opposition in Latin America. The leadership-training programs seem devoid of the social concerns with which Latin American women in particular had embued earlier inter-American women's conferences.

In Latin America, student movements, often acting in conjunction with other groups, have provided the political and intellectual matrix from which the leadership of reform and revolutionary movements has emerged. In the 1960s more young people were matriculating than ever before in history; in many countries (as was noted in chapter 3) young women were entering higher-education institutions in record numbers. Yet, as Elsa Chaney points out in her study of women in Chile and Peru, in the 1960s women were not visible in the leadership of student politics: "by and large, women miss out on this crucial start toward a political career."[79] Two factors were important. First, most women students were preparing for "feminine" careers such as teaching and nursing, and these "feminine" faculties were "isolated from student politics."[80] Second, when women were present in demonstrations, it was "to supply food to the males who would assume the leading roles, make the policy decisions, and occupy the buildings."[81]

Giovanna Merola points out that in Venezuela young women were part of both urban and rural guerrilla groups. But the record of their presence is obscure, partly by virtue of the clandestine nature of guerrilla activities but also because they were not seen as the heroes or leaders of the guerrilla bands. The same was true of women in the Mexican student movement. In Havana the heroines of the Cuban Revolution had been relegated to special sector positions: Vilma Espín to head the FMC; Haydée Santamaria to direct the cultural ministry, *Casa de las Americas*.[82] In the early 1960s the young woman who was to become the female symbol of the new generation of revolutionaries was in Havana, preparing to participate in what was perhaps the most quixotic rural guerrilla expedition of the era.

Haydée Tamara Bunke Bider, best known by her revolutionary pseudonym Tania, was born in Buenos Aires in 1937. Her parents fled to Argentina from Nazi Germany in 1935, where her mother's Russian-Jewish heritage and their political convictions—both were ardent anti-Fascists and committed to the Communist cause—put them in mortal jeopardy. In 1952, when Tania was fourteen, they moved to East Germany. Tania was well-educated and active in East German youth groups; her preuniversity school was named for Clara Zetkin, a pioneering Marxist revolutionary and feminist who founded the Woman's Socialist International in 1907.[83] By the time she was sixteen, her bilingualism in Spanish and German and her enthusiasm for politics led to work as an interpreter for international youth groups; in 1957 she traveled to Moscow for the VI Youth Festival. At Humboldt University in East Berlin she joined the International Student Union and befriended many students from Latin America;[84] when she turned twenty-one she was recruited by the East German Ministry of State Security as an agent.[85] In December 1960 she represented the Free German Youth Association at a reception celebrating the signing of new trade agreements between East Germany and Cuba. Ché Guevara headed the Cuban delegation, and Tania accompanied the delegation to Leipzig as interpreter. Shortly thereafter, Tania became the interpreter for the touring Cuban National Ballet and received an official invitation to Cuba.

She arrived in Cuba less than a month after the Bay of Pigs invasion. She found work at the Ministry of Education as a translator, joined the militia, and threw herself into the work of post-Revolutionary Cuba. Later biographers presented this period of her life in highly romantic imagery: "Late in 1961 Tania met Ché Guevara again. As a member of one of two volunteer brigades, she spent a day doing construction work on a school for the International Student Union in Havana. One brigade was made up of women; the other included the Minister of Industry himself, Ché Guevara. Almost immediately the brigades challenged each other to a contest to see which could work faster. Good-natured heckling followed, but when Ché's team began to win, he switched sides and the game ended in a tie. After the workday was over, Tania entertained her fellow workers on the guitar, teasing with a smile, 'I'll bet you can't beat me at this, *comandante*.'"[86]

In fact, Tania saw Ché often in her capacity as an interpreter for East German delegations meeting with Fidel Castro and Guevara and as a fellow Argentine and friend. In 1963–64 she withdrew from her interpreting activities to devote nearly full-time study to the skills she would need to undertake an unspecified mission in South America. She learned "to decipher codes, write invisible messages, use radio transmitters, and establish a new identity."[87] At the end of March 1964, Ché, whom she described as "la mayor emoción de mí vida,"[88] disclosed the project and what her role would be. She was to go to Bolivia and "establish relations inside the armed forces and the bourgeois government, travel to the interior of the country and study the forms and structures of the exploitation of the miner, the peasant and the Bolivian worker in order to know directly their hardships, and finally, to wait for a contact which would indicate the moment to join in the struggle for which she was making preparations."[89]

At the time of Tania's departure, first for East Germany to create an identity unconnected to Cuba, and then to Bolivia, Ché's position within Cuba was difficult. He disagreed with Castro over the question of the degree of reliance on Soviet aid, which he saw as selling out to another imperialist power; Castro saw the alliance with the USSR as vital. In 1965 Ché left Cuba for the Congo, "where it was his intention to remain for several years, helping the Congolese and other African peoples organize revolutionary struggles against colonialism and imperialism."[90] The question of Cuba's giving aid to guerrilla movements in other countries came to a head at the Tricontinental Congress held in Havana in 1966, where the Soviets called for a public policy of peaceful coexistence and sought to tone down Castro's commitment to revolutionary war.[91]

However, to Castro as well as to Ché Guevara, the time to inaugurate a guerrilla *foco* in South America seemed ripe. The United States was becoming ever more deeply involved in Viet Nam and the Johnson administration's decision to send U.S. marines into the Dominican Republic in 1965 had proved highly unpopular at home as well as abroad. Local guerrilla movements, workers' strikes, and land-recovery actions by peasants seemed to indicate a responsive atmosphere in many areas of Latin America. The plan was to establish a site in northwestern Bolivia "which would ultimately serve as a training ground and command post for a continent-wide war for the liberation of South America."[92] Ché departed for Bolivia in November 1966.

Tania, under the name Laura Gutierrez Bauer, had done her work well. Left mostly to her own devices in what was an exceedingly difficult assignment, she made friends in the highest circles of the Bolivian government and among the military, secured vital documents (including signed, blank letterheads from the Ministry of the Interior) and information, and, using her "cover" as an ethnologist, traveled extensively in the interior. An incidental result of her work and her interest in folkloric music and the intricate designs on the clothing of indigenous Bolivians was "the first exposition to display native Bolivian clothing in La Paz."[93] When the guerrilla leaders began to gather, she secured living quarters, food, and clothing for them. The men included army majors and highly placed officials from Cuba, the Peruvian guerrilla leader Juan Pablo Chango Navarro, and sympathetic Bolivians such as Moises Guevara, a Maoist strategist. A headquarters was established in the Santa Cruz area in the southeastern part of the country.

The euphoria created by Ché's arrival in December and the call to action after the long planning period dissipated quickly as the rigors of the Bolivian countryside took its toll. The first expedition, intended to be a training exercise, proved to be a grueling forced march during which two men were drowned crossing a river. At that time, Tania's assignment was to act as a courier between La Paz and the guerrilla encampment, bringing information and making contact with sympathizers. At the beginning of March she brought the French guerrilla strategist Regis Debray and Argentine Ciro Roberto Bustos to the camp, leaving her jeep in nearby Caimiri. Two weeks passed while they awaited the return of Ché and his men from the training exercise.

By the time Ché returned to camp on March 20, the carefully laid plans and layered security precautions were disintegrating. The camp itself was in disarray; two deserters from the guerrilla troop had talked to government authorities, revealing the aims, location, and strength of the guerrilla band; and Tania's jeep, which contained "Laura's" address book and other incriminating documents, had been discovered and searched by police. A biographer writes: "Had events not already caused serious damage to the guerrillas, she alone would have borne responsibility for the ensuing disasters."[94] Daniel James, in his preface to Ché's Bolivian diaries, states that Tania Bunke was a double agent from the time she "first set foot in Cuba until her death in Bolivia," with the specific mission of "keeping her eye on the unpredictable Castro people."[95] She was recruited by Guenther Maennel, an East German official who later testified that "I myself assigned Tamara Bunke as an agent against Guevara. Through her, East Berlin and Moscow were kept informed of Guevara's thoughts and decisions." Even if Tania's ultimate loyalty lay with Moscow rather than Havana, her chief task was passing information. It is not clear that she set out to sabotage the Cuban-inspired guerrilla force in Bolivia; as the Hendersons point out, she could have accomplished that without personal involvement. The history of her engagement in building the Cuban Revolution and her personal admiration for Ché Guevara make it possible that leaving the jeep in Caimiri was unplanned. The tragic saga of the guerrilla band is rife with similar lapses in judgment, among which were picture-taking sessions at the secret campsite and repeated attempts to recruit indifferent if not outrightly hostile peasants.[96] Additionally, the U.S. press made much of "fingering" Tania as a double agent working with the KGB; see for example, Benjamin Welles's article in the *New York Times*, July 15, 1968, "Blunders by Woman Spy for Soviet Trapped Ché Guevara." The peril in which the guerrilla force found itself was compounded by the March 23 ambush of a military platoon, in which seven Bolivian soldiers died and fourteen were taken prisoner, treated for wounds, and released. The location of the camp was exposed, and the next day military planes bombarded the region with napalm.

From that moment on, for the next seven months, the band was on the run. The odds were incredible: Ché's group numbered approximately forty-seven, including noncombatant visitors; over two thousand Bolivian troops were deployed in the "Red Zone," augmented by the CIA, the Green Berets (the U.S. Marine Corps's elite counterinsurgency unit), and arms, ammunition, transport vehicles, and counterrevolutionary experts from the United States. At no time did the guerrillas have much success in rousing local support for their activities; to the peasants, retaliation from the military seemed more certain than the promise of revolution. Perhaps more important, the band had almost no time to develop a local base of support.

Pombo, one of the survivors of the expedition, described Tania's role in camp: "The first thing she did was sew for the comrades and attend to a number of problems with buttons and things like that which women always do better than men. Moreover, she was a big help to me in the distribution and control of food." [97] She was also the principal analyst of radio news broadcasts both within Bolivia and from Argentina and Radio Havana. The only woman in the camp, she received special protection; according to the testimony of two deserters, Antonio, a Cuban who was in charge in Ché's absence, threatened that anyone who got close to her hammock would be shot.[98] At first, Antonio also resisted her request to be allowed to serve guard duty but relented in the face of her continued demand to do so and the needs of the camp. When Ché returned, Tania was made a member of the high command. Pombo observed, "I believe that the greatest moment for her must have been when Ché gave her the honor of being considered one more fighter—when he gave her an M-1 rifle."[99]

In his diary, Ché recorded that Tania's "presence in the group served to show that a woman could endure what those miserable guys who had given up couldn't. She never lost her spirit."[100] Wearing oversize men's military boots, which gave her constant problems during the endless marches, she held her own with the column until she became ill. Ché made a decision to split the group, taking the vanguard toward Muyupampa and leaving those slowed by illness and a few recent recruits under the command of four seasoned guerrillas to serve as a rear guard. As the military net tightened around them, the rear group struggled to survive: maintaining silence, cooking what little food they had only at night under crude shelters, and lying low during the day.[101] They were almost constantly under fire and in threat of ambush.

By the end of August the rear guard consisted of only nine survivors and had been completely cut off from Ché's group. They sent emissaries to the house of a peasant they had contacted earlier, Honorato Rojas. At the time, Ché noted in his diary: "This peasant is typical; capable of helping us but incapable of foreseeing the risk involved and, therefore, potentially dangerous."[102] Rojas agreed to give them food for the money they gave him and to guide them to a river ford, the Vado del Yeso, the next day. He led them straight into an ambush, which was prearranged with the Bolivian troops; Tania was the second to fall as the guerrilla band stepped out of the riverside shrubs into the water.

Tania was killed on August 31, 1967; her body was discovered downstream six days later. On September 7, Ché wrote in his diary: "Radio La Cruz del Sur announced finding the body of Tania the Guerrilla on the shores of the Rio Grande." And on September 8: "The radio gives news that Barrientos [the president of Bolivia] was present at the burial of the remains of Tania the Guerrilla, who was given a Catholic funeral, and that he then went to Puerto Mauricio, where Honorata Rojas lives."[103] One month later Ché's group was ambushed; the wounded Ché was executed on October 9 by a Bolivian army officer.

Why did the Bolivian government give Tania a public "Christian burial"? She was the only one of the fallen guerrillas so singled out; the others were buried in mass graves in the interior. Clearly, the government used the occasion to publicize this particular victory over the guerrilla forces. But it seems more complex than that; it seems as if the government wished to demonstrate, through their special consideration of this female guerrilla, its own claim to Christian virtue and reverence for womankind. Tania herself was no Christian, nor were her parents. The government definitely did not want to create a female martyr. By their apparent selflessness in providing a proper funeral, the church and state in Bolivia could depict her as a misguided daughter of

God and appropriate the occasion of her heroic death, depriving Tania, in death, of her potential as a martyr.

But if El Ché became the guerrilla of myth and legend, Tania was *la guerrillera*, the female guerrilla. Her image was inscribed by the words of Antonio Arguedas, a former minister of Bolivia who resigned after Ché's execution: "When Tania entered the water the soldiers in hiding got their first glimpse of the woman whose imperative voice was already familiar to them. This blond woman, thin from the privations of the struggle, was wearing camouflage battle trousers, soldiers' boots, a faded blouse with green and white stripes, a rucksack, and a submachine gun. The first shots from those in ambush were heard. Tania raised her hands to bring the weapon over her head into firing position. Vargas, a soldier, shot her in the lung, and Tania fell into the water, together with the Peruvian doctor, Negro." [104]

Thirteen years after her death, the power of her image remained undiminished: In the January 1980 issue of *fem*, Mexican author Elena Urrutia wrote: "The armed struggle could be considered the ultimate closed barrier to woman; nonetheless, woman has participated in it effectively and also heroically: and Tania the Guerrilla is a clear and close example." [105] Urrutia was reviewing a book by Cuban journalists María Rojas y Mirta Rodriguez Calderón, *Tania la Guerrillera*, published in 1978. In 1970 Rojas and Rodriguez Calderón had published a compilation of interviews, photographs, letters, and documents, many of which were provided by Tania's parents, titled *Tania la Guerrilla Inolvidable* (*Tania, the Unforgettable Guerrilla*), a title bestowed on her by Fidel Castro in commemoration of her life. If the Bolivian government hoped to bury Tania, these Cuban women were equally intent on enshrining her memory.

In July 1967, as Tania and Ché were locked in their desperate struggle in eastern Bolivia, Fidel Castro convened the first OLAS (Latin American Solidarity Organization) conference in Havana. Communist and non-Communist revolutionaries from every country in Latin America attended. The schisms that had surfaced at the Tricontinental Conference were even more in evidence. Castro remained firmly committed to the support of revolutionary struggle and held up Vietnam as an example of a small, poor nation successfully standing off the military force of the United States. The conference hall was hung with an enormous portrait of Simón Bolívar at one end and an equally large mural of Ché, whom Castro proclaimed the leader of the continent-wide guerrilla movement, at the other. Dozens of journalists from all over the world were invited; American reporter Lee Lockwood observed that "the conference was clearly intended as a propaganda send-off for a new 'international' of Latin American revolution. In unequivocal language it ratified Fidel Castro's thesis that the armed struggle is the only road to self-determination for the peoples of Latin America, and it officially condemned the USSR for its opposition to, and even subversion of, the guerrilla movements already existing in Latin America."[106] Part of the intransigence of Castro's position on the issue of armed revolution in Latin America in the face of its major benefactor's official disapproval must be understood as Cuba's perception that its own long-term survival as a nation depended on the appearance of other Socialist nations, friendly to Cuba, within the Western Hemisphere.[107]

There were several points of friction between the Cuban position and that of other Latin Americans. Most of the Latin American Communist parties had long since resigned themselves to vying for electoral support and legitimacy as a political party. This had indeed been the strategy of the Cuban Communist party prior to the revolution of 1959; it did not join forces with Castro until 1961. The Cuban thesis of armed struggle threatened the very legitimacy the Soviet-aligned Communist parties sought.[108] Another point of friction was the deep resentment felt by revolutionary nationalists toward Cuban attempts to establish a control center for revolution in Havana, one of the purposes of the OLAS conference. Revolutionary imperialism was no more welcome in Latin America than any other form of imperialism.

The bitter exchange that took place in the spring of 1967 between Castro and the Venezuelan Communist party (PCV) illustrates the situation. The Cuban government was providing both moral and material support for the guerrilla force headed by Douglas Bravo, a group that openly dissented from the PCV. The murder of Julio Iribarren Borges, brother of the Venezuelan foreign minister, in March 1967, brought matters to a head. In Havana a spokesman for the Venezuelan FALN (Armed Forces of National Liberation) took credit for the terrorist action. In Venezuela the PCV condemned the action and tried to disassociate itself from Cuba and the terrorist left. Castro responded by denouncing the PCV as pseudo-revolutionaries. The PCV shot back: "The PCV asserts its right to form its own policy without interference from anyone. Because Cuba has traveled a hard revolutionary road honorably, she is for us an example and an inspiration; but what we have never been, are not now, and shall never be are Cuba's agents in Venezuela, just as we are not agents of any other Communist party of the world. We are Venezuelan Communists."[109]

At the time of the exchange dozens of members of the PCV were prisoners in Venezuelan jails, and the PCV was operating as a clandestine organization. The response of counterrevolutionary forces to the threat of revolution was increasingly violent in many areas of the hemisphere. In Bolivia it was not only Ché's column that was under attack but any group suspected of association with revolutionary activities. Domitila testified to the situation at Siglo XX in 1967: "Suddenly we began to hear that there were guerrillas and that the government was going to take strong measures against them and anyone who supported them."[110] She asserted that at first the mining community thought that the presence of guerrillas was a rumor, or perhaps a pretext to continue carrying out "blood massacres and white massacres," a term by which they referred to the massive layoffs of mine workers that were depriving hundreds of men of the means to earn a living. Then they received a manifesto from the guerrillas that, in addition to outlining a political analysis of the situation, proclaimed the right of the workers to have an armed force to protect their rights against the armed force of the government.[111]

At Siglo XX the miners broadcast the manifesto and threatened to aid the guerrillas if the government did not pay the wages owed them. A meeting of the heads of the mining union was called for June 25, 1967, to discuss the manifesto further. Domitila described the ensuing events: "But the day before, at dawn on the 24th, which is the traditional feast of San Juan, when there are bonfires and we all have the custom of drinking with the neighbors, of singing and dancing, the army entered and killed a lot of people. And all of us who, according to them, had supported the guerrillas, were arrested, beaten, mistreated, and several were killed. For example, I lost my unborn child in prison because they kicked me in the stomach, saying that I was the liaison with the guerrillas. So, many of our comrades and even some of our children went with Ché, because many of us have lost our most beloved ones for the sake of Ché's guerrillas in Bolivia."[112]

At the time of the San Juan Massacre, Domitila and most of the miners had no idea that Ché Guevara himself was in Bolivia. Only when the photograph of his corpse was published in the papers did they know that he had been with the guerrillas. Violent repression was nothing new to the mining community, but the ferocity of the full-scale military attack on a sleeping community indicates the anger and frustration felt by the military as Ché and his band continued to elude them. It also indicates the seriousness with which the revolutionary threat was taken by the governments of the hemisphere.

The eradication of Ché and his column, together with the increasingly heated ideological splits among the left, marked a turning point in revolutionary strategy in Latin America. The rural *foco* outlined by Regis Debray in his *Revolution within the Revolution* and advocated by Fidel and Guevara had proved vulnerable to counterinsurgency forces. In Brazil, Carlos Marighela was developing the theory and practice of urban guerrilla warfare.[113] Marighela was a long-time member of the Communist party of Brazil (PCB), but in 1967 he attended the OLAS meeting in defiance of the wishes of the PCB. In 1968 he and Mario Alves established a pro-Cuban Communist party and launched Action for National Liberation (ALN), which carried out bank robberies in São Paulo and Rio de Janeiro, getting away with almost $2 million in a two-year period, and staged a number of armed raids. In pamphlets and letters distributed from secret posts, Marighela outlined his revolutionary strategy, which was the adaptation of the rural *foco* to urban conditions.[114]

Of their initial actions Marighela wrote: "Brazilian urban guerrilla warfare started from nothing, since we had no weapons, ammunition or money, and were obliged to take them by expropriations."[115] The robberies, kidnappings, and capture of arms, ammunition, and explosives evoked a wave of terrible repression on the part of the military government. Civil liberties were revoked in Institutional Act No. 5 on December 13, 1968; death squad activities increased with tacit acceptance by officials, and disappearances and the torture of political suspects were daily occurrences. Marighela stated: "For the first time the dictatorship has defined as revolutionary acts terrorism, bank raids, execution of foreign spies, attacks on barracks and the capture of arms and explosives. In their attempt to prevent revolutionary activity through violent laws, the enemy has become more cruel, using police terror."[116] Marighela believed that the government actions had provoked greater sympathy for the revolutionaries: "Students carried out memorable mass demonstrations. . . . The clergy—or rather priests and members of various grades in hierarchies of every religious organization—intellectuals and Brazilian women demonstrated against the military dictators and North American imperialists. The result is that the urban guerrilla movement and psychological warfare are proceeding successfully."[117] Marighela's central departure from the Cuban model of the rural *foco* was his belief that the urban revolution must precede the rural one.[118]

Women, present mainly as exceptional heroines or as *compañeras* in the rural movements, were omnipresent in the urban guerrilla movements of the late 1960s.[119] This was partly because of the linkages between student groups and the militant left; women now had a significant presence in the universities of Brazil, Uruguay, Argentina, Mexico, and Chile. The years 1967 and 1968, which were key years in the resurgence of feminist thought among young women students in Europe and the United States, were years of intense political engagement for their counterparts in Latin America. Giovanna Merola comments: "By the end of 1968, all existing women's groups in Venezuela had disappeared. During this period, Venezuelan women were strongly involved in political parties, and they defined women's issues only within the context of class struggle."[120]

Angela Neves-Xavier de Brito describes the political left in Brazil at the time as divided roughly into two groups: the nonmilitarist, which was more directed toward mass action and included the PCB, and the militarist, represented by the ALN and Marighela, among others. Of the participation of young women in these groups, she writes: "The organizations that were more directed toward mass action certainly had feminine sections intended to politicize the mass of women habitually kept apart from politics. The problems of women were explained by the class struggle. In the militarist groups an egalitarian relationship predominated, however. Thus, the woman is a combatant, an activist, and combatants, like angels, have no sex. Thus, women were included at the expense of their specificity, striving to imitate the behavior, attitude, and language of their masculine comrades whose positive identity seemed to them a model that was both ideal and unattainable."[121]

Despite the egalitarian rhetoric, men rose to leadership positions, and women were excluded from policy and decision making. De Brito observes: "Being unable to escape the ideologically charged reality of the society that these groups wanted to combat, but of which they were a part, most women activists were content to occupy a subordinate role and to participate in the secondary tasks assigned to them."[122]

It was among the Tupamaros of Uruguay that women apparently played the most truly egalitarian role. It was a role not accounted for by the sardonic comment attributed to a Tupamaro by a journalist in response to a query about the place of women in the movement: "First let me tell you, a woman is never more equal to a man than behind a .45 pistol."[123] The sense of egalitarianism more likely derived from the Tupamaros' resistance to hierarchy in any form and their philosophy of "no heads, no heroes, no names." The Tupamaro movement arose in the early 1960s but did not become widely known until 1967–1968.

Uruguay had a long history of progressive social reform and democratic electoral practice, but by the late 1950s economic stagnation threatened the nation's highly regarded social welfare system. Inflation, unemployment, trade imbalances, and a declining population led to increasing frustration among the Uruguayan people; the government responded to strikes and other demonstrations of protest with repression. In 1962 the Tupamaros formed among disaffected members of the Socialist party who believed that the ballot box could never lead to socialism. The appearance and rapid spread of an insurgent movement in Uruguay came as a surprise to Uruguayans and the rest of Latin America.[124]

The Tupamaros were unusual in a number of ways. Though committed to the use of violence, their early exploits were remarkable for the lack of bloodshed, and they enjoyed wide public support and a Robin Hood–like image. They used Marighela's tactics of urban guerrilla strategy: extreme secrecy safeguarded by each member knowing only a handful of others, expropriations of monies and weapons, and kidnappings but, unlike the Brazilian guerrillas, rarely resorting to bombings and assassinations. Although torture, beatings, and imprisonment of strikers and political dissidents were escalating rapidly, until 1968 the toll directly attributable to Tupamaro actions was three: two Tupamaros and one policeman.[125] One of their most widely publicized actions was "Operation Pando" in which simultaneous bank holdups were staged in the city of Pando on October 8, 1969; it was "offered in homage to that great American, Ché Guevara, assassinated two years ago today in Bolivia, as tangible proof that his fight was not in vain."[126]

Most of the women who participated as "soldiers," that is, in the actual bank robberies and kidnappings, were young. Thirteen who escaped through a prison chapel in 1968 were between the ages of twenty and twenty-three. The majority of male soldiers also were young, many in their late teens. But the lines of support in the larger population involved men and women of all ages and walks of life: "Nobody knows who is or is not a Tupamaro. Nobody can be sure whether a member of their family or staff is involved. The dreamy-eyed daughter, the studious, respectful smartly-dressed son, the dull clerk, the sensible housewife, the milk-boy, they all could be—and probably are—Tupamaros." One of the reasons for the early success of the Tupamaros was that their obvious middle-class background protected them from immediate police attention, "whereas trade-union leaders, student leaders and so on are usually earmarked as potential trouble-makers and swept up at the first excuse."[127] The ability of the urban guerrillas to melt into the general population was a crucial difference from the situation of rural guerrilla, where the members of the group were committed to a full-time armed status. Another factor is the fact that urban Uruguay lacks the racial demarcations of Brazil and the Andean countries. In contrast, the Tupamaros and similar urban groups were supposed to carry on with their daily lives; it was the most effective camouflage they possessed. And it undoubtedly contributed to the ability of women to participate more fully than was possible in the rural movements. Moreover, although the urban guerrilla movement employed military language ("soldiers," "operations," etc.), it did not involve uniforms or barracks-style living or other military activities so strongly identified with masculinity; women could belong as women, not as women who were like men.

In the aftermath of Operation Pando, 42 women and 106 men were captured and imprisoned. Many were tortured. Tupamaros on the outside kidnapped the British ambassador to Uruguay, Sir Geoffrey Jackson, and swore to hold him until the release of the imprisoned guerrillas. Eight months later the Tupamaros brought off a remarkable escape plan in which the women crept through the sewer system under the prison; the men escaped in similar fashion through a tunnel from the men's prison. The Tupamaros sent out an announcement that Geoffrey Jackson would be set free: "By our action in releasing Mr. Geoffrey Jackson we reaffirm our intention of avoiding useless suffering."[128] They also asserted that nearly a thousand Tupamaros were involved in the rescue, a significant number in a national population of 2.5 million.

The Tupamaros adopted as a rallying cry a slogan from Uruguayan history: "A nation is for everybody or it is for nobody."[129] They adopted the name

Tupamaro for the National Liberation Movement from a band of Uruguayan gauchos who fought against the Spanish during the Wars of Independence in the early nineteenth century; the gauchos, in turn, had taken it from the legendary Tupac Amarú, Incan hero of the Peruvian resistance against the Spanish in the eighteenth century. Uruguayans also knew that *tupumaro* was the Guaraní word for a large, ungainly, and extremely noisy bird; as one reporter observed, "Noisy birds are difficult to suppress and the Tupamaros could, like the geese who saved Rome, perform a useful service for their country." [130]

By 1970 the hope of the Tupamaros to avoid violence was moot. The government passed a decree abridging Uruguay's long-standing freedom of the press. The deteriorating situation was described in a Tupamaro communiqué: "To pretend that proper elections can be held under a system of political detentions, press censorship, systematic persecution of public militants, a total absence of individual rights, and repression and violence practiced on all and sundry with the blessing of authority, is simply to practice a monstrous fraud on the people." [131] The Tupamaros wrote in support of the *Frenté Amplio* (Broad Front), a coalition formed by Socialists, Communists, and Christian Democrats, which garnered enough votes to break the hegemony of the Colorados, long the majority party. Violence on the part of both the government forces and the revolutionaries continued to escalate, and on August 9, 1970, whatever remained of the Tupamaros' efforts to maintain a nonviolent image was effectively destroyed by the kidnapping and assassination of Dan Mitrion, who was in Uruguay as the chief U.S. advisor to the Uruguayan police.

Between 1971 and 1973 the full force of the Uruguayan military, which now contained units specially trained in counterterrorist tactics, was unleashed against the Tupamaros and all who were suspected of connections with antigovernment political activity. Tortures, beatings, and death squad murders and disappearances were daily events. The brutal repression seemed doubly stunning in the "Switzerland of the Americas," as Uruguay was romantically dubbed in earlier textbooks. By the end of 1973 the Tupamaros were effectively crushed.

In her sympathetic 1970 chronicle, *The Tupamaro Guerrillas*, María Esther Gilio quotes from a Tupamaro communiqué: "Now the Poor of America are really making their voice heard. History will no longer be able to ignore them as they are now the ones who are writing history." [132] The focus on the poor, prompted by the apparent failure of developmentalist schemes to alleviate or even slow the growth of poverty, was not confined to the revolutionaries. On August 24, 1968, Pope Paul VI convened the Second Latin American Episcopal Conference at Medellín, Colombia. In the years between Vatican II and Medellín, numerous preparatory meetings had been held all over Latin

America. By the time of the May 1968 meeting in Brazil a new, activist analysis was emerging that represented the growing commitment of many clergy to engaging the church "in the process of change in Latin America." It was also clear at the Brazil meeting that these members of the church had assimilated the socioeconomic analysis of most Latin American social scientists, which posited that underdevelopment in Latin America is the by-product of the capitalist development of the Western world. These two concepts were crucial in the formulation of what would become known as liberation theology, with its radical "preferential option for the poor." [133]

The clerics assembled at Medellín were responding to the violence perpetrated by both the revolutionary left and the counterrevolutionary forces: "The poor are oppressed by the institutionalized violence of internal and external colonial structures." [134] Both capitalist and Communist models of development were denounced: "The developmentalists and technocrats emphasize economic progress at the cost of the social well-being of the majority"; furthermore, "they urged popular participation in government and stressed the need for consciousness raising among the poor, who are the agents of change." [135] The Medellín Documents, which stated the conclusions of the conference, reverberated among the priests, nuns, and organizations working with the poor and grass-roots groups throughout Latin America. [136] The results of Medellín were enormously controversial. In assuming a voice of conscience, a commitment to the politics of change, and a defense of the poor, the church was in many cases pitting itself against national governments and undermining old church–state alliances. The hierarchy of the Brazilian and Chilean churches led the way in this effort; in many other countries the church hierarchy remained loyal to its traditional allegiances, and liberation theology was more influential among the pastoral clergy whose mission was among the people.

Medellín inspired many religious people to dedicate themselves to work among the poor, and it was here that women—nuns, laywomen, congregants—were most visible. Women were mentioned specifically only once in the Medellín Documents, as part of a multitude of groups seeking justice throughout the continent. [137] Sally Yudelman comments: "Although the bishops' call for liberation, radical as it was, did not envision a new role for women (the church has historically been conservative, even reactionary on all issues relating to gender roles and the family), it had an impact on them. Thousands of poor women participated in literacy and other types of consciousness-raising programs which led them to question the conditions in which they lived." [138]

In Chile, Medellín reinforced evangelical efforts among the urban and rural poor that were already underway. Many women religious left their original work, which was often in schools and hospitals that served the middle classes, to take part in the direct apostolate, the carrying of the Christian message into the world, among the marginal sectors of Chilean society.[139] The first efforts of those involved in the direct apostolate was to establish primary communities, *communidades de base*. The concept was to involve the laity in every aspect of the mission. In Chile hundreds of laypeople, men and women, were trained as catechists, a process that involved imparting literacy and learning about and questioning the world around them. In the words of Freire, "Each student must acquire an active role in creating his own awareness of the surrounding world. This process (*conscientizacion*) is intended to develop in each person a critical awareness of society as a human, and therefore changeable, product."[140]

Female members of religious orders were among the first Latin Americans to become conscious of the disadvantages created by their gender. Sister Katherine Anne Gilfeather writes: "The religious woman engaged in pastoral action in Chile knows her own capacity, her professional preparation, and the success she has enjoyed in exercising responsibility for the People of God. At the same time she is becoming more and more conscious of the lack of theological and psychological bases for those restrictions which have reduced her to a secondary position in the Church. This gap between ecclesiastical structures and changing cultural mores continues to produce enormous tensions among these women, particularly those most dedicated to pastoral action who are more vulnerable to the experience of two coexisting realities in constant warfare."[141]

The catechists also learned organizational skills, which they employed not only in extending the outreach of the evangelical effort but also turned to active use in attempts to resolve community problems from land use to food costs. Elvia Alvarado, a Honduran woman who began her activism through her involvement in the rural housewives' program established by Caritas, the social action arm of the Catholic church, puts her understanding of Catholic activism thus: "I don't think God says, 'Go to church and pray all day and everything will be fine.' No. For me God says, 'Go out and make the changes that need to be made, and I'll be there to help you.'"[142]

From the beginning, the rural housewives' clubs, known by their acronym CAC (*clubes de amas de casa*) were closely linked with the peasant movement for agrarian reform. In Honduras most of the nation's wealth lay in the hands of foreign companies—United Fruit, Standard Fruit, Rosario Mining Company—a situation that was reinforced with the establishment of the Central American Common Market in 1961. A massive strike by banana workers against United Fruit in 1954 resulted in agreements on the right to strike and collective bargaining. But it was land reform that the peasant leagues sought, a land reform that would, in fact, demand that any land, state or private, that lay idle or was poorly utilized be expropriated and turned over to landless people.[143] Catholic church workers had been involved in the organizational efforts of the peasant leagues since 1963.

The emphasis of the CAC, which adopted the slogan "The liberation of the people begins with the liberation of women" in the 1970s, was on the rights of women as citizens and their ability to become involved. The Caritas program was founded as an expression of the humanitarian philosophy of the post-Medellín church and its call to social action.[144] The CAC program trained local women, who then organized women's groups in the villages where they lived. The programs did not abandon the Catholic commitment to the family as the nucleus of society and the woman as the heart of the family, and they included traditional activities such as child-feeding programs, sewing, nutrition, and health care; but training also incorporated discussions of social and economic conditions and concepts of class and social justice.[145]

Laymen, laywomen, and church workers were involved in the organization of the Unión Naciónal de Campesinos (UNC) in 1970, a militant, nationwide union that organized petitions and carried out demonstrations, land occupations, and hunger marches to pressure the government agrarian reform agency to respond to their needs. The agrarian reform laws of 1962, 1972, and 1975, were passed primarily as a response to pressure from the peasant leagues and their urban allies.[146] It was this involvement in political actions that brought Catholic nuns and clergy as well as laypeople into direct confrontation with counterrevolutionary forces in state after state. In Honduras, by 1975, CAC claimed a membership of twenty-five thousand, with more than one thousand chapters, and UNC had a membership of approximately thirty-eight thousand. In May a nationwide attempt to occupy unused land on some 126 farms was repelled by force; and in June, UNC organized a hunger march from all over the country to the capital city: "One column had just reached Jutiagalpa, a small town in Olancho, when the army moved in to stop it. Aided by some local ranchers, the soldiers attacked while the marchers were meeting at a training center. Five peasants were shot to death. Nine others— students, priests and peasant leaders—disappeared. Their mutilated bodies were found a week later on a farm near Horcones."[147] The massacre of Horcones combined with internal political tensions brought the first period of CAC's organizational growth to an abrupt halt in 1975.[148]

In Brazil, following Vatican II, the church also made a strong commitment to agrarian reform and to alleviating the pressures of poverty in the devastated Northeast. For her book *Brazilian Women Speak*, Daphne Patai interviewed twenty women, one of whom was an older nun working in the Brazilian Northeast.[149] "Sister Denise" originally taught in a convent school; most of the nuns of her order were either in health work in hospitals and clinics or taught in church schools. She relates: "After Vatican II, many sisters, including me, began to ask questions: what answer can we give to those people who live marginalized lives, those people who are actually forgotten by society, who are humanity's leftovers? It's a call heard throughout Latin America. . . . So some of us decided to go outside of the comfortable school structure. A few sisters began to take the first step, to move to the outskirts of the city, the periphery, and to the rural areas." [150]

If the new commitment to social action on the part of many religious people had an important impact in poor communities, the experience of living in slums and poor rural towns was transformational for many of the nuns. Even those members of religious orders who are engaged in teaching and health work are usually insulated from the communities around them, their lives structured and largely sequestered within the convent unit: "Our whole world was there, inside the convent." [151] Sister Denise tells of the changes: "When we left to work among the people, we had to dismantle the structure we carried within us—our own culture, our language, our way of being, including our very clothing."

Gradually, the nuns realized that their tutelary approach to their mission also should be altered: "We still had that view—of teaching, dominating, of giving orders. And little by little we began to notice that it was the people who were teaching us to follow a new path in the life of the Church. I wasn't expecting that." [152] Twice a year Sister Denise and the three sisters she lived with met with others doing similar work. One of the results of these sessions was a rejection of traditional charity work: "When we were in the convent school, once in a while we'd leave the schools to do catechism, and we'd see the situation of the poor. We used to feel pity for them, we'd always take some food, some clothing, and then we'd feel calmer. . . . But with the call of the Church, of Vatican II, we saw that we couldn't go on that way, given the system in which we're living, a capitalist system that wants the poor always to continue being poor so the rich can get richer." [153]

The gradual change in the sisters' ways of living among the poor was for Sister Denise a return to her origins but with the profound distinction that she now perceived the value of her early life and questioned the worth of her work in the convent, which mainly served the upper and middle classes: "I was born into a poor family, too, in a tiny town, to a very large family, a patriarchal family. My father married four times; he had forty-three children. I'm the twentieth child. It was a very good experience for me to have all these families." During her years in the convent she had felt embarrassed at her background, but when she moved from the convent to the poor suburb, "I began to sense again the value of my life when I used to be at home." [154]

Sister Denise also spoke about the secondary position of women within the church hierarchy, but as she was being interviewed in 1983, she may have interjected some of the sensibilities of the new women's movement into her memories. "When I was young and knew I wanted to enter the convent—this was before the Vatican Council—I used to think, 'But why can't a woman be a priest?' But many things in this Church will have to change. Many. Starting with the priests. Why shouldn't the Church, in this day and age, let priests marry? The Church should leave people free." [155]

The base community with which she and her three colleagues worked celebrated its twelfth anniversary in 1982. New members were interested in learning about the origins of the community, so a play telling the history of the community was staged at the celebration. Sister Denise comments: "That's something we very much like to do, to stir the people's memory, because the people have been lost to history. But in the work we do, they remember their memories, they recapture their history." [156]

Under the leadership of the Centro Bellarmino, the Chilean church and lay community were, along with members of the Brazilian Roman Catholic church, among the first in Latin America to engage in direct pastoral activism among the poor. The growing concern of the church with the increasing alienation and marginalization of large sectors of the Chilean population was shared by Chilean political leaders. The need for reforms that directly addressed disparities of wealth and opportunity seemed acute; the peaceful succession of elected governments, which had earned Chile the reputation as one of the most democratic of Latin American nations, masked deep problems.

In 1964, Eduardo Frei was elected president of Chile on the Christian Democratic ticket. The campaign of 1964 was acrimonious, pitting the centrist Christian Democrats against the Marxist Frenté de Acción Popular (FRAP). FRAP sought to create a Socialist society in Chile; the Christian Democrats sought fundamental change but emphasized peaceful, legal methods—their slogan was "Revolution in Liberty." [157] During the campaign both Marxists and the Christian Democrats "promised agrarian reform, rural unionization, and enforcement of labor law in the countryside." [158] For thirty years Chile had prided itself on its political stability, a stability that rested on political and economic accommodations agreed on in 1932. Governmental support for effective agrarian reform threatened to undermine the power of the landholders and laid the ground for dismantling the old political coalition.

Frei was one of the leading Latin American proponents of the Alliance for Progress, and he actively sought to implement the reforms proposed in the Alliance in Chile. However, by the mid-1960s the government of the United States withdrew both concrete and moral support from the Alliance. In 1967, President Frei, in an article titled "The Alliance That Lost Its Way," expressed his disillusion with the promises of the Alliance. He saw that Washington was interested in it only as a propaganda weapon in inter-American relations, not as an instrument of multilaterally supported reform. Frei recognized that the proposed reforms, if carried out, were potentially revolutionary for the people: "The Latin American revolution has clearly defined objectives:

the participation of the people in the government and the destruction of the oligarchies; the redistribution of land and the ending of the feudal or semi-feudal regimes in the countryside; the security of equal access to cultural and educational facilities and wealth, thus putting an end to inherited privilege and artificial class divisions. Finally, a main objective of the revolution is to secure economic development. . . . These are precisely the same objectives as those of the Alliance."[159]

The Frei years (1964–1970) saw unprecedented organizational efforts in the countryside and poorer urban neighborhoods of Chile, not only by Catholic pastoral action groups and agencies affiliated with the Alliance for Progress but by Protestant groups, political parties, unions, and numerous revolutionary groups, including the radical *Movimiento Izquierda Revolucionario* (MIR), perhaps the best known of the armed revolutionary forces in Chile; its leadership was drawn from the students of the university in Concepción. The Christian Democratic administration gave strong support to both *campesino* and union organizational efforts; between 1965 and 1970 the number of people involved in *campesino* cooperatives increased thirtyfold, and union membership (industrial and plant unions, professional and craft unions, and agricultural unions) more than doubled.[160] Impressive gains were made in health and educational programs. But it was the expropriation and distribution of land that evoked the fiercest response from the Chilean elite.

By the elections of 1970 both right- and left-wing factions had deserted the Christian Democratic party. Three candidates led the electoral race: Christian Democrat Radomiro Tomic; Jorge Allesandri, an "independent" who appealed to the alienated conservative voters; and Salvador Allende, a long-time distinguished leader of the Socialist party who was the nominee of the *Unidad Popular* (UP), a leftist-Marxist coalition that promised "a transition to socialism." Salvador Allende emerged with a slim plurality. Historian Brian Lovejoy writes of the unfolding events: "Proclaiming that with him the people [*el pueblo*] of Chile entered into the presidential palace, Salvador Allende received the presidential sash on November 3, 1970. Less than three years later Allende's body would be carried from La Moneda, testimony to his unsuccessful struggle to take Chile down the peaceful road to socialism."[161]

Salvador Allende's plans to create a more equitable social, political, and economic system in a short time were set forth in an unpropitious climate of increasing violence and factionalism within Chile and were faced with the implacable opposition of the Nixon administration in Washington, which used every means at its disposal, both covert and diplomatic, to undermine "the first elected Marxist government in the hemisphere." Women of the popular classes and women of the upper and middle classes became emblematic of the political polarization that ensued.

In Chile in the 1960s and early 1970s, women's formal political participation was generally through the women's sector of a particular party. A male reporter for *El Mercurio*, a conservative newspaper, summed up the situation thus: "The woman constitutes a political world apart from the male. . . . When the woman speaks in the marginal settlements around the cities or in the countryside, she does so in language of the heart. In Parliament they fulfill their role in another style [than the men]. Whether they are Radical, Christian Democrat, Communist or Socialist, they are the untiring 'ants,' valiant and tender. The men will be preoccupied with problems as abstract as constitutional reform. The women are fighting for kindergardens, for drinking water in the *poblaciones*, for day care centers."[162]

Elsa Chaney's pioneering study of women's political participation in Chile and Peru, carried out during the late 1960s and early 1970s corroborates the observation: "This does not mean that women lack all influence. Rather, certain boundaries have been established designating women's legitimate professional and political activity. They are confined in professions and public office to tasks analogous to those they perform in the home."[163] Chaney employed the term *supermadre* (supermother) to describe her observation that female political activity tended to be extensions of the female role in the home.

During the early 1970s political refugees from elsewhere in Latin America came into Chile, attracted by the open political climate and the opportunity to work to build a Socialist country. Many Brazilian activists were among the political refugees; the late 1960s and early 1970s were a time of harsh repression at home. A Brazilian woman's description of her experience testifies to the sharp division of political roles by gender that characterized Chilean politics regardless of ideology: "Suddenly, we arrive in Chile, and we are displaced, unlike the men. They quickly reestablished themselves because they came with reputations as revolutionaries with a political entrée. The fact that they were coming into another 'macho' culture made it all the easier for them to make contacts. As a result, we stayed in their shadow."[164] She comments that the Chilean left, "even during the period of intense struggles under Allende did not 'break free from the traditional conception of the Latin American Left on the problems of women.'"[165] Chaney concurs: "In spite of widespread anticipation that women would play an important role in his government, Allende waited two years to appoint a woman to cabinet rank, and she lasted only a few months. . . . the effort appears to this observer as an attempt to create some high status but marginal posts for women so that an important ministerial portfolio need not be wasted on them."[166]

The expectation that the Allende government's "peaceful path to socialism" should be revolutionary for women sprang in part from the Socialist tenet that all people, regardless of their sex, would benefit alike under the new regime. It also derived from Allende's understanding that to realize the goals of the revolution women must be involved at all levels of responsibility.[167] In the years in which he had run for office Allende had not fared as well among women voters as he had among males, a phenomenon accounted for by the "well-documented conservative tendencies" among women in each social class.[168]

There were, however, nuances of difference in the effect for women of the reforms instituted under the Frei and Allende administrations. An example may be taken from the agrarian programs of the successive regimes. The reforms instituted under the Frei regime had in practice, if not intent, discriminated against women by limiting benefits to heads of household and permanent workers, both of which categories were seen as male. Women were not defined as "heads of households," though in fact they often were, and their seasonal work was deemed "temporary."[169] Under Allende the program was extended to include temporary workers, and adult men and women alike could become members of the collective farms being established by the government. The effect of the UP's agrarian reforms was to create a new avenue of economic opportunity for poor rural women, but in the exceedingly brief time the cooperative experiments were in place, attitudes toward female participation in decision making remained unaltered. The strongly gendered political ethos that marked Chilean politics elsewhere prevailed in the collectives: "The role of women was seen as working in activities complementary to, rather than competitive with, men's and heavy ideological pressure was exerted on women to stick to their traditional roles."[170] A survey carried out by the University of Wisconsin in 1970–1973 showed that "ninety-three percent of women in reformed farms reported that women were excluded from decision-making in all areas."[171]

Allende did succeed in winning increased support among urban women of the popular classes, which proved critical in the plebiscite of 1971; Chaney states that it was the women's vote that pushed the UP program over the top in that election. During the late 1960s numerous *centros de madres*, or mothers' centers, formed with the support of various religious and political groups, including the Christian Democrats and Catholic activists. Many of these centers became highly politicized in the climate of the early 1970s. The radical Catholic leadership in Santiago organized "Christians for Socialism," which called for members of base communities "to make an active commitment to the transition to socialism and to parties of the left."[172] Women of the *barrios* regularly turned out for demonstrations and rallied in support of the Socialist program of the UP. Socialist and Communist women were also actively encouraging organization among women of the poorer sectors and were engaged in planning a world congress of women representing the Socialist countries. Brazilian exile Angela Neves-Xavier de Brito writes that even this activity (the mass organization of working-class women in the *centros de madres*) failed to awaken the Chilean left to the political importance of women: "It was said that the Centros de Madres were only a structure inherited from preceding governments, 'paternalistic and authoritarian, inspired by traditional values,' and consequently, there was fear of 'not being able to control them.'"[173]

This concern with "not being able to control" women once they are roused is a refrain that echoes over time and across cultures and the political spectrum, but it was particularly telling in contemporary Chile. In 1971 middle-class women in Santiago turned out in a resounding demonstration, "the march of the empty pots and pans," ostensibly to protest the food shortages brought on by the deteriorating economic situation. Similar demonstrations continued throughout 1972 and received widespread publicity: In the North American press the message was that the Marxist Allende government could not feed its people. The women involved in these demonstrations lived in the well-to-do districts of Providencia and Los Condes of Santiago; they felt threatened by the very idea of a Socialist government. Allende repeatedly attempted to allay these apprehensions by stating that his revolution was peaceful and involved "moral achievement, generosity, a spirit of sacrifice and dedication to achieve a new life for all Chileans within the framework of the nation's free institutions."[174]

To what degree these early demonstrations by upper- and middle-class women were spontaneous is open to speculation. We have looked at the ways in which women may organize when their ability to fulfill their traditional, valued function as nurturers is countervened;[175] and there are countless examples of women organizing around bread-and-butter issues. But these women were not poor, and even if their early demonstrations were born out of frustration at not being able to feed their families in the manner to which they were accustomed, by late 1972 there were clear parallels to the situation as it had developed in Brazil in 1964.

Michele Mattelart opens her article "Chile: The Feminine Version of the Coup d'Etat" with a quote from a Brazilian engineer: "Once we saw the Chilean women were marching, we knew that Allende's days were numbered."[176] The man, speaking to a reporter for the *Washington Post* in 1974, claimed that members of Brazilian right-wing anti-Marxist organizations lent support to efforts to overthrow the Chilean government in two ways: planning antigovernment demonstrations by women and establishing an institute, the Center for Public Opinion Studies, similar to the Brazilian Institute of Research and Social Studies.

The ideological struggle, viewed through the prism of women's political activities, reveals a great deal about the bitter political situation that was building to crisis proportions in Chile in 1972–1973. First, although the UP coalition has been criticized for not addressing women's issues or for paying only lip-service to them, in fact the analytic perspective of Allende and his government predisposed them to seeing issues in terms of class, and class interests were presumed to be the same for both sexes. Additionally, in 1972 most Chilean men and women, whatever their ideological position, accepted traditional ideas about women's role. This included the president, who often spoke of women in mother images: "When I say 'woman,' I always think of the woman-mother. . . . When I talk of this woman, I refer to her in her function in the nuclear family. . . . the child is the prolongation of the woman who in essence is born to be a mother."[177]

But it is necessary to distinguish between the acceptance, by the political left, of traditional ideas about women's role in society and the promotion, by the political right, of an idealized generic notion of womanhood as part of its campaign to mobilize women on a cross-class basis. The conservative response to the reformist agenda of the UP and President Allende's promise of "a peaceful path to socialism" was vociferous, and the ardor of the "Christians for Socialism" was more than met by the passion of the right-wing Catholic movement "Tradition, Family and Property" (TFP).[178] Viewing women as inherently conservative was central to the tactics of TFP; women were to be mobilized on the basis of their connection to preserving life, to nurturing, to sustaining the family. This presentation of women has the effect of removing the individual woman from her historical life circumstances, of taking away the specificity of her experiences, decisions, actions.

Both the military and the TFP rejected the post-Medellín commitment of the church to the poor, viewing organizing efforts by and among the poor, legal aid, and support of strikes and demonstrations as subversive, perversions of the religion they were raised to honor and defend.[179] Priests who participated in these activities were denounced as Communists and lost the protection their clerical status once provided them; similarly, women activists on the left were viewed as "unnatural," creatures who forfeited the reverence supposedly accorded womanhood.

By March 1972 the women's antigovernment demonstrations had developed a distinct pattern. Once or twice a month, usually in the evening hours, women gathered in the residential neighborhoods of Chilean towns and cities carrying cookpots, which they beat with lids or ladles. Most of the participants were women of the bourgeoisie, though women from the working classes and poorer *barrios* marched as well.[180] In 1972, *Poder Femenino* (Feminine Power) was established as the women's branch of the extreme right-wing organization Fatherland and Liberty. Their declared mission was to "save our homes from Communism."[181] Demonstrations organized by Poder Femenino were often escorted by helmeted paramilitary units armed with chains.[182]

Women of *Poder Femenino* actively sought the intervention of the military to "restore order." They spread vicious rumors about Allende's personal habits and sought to manipulate other women by rousing apprehensions that the UP government could not provide food or protection from social chaos. Above all, as the Brazilian women marchers had done earlier, the Chilean women marchers lent legitimacy to the idea of a military coup d'etat "to save the country" from chaos/communism. Mattelart describes one of the activities the anti-UP female demonstrators used in attempting to provoke the military to intervene: "Many times women went to the Military Academy to throw grain at the Chilean soldiers, thereby treating them like hens, chiding them for weakness and lack of virility."[183]

Extreme political polarization marked Chile by 1973. Militant groups to the left of the UP government carried out land expropriations and political actions without regard to the government reform program. Right-wing paramilitary groups countered with escalating violence. The Chilean economy was severely crippled by the domestic situation and the successful destabilization campaign orchestrated in the international financial community by U.S. secretary of state Henry Kissinger. The last major women's antigovernment demonstration was carried out on September 5, 1973. Flyers "summoned all Chilean women to an affair of honor!" They also declared: "Mr. Allende does not deserve to be President of the Republic. Mr. Allende has led the country into a catastrophe. We don't have bread for our children! We don't have medicine for those who are sick! We don't have clothes to wear! We don't have a roof to put over our heads!"[184]

Six days later, on September 11, 1973, the UP government was overthrown in a bloody coup d'etat led by the Chilean military. In the brutal battle that ensued President Salvador Allende lost his life. The euphoria with which those who had opposed the government greeted the military intervention— and especially the release of foods and dry goods that had been hoarded by antigovernment forces to heighten tensions—evaporated as the most ruthless regime in Chilean history moved to establish itself in power. In the immediate aftermath of the coup more than five thousand Chileans were "disappeared." Many were later discovered to have been tortured and then murdered, buried in mass graves. Bodies floated down the Mapuche River; death squads operated freely against anyone accused or suspected of or associated with political organization among the poor or labeled with broadly defined "left" tendencies. Thousands sought political asylum abroad. Congress was closed; civil liberties and freedom of the press were suspended indefinitely.

The philosophical underpinnings of the new regime, led by General Augusto Pinochet Ugarte, were adopted directly from the TFP, whose primary tenet is the sanctity of private property; in this construct, women and children are considered the property of the male head of household.[185] The generic "woman" was now the "Valiant Chilean Woman," defending her home and children against Marxism. A National Secretariat of Women was established, which promoted the ideal of the "natural" woman as homemaker and mother.[186]

In both the domestic and the international press the role of women in the coup d'etat received great play. *Los Angeles Times* columnist David Belnap proclaimed, "The hand that rocks the cradle rocked the ship of state of Chile's late Marxist President Salvador Allende until it overturned and sank."[187] To what extent did women act on their own behalf in Chile between 1970 and 1973? To what extent were women "used," pushed to the front of demonstrations organized by both the left and the right? Certainly, women of the poorer *barrios* turned out in pro-UP demonstrations with their men, and there is evidence that Allende was successful in increasing his support among poor and working-class women during the early part of his administration.[188] Women also were active in MIR and other militant left-wing revolutionary groups that stood to the left of the administration. Working- and middle-class housewives were truly squeezed by inflation, food shortages, and the breakdown of the economy, most dramatically pointed up by the truckers' strikes that paralyzed the country in 1972 and 1973, and they had cause to fear the disruption of their way of life. That they were responsive to the call of the *Poder Femenino* does not necessarily mean that they were "dupes" of the right any more than the women of the poor *barrios* who marched in solidarity with their men were dupes of the Communists.

The female leadership of *Poder Femenino* had no doubt that they were acting to protect their class interests. They were members of Chilean families who had long exercised economic and political power in the nation; in the aftermath of the coup many donated jewelry and money to fund the national reconstruction program of the military junta. *Poder Femenino* played a crucial role in the coup. Many of its members were the wives of military officers and could call for military intervention while their spouses kept apparent faith with their pledge to uphold the constitutional role of the military. And yet there is evidence that the women of *Poder Femenino* too were used as a front by the TFP and Liberty and Fatherhood to openly defy the government, when it might have been dangerous—and certainly would have been treasonous— for their male counterparts who held official positions to do so.

In addition, later investigations revealed international involvement across the political spectrum. TFP, the Center for Public Opinion Studies, and the truck strikers all received funding and support from the Central Intelligence Agency of the United States. MIR and other revolutionary organizations received arms, monies, and strategic support from outside the country. Perhaps the point is not that Chilean women—and men—were manipulated but that in the precarious political climate of the early 1970s Chileans sought whatever support they could to further what they saw as their own political interests. Salvador Allende's commitment to running an open government allowed opposition forces to function freely. Few Chileans foresaw or could have imagined the bloodshed and repression that was unleashed against the Chilean citizenry in the days, months, and years following the coup d'etat, a repression that proved not to be an aberration but a fundamental part of the national reconstruction plan.

Elsewhere in the hemisphere the first stirrings of the new women's movement were being felt, but there is scant evidence of this in the Chilean instance. Women of the political left eschewed feminism as bourgeois, and feminism and feminists were anathema to TFP; the essence of *Poder Femenino* was the defense of an idealized woman-mother. In no case did women's political activity within their political groupings translate into political leadership by women.

In 1972 some of the Brazilian women who had accompanied their men into political exile in Chile formed the *Comité de Mulheres Brasileiras no Exterior* (Committee of Brazilian Women Abroad). De Brito comments wryly on these first attempts at consciousness raising, noting that the women political activists considered themselves "liberated" and the majority of women, who lived at home and were the wives and mothers of male activists, unenlightened. Thus, the women's groups replicated the hierarchical structure of male-dominated political organizations. Furthermore, she points out that specific problems such as discrimination in work, divorce, and abortion, were often used as lures to get women involved on behalf of a particular party.[189] In retrospect, she concludes, "Our relationship with the other women was shabby."[190] The Brazilian women of de Brito's circle did not seriously confront the ideas of the new women's movement until after the coup d'etat. Foreign-born political exiles were among the primary targets of the military junta, and many of those who were not caught up in the initial political detentions and disappearances fled to a "second exile." It was in that second exile— in France for the women who formed the Comité de Mulheres Brasileiras no Exterior—that these women activists first came into contact with the ideas of the emergent women's movement.

In Latin America, as in the United States and Europe, it was the experience of the woman activist from which the new women's movement took its social conscience and forced open the narrow politics of women's rights. In the 1970s the tension between the women who emerged from the New Left and those who saw equal rights as the desirable goal created a transformational feminist dialectic, which will be explored in chapter 7.

7. National Liberation, Redemocratization, and International Feminism, 1974-1990

For me, a woman who becomes politically conscious of being a woman is a feminist. What feminism does is to develop our consciousness of oppression and exploitation into a collective phenomenon, capable of transforming reality, and therefore revolutionary.[1]

The speaker is a Chilean woman, a former leader of MIR (Movimiento de Izquierda Revolucionario) now living in exile, in attendance at the *IV Encuentro Feminino Latinoamericano y del Caribe* held in Taxco, Mexico, October 1987. Until recently, most women as well as men of the political left subscribed to the prevailing ideology that class was overwhelmingly the most important tool of analysis, and they expressed scorn for those who sought equal rights or equal roles within the revolution itself. In the 1970s and 1980s with the advent of the new woman's movement and the international attention to and support for women's issues during the United Nations Decade for Women (1976–1985), a potentially transformational gendered critique of social, political, and economic programs that spans the political spectrum emerged. Initially perceived as emanating primarily from Europe and North America and therefore foreign to Latin American reality, the new feminism in Latin America has become a primary vehicle for social criticism. It is visible in liberation movements in Nicaragua, El Salvador, Guatemala, and Peru and in the redemocratization efforts in Brazil, Argentina, Paraguay, and Uruguay.

In examining the history of feminism in Latin America we have seen that women have been most successful in putting forth their programs during periods of general political reform and change: in Uruguay during the Batlle reforms, in Cuba during the Machadato (1929–1934), in Brazil at the fall of the Old Republic in 1932, in Guatemala and Venezuela in the mid-1940s. However, women living in countries that experienced profound social revolution, such as Mexico (1910), Bolivia (1952), and Cuba (1959), found that the insistence on articulating programs solely in terms of class or "the people" served to perpetuate traditional patterns of male leadership. The *foco*[2] style of organization adopted by many Latin American revolutionary groups in the years after the Cuban Revolution further encouraged traditions of male elitism and hierarchy within Latin American revolutionary movements, with women, even women who fought side by side with men during the revolution, relegated to subordinate positions.

Perhaps the most important legacy of the UN Decade for Women is that political parties and governments seeking legitimacy and claiming the right to speak for all of the people have found it politically advantageous to address women's issues. The Cuban case provides an interesting example. In the early 1970s, Cuba and its charismatic head of state Fidel Castro were seen by thousands of Latin Americans and many North Americans as politically exemplary: Socialist in ideology, vehemently anti-Yankee, supportive of proclaimed national liberation movements from Vietnam to Angola to El Salvador. The Cuban government paid special attention to women from the start, with the establishment of the FMC (Federación de Mujeres Cubanas, or Federation of Cuban Women) in 1960 with a mandate to integrate women into the political and economic life of the country. Both the mandate and the structure of the FMC recall the efforts of the Mexican and Bolivian governments to incorporate women into their programs.

More important, the Cuban Communist party, "like its counterparts elsewhere in Latin America, strongly advocated organizing among women."[3] In 1959 existing women's associations in Cuba were augmented by new women's groups formed to support various proposals of the revolutionary government. "In an effort to bring the voice of our women—revolutionary women—to our sisters throughout the continent" Cuba sent a delegation of seventy-six women to the First Congress of Latin American Women, held in Chile in November 1959.[4] The congress was sponsored by the Moscow-based International Democratic Federation of Women (WIDF). On their return to Cuba the women set up an umbrella organization called the Congress of Cuban Women for the Liberation of Latin America. In August 1960 this group was renamed the FMC by Fidel Castro and became "the single, all-encompassing women's organization in Cuba."[5]

Vilma Espín, who has led the FMC since its inception, is the wife of Raúl Castro. Espín graduated from MIT with a degree in chemical engineering in 1956 and joined the revolutionary movement after meeting with Fidel Castro in Mexico that same year. She participated in the underground movement and fought with the guerrilla forces. In an interview in 1972, Espín discussed the position of women in Cuba and the liberation of women:[6] "In my opinion, the liberation of women in Cuba cannot be separated from the liberation of society in general. There can be no liberation for a social group constituting half of humankind, as long as exploitation of man by man continues, as long as the means of production are owned by an exploiting minority." Espín's words reflect the traditional attitude of the political left in Latin America toward women, as do her comments on feminism: "Unfortunately many feminist groups take away forces that could strengthen the genuinely revolutionary movement."[7]

In the areas of the education and incorporation of women into the work force, the achievements of the FMC during the first ten years of the revolution were substantial. The literacy campaign, one of the first projects to which the FMC put its energies, ultimately reached more than 700,000 Cubans.[8] By the mid-1970s approximately 70 percent of Cuban women belonged to the FMC, and its activities were closely watched by women elsewhere. The Cuban women hosted several international congresses of women.

As the new international women's movement gained strength, a gendered critique was also emerging within Cuba. Women were working in greater numbers than ever before; options for women, especially for rural women, had increased; educational opportunities for all Cubans were greatly improved. But in 1974 women comprised only 13 percent of the membership of the Communist party, which is the policymaking body of the Cuban government. And women's employment continued to be concentrated in teaching and health care, retail trade, and secretarial work. Most of all, working women continued to bear women's traditional familial role as mother, wife, homemaker; to work "the double day." In short, the problems women in Cuba faced were much the same as those faced by women elsewhere. What was special in the Cuban situation was that (1) there was an expectation that the state was morally responsible for creating social justice for all, including women, and (2) there already existed a national women's association, the FMC, that could act as a forum for the discussion of women's issues and could respond to the concerns of Cuban women.

At the second National Congress of Cuban Women, held from November 25 to 29, 1974, resolutions prepared prior to the congress included demands for more child-care centers and six-day-a-week boarding schools, as well as the acknowledgement that housework is not women's work but family work and that children should be raised in a consciously nonsexist way.[9] The resolutions reflect the strain women felt in trying to carry out the demands made on them in the work place and at home. On the last night of the congress, Fidel Castro gave the closing address, in which he stated that "the work of the Revolution is not complete—there must be real equality for women." As one observer noted, "While there is much work still to be done in the area of people's consciousness and sexual attitudes, the liberation of women now has the prestige of the Revolution solidly behind it—an important factor in today's Cuba."[10]

With the exception of the concept that children should be raised in a nonsexist manner, there was little in the content of the formal resolutions that deviated from the FMC's historical role as the government branch that organized and mobilized women on behalf of the state. But the debates prior to, during, and following the congress were broader. In 1974 a proposal for an extensive revision of the Family Code was put forth. Based on the ideal of complete equality between women and men in marriage, divorce, and the family, it stated that both partners have the same obligations and duties concerning the protection, upbringing, support, and education of their children.[11] The most discussed clause in the new code proposed that men share responsibility for domestic tasks.[12] In 1975 the First Congress of the Communist Party of Cuba (PCC) adopted a platform on "the full exercise of women's equality."[13] The Family Code, including the provision that men whose wives work do half of the housework and child care, was enacted the same year.[14]

The revision of the Cuban Family Code, the campaign to degender work roles within the home and in the marketplace, and the open discussion of women's lack of representation within the PCC may be seen as marking a turning point in Cuban postrevolutionary history. The women were putting forth, however tentatively, a critique of the Cuban system, in which politics continued to be dominated by men and male–female relationships remained traditional. Although the issues raised at the second congress were squarely in line with the issues being brought to the fore by the new international women's movement and although blame for the lack of adequate child care facilities and boarding schools fell not on the Cuban regime but on the economic duress imposed on all Cubans by international capitalism, nevertheless, what the women were saying was a criticism of the status quo within Cuba. It is difficult to think of any other constituency within Cuba since the Revolution that has mounted a campaign to change attitudes, gain more political representation, and improve its position. Moreover, the issues raised at the second congress received serious attention from the government and national press as well as coverage in the international press.[15] Fidel Castro and the 1975 PCC congress, by acknowledging the justice of women's concern, could proclaim their openness to constructive criticism: "We live in a socialist country, we made our revolution sixteen years ago, but can we really say that Cuban women have in practice gained equal rights with men and that they are fully integrated into Cuban society?"[16]

Another important point about the 1974 Cuban women's congress and the discussion and passage of the Family Code in 1974–1975 is that the Cuban government was consciously placing itself in the vanguard of the new women's movement with respect to women of the Communist bloc and nonaligned nations. American writer Margaret Randall, who attended the second congress, wrote of "the deep internationalism felt by Cuban women. Sixteen years have taught them that they are part of a world community, fighting for final liberation from colonialism, neocolonialism, imperialism, resisting and fighting imperialism. . . . Cuban women have studied the situation in Vietnam, in Chile, in the African countries."[17] Delegates invited to the second

congress of Cuban women included Ha Thi Que, president of the Vietnam Workers party, and Bui Thi Me, vice-minister of public health of the
Provisional Revolutionary Government of South Vietnam; Luisa González,
founding member of the Communist party in Costa Rica; Ana María Cabral,
who saluted the Cubans who struggled alongside her people in Guinea-
Bissau; Khmer women from Cambodia; Soviet astronaut Valentina Teresh-
kova; North American Angela Davis; and Fatima Bettahar from the Union
of African Women, who shared her joy at being in this "first free territory in
America." [18]

The international character of the Cuban congress echoed the internationalism of the new woman's movement, which has its roots in Western
political traditions of democracy, and one of the purposes of the Cuban
women's congress was to establish a revolutionary countervoice to that tradition. In 1972 the UN General Assembly proclaimed that 1975 would be
International Women's Year (IWY) with a world conference to be held in
Mexico City June 19 to July 2, 1975. Latin American women have had a long
history of transnational interaction: the Latin American scientific congresses
of the 1890s; the Primero Congreso Femenino in Buenos Aires in 1910; the
numerous conferences held in Lima, Mexico City, São Paulo, Santiago, and
Caracas in the 1920s and 1930s; the founding of the United Nations; and the
postwar participation in the Primero Congreso Interamericano de Mujeres
in Guatemala in 1947; and the reformation of the Interamerican Commission
of Women (CIM). They were well represented on the United Nations Commission of the Status of Women, which began formulating the plans for the
IWY in 1965.

Throughout the planning period for the United Nations Decade for
Women, CIM played an important role, both in drawing up position papers
and as a model for regional organizations of women elsewhere in the world.[19]
The issues that dominated the opening discussions at the IWY conference in
Mexico City are outlined in CIM reports presented to the Twenty-First and
Twenty-Second Sessions of the United Nations Commission on the Status
of Women in 1968 and 1969, respectively. CIM was a specialized organization of the Organization of American States, housed in Washington, D.C.,
and largely financed by North American monies. Its representatives were
government-appointed. Thus, it might be expected that it would be thor-
oughly establishment in its political perspective, and CIM was supportive of
reformist rather than revolutionary strategies. But in this period CIM was
working closely with the International Labor Organization (ILO), and this
fact, combined with CIM's special focus on women, meant that the commission was primarily concerned with issues and problems confronting women
and work in the hemisphere: poor women, migrant women, rural women—
women disadvantaged not only by the class to which they had been born

but by their ethnicity and geographical locus and who, relative to their male counterparts, had less access to resources and fewer possibilities of social or economic mobility. As this information accumulated, the reports of CIM became increasingly critical of the political systems and national and international economic order that perpetuated the conditions under which the majority of women in the hemisphere lived out their lives. By the early 1970s, CIM meetings were often the site of bitter political debates that presaged the "first world–third world" dichotomy of the IWY Mexican conference.[20]

If the politics of women's issues provided an acceptable avenue for self-criticism within the Cuban context, especially with the wider aim of bolstering Cuba's claim to the leadership of nonaligned nations, in other areas of Latin America the international women's movement provided a certain degree of *sombra* (shade, or protection from political repression). One of the most striking instances of the legitimization of political activity by women during the IWY may be seen in Brazil.

In 1974 the administration of Brazilian president Ernesto Geisel took the first steps toward *abertura*. Literally meaning "opening," the term *abertura* signifies the highly tentative reopening of politics to the civilian sector. Under strong international and domestic pressure to move away from the legacy of state violence against the populace, and anxious to restore international legitimacy to the Brazilian government and to the Brazilian military, the Geisel regime apparently viewed the woman's movement as a relatively safe way to express their newfound commitment to a more open society. Thus, in 1975 the government permitted women to stage public demonstrations in Rio de Janeiro, São Paulo, and Belo Horizante in honor of the IWY. The women's marches proved to be the largest public demonstrations since the hard-line military crackdown of 1968. In her study *The Politics of Gender in Latin America: Comparative Perspectives on Women in the Brazilian Transition to Democracy*, Sônia Alvarez describes the situation thus: "Even when women were organizing campaigns against the rising cost of living or for human rights in Brazil, the military allowed women's associations greater political leeway than was granted to many other social movement groups. The Feminine Amnesty Movement, which called for the release of political prisoners, was allowed to organize in the mid-seventies when a 'mixed' movement of that sort might have been actively repressed."[21]

The endorsement by the Brazilian government of the goals of the United Nations Decade for Women—equality, development, and peace—opened the door for further organizing by Brazilian women. Groups that had previously organized around "feminine" issues, such as child care and maternal health, and neighborhood associations in which women came together to work for better housing, clean water, and lower food prices gradually began to insert the discussion of their specific disadvantages as women into their meetings.

A more explicitly feminist position was taken by some middle-class women, usually professionals such as teachers and academics, who sought to articulate "a critique of existing discrimination against women of all classes."[22]

In this early period of renewed public political activity by women, Brazilian women activists, like their counterparts throughout Latin America, were deeply divided on the question of feminism. In the Latin American context of the 1970s use of the term *feminism* was highly problematic because of its association with women of the urban upper-middle and middle classes in Latin America and its identification as "foreign," another example of European and North American ideological imperialism. Cuban leader Vilma Espín, for example, has always taken great care to avoid the label "feminist."

What came to be the primary voice of the new women's movement in Brazil was delineated by women of the political left. The militant women tended to be younger than the women professionals. Their network was based on their former political alliances within Brazil and, for a number of them, on friendships established while living in exile.[23] For these women especially, the new women's movement provided a relatively safe or "respectable" opportunity for political activity.[24] They denounced the feminism espoused by more politically moderate women and insisted that the only "legitimate" Brazilian feminism was one that placed women's oppression within the global struggle for social justice. In practice most of these women avoided the term *feminist* altogether, but their definition of a "legitimate" feminism as a political activity that augmented the forces of the political left was generally adopted by Brazilian intellectuals and political activists; other strands of feminism were "totally unacceptable, alien, the struggle of bourgeois lesbians against men."[25]

The periodical or women's journal has served as a primary vehicle for the discussion of feminism in Latin America since the nineteenth century, and with the reemergence of "the woman question" in the 1970s, a number of new publications appeared. The first Brazilian periodical of the new women's movement was *Brasil Mulher*, published in Londrina, Paraná, in October 1975.[26] Its editors were women who had been imprisoned for their political activities and who were associated with the Feminine Amnesty Movement. Their opening editorial stated: "This is not a woman's newspaper. Its objective is to be one more voice in the search for and reconquest of lost equality. Work which is destined for both men and women. . . . We want to speak of the problems that are common to all the women of the world."[27]

The first avowedly feminist periodical to appear was *Nos Mulheres*, founded in 1976 by university women and former student movement participants in São Paulo: "We women decided to create this feminist journal so that we can have our own space, to discuss our situation and our problems. And also, to think about solutions together."[28] The women who edited and wrote *Nos Mulheres* first met at a series of debates sponsored in São Paulo by the *Centro de Desenvolvimento da Mulher Brasileira* (CDMB, Center for the Development of Brazilian Women) during 1975 and 1976. The origins of the CDMB illustrate one of the most remarkable features of the new women's movement in Brazil, the role played by the Brazilian Catholic church. Since Medellín in 1968, the church had increasingly focused on the problems of the poor; in September 1975 the episcopate of São Paulo sponsored a meeting to discuss *o povo e seus problemas* (the people and their problems),[29] during which "participants called attention to the specific problems confronted by poor and working class women, the lack of adequate maternal-infant health care, and other gender-specific needs and decided to hold a separate meeting to honor Paulista women during International Women's Year."[30] The conference, *Encontro para Diagnastico de Mulher Paulista* was held in October 1975 with sponsorship from the United Nations and the Metropolitan Episcopal Tribunal of São Paulo. It was from this meeting, which included representatives of neighborhood associations, unions, church-affiliated groups, and research and academic institutions, that the CDMB emerged with a commitment to address the problems raised at the conference.

In 1975, as the politics of *abertura* merged into the politics of *distensão* (decompression) in Brazil, the continuing danger of political visibility should not be underestimated. The political left, student movements, and labor organizations were viewed as highly suspect and subject to violent repression; it was in October 1975 that journalist Valdimir Herzog was arrested and died "under interrogation" in the custody of the Second Army in São Paulo. In this precarious political atmosphere, the Brazilian Catholic church played a crucial role for the women's movement.

Two decisions, taken by the church after Vatican II and Medellín, were key: first, the decision to provide institutional sanctuary for opposition groups, and second, the creation of Christian base communities throughout Brazil. The Christian base communities, or CEBs (*comunidades de base*), were established at the grass roots level in the poorest neighborhoods and provided an organizational structure that encouraged collective action to procure potable water, decent housing, and other daily needs. Women were overwhelmingly the principal participants in the CEBs.[31] The power of community organizing, leadership skills, participation in literacy workshops that often incorporated the principles of Freire's pedagogy of the oppressed, and the spirit of liberation theology imbued the CEB members with a sense of their ability to change their situation.

In 1975 in São Paulo, women were able to use the shelter provided by the church and the international attention provided by IWY to organize and articulate a politics of opposition, a position that would have been appreciated by their Socialist and anarchist-feminist forebears. Furthermore, it appears that the women's demonstrations served President Geisel in his efforts to disempower the hard-line military.[32] Alvarez writes: "Here, an age-old stereo-type seems to have worked to women's advantage. The institutionalized separation between the public and the private may have, in an ironic twist, served to propel women to the forefront of the opposition in Brazil."[33]

In contrast to Brazil and Cuba, with their long histories of middle-sector political activity by women and men, most analysts believe that Peru did not experience a true opening of the political process to middle-sector reform until the nationalist coup d'etat of 1968 that brought General Juan Alvarado Velasco to power: "The armed forces—a quintessentially middle-class institution—were finally able to undermine the oligarchy's power and undertake reforms in Peru."[34] Between 1968 and 1975 the military government undertook a number of far-reaching reforms, many of which had been advocated by APRA and the Peruvian left since the 1930s, including agrarian reform, expansion of the educational mission of the public schools, worker participation in management and profit, and nationalization of key economic sectors. At the same time, profound demographic changes, already underway, were accelerated by massive migration from the Sierra to the coast and rapid population growth.[35]

In 1968 women's issues were not a special consideration of the military administration, but by 1971 the new women's movement was making itself felt. Peruvian feminist Virginia Vargas, a founder of the *Centro de la Mujer Peruana Flora Tristán*,[36] writes that in retrospect, "the central characteristic of the seventies with respect to women was the incorporation of women into the social and political struggle in a much more permanent and more comprehensive form than in the past." It is possible to distinguish two stages in the rise of the modern feminist movement in Peru 1970 to 1976, and 1977 to 1986. At the beginning, between 1970 and 1976, there began to be a more widespread understanding of the need to reappraise the value of women. A series of women's organizations arose that were dedicated to *capacitación* and the dignifying of traditional women's work.

Peruvian neighborhood associations were headed by men and institutionally linked to the Velasco government; they did not initially provide the grass roots networks for poor women that the Brazilian associations did. However, for women of the middle sector, incorporation into unions, teachers associations, government job-training programs, and increased participation in political parties in the early 1970s gave ever greater numbers of women experience in collective activity and a heightened awareness of the degree to which they were unequal partners in these enterprises. Vargas writes: "Although women did not begin the recovery of their just rights in this early period, a space was being created in which they could question established rules.[37]

The term *reivindicación* that Vargas uses to express "the recovery of their rights" is derived from the discourse of Latin American revolution and has particular political overtones important to understand in the context of comparative feminism. The politics of *reivindicación* assume that what is being sought or fought for—justice for women or the right of indigenous people to land—are rights that already exist and were once held; they are in a sense inherent but have been taken away or lost. This is a concept quite different from the idea of winning equal rights or breaking new paths for women, both of which are progressive concepts long predominant in North American and European feminist thinking. In Peru, *reivindicación* also invokes the folk belief in Pachamama, the primordial Andean mother-goddess in whose matrilineal realm women were empowered.[38]

In Peru, as in Brazil, the first public conferences on "the woman problem" were held under the auspices of the Catholic church. In October 1971, Peruvian lawyer Rosa Dominga Trapasso organized a series of talks titled "La mujer en la sociedad actual," which were held in the Center for Social Advancement of the archbishopric of Lima. Plans for an organization to aid women's advancement came to nothing, but Trapasso began collecting and copying bibliographic data on women for distribution to women who began to meet in small groups to discuss feminism and the new women's movement. In 1972 a conference, "once again attended primarily by distinguished male and female social scientists and middle-class intellectuals,"[39] met to discuss women's issues.

A number of points should be taken into account in assessing why the Catholic church, historically so hostile to nontraditional activities by women, should grant its support, at least in the form of offering space for women meeting to discuss "the woman problem." First, the church is not monolithic: it is diverse and reflects the political divisions of the larger society. Second, the Peruvian Catholic church, like the entire Latin American Catholic church, was deeply affected by the message of liberation theology. Those branches of the church most closely involved with social work, as for example, those associated with the archbishopric of Lima's Center for Social Advancement, were especially concerned with issues of social justice, and this included women. Third, these middle-class Peruvian women and men were at least nominally Catholic: both they and the church had a powerful interest in aligning with this new liberation movement.[40]

Additionally, these early meetings were not defined as feminist. The first avowedly feminist group of the new women's movement was ALIMUPER (Action for the Liberation of Peruvian Women) founded in 1973. It was, in Vargas's words, "greatly misunderstood by women as well as men." ALIMUPER maintained a separate identity from the new women's organizations linked to the state apparatus, which tended to be "traditional and patriarchal, but which nonetheless served a purpose."[41] In 1973, ALIMUPER staged a public demonstration at the Lima-Sheraton Hotel to protest the Miss Peru contest being held there.[42] Eventually, the group divided over the debate on the primacy of gender versus the primacy of class in understanding women's oppression, a debate that raged throughout the new women's movement everywhere.

From October 24 to 28, 1974, the *III Seminario Latinoamericano de Mujeres* convened in Lima. Local arrangements were made by the women's section of the *Partido Comunista del Peru*, the *Unión Popular de Mujeres Peruanas*. International support came from UNESCO and from the WIDF (International Democratic Federation of Women).[43] The purpose of the conference was to prepare position papers for presentation at the forthcoming IWY meeting in Mexico City.

Catholic women, Communist women, radical feminists, government workers, the splits and splinters in the new women's movement accurately reflect the ethnic and racial divisions and class struggles in Peruvian politics and society in the era. While the Catholic and Communist groups in particular sought to organize among women and families of the *barrios* and *pueblos jóvenes*, it should be noted that nearly all of the women initially involved in the new movement were ethnically Hispanic, urban, and middle class. In her study of socialist feminism, Cornelia Butler Flora writes: "In Peru, the new feminist movement, begun in 1971, grew and developed like a many-headed hydra."[44]

The politics of the women's movement in Peru are particularly illuminating in trying to understand the issues and concerns that Latin American women brought to the World Conference of the International Women's Year in Mexico City, June 19 to July 2, 1975. Many of the divisions among women that were to emerge so dramatically in Mexico were present in the Peruvian polity: divisions of race and ethnicity, between reformists and revolutionaries, between women of means and poor women. In Peru and throughout Latin America, first world and third world women coexist, if by "first world" we mean those who control wealth and by "third world" those who are in unwanted dependency. The preconference preparations held in Peru under the auspices of the Peruvian Communist party, with international support from Geneva-based UNESCO and the Moscow-based WIDF, indicate the unusual partnership of international funding agencies that became a hallmark of the decade and presage the anti-Americanism that marked the Mexico meeting. In 1974 the strongly nationalist left-wing Peruvian military government was actively pursuing a foreign policy independent of Washington; hosting the *III Seminario* was one more way to emphasize its nonaligned position.[45] The women who attended the *seminario* were not part of the government-appointed delegations to the UN conference but were planning strategies for the Tribune of Non-Governmental Organizations (NGOs), which met simultaneously with the official UN conference in Mexico City.

The formal genesis of the IWY and the emphasis on women and development "grew out of a proposal made by a group of women's organizations at a 1972 meeting of the UN Commission on the Status of Women in Geneva, Switzerland."[46] A multiplicity of activities lay behind that action, including the United States's declaration of commitment to aiding "the poorest of the poor." In 1970, Ester Boserup's influential study *Women's Role in Economic Development* revealed the critical need for more reliable information on women, especially rural women involved in agricultural production, so that more equitable policies and practices might be designed. Within Latin America, liberation theology, although not specifically envisioning a new role for women, created an atmosphere receptive to grass roots social change. The passage of the Percy Amendment by the U.S. Senate in 1973, which tied Agency for International Development and Inter-American Foundation monies to proof that the applicant country's project would give special consideration to poor women, backed up the UN declaration with economic clout.[47] Margaret Mead, as president of the American Association for the Advancement of Science, put the prestige and resources of the AAAS to work to get the IWY off the ground and organized a series of seminars, held just prior to the formal conference in Mexico City, to address women's issues.

The Mexico City *Conferencia Mundial del Año Internacional de la Mujer* met from June 19 to July 2, 1975, and consisted of two main meetings: the UN IWY conference, which was attended by delegates from 133 countries, half of whom were men and many of whom were female relatives or spouses of heads of state, such as Imelda Marcos of the Philippines and Ashraf Pahlavi, twin sister of the shah of Iran; and the Tribune, where representatives of nongovernmental organizations and interested individuals convened. The UN conference drafted a World Plan of Action for the UN Decade for Women, 1976–1985, with the three themes of equality, development, and peace.

It was at the Tribune sessions that Latin American women made their presence felt most strongly. Of the approximately six thousand people who attended the Tribune the vast majority were "self-selected individuals from South, Central and North America,"[48] including an estimated two thousand Mexican women. Sessions were in English or Spanish. Topics at the thirty-five formally convened Tribune sessions included "Law and the Status of Women," "Health and Nutrition," "Agriculture and Rural Development," "Education, Women at Work," as well as women in public life, population and planned parenthood, the family, third world craftswomen and development, and peace and disarmament. As one participant put it, the Tribune was "unhindered by the formal procedures of the main meeting." An additional 192 informal meetings were called "on every conceivable subject":[49] "Women and Imperialism," "Puerto Rican Women," "Women of the Fourth World," "Feminist Cause," "Japanese Feminists," "Coalition Task-Force on Women and Religion," "Global Speak-Out," "Women to Women Building the Earth for Children's Sake," "Self-Help Clinics," "Replacing Male-Dominant Language Elements," "International Association of Volunteer Education." In the words of one participant, "When you're talking about Mexico, you have to understand the Tribune was its soul."[50]

Hanna Papanek, writing about the IWY conference, notes that in addition to the Mexican women in attendance (which included rural women and urban women who came to speak about specific grievances), "there were also very large groups from other Latin American countries."[51] Papanek speculates that the predominance of women of the Americas at the Tribune meetings reflected the fact that would-be participants from Asia, Africa, and Eastern Europe were handicapped by distance and cost. Although this undoubtedly was an important factor, we have seen that there were extensive preparations made for the UN meeting in many places in Latin America in the years prior to the Mexico meeting, that there was some governmental support available for women to organize, and perhaps most important, that there is a long history of Latin American women's participation in international meetings to discuss issues of feminism and peace. In its role as a countervoice to the official UN meeting, the Tribune recalls the *Primero Congreso Interamericano de Mujeres* held in Guatemala City in 1947.

The debate that dominated women's politics during the first half of the UN Decade emerged at the Tribune sessions; as the reporter for the feminist journal *Connexions* wrote: "It was in Mexico that the incredibly diverse situations in which women live were first shared and that the term 'women's issues' began to be more broadly defined."[52] The lines of contention were drawn between first world women and third world women. The most visible protagonists in the debate were Betty Friedan, whose book *The Feminine Mystique*, published in 1963, was the touchstone of the new women's movement in the United States, and Domitila Barrios de Chungara, who came to Mexico City representing the Housewives Committee of Siglo XX, an organization of Bolivian tin miners' wives.

Barrios de Chungara's invitation from the United Nations to attend the Tribune (which included travel arrangements and accommodations) was made at the instigation of a Brazilian cinematographer who filmed the Housewives Committee for a UN-sponsored project on women leaders in Latin America in 1974. Barrios de Chungara described her mission to the *Conferencia Mundial del Año Internacional de la Mujer* thus: "I'd left my *compañero* with the seven kids and him having to work in the mine every day, I'd left my country to let people know what my homeland's like, how it suffers, how in Bolivia the Charter of the United Nations is not upheld."[53]

Domitila Barrios de Chungara hoped to speak with women who had problems similar to her own, and with women who had worked successfully to overcome problems in similar circumstances. The Tribune agenda as envisioned by North American, European, and middle-class intellectuals from around the world was alien to her experience and her needs. She was confounded by the concerns she heard expressed: the problems of prostitutes, the lesbian experience, the need for equal rights, the idea that men were responsible for war, that men abused women:

That was the mentality and the concern of several groups, and for me it was a really rude shock. We spoke very different languages, no? And that made it difficult to work in the Tribune. Also, there was a lot of control over the microphone. So a group of Latin American women got together and we changed all that. And we made our common problems known, what we thought women's progress was all about, how the majority of women live. We also said that for us the first and main task isn't to fight against our *compañeros*, but with them to change the system we live in for another, in which men and women will have the right to live, to work, to organize.

Barrios de Chungara's perspective on birth control illustrates what different approaches to problems women of different cultural, economic and political backgrounds had; in her eyes, "they [other women] wanted to see birth control as something which would solve all the problems of humanity and malnutrition. But in reality, birth control as those women presented it, can't be applied in my country. There are so few Bolivians by now that if we limited birth even more, Bolivia would end up without people. And then the wealth of our country would end up as a gift for those who want to control us completely, no?"[54] For her, numerical strength was the principal weapon the miners and Housewives' Committee possessed in their struggle with the Bolivian government, and she projected the vision of a less populous Bolivian nation as a weaker Bolivia, more vulnerable to international exploitation.

A remarkable aspect of the Mexico meeting is not that there was dissension among the thousands of women gathered but that women from all walks of life—especially women from all regions and backgrounds in Latin America—came together and that they made themselves heard, as Barrios de Chungara asserted: "I stated my ideas so that everyone could hear us, through the Tribune."[55]

Domitila Barrios de Chungara and the women she spoke for dismissed as irrelevant the concerns of feminists over reproductive rights, political and economic equity with men, the subordinate position of women within the family. Betty Friedan led the attempt to explain and defend the feminist position and the need to include their platform in the World Plan of Action. The result was a clash between Barrios de Chungara and Friedan; in Barrios de Chungara's account, Friedan asked "that we stop our warlike activity," said that "we were being manipulated by men," that "we only thought about politics," and that "we'd completely ignored women's problems." A predictable result of the noisy debate, a result Friedan was attempting to avoid, was the response of the international press, which leaped upon the dissension with headlines such as "Catfight among Women in Mexico" and "Fighting Feminists Find No Common Ground." Betty Friedan was depicted as a harridan, representing a brand of North American–European feminist imperialism, and Domitila Barrios de Chungara was presented as a simple woman of the people. The intent of the press coverage was not so much to elevate Barrios de Chungara whose message, after all, was revolutionary in its portent as it was to pillory feminists and exacerbate the tensions among conference participants.

Ultimately, it was not the press coverage that mattered. After the Mexico City meeting, and especially after the publication of *Let Me Speak! Testimony of Domitila, A Woman of the Bolivian Tin Mines*, Domitila Barrios de Chungara became the symbol that the vital issues for women to be addressed by the UN Decade for Women could not be defined solely by upper- and middle-class women, privileged women, specifically women whose lives were eased by the labor of other women. Her denunciation of feminists, whom she saw as exclusively of the exploiting classes and interested only in becoming like men, challenged women with a feminist perspective to examine their position vis-à-vis other women. Gradually, a shift took place. Within the Western Hemisphere, Latin American women redefined feminism, opening up the understanding of what feminism could mean. In the constant stretching of boundaries of what should, must, be the concern of all politically aware women to include matters of daily life and death—potable water, noncoercive health care, decent housing, daily bread, the right to organize—the concept of what it means to be feminist also expanded far beyond the narrow confines of "equal rights."

If in 1975 the political understanding and agenda of Domitila Barrios de Chungara and the political understanding and agenda of Betty Friedan appeared to be irreconcilable and irremediably divisive, by the end of the decade a cross-fertilization of ideas had occurred: Women of diverse cultures and ethnicities and social and economic strata became aware of the urgency and immediacy of one another's concerns; women of relative privilege could understand that in their concern for less privileged women what was needed was not leadership or instruction but respect and support for the projects of these women; and women involved in grass roots activism gradually began to understand the ways in which their gender affected their life situations. Over time, the ideas put forth by Barrios de Chungara and by Friedan informed the politics and understandings of the whole women's movement, though the divisions among women of different ethnic and class backgrounds not only persisted but deepened in the desperate economic climate of the late 1980s.

At the conclusion of the IWY conference, the World Plan of Action was adopted. The weight carried by the voices of women from Latin America and elsewhere in the third world is clear in the document, which begins by reaffirming the commitment of the United Nations to "the dignity and worth of the human person, in the equal rights of men and women and nations large and small" and continues with the assertion that "the last vestiges of alien and colonial domination, foreign occupation, racial discrimination, apartheid and neo-colonialism in all its forms are still among the greatest obstacles to the full emancipation of and progress of developing countries and all the peoples concerned."[56] The desire by feminists to include "sexism" among the obstacles to full emancipation and to specify "women" rather than employ the generic term "peoples" was defeated after hours of impassioned debate; the coalition that prevailed was formed by an alliance between the Soviet and East European delegates and representatives from Africa, Latin America, and some Asian countries. The resistance to targeting sexism as a pervasive problem directly reflects the importance of traditional Marxist analysis in the thinking of these delegates and the belief that revolutionary change would create equality for all, including women. It also reflects the determination to reject thinking that potentially divides the forces of revolution as well as an antipathy to the reformist politics put forth by women from the United States.

In addition to the adoption of the World Plan of Action, a number of resolutions were passed. One addressed the situation of women in Chile: "Considering that a number of intergovernmental and non-governmental organizations that have visited Chile either for humanitarian or investigative purposes have reported the systematic violation of all basic human guarantees regarding liberty and the fundamental economic and social rights; Deeply concerned about the reports of degrading and humiliating conditions of women prisoners. . . .; Demands that the Chilean authorities immediately abstain from any political executions, torture, persecution, oppression and the denials of liberty which continue to be reported."[57]

The impact of the IWY conference in Latin America is readily apparent in the immediate aftermath of the Mexico City conference. The large numbers of Latin American women who participated, the publicity the meeting received, the fact that the conference took place in Latin America, and the fanfare that accompanied the opening of the UN Decade for Women all combined "to focus the attention of governments and citizens on the position of women within each country."[58] The IWY and the Decade for Women gave a new legitimacy to women's issues. Additionally, international donors became more willing to support women's organizations concerned with poverty and development. The USAID and Inter-American Foundation broadened their commitment to programs for women; European government aid agencies increased their support (although their impact was negligible in the Western Hemisphere); specialized agencies of the United Nations such as the UN Voluntary Fund for Women (founded at Mexico City), the Inter-American

Development Bank, and private and church-related European and U.S. foundations all contributed.[59]

The dispersion of the ideas brought forth at the IWY among broader sectors of the populace, especially among women of the popular classes, is illustrated in the account of Magaly Pineda, a sociologist who has long been politically active in the Dominican Republic:

> Especially after 1975 women who had begun to learn words like discrimination and sexism began a process of change. The growing international feminist movement had a vital impact. However distorted and/or minimized, news of "crazy" women demanding freedom, equality, and participation in countries all around the world did not fail to reach the ears of Dominican women. The "officialization" of the theme of women through the declaration of IWY extended the radius of influence. Through radio and newspaper accounts echoes of the IWY reached even the most isolated regions of our country. Those of us who, as militant feminists, spent that year speaking all over the country—both in cities and in the countryside—were astonished at women's receptivity to the idea of their oppression.[60]

In the wake of the IWY women's organizing efforts received government support in a number of countries, including Mexico and Brazil. In Peru the Valasco government helped establish CONAMUP (Comision Nacional de Mujer Peruana).[61] CONAMUP was intended to serve as an umbrella for women's organizations throughout Peru, uniting neighborhood, professional, and union women's organizations;[62] however, some of the members threatened to expand their mandate, and CONAMUP was dissolved by the more conservative military government that succeeded Velasco. A number of its members went on to assume leadership positions in subsequent feminist groups.

By 1977 a wider acceptance of a feminist political critique is visible in the new women's movement in many areas of Latin America. From the beginning, activist women's strong commitment to the ideals of the political left imbued the movement with a sense of participation in the common struggle for social justice and national liberation: "At first we did not give ourselves much thought apart from considering the politics of class struggle and criticizing groups of petit bourgeois which fought only for their own liberation. Our fundamental preoccupation was how to reconcile feminism with the positions of the left."[63] In Peru, as was true elsewhere in the hemisphere, the steps toward self-definition as *feministas* was gradual and tentative: At the end of 1978 a collection of organizations with *una intención feminista* (a feminist intent) were formed. There appeared, besides ALIMUPER, organizations like the Movimiento Manuela Ramos (the name Manuela Ramos signifying "everywoman"), the Centro de la Mujer Peruana Flora Tristán, Mujeres en Lucha, and the Frenté Socialista de Mujeres.

One of the crucial issues for women activists in their progression from defining themselves solely within the left to the development of separate women's organizations and, ultimately, to defending the autonomy of the movement on its own terms was abortion. Throughout most of Latin America, abortion is the most common method of limiting births; in most of Latin America it is illegal, and even where legal it is often inaccessible to poor women. Throughout Latin America unsanitary and badly performed abortions result in the death and mutilation of thousands of young women each year; it is the primary killer of young women between the ages of fifteen and thirty-five.[64]

Governments and political parties of all persuasions avoid discussing the legalization of abortion, which is adamantly opposed by the church and goes against the grain of nationalist policies wherein a large population is seen as desirable. Moreover, many women who are able to reconcile their feminist sympathies with their Catholicism on other issues cannot do so on abortion. The decision by some women's groups to stage public demonstrations on behalf of "free abortion on demand" produced shock waves in Catholic Latin America.[65]

Abortion is quintessentially a "woman's issue," and it proved to be the cause that pointed up for many women, particularly those involved in the political left, the need for an autonomous feminist political presence. Founders of the Centro de Flora Tristán described their experience: "When we began to fight for our own rights we found that the support which we had been giving to the social struggle at all its levels brought no correspondent level of support [to our causes]. In the march for abortion we were only fifty women, subject to the laughter of our *compañeros* and the aggression of passers-by. . . . This period was important to us because we learned to organize ourselves, to act in the streets . . . and we discovered the political character of the feminist movement."[66]

The experience of the Peruvian women seeking to reconcile their growing feminism with their position in the political left was shared by women activists throughout Latin America, with the result that "the dialectic between class-specific issues and gender encompassing issues informs both the theory and practice of Latin American socialist feminists."[67] Vargas describes the evolution that occurred: "A few organizations at first, and then others began to define themselves as feminist. . . . In response to our definition, the parties began to create women's commissions. The intent was supposedly to neutralize or coopt the feminists; nevertheless, we had succeeded in each one of the parties in opening a very important space for women who are working from within, with an increasingly clear feminist position."[68]

Nearly all of the newly founded women's groups served as information centers, gathering and distributing material on women's issues. As Magaly

Pineda indicates in her description of the Dominican situation, the ideas of the IWY spread in spite of the distortions published in the mainstream press. The World Plan of Action addressed the potential of an alternative women's media in breaking down stereotypes, improving the image of women, and encouraging education and independence, and it is in alternative publications and the innovative use of film and radio rather than in the mainstream press that we can most clearly see the impact of the new women's movement. One of the first feminist groups with a global perspective was ISIS, named after the Egyptian goddess of fertility. ISIS founded the Women's International Information and Communications Service with offices in Geneva and Rome and publishes the quarterly *ISIS*, which has had a significant presence in Latin America since 1979, when it established an office in Santiago and began issuing a Spanish-language edition. Moreover, *ISIS* has published a number of special issues on Latin American topics, such as "Rural Women of Andean America," which appeared in the summer of 1987.

One measure of the spread of the women's movement in Latin America during the UN Decade is the number of newsletters, feminist journals, and women's movement periodicals that appeared, indicating the presence of women's groups, however small; no region of the vast continent is unrepresented in the literature.[69] Moreover, although the periodical has been an important vehicle for the exchange of ideas in Latin America, in the past, feminist periodical production was often ephemeral: short-lived and irregular, typically sustained by the efforts and financial resources of a crusading individual. Contemporary feminist literature, in contrast, is distinguished by its continuity. One of the earliest and most notable of these journals is *fem*, a "bi-monthly feminist publication" produced by a collective editorship (*Nueva Cultura Feminista*) in Mexico City; it has appeared without interruption since 1976. The subjects it addresses provide a microcosm of the concerns of Mexican feminists over the years: abortion (Winter 1977), work, sexuality, feminism, language, family, education, mothers and children, women writers, the history of women in Mexico (Fall 1979), women in the struggle for social justice.[70]

In Brazil, both *Brasil Mulher* and *Nos Mulheres*, discussed above, continued to publish for nearly a decade. *Brasil Mulher* originally rejected feminism in favor of utilizing the traditional image of woman as mother and "natural" pacifist in order to legitimate women's work on behalf of amnesty, but by the late 1970s the editors had incorporated feminist analysis into their political analysis.[71] The journal was directed to women of the popular classes, especially female factory workers and domestic workers in São Paulo; it reported a circulation of ten thousand readers in 1980. At mid-Decade, two Brazilian scholars observed that *Brasil Mulher* and *Nos Mulheres*, despite their distinct origins, "actually have basic positions in common," including the call to end the military dictatorship and a belief "that capitalism is the origin of numerous forms of the oppression of women."[72] Both journals seek to break class barriers between middle-class "women of conscience" and the working-class women "most oppressed by the double exploitation of sex and class." Both journals strongly oppose governmental attempts to regulate the conception of children and insist that women must retain the right to decide when they will have children and how many, and both condemn the distribution of "birth-control devices without regard for the health of women."

Another difference between the publications of the new women's movement and earlier feminist writing is that the literate audience in Latin America had expanded dramatically in the post–World War II years: in the 1980s illiteracy no longer presented the nearly absolute barrier between rich and poor and middle-sector women that it did in 1950. Moreover, the literacy campaigns of the 1970s frequently incorporated the ideas of the women's movement, as may be seen in this excerpt from a Nicaraguan literacy workbook: "Exercise A. 1. Let's read the sentences. Nicaraguan women have traditionally been *exploited*. The Revolution now makes their liberation possible."[73] Furthermore, modern technology—especially the ubiquitous Xerox machine—facilitates the inexpensive reproduction of material and helps bypass the in-house censorship to which mainstream publications are routinely subjected in many nations. The greater accessibility of print materials, which typically include wonderful and powerful cartoons and comic-strip style discussions on issues such as work, health care, and housing,[74] as well as poetry and prose articles, is complemented by the establishment of women's radio networks and by cinematographic work with a strong feminist message.

Brazilian women have been leaders in the innovative use of film and have succeeded in incorporating the concerns of the women's movement into the wildly popular *telenovelas*, which are long-running television "novels" watched by Brazilians of every walk of life and syndicated throughout the world.[75] In form, the *telenovela* is a cross between a soap opera and a series such as BBC's Masterpiece Theater; the stories may be historical or contemporary but are grounded in Brazilian life. In her book *Mulheres em Movimento*, María Lygia Quartim de Morães describes how Regina Duarte, the most popular television actress in Brazil, became "a symbol of the fight to change women's status in Brazil." In her role as heroine of the *telenovela Malu Mulher*, Duarte played a divorced sociologist who supports a teenage daughter and lives through "situations of homosexuality, abortion, racism, and extramarital relationships." The series traced the feminist movement in the main urban centers of the country and was a great success in Brazil—and also, notes Morães, in Cuba, France, and Sweden: "In a country where even the poor have access to and religiously watch the prime-time *novelas*, this change in women's image is indicative of the growing mobilization and organization of feminist and working class women."[76]

Using the political *sombra* provided by the UN Decade and garnering what financial support they could, the efforts of Latin American women in publishing and broadcasting their message is impressive. Characteristic of the period is the heightened awareness of political conflict in other regions of the hemisphere. Problems of distribution and the severe censorship imposed in some countries (notably in Brazil and the Southern Cone during the 1970s) was offset to some degree by the expanding women's networks and numerous conferences held under the auspices of the women's movement. The traditional transnationalism of the Latin American women's movement and feminist writing is clearly reflected in the pages of the new women's periodicals.

The Winter 1980 issue of *fem* provides an illustration of the deep concern of the new feminist movement with the broadest political issues. Dedicated to *America Latina: la mujer en lucha* (Latin America: women in struggle), in this issue women fighting in national liberation movements in El Salvador and Nicaragua and women protesting the brutal authoritarian regimes in the Southern Cone are seen as united in a common fight. The editorial is dedicated to women in Argentina, Bolivia, Brazil, Chile, Ecuador, Peru, Paraguay, and Uruguay:

In Argentina women confront the dictatorship from inside the prisons, or as mothers of prisoners and the disappeared; in Chile they organize to denounce repression, to open up ways of action and to oppose themselves to the model of femininity promoted by the Pinochet regime[77]; Uruguayan women in exile bring to the attention of the world the situation which imperils their country; in Paraguay women denounce the oldest dictatorship on the continent and defend the right of the mother and child; in Brazil, which since 1964 has been an enclave of imperialism in the southern hemisphere, women are trying to make good use of the recent political openings; in Peru teachers are on strike and *amas de casa* [houseworkers] are mobilizing; in Ecuador there are *campesinas* who not only participate in strikes and militant actions but who are seeking new forms of cooperative organization; in Bolivia the *compañeras* of the miners provide an example of the most combative women on the continent, and today are forming women's fronts within the major political parties.

Latin American women are repressed, but not resigned, and today we are on the march. Thus you may see us on the speakers' platform, in the classroom, in the factory, in the countryside, in the city and in the mountains. We fight for voluntary maternity, for full juridical and economic equality, for full participation in production and in politics."[78]

What is striking about the *fem* editorial is not its political orthodoxy but its spirit of inclusivity: it does not discriminate between the mothers' movements and the national liberation movements, which are quite different things, carried on by women with different values and different class backgrounds. It is a declaration of solidarity not only with the revolution and not only with women who could be defined as socialist-feminist (which the *madres* certainly could not be) but with the plight of women throughout the continent. The *fem* editorial presages the tolerance for diversity, the acceptance of difference, that became the keystone of Latin American feminism in the 1980s.

From its first issue, *fem* brought together information on women throughout Latin America and envisioned its audience as the Spanish- and Portuguese-speaking population of the entire hemisphere. Its international vision was reinforced by the participation of women from Chile, Argentina, Central America, and Uruguay who came to Mexico City as political exiles[79] and who were prominent among the writers and editors of *fem*. The *fem* editorial also demonstrates the extent to which the politics of the women's movement are a gendered manifestation of contemporary politics, intimately linked, within Latin America, to the push for social change, whether expressed in revolutionary or reformist terms. Feminism is a potent social criticism that has its own dynamic; it is this quality that has made it so rapidly acceptable to women of the popular classes. Politically involved Latin American women have been at the forefront of the international women's movement in recognizing and articulating this.[80]

The growing importance of women's issues in Latin America is apparent in the national liberation movements in Nicaragua, El Salvador, and Guatemala. In *Women in Revolutionary Movements: The Case of Nicaragua*, Norma Chinchilla states, "The participation of women in Central American revolutionary movements has surpassed, in quantity and quality, all previous examples from the history of the Western Hemisphere."[81] It is estimated that at the time of the overthrow of Somoza in July 1979, 30 percent of the 15,000-member guerrilla forces were women."[82] The unprecedentedly high number of women engaged in armed combat was in large part due to the broad popular base of the coalition formed to oust the Somoza dictatorship. Like the popular front in Nicaragua, which was composed of liberal democrats as well as Sandinistas, AMPRONAC, the Association of Women Concerned with the National Problem, was founded in 1977 on the "joint initiative of women from the FSLN (Frenté Sandinista de Liberación Nacional) and the bourgeois opposition."[83] There were approximately sixty original members. AMPRONAC published a declaration of its composition and purpose in November 1978: "[Our] members are free to adopt different political ideologies but their participation in Ampronac must be determined by the following objectives: (1) To encourage the participation of women in the resolution of the problems of the country; (2) to defend the rights of Nicaraguan women in all sectors and in all aspects; (3) to defend human rights in general."[84] The social status and respectability of some of its founders, as well as the mild tone of its declaration, allowed AMPRONAC to operate openly; Somoza had recently lifted martial law and censorship, and AMPRONAC received considerable coverage on television and in the press. AMPRONAC played a key role in denouncing the role of the National Guard in the disappearance, imprisonment, rape, and torture of Nicaraguan citizens; and it organized demonstrations and marches in collaboration with church leaders, demanding: "Where are our peasant brothers? What do the assassins say?"

In the months leading up to the overthrow of Somoza, the women of the FSLN and the women of the moderate opposition were increasingly divided over the use of AMPRONAC as the base for the mass mobilization of women: "In July 1978, after a series of national meetings, a special conference of 150 delegates representing 1,022 women from nine cities, adopted by a large majority the orientation proposed by the Sandinista supporters."[85] As the figures show, the subsequent success of AMPRONAC in mobilizing women was notable, but the achievements of the Nicaraguan women in the months following the revolution were even more remarkable. Nicaragua was devastated: an estimated forty thousand people died during the fighting, and thousands more were wounded; children were orphaned, many were homeless, and food was scarce. In response to the desperate situation the country faced, and with the full support of the FSLN, AMPRONAC reorganized itself into AMNLAE (Asociación de Mujeres Nicaragüenses 'Luisa Amanda Espínoza'), the Association of Nicaraguan Women Luisa Amanda Espínoza, named after the first female FSLN fighter to fall in combat. The reorganization of the women's group parallels the consolidation of Sandinista power in the governing revolutionary coalition.

AMNLAE undertook the task of building a massive women's organization based on local committees, including women workers, peasants, and housewives. By the spring of 1980 it had seventeen thousand members. AMNLAE was crucial to the success of the literacy campaign, to the establishment of crèches and health care centers, and, in the ensuing years of the U.S.-backed counterrevolution, to the defense of the revolution.

The contributions of Nicaraguan women to the success of the revolution and to the consolidation of power by the Sandinistas was direct and highly visible; how women's interests would be represented in the Sandinista state was a central question.[84] The fact that the Nicaraguan Revolution took place during the rise of the new feminism in Latin America, and that the revolution was committed to political pluralism, promised special attention to women's issues, as did the slogan: "No revolution without women's emancipation: No emancipation without revolution." Unlike other revolutionary movements, the Sandinistas did not denounce feminism as "counterrevolutionary." One of the first decrees of the new government prohibited media exploitation of women as sex objects, and a number of women veterans were appointed to senior positions in the administration. Yet, as Minister of Defense Tomás Borge acknowledged in an address in October 1982, "all of us have to honestly admit that we haven't confronted the struggle for women's liberation with the same courage and decisiveness [as shown in the liberation struggle]. . . . From the point of view of daily exertion, women remain fundamentally in the same condition as in the past."[87]

Perhaps because the revolution took place at the time it did, the expectations of the new government's ability to transform Nicaraguan society, and women's role therein, were exaggeratedly high; certainly, the overall hopes for a more egalitarian society were sharply reduced by the continuous stress of civil war and economic duress. The new Nicaraguan government did enact measures designed to bring women into the political process, to educate women for the work force, and to strengthen the family—that is, to support those factors that in turn bolster the interests of the state. The potential effect of these measures—unrealized in the economic chaos that deepened daily—is to improve the lot of the poorest women in society, without challenging "the prevailing forms of gender subordination."[88]

Throughout the hemisphere, in Latin America and in the United States, the overthrow of the Somoza regime and the establishment of the Sandinista government was closely watched. The political sympathies of many Latin American feminists lay with the Sandinistas; the presence of Cuban and Eastern Bloc personnel in Nicaragua, the bellicose stance of the Reagan administration in Washington, and the proclaimed goal of the Sandinistas to construct a revolutionary path that would be truly Nicaraguan, not Communist and not capitalist, represented the classic contemporary revolutionary situation, with superpower surrogates involved on opposite sides in an ostensibly independent third world movement for national liberation.

One aspect of the meaning of the Nicaraguan Revolution elsewhere in the hemisphere is revealed in Virginia Vargas's assertion that the "first public demonstration (in Lima) in which women marched as women" was in protest of the Somoza dictatorship in Nicaragua. Vargas uses the event to identify the point at which Peruvian women active in various areas of the women's movement "recognized the need to join forces": "We formed the Committee of Coordination of Organizations, named at the time (1978) 'Femeninas' and later changed to 'Femeninas y Feministas,' which is now the Coordinating Committee of Feminist Organizations."[89]

Vargas's material is of special interest on several levels. One, it shows the evolution of women activists in Peru, who emerged from the political left, away from resisting the label "feminist" toward deliberate use of the term to describe themselves in the years between 1978 and 1982. Second, it underlines the sense of connectedness with the struggles of women, and men, throughout the hemisphere expressed in the Latin American feminist press and in the international conferences of the period. And third, it offers a telling example of the ways in which activist Latin American women have used extranational incidents—in this case the struggle to overthrow a notoriously repressive and corrupt Central American regime—to demonstrate against repression and dictatorship, which, expressed in terms of local politics, might well put the demonstrators at risk of harsh retaliation.

The response of counterrevolutionary governments to the challenge of international feminism as articulated by socialist-feminists in Latin America may be seen in the attempt of the ruling junta in Chile to define women's role. In numerous speeches delivered after the coup d'etat that overthrew the elected civilian government and brought the military to power in 1973, President of the Republic General Augusto Pinochet described the family: "The family is the basic unit of society. It is the first school . . . , the mold in which the moral character of each citizen is founded. . . . The Nation is truly the reflection of the hearth."[90] According to this doctrine, the Chilean woman must understand the importance "of her mission, the superior destiny of her maternal vocation, her role as wife and educator." If she does not, if she "rejects her feminine identity," she can easily fall into error: "Animals do not form families. They unite temporarily in order to procreate. . . . The animal has no spiritual liberty, simply instincts. . . . [For humans] the family is an institution of natural order. It is necessary to inculcate in woman the fundamental importance—for the future of society—of making a home. It is especially important to insist—as we already have in speaking of patriotic values—on the dignity which emanates from the concept of service."[91]

The quotations in the passage above are taken from a booklet published in 1982 by the National Women's Bureau (*Secretaría Nacional de la Mujer*) in Santiago. That the national women's bureau in Chile should be a conduit for antifeminist propaganda (in the booklet, feminism is defined as the reverse of machismo: "the desire to impose female dominance over men") demonstrates the way in which governments can appear to be supportive of women's issues—in this case, by giving financial support to a national women's bureau—while utilizing an agency to its own ends. The cooptation of the forms of the new women's movement and the perversion of its spirit are particularly discernible in government-created agencies, and they have been a primary reason, in Latin America as elsewhere, for the important role played by NGOs, the independent feminist press, and unaffiliated research groups.

The Winter 1980 *fem* editorial refers to Chilean women organizing to denounce repression and "to oppose themselves to the model of femininity promoted by the Pinochet regime." Equating womanhood with motherhood is a common strategy in totalitarian regimes. It has the effect of removing women from their particular historical and cultural context, making them subject to unchanging "laws," here defined as raising children in the home within the order prescribed by the military government, and of "alleviating and enduring the sacrifices demanded by the nation."[92] In the Chilean instance, the definition of woman's "natural" role has another, more pernicious purpose: women who criticize the regime, who oppose the state, who choose to move beyond the constricts of woman-only-as-mother, may be seen as "unnatural." The reference to animals in the tract *Valores patrios y valores familiares* is not rhetorical; the nonhuman analogy is extended to cover Marxists, "who negate the idea of God, of patria, of liberty and human dignity."[93] Thus, the "inhuman" treatment meted out to women identified by the Pinochet regime as dissidents—the rape, torture, and murder of thousands of Chilean women, documented by testimony and human rights organizations—derives directly from and is justified by the regime's definition of woman's "natural" role.

The military regimes in Argentina, Uruguay, and to a lesser extent Brazil promoted a similar identification of mother with nation. It was in this atmosphere that the protest movements known as the mothers' movements were formed; as described in the chapter on women and history, the mothers' movements were consciously constructed to appeal to an international audience in hopes of bringing their plight and the crimes of the military against the citizenry to light.

Focusing attention on women and their role in national political struggles within the Western Hemisphere was the intent of the *fem* editorial cited above: in 1980, the nations of southern South America—Chile, Argentina, Uruguay, and Paraguay—were all suffering grievous military repression; in Brazil, the military dictatorship was still firmly in power, although the reopening of the political process to the civilian sector was under way; in Guatemala, government troops burned indian villages; in El Salvador, death squads murdered and "disappeared" hundreds of men, women, and children. Terrorism and counterrevolutionary force scarred the Andean nations, especially Peru and Colombia. In Mexico opposition parties were denied access to national media, and rumors about the torture and murder of members of peasant and Indian organizations in rural areas went unanswered.[94] In Washington, the Carter administration spoke out against human rights abuses while Congress continued aid to the Salvadoran military. The diplomatic hegemony of the United States was severely weakened, and attempts by Washington to assert its program in Central America were under attack at home and abroad.

It was within this heavily charged political atmosphere that the next series of international women's conferences were held. The mid-Decade conference that met in Copenhagen, July 14–30, 1980, was preceded by numerous preparatory conferences at the national level. Women's bureaus were formed as government responses to the IWY in several countries. In Cuba, where the FMC was again seeking to provide a countervoice to feminism, as it had done prior to the IWY meeting in Mexico City, the Third Congress of the

FMC convened. By 1980, FMC membership claimed 80 percent of all Cuban women over fourteen, or approximately 2.5 million members. Speaking at the close of the FMC congress on International Women's Day, March 8, Fidel Castro lauded the international work of Cuban women: "Our federation has undertaken a lot of important internationalist work in the Women's International Democratic Federation, and also in the United Nations, with IWY and the International Year of the Child. . . . The FMC has earned a great deal of prestige internationally, in international bodies, in women's organizations in other countries—countries of both the socialist camp and the capitalist camp—liberation movement organizations and organizations of underdeveloped countries. I think that our federation has contributed enormously to the foreign policy of the revolution." As examples of the work of the FMC in the international arena, Castro praised the 1,500 Cuban teachers and health care workers who "have gone to the aid of the Sandinistas in Nicaragua," and the cadre schools staffed by the FMC and attended by students from Namibia, South Africa, the Sahara, and national liberation movements elsewhere: "This is an important international service we are providing: helping train cadres from women's organizations in countries where there are liberation movements and Third World countries that need them."[95]

The extent to which the national women's commissions, established in the interim between the Mexico City meeting and the mid-Decade conference, were creatures of their governments was clear in Copenhagen. The conference was consumed by national political divisions to the near-exclusion of women's issues. The emblematic division came with the call by supporters of the Palestine Liberation Organization to condemn Israel and Zionism as racist and, by extension, to condemn Israel's ally, the government of the United States. African, Latin American, and Middle East delegates disrupted sessions and boycotted talks. As internationalist Charlotte Bunch predicted, Copenhagen was used both internationally and domestically by governments to promote their own images or needs: "This traditional approach to international discussions allows governments to deflect attention from their own responsibilities for perpetuating female subordination, while stifling the possibilities for innovative solutions to national and global problems."[96]

In addition to the official governmental delegations to Copenhagen, some ten thousand women representing nongovernmental organizations (NGOs) attended, of whom approximately seven thousand were Europeans. At the NGO sessions, the issue of dependency was as bitter and divisive as the PLO–Israeli dispute. The plea by feminists from the United States and Europe to concentrate on issues of importance to women was denounced as a ploy to keep the PLO and dependency issues off the agenda, and the line espoused by the FMC, the USSR, and the Eastern Bloc nations prevailed. The struggle as to who could dominate international discourse—first world or third world nations, Communist states or capitalist states, developed or less-developed nations—was articulated in women's voices. What was striking was not the fact that these divisions should be manifest in the international women's movement but the degree to which the post–World War II East–West dichotomy was dissolving under the challenges raised by Africans, Asians, and Latin Americans.

It seemed to some that the negative publicity and din of dissent that surrounded the Copenhagen conference demonstrated the hopelessness of an international women's movement that sought to address the cross-cultural commonality of women's subordination. Within Latin America, however, the early 1980s were a time of extraordinary growth for the women's movement and the politics of feminism. In July 1981 the *Primero Encuentro Feminista Latinoamericano y del Caribe* met in Bogotá, Colombia. Plagued by meager financial resources and political dissension among the organizers, the *encuentro* was two years in the planning. The decision to call the meeting a feminist conference differentiated it from previous international women's meetings in the region, as did the insistence that it was Latin American and Caribbean—not, in other words, hemispheric. This point was underscored by the choice of Spanish as the "language of communication."[97] Two hundred fifty women, from Brazil, Chile, Colombia, Curaçao, Ecuador, Mexico, Panama, Peru, Puerto Rico, the Dominican Republic, and Venezuela, as well as from the United States, Canada, and several European nations, attended.

Reporting on the conference afterward, an observer wrote:

One of the most striking features of the conference was the heterogeneity of the participants, as reflected in the wide age and diverse political experiences, degree of familiarity with feminist issues and writing and general cultural sophistication of the women. The Colombian organizers, in striving to guarantee a feminist perspective for the *encuentro* could control only the qualifications of Colombian women. Among those from other countries were women who had never before left their homes, never confronted the issue of lesbianism, never heard of a self-help clinic. . . . At the other end, there were women who, as feminists struggling to widen the movement's base had formed a Feminist Party (Spain), created alliances with receptive political parties (Mexico), or were experimenting with the coordination of womens' groups (Peru).

The first day and a half of the Conference were spent in a general plenary at which representatives of each country described the state of its feminist movement and the activities of the feminist groups represented. Those of us who had some experience working in Brazilian women's groups (*SOS Mulher* in São Paulo; *APEM*, a Women's Studies Association, and the *Colectivo de Mulheres* in Rio de Janeiro; and the Center for the Defense of the Rights of Women in Belo Horizante) presented a brief analysis of the growth of the women's movement in the context of the current redemocratization process, and then concentrated on the problem of violence to women in Brazilian society. We discovered that the majority of Spanish-speaking Latin American women had little knowledge of the Brazilian women's movement. . . . In addition we discovered that besides Mexico, which has a center for rape victims, no other Latin American country has begun to recognize the enormous problems of battered women victims, or murdered wives (a prevalent Brazilian problem).[98]

The third and fourth days of the conference were devoted to three workshops. Two Puerto Rican women presented a workshop on sexuality and health, in which they described self-help examinations, the reproductive system, and the risks and advantages of a variety of birth control methods. The most heavily attended workshop of the conference was one on feminism and politics, which focused on "the universal dilemma facing the current movement—the relationship of feminists to organized political parties and groups."[99] Although there was general agreement that women's secondary status is attributable to economic dependence, the "Women and Work" session was canceled because of low attendance. Leni Silverstein, who teaches at Pontificado Universidade Católico (PUC) in Rio de Janeiro and who attended the conference in her capacity as a founder of the *Centro de Mulheres Brasileiras*, commented: "The cancellation reveals a marked division between academicians and activists . . . it is not so surprising that in precisely that area to which the greatest intellectual scrutiny has been devoted (women and work) there was decidedly less activist involvement. The apparent separateness of the majority of Latin American researchers on women from the feminist political movement [was] further emphasized by the fact that women academicians researching and publishing on women were either expressly discouraged from attending the conference or not invited to attend."[100] Two resolutions were passed: (1) to hold a second conference in Lima in two years and (2) to initiate an international campaign protesting violence against women.

The Bogotá conference stood in remarkable contrast to the world conference at Copenhagen; in the words of Ana María Portugal, "Bogotá was a fiesta."[101] Deliberately unstructured, with plenary sessions rather than workshops and a "Caribbean ambience," from the moment the conference began "it was faithful to the autonomous feminist vision of the Colombian organizers." What emerged was the need to clarify and agree on a course of action more fitting to a movement that had to nurture itself in the reality of Latin America, a feminist movement that proclaimed itself in all of the tones of democracy, antiauthoritarian and outside the classic political structure.[102]

Perhaps the central discovery for the women who attended the *Primero Encuentro Feminista* was the state of feminist activity elsewhere in the region. The free flow of ideas from one place to another is not a given; in the Latin American context, communication between different regions of a single country is often imperiled by numerous factors, including illiteracy, lack of fluency in the dominant language, lack of facilities such as libraries and bookstores outside major urban areas, a weak domestic publishing industry, and official indifference, if not hostility, to aiding the distribution of information on issues not directly relevant to the aims of the state. The barriers between nations in this respect are even greater. As Leni Silverstein pointed out, most Spanish-American women had little idea of what was going on in Portuguese-speaking Brazil. In the 1980s the crippling effects of inflation and the international debt further exacerbated the problem, making books and magazines published outside a country prohibitively expensive.[103] Material published about what is going on in Latin America and the Caribbean is more easily accessible in the publications, libraries, archives, and universities of the United States and Europe. Within a country, grass-roots work, television, radio, and film may be means of reaching less literate or illiterate audiences with ideas that are not part of the mainstream, whereas the primary means for the international communication of noncommercial ideas is by print.

The realization of the need to create a means of communicating information on women's activities in various national communities inspired the establishment of *Mujer*/Fempress, with offices in Santiago and correspondents in Argentina, Bolivia, Brazil, Costa Rica, Ecuador, Mexico, Peru, the Dominican Republic, Uruguay, and Venezuela. The Mexican connection is particularly important because, within the Latin American context, Mexican women have the greatest access to information from other countries. *Mujer* set out to reproduce and distribute recent articles on women's issues from throughout Latin America:

The clippings arrive thanks to the journals with whom we exchange materials, the clipping service of G. Saelzer of Mexico, the work of the correspondents and the sense of sisterhood of all women, who, from their own countries, send us articles which have appeared in the national press.

This publication seeks to aid those who are working to improve the condition of woman and raise their levels of conscience, within the framework of social justice and political democracy.

Our work will be useful to organizations as a resource to consult and discuss; to researchers; in making information available that is otherwise difficult to obtain by other means; and will reflect the important developments which are occurring in Latin American and Caribbean countries with respect to women. And it is useful in the way in which its articles are broadcast or reproduced by media sensitive to the theme of woman, from an alternative perspective.

FEMPRESS was conceived to strengthen and increase the means of alternative communication among women. Write for MUJER, reproduce and circulate copies of its articles, taking care always to cite the source.[104]

Financial support for the production of *Mujer*/Fempress comes from several sources, including ILET (Instituto Latinoamericano de Estudios Transnacionales); SIDA, a Swedish aid agency; the Norwegian Ministry of Development and International Cooperation; and the North American Methodist church. In the years since its inception it has succeeded in carrying material on nearly every aspect of the women's movement and feminism in Latin America, and it has published more than twenty special editions on topics ranging from maternity and abortion to rural women, Central America, domestic employment, prostitution, disarmament, democracy, woman as head of the household, aging women, young women, and women who are part of a couple. No region has gone unrepresented. *Mujer* also regularly carries notices of conferences ("Actividades de la Asociación Latinoamericana para el Desarrollo y la Integración de la Mujer"), and of new publications ("Mujeres Uruguayanas han dado a luz el *Cotidiano Mujer*" [Uruguayan Women give birth to *Cotidiano Mujer*]).

The impact of Fempress and the breadth of its audience is visible in its content and in letters to the journal, such as the following from a women's center in La Paz, Bolivia: "We recently received a copy of *Mujer*, which lists us as part of the Women's Radio Network Circle [*Ciclo Rede Radiofonica de Mujeres*]. We wish to thank you for including us in the register, and to let you know that we are in full production, and planning a second cycle in our series which addresses the problems of migrant Aymara women."[105] The productions referred to in the letter are a series of booklets, "Nuestros Leyes"; three videos (they note that they are in Betamax) about sexuality; and fifteen radio programs for the series "the Voice of the Kantutas."[106]

Latin American women involved in the international women's movement have been innovators in experimenting with alternative means of communication that reach across the class and racial divisions of their particular national and regional communities, and their work has inspired similar production by others, such as the Pan-Asian Women's Association and groups of sub-Saharan women in Africa. The use of radio, video, and film to bridge barriers of language, dialect, ethnicity, and geography is augmented by the production of illustrated booklets and comic books that address woman's issues. General interest comics and pulp picture booklets, sold in streetside kiosks all over Latin America, are cheap, enormously popular, and read by people of all walks of life. An example of the adaptation of this form by feminists may be seen in the pamphlets published by the *Centro de la Mujer Peruana Flora Tristán*, among which are *From Girlhood to Womanhood* and *Knowing Our Body*.

Isis, also published in Santiago, differs from *Mujer* in that its articles usually are researched and written for the journal. *Isis* frequently publishes "testimonios," wherein, for example, Andean peasant women testify about their lives, and the *Isis* writer places the testimony in a political and cultural context.[107] The efforts of the international women's press are visible at the national level. The pioneering work of *fem* in running articles on the women's movement in Brazil or Peru as well as in Mexico, reporting on international as well as local women's meetings, and publication of interviews with international figures such as Hebe de Bonafini, leader of Las Madres de Plaza de Mayo, was replicated by many of the new feminist publications that were beginning to appear in the hemisphere.

The *II Encuentro Femenista Latinoamericana y del Caribe* was held July 19–22, 1983, at a resort near Lima, Peru. The Peruvian organizing collective, with representatives from seven women's groups,[108] faced almost insurmountable obstacles in bringing the conference about. They wished to maintain the criteria of self-financing established at Bogotá to deflect any suggestion that the *encuentro* was being manipulated by outside interests, but circumstances were difficult: "[Financial independence] is hard for countries like ours which confront the deepest economic recession of modern times and particularly for Peru, in a year in which natural disasters [a flood totally destroyed the planned conference site] and disasters of other types [the steady erosion of the standard of living, inflation, unemployment, terrorism] occur. Planning was a fight against existing political conditions and also against time."[109]

The theme of the conference was "Patriarchy in Latin America." More than six hundred women attended, from every country in the region except Cuba and Nicaragua. Many women came from the interior of Peru; the largest foreign delegations were of Chilean, Colombian, and Dominican women. Unlike the Bogotá conference, this one was carefully structured, with workshops, panels, and exhibits—an organizational decision that was harshly criticized by those who preferred the informal encounter in Colombia. The presence of numerous academics, social workers, writers, journalists, and women doctors and lawyers also prompted dissent: "This is a game for professionals!" A significant number of women came as observers, "to see what the feminists are planning." They represented various political parties, unions, and their own curiosity. And finally, the *feministas clasistas* (Marxist feminists) came, insisting that "the class struggle is the decisive factor before we can speak of feminism."[110]

The conference opened with an address by Roxana Carillo, who stressed the importance of the meeting "particularly in this moment in which the crisis in Central America threatens world peace and the current situation in Peru tends to a narrowing of democratic freedoms."[111] Carillo specifically warned against the temptation to consider women's demands as secondary and emphasized that feminism does deal fundamentally with the issue of the distribution of power. The results of the work of *Mujer*/Fempress and ILET were presented in a workshop. Adriana Santa Cruz, an editor of *Mujer* and coordinator of a network of alternative media for Latin American women, talked of the expanding work in publications, films, and radio.

It was at the session "Patriarchy and Power" that the tensions that were barely concealed throughout the conference (one Mexican feminist commented that she felt as if she were at a "disencounter") surfaced. Shouting

"¡No hay feminismo sin socialismo!" (There is no feminism without social-ism), a group of about seventy women disrupted the session. Ana María Por-tugal, a founding member of the Centro de Flora Tristán and a coordinator of the Peruvian meeting, writes of the confrontation:

The slogan was intended to reignite the old polemic of the seventies, when to be a feminist in this continent was to fall out of grace with the party.

But not for nothing have ten years passed, and for us, seasoned veterans strength-ened by former political "excommunication" and acts of contrition, it is time to break the cords that tie us down. The women at the conference responded that they would no longer give in to blackmail, guilty conscience, or labels of being "petit bourgeoise." "We ought not to fall into the game of conciliation," a Colombian woman confronted the shouted proclamation, referring to a feminism that, in order to obtain the *nihil obstat* of the central committees [of the political left], must declare itself "revolu-tionary," "anti-imperialist," "political," "of the masses," "identified with its own class interests," "not outside of society, etcetera, etcetera.[112]

Portugal uses the Latin term *nihil obstat* to connote the idea of official censor-ship, in this case by the central committees of political parties; it is taken from the practice of the Catholic church, where it stands for permission to publish a book, granted by the official censor who has certified that the book contains nothing contrary to faith or morals. The reference and the connotation would be immediately recognizable to an audience of Latin American women.

The point is that many Latin American feminists, while committed to the struggle for social justice and the search for true democracy, had come to believe that patriarchy is not restricted to the elites (the *pequebu*) but is a cross-class phenomenon. Women of every class and every group are subordi-nate to their male counterparts, usually most visibly in their earning power and relative lack of mobility because of their maternal role. Fietta Jarque, reporting the *II Encuentro* for the Lima journal *El Observador*, put it thus:

The women at the meeting arrived at the following conclusions: feminism is a project which transforms the hierarchical relations of the sexes; it is an understanding about the quality of human relationships in society, and therefore, a door to overcoming the position relegated to women; feminism is connected to the processes of trans-formation and liberation in each one of our countries; the feminist movement must be autonomous; the contradiction of gender is present in the lives of all women, whatever her class, race or age, and whatever the economic system in which she lives; feminism confronts patriarchal power from the private sphere to the antiimperialist fight against capitalism."[113]

The conclusions reported in Jarque's article emerged from the concrete experiences expressed by the women who attended the conference, not only those of women intellectuals who fought for recognition within the politi-cal parties. "Women should have their own space," related Josefa Ramirez, a Peruvian woman of the *altiplano*. "They need their own organizations since the male leaders tend to take over when they are together with women." Dominican women spoke of popular education as a means of raising the political conscience of rural women: "consciousness-raising is an irreversible process," and feminism, as an understanding of subordination, "is tremendously subversive."[114]

A dissenting document was drawn up, primarily by women representatives from the popular front, which concluded "¡No hay feminismo sin socialismo!"

While the debates raged among women in attendance at the conference, there were others, not in attendance, who denounced the whole idea of the conference. In her book *When Women Rebel: The Rise of Popular Feminism in Peru*, North American writer Carol Andreas, who has spent most of her adult life working as a political activist among the poorest sectors of Peruvian society, accused II Encuentro of elitism and charged that the organizers had excluded the indigenous women who were the subjects of slide shows and videos shown at the conference. Andreas speaks from a political perspective to the left of established Socialist and Communist parties; for her and those who agree with her, the only valid political expressions (including feminism) are those that emerge directly from the poorest of the poor:

The women of the high sierra, like the women of the tropical rain forest, have never had anyone they could trust to represent their interests in the Peruvian government. . . . The campesino union, which recently began to recognize the rural women's right to a voice in deciding their own future, did so only after many women of the sierra [turned] to open insurrection against the state. In the central provinces of Ayacucho and Apurima, it was the guerillas of Sendero Luminoso who began, in the 1980s, to provide a dramatic outlet for women's frustration and anger against the powerful men who controlled their destinies. The senderistas organized a *Movimiento Femenino Popular*, and members of the movement engaged in public debates challenging other maoists who insisted that "the woman" question did not merit the attention the senderistas were giving it.[115]

Andreas's description of the rise of a gendered critique among rural women of the high Andes is compelling, and it echoes the Dominican women's assertion that feminism is revolutionary not only in its potential challenge to power relationships between men and women but in analyzing any system of dominance. However, her bitter criticism of the women who put on the *encuentro* is a gratuitous repetition of a familiar litany of allegations (most often leveled by more conservative critics than Andreas) against feminists as "teachers" who would raise other less-enlightened women's consciousness, scholars who "study" other women, women who are concerned with the politics of sexuality instead of the "true" needs of poor women (who are presumed to be exclusively concerned with clean water, shelter, adequate food, the politics of survival). Such images of women are in fact stereotypes that do serious disservice to women of all walks of life.

Contrary to Andreas's charges, women organizers from the *pueblos jovenes*[116] and rural women from the interior of the country were involved in both the planning and the realization of the *encuentro*. Others, like Rosa Dueñas, a grass-roots organizer from one of the "new towns" near Callao, hitchhiked into Lima and attended the conference "illegally," with the complicity of those who had paid the $50 registration fee. Dueñas, who is a Quechua/Peruvian, spoke passionately of her belief in *feminismo popular*, the grass-roots feminism that springs from the daily life experience of women, in solidarity with the people.[117]

For most women who attended the *II Encuentro*, establishing ties with women "doing the same work we are" was the most important aspect of the conference. In this respect the conference provided a special opportunity for the many women who were living in exile to meet with their countrywomen and other Latin American women. Seventy Chilean women attended; they came from the United States, England, Spain, and Switzerland, as well as from Chile. Chilean women led seven of the nineteen workshops; they described their work within Chile and their experiences in exile. They were able to use the conference as a means of letting the international community know what the consequences of Pinochet's policies were for women and for the political opposition within Chile.

Ana María Portugal titled her summation of the conference "No feminism without socialism?" She writes:

A sense of discomfort pervades. In order to recover a space beyond the polemics over the "correct line" it will be necessary to accept the existence of different focuses and positions, in order to erase the tension.

A happy ending? It depends. . . . We still need to get rid of old polemics and blackmail. Some questions also need to be resolved about the type of *encuentro* most adequate to meet feminists' expectations (many of us feel as if we have attended a sort of multitudinous congress of women where there were also feminists).

But the fundamental resolve is written and proclaimed. That is, that feminism is a social movement that is pledged to the fight to change the system. A fight in which our specificity as women is manifest, and that, therefore, is revolutionary. That the class struggle and the feminist struggle are two currents which converge on a single historical objective: to fundamentally change the system, but that, many times the feminist struggle is not necessarily going to coincide exactly with the immediate goals of the class struggle. Therefore, we cannot accept the false proposition that "there is no feminism without socialism." Feminism already exists, it is a struggle which has been carried out across the centuries and which will continue as long as there are women alive who are subjugated, as much in capitalism as in socialism.[118]

The Lima meeting may be seen as a watershed in the history of feminism in Latin America. While in no way disavowing their commitment to the struggle for social justice, Latin American feminists were asserting that feminism and the issue of women's subordination has its own validity and its own history and that, although socialism and democracy as ideals posit the equality of men and women, in no existing system, socialist or capitalist, has such equity been realized. Portugal's eloquent defense of the feminists' position is also a plea to move beyond rigid ideology, to build toward a future that can embrace a multiplicity of feminist perspectives. That this position should be articulated in Lima is no accident; unlike the Mexican, Argentine, Chilean, Venezuelan, and Brazilian situations, with their long histories of middle-class women's movements, in the Peruvian setting the development of a widespread, viable feminist movement among women of the middle sector barely preceded the appearance of women's collectives among the urban poor and the rise of *feminismo popular* alongside rural resistance movements. The profound social dislocations of contemporary Peru were vividly apparent at the *II Encuentro*; for Peruvian feminists the need to deal with such divisions is not rhetorical—it is essential to survival.

In attempting to better understand Peruvian reality, historians have rejected the old concept of the "Two Perus" (connoting coastal and sierra, Spanish and indigenous, rich and poor) in favor of the concept of *raizes mutuas*, literally "mutual roots," which suggests a more complex and dynamic heritage. The recognition of plurality, the *raizes mutuas* of feminism, is addressed in the first issue of *Viva*, which began publication in 1984 under the auspices of the Centro Flora Tristán:

We are living in cruel times. Times of violence and of death. To live today in Peru is a risk . . . it is a life lived amidst ceaseless, daily bloodshed. What part of this cruelty does not touch [us as] women?

The appearance of *VIVA* is not casual. At the present moment, the women's movement is confronted with a reality which seizes our conscience and calls for the direct defense of the ideals of feminism, which are based not only on the struggle to change social and economic structures, but which denounce sexism, racism, torture, and terrorism in all of its forms, fascism and militarism, and patriarchal values which preclude the hope for justice and equality.

VIVA announces a new tribune for debate, opinion, clarification and information about the questions, successes and themes raised by women who have an engagement in feminism, whether it be militant or not. An engagement which in our country assumes diverse forms and expressions, because the women's movement is plural and democratic.[119]

The *Viva* editorial represents a central contribution of Peruvian and Latin American feminists to the international women's movement. Feminism in Peru is a multiplicity of expressions that reflect the broader political spectrum and the divisions that exist in every Latin American country—and in countries across the globe—but are especially stark in the Peruvian polity. The editorial may be seen as a metaphor for the hope—and the immense problems—faced by the new women's movement and, by extension, other social reform movements. It is also an early indicator of the direction Latin American feminist thinking took after 1983, which is an acceptance and pride in multiplicity and a rejection of the only-one-right-way-to-think politics of the early and mid-1970s. It is born out of the direct political experience of women in Brazil, Mexico, Argentina, Bolivia, Ecuador, Venezuela, Colombia, Uruguay, Costa Rica, and Peru. It includes the researchers who were so damned earlier, and it includes an understanding of how manipulated women were in the loud condemnation of other women—who could be a feminist and who could not, who was dismissed as "petit bourgeoise," and so forth. The mainstream of the early women's movement in Latin America adopted not only the critical analysis but the prejudices of the political left and incorporated them into their own politics. What the Peruvian women were expressing was the perception that gender did give them links with other women and that links with other women in society were crucial not only to the hopes of the women's movement but to the future of Peruvian society. It was a move toward legitimatizing a variety of women's voices, a move away from the politics of delegitimization that had threatened the international women's conferences from Mexico City to Copenhagen to Lima.

"Every new movement in Latin America picks up and blends with what preceded it. As the notion of feminism has spread from a middle-class movement, it increasingly recreates itself—from middle-class women disputing the boundaries of gender, to poor women defending their family and economic rights." [120] The constant reinvention of feminism is visible in many aspects of the contemporary women's movement in Latin America. Gisela Espínosa Damian, a Mexican feminist and economist who worked with CIDHAL (Communication, Exchange and Human Development in Latin America), a center for popular education located in Cuernavaca, describes the progression "toward a new dimension of feminism" in Mexico: "The decade of the 1980s heralded a new opportunity for developing the women's struggle." [121] Damian pinpoints the First National Women's Meeting held in Mexico City in November 1980 as the breakthrough "where the seed was sown for a discussion of the women's problem on a huge scale." The meeting was attended by more than a thousand women, including rural women, factory workers, office workers, women from barrio organizations, and housewives, and was followed up with regional meetings across the country. Women workers' committees and, in the south and southeast of the country, peasant women's conferences were set up. The campesina and worker's organizations, like the middle-class feminist organizations, had long roots in the history of Mexican women's movements and in their relationship to the government. A different coalition was represented at the First National Meeting of Women of the Popular Urban Movement; five hundred women met in Durango in 1983, and a second congress was held a year later in Monterrey. The drive and vitality of the urban women's movement was apparent in the aftermath of the great earthquake of September 19, 1985; women from the poor urban suburbs were at the center of the new political forces that supported the candidacy of Cuauhtémoc Cárdenas and gave serious challenge to the PRI candidate in the elections of 1988.[122]

The interactions between the rapidly spreading politics of the new feminism and the forces of political change are also observable in the Brazilian polity, and the phenomenon is intimately linked to the politics of redemocratization. Carmen Barroso and Cristina Bruschini state:

. . . the transition to democracy presented new opportunities and new risks for Brazilian feminists. A growing crisis of legitimacy, and a deepening economic collapse brought a gradual end to the military regime, starting with the election of opposition state governors in 1982. The coalition now in power is a blend of disparate political forces, including some progressive sectors. Some feminists have entered party politics and are lobbying from inside for gender-specific issues. Others are very reluctant to do so, either because they have joined the other progressive party which has remained in the opposition, or because their view of feminism attaches no relevance to state policies. Some of the "opposition feminists" work in middle-level posts of the government bureaucracy where they have been trying to implement a feminist agenda. This has been facilitated by the need of the current regime to maintain its broad social basis of support, and the resulting courtship of the women's movement.[123]

Like Damian in Mexico, Barroso and Bruschini were involved in popular education projects among women of the urban poor; between 1981 and 1983 they participated in a sex education project developed by feminists from the Carlos Chagas Foundation in collaboration with small groups of women from the outskirts of São Paulo. Although the women from the Carlos Chagas Foundation provided information and materials, the decision to focus on sexuality came from "the demand for discussions on sex education and gender relations voiced by women in the grass-roots movements."[124]

The five booklets developed deal with male and female physiology, birth control, childbearing, self-examination, and sexual pleasure. Barroso and Brushini note with satisfaction that the booklets have since been shared with thousands of women assembled in small groups throughout Brazil and in many other countries. The rapidity with which a feminist understanding of sexual politics was absorbed by women of the urban poor underscores MacKinnon's observation that "sexuality is to feminism what work is to marxism: That which is most our own, yet most taken away."[125] Barroso and Bruschini affirm that "(the women's) asserted interest in sexual politics is part of a movement that is spreading in all of Latin America, with no respect for the hierarchy of needs established by the well-meaning but misguided 'bread-first' school of thought." The 1983 position papers on women's health drawn up by the Brazilian government "prominently featured the reproductive rights discourse of the women's movement." Barroso and Bruschini conclude: "By 1985, in Brazil, the issues of female sexuality and reproductive rights have come out of the closet."[126]

Financing such projects is always a delicate issue for Latin American feminists. Government funding is often unobtainable or unsought for fear of co-optation or accusations thereof; funding from international agencies carries the same problems of possible co-optation plus the possibility of being infiltrated or used as a front for information gathering (as AID projects were in the 1960s) or being charged with participating in cultural imperialism. And raising funds independently in inflation-strapped economies is enormously difficult, as the Peruvian women reported at the *II Encuentro*. The Carlos Chagas Foundation project on sex education was funded by the Ford Foundation, which, in Brazil, has supported many progressive initiatives, including some of the most radical feminist groups. Barroso and Bruschini explain the acceptance of Ford support:

> During the early years of the military dictatorship in the 1960s the Ford Foundation established a liberal reputation for supporting professors who had been expelled from the universities under the accusation of being Leftists; in spite of that, in the 1970s, most feminists were hesitant to approach the Foundation fearing that the motives behind their interest in the women's movement were to act as an intelligence service or as an attempt to control, co-opt or neutralize the movement. In recent years, these doubts have given way to a more pragmatic approach. Given the fact that Ford officials have made no attempts to intervene in the group's policies and practices, and that the information collected through grantee's reports is public anyway, feminist groups felt that there was no reason not to accept the Foundation's support for projects that otherwise would not be feasible.[127]

In Uruguay, as in Brazil and Argentina, the early 1980s was a period of transition from military dictatorship to civilian government; and in Uruguay, as in Brazil, the new women's movement was at the forefront of the forces demanding a return to democratic politics. In April 1984 the *Grupo de Estudios sobre la Condición de la Mujer en Uruguay*,[128] an independent women's studies group that had been documenting the history of women in Uruguay and collecting information on the status of women in the country since 1979, published the first edition of *La Cacerola* (*The Casserole*). They wrote on the origin of the name:

> The chosen name has many meanings, but one above all: in these months of perilous transition to democracy, the Casserole has been converted into a symbol of liberation for the Uruguayan people.
>
> The name refers to the street protests when the streets resonated with the sound of casseroles being beaten with spoons; the demonstrations against the military regime were called "cacerolazos."
>
> Thus, from the center of the home, from the kitchen, emerged the humble casse-

role, ancient symbol of female oppression, today the symbol of national liberation. From the private space, the hearth, the resistance brought it into the public realm, the street. A resistance where everyone, great and small and young and old, men and women, participated. A resistance spontaneous and collective, made with casserole in hand. From this comes the name, chosen and assumed not without fear that its meaning is obvious while we are still living under the dictatorship.

Of course we do not have permission to print and the only security we have is that the Ministry did not tell us not to publish—although this is beside the point as we did not wish to ask, in these times when Uruguayans try to ask as little as possible from the military government.

The subterfuge we used to edit this revista is to call it "a free bulletin for internal consumption only," by which means we escape censorship as well as the need for permission. For all of this, we were a little uneasy, but the name was irresistible. *La Cacerola* is a surprise, a conspiratorial wink. Ninety percent of all Uruguayans will understand what the casserole means.[129]

La Cacerola appeared as tensions between the military and the civilian sector were reaching a crescendo. In May 1984 the military announced plans to prolong the "transition period," which would have the effect of prolonging their stay in power; the plan was denounced by the civilian political parties. The precariousness of the political situation into which *La Cacerola* was launched is illustrated by the June 1984 arrest and imprisonment of Wilson Ferreira Aldunate, leader of the National party, on his return from exile. Only as the promised election date of November 25 approached did the ever-widening protests against the military diminish; no one wished to jeopardize the first open elections in a decade. On November 25, civilian Julio María Sanguinetti was elected president of Uruguay.

In the ensuing months *La Cacerola* added its voice to the impassioned discussions surrounding redemocratization. Redemocratization, in the full Spanish or Portuguese sense of the word, suggests far more than the mere replacement of military governments by elected officials; it implies deep, often agonizing appraisals of national character and raises intense debate over economic versus political democracy.[130] Referring to the legal battles of the early Uruguayan feminists who had succeeded in gaining suffrage and other reforms, *La Cacerola* states: "Today we know that the legal conquests were but half the battle. Today we are fighting for real equality of opportunity and participation."[131] The cover of the publication shows a casserole at full boil, with its lid popped off and steam rising from the contents. The casserole is also used to invoke the diversity of women—"the casserole may be of iron, of earthenware, of aluminum or of steel"—and recognition of the fact that more than 40 percent of Uruguayan women are exclusively homemakers. The editors honor this role, while insisting that women should have the opportunity to choose freely, "unconstrained by social or authoritarian traditions."[132]

One of the issues that always must be considered in weighing the importance of the feminist press, especially an alternative publication such as *La Cacerola*, is how many people does it reach? In a column titled "Who Eats the Casserole?" the editors estimate their readership at between fifteen thousand and twenty thousand people, an excellent distribution in a country with a population of slightly less than 4 million. And they add that when the material they publish begins to be broadcast on the radio and printed in daily newspapers and magazines, "there will be no further need for us."[133] They are still in production.

Between 1980 and 1988, 153 women's periodicals with a feminist or women's-liberationist perspective came into publication in Latin America; only 46 had existed in the preceding decade.[134] In 1984, ILET published a booklet that gave examples of the new women's press from every country: *Brujas* (*Witches*) and *El Largo Camino* (*The Long Road*) from Argentina; *El Pan de Cada Día* (*Daily Bread*) from Bolivia; *Mulher e Saude* (*Woman and Health*) and *Mulher Libertação* from Brazil; *Amistad y Esperanza* (*Amnesty and Hope*) from Chile; *Emancipación* from Colombia; *Golondrinas* (*The Swallows*), published in Costa Rica by Chilean women in exile; *La Mujer* from Ecuador. In Central America, women's groups involved in the national liberation movements published journals intended to promote solidarity with the revolutionary movements: *Boletín Internacional de AMES* (*International Bulletin of the Association of Salvadorean Women*) in El Salvador; *IXQUIC*, which cataloged the disappearances, assassinations, and death squad activities suffered by women and their families in Guatemala; *Somos* (*We Are*), the journal of AMNLAE in Nicaragua.

fem was but one of numerous journals listed from Mexico; *Mujer y Actualidad* (*Women and Reality*) took a strong feminist line in Honduras; *Noticiero de la Mujer* (*News of Women*), in Panama. In Peru, journals from areas other than Lima were appearing such as *Las mujeres de los barrios populares del Cusco* (*Women of the Barrios of Cusco*). In the Dominican Republic, journals representing a feminist perspective, *Quehaceres* (*What's Happening*) appeared alongside journals advocating national liberation such as *Mujer Adelante!* (*Women Forward!*). In addition to *La Cacerola, Ser Mujer* (*To Be Woman*) is listed from Uruguay; *La Mala Vida* (*The Bad Life*) and *Mujeres de Lucha* (*Women of the Struggle*) were in print in Venezuela. Six countries, Argentina (twenty), Brazil (twenty), Chile (twenty-one), Colombia (twelve), Mexico (twenty-four), and Peru (nineteen) account for more than 70 percent of the journals published.

The proliferation of feminist and women's journals is one indication of the spread of the ideas of the women's movement in the region; the creation of women's associations that incorporate a gendered critique into the analysis of their specific situations has been equally dynamic and is apparent in every sphere of life. Grass-roots organization along gendered lines is part of a larger picture: "Church groups, labor organizations, political action committees. Village potable water associations, communal labor arrangements, cooperatives. Youth groups, squatter associations, worker-owned businesses. Ethnic burial societies, tribal federations, microentreprenuer group credit associations. . . . In every Latin American country, such organizations pepper the social landscape, connecting the poor to each other in unprecedented ways. With widening education and the advent of mass media, new ideas and ideologies have transformed the earlier ethnic and village bases of social organization."[135]

Organizations of rural women, women factory workers, and women of the poor suburbs have long roots, and over the years they have received organizational support from the Catholic church; Mormon, Adventist, and other pentacostals; the political left; and governmental and international agencies such as AID and UNESCO.[136] But new groups arose in the 1980s; for example, in the light of the attention being paid to all areas of women's work, women domestic workers have organized on an unprecedented scale. Female domestic workers comprise the single largest category of women workers in several Latin American countries. In Uruguay, with a relatively homogeneous population, there were an estimated ninety thousand female domestics in 1984, many of whom had previously held factory jobs but been laid off as the economic crisis deepened in the mid-1980s.[137] Domestic work has always been particularly resistant to protective organization because of its isolated nature, the youth of the workers, their unfamiliarity with urban life if they are rural-to-urban migrants, and the patroness–client relationship that frequently characterizes employer–employee interactions. The emergent domestic workers organizations, begun on a local scale, received significant support from feminist organizations.

The UN World Conference in Nairobi, July 1985, was held to assess "the progress achieved and the obstacles encountered" in attaining the goals of the Decade for Women.[138] Thirteen thousand women attended, with three thousand delegates at the UN sessions and ten thousand attending the NGO forum. The emphasis at both the formal conference and the NGO forum was on strategies for the implementation of the objectives of the Decade; the NGO also explored specific issues of equality, development, peace, education, employment, and health. Claudia Hinojosa, a founder of *fem* and an innovator in feminist radio programming in Mexico, attended both the Copenhagen and Nairobi conferences. She contrasted the atmospheres of the meetings: "I think there is a much greater sensitivity to differences in Nairobi than in Copenhagen. I think that we've learned that all issues are women's issues. More and more, women are pointing out that to speak about national liberation, pacifism or new alternatives to development, we have to deal with feminism. I think this comes partly as a result of the networking that women have done since 1980, and of the incorporation of very diverse types of women into the feminist movement. . . . The voices of Third World women, women of color and working class women have been integrated into a feminist discourse."[139] Another participant observed, "Although issues like the global economic crisis and the desire for world peace have been prominent themes throughout the Decade, a broader internationalist perspective was adopted in Nairobi. It is part of a growing understanding that we are all in this together."[140]

In August 1985 the *III Encuentro Feminista Latinoamericano y del Caribe* was held in Santos, the port city of São Paulo, Brazil. The conference was attended by 950 women, of whom some 300 were Brazilian. Because most international funding available for women's conferences was directed toward Nairobi in 1985, the Brazilian women had difficulty getting financial support. An important consideration for the organizers was that most of the women who could go to Santos could not have traveled to Kenya. A grant from the Ford Foundation made one hundred fellowships available to women representatives from poor rural and suburban grass-roots organizations.

The structure of the conference was like that of Bogotá, with plenary sessions and workshops, music and dancing, in an informal atmosphere described by the *Centro Informação Mulher* (Brazilian Women's Information Center) as "four days of free and convivial communion."[141] At Santos, the acceptance of diversity, increasingly apparent in the Latin American women's movement since Lima in 1983, was explicit: the theme of the conference was "Our Feminisms." The topics addressed reflected central concerns of Brazilian feminists: violence to women, racism, communication and the arts, and feminism and institutional power. The discussion of what the relationship between the feminist movement and the state should, or could, be was of special concern to women from Brazil, Argentina, and Uruguay, who wanted the women's platform to be honored in the redemocratization process but were wary of becoming a party to governmental efforts to mobilize popular support and were suspicious of the sincerity of political leaders' professed commitment to women's issues.

The issue of racism, both in the larger society and within the women's movement itself, was brought forcibly to the attention of the conference. Brazilian feminists live in a multiracial society with a history of enslavement of indigenous and African peoples, where the quip "money whitens" describes census categorizations and the myth of Brazil as a racial democracy is the official line; they are painfully aware of their own legacy of discrimination based on class and color. In the 1930s, Pagú wrote of the triple oppression of gender, race, and poverty, and Brazilian feminists of the new women's movement continue efforts to understand their and their society's racism and to break down—or at least to point out—the burdens borne by poor women of color.[142]

But the fact that racism was a topic of discussion within the conference and that women representatives from grass-roots and *favela* organizations, many of whom are of Afro-Brazilian heritage, were participating in the discussion was lost in a blaze of devastating publicity. During the inaugural ceremonies of the meeting, a busload of poor black women from Rio de Janeiro, a journey of some eight hours, arrived at the gate of the conference facility and demanded admission to the meeting. Two of the women already had tickets; after heated discussion the conference directors said that they might elect five more to represent their group. The women refused, saying it must be all or none. When the directors did not accommodate this because of the commitment they had made to their sponsors and their wish to adhere to the idea of representative participation, the busload of women set up an "alternative" conference "outside the gates," claiming exclusion from the conference and protesting the alleged class bias of the organizers.[143]

Front-page headlines in the Brazilian press and sensational television stories denounced the feminist conference as racist and insensitive to the needs of the poor. Within the conference the situation was the subject of heated debate and nearly shipwrecked the meeting. Television cameras and newspaper reporters eagerly recorded the dramatic image of the poor women's "outside the gates" conference. Gradually, as women from the conference talked with women from the bus, it became clear that the bus had been hired by the conservative newspaper *O Jornal do Brasil*, which also controls one of the major television networks in Brazil, and had been dispatched with its occupants to Santos. Television and newspaper coverage of the staged confrontation was arranged well in advance.[144]

Efforts to disrupt women's conferences reflect the seriousness of the debate and the understanding that the stakes are high. Quite aside from the troublesome topics of sexuality, right to control over one's body (which includes the right to abortion and birth control information), pornography and its link to violent treatment of women, and rights within (and without) marriage, at its core feminism is a profound questioning of power relationships, not only between men and women but, by extension—as Latin American women have insisted repeatedly—of all patriarchal systems. Historically, feminists have been subject to attack from both the left, where the Maoist sympathies of critics like Carol Andreas locate her, and from the right, represented in the Brazilian case by the national media. In the 1920s feminist congresses were disrupted in Mexico City and their message distorted in the press; during the UN Decade, the Mexico City, Copenhagen, Lima, and Santos conferences were similarly plagued, as were meetings of the National Organization of

Women in the United States.[145] In Brazil in 1985, the serious issues raised by the conference received only perfunctory coverage, and efforts to discredit the feminist organizers in the eyes of the public succeeded.[146] The lesson to be taken is to read such denunciations with caution and beware of the implications for women and for the women's movement.

One of the first concerns of the UN Decade for Women was to gather information about women's activities—their work, their daily lives—to ensure that development programs, legislation, and so on would no longer be based on assumptions about what women needed (much less wanted) but could be based on an understanding of women's reality. Within the context of Latin America it was also necessary to ensure that programs would no longer be based on unproven assumptions about women or on assumptions constructed from a first world perspective about Latin American reality. The effort to collect and assess valid information on women was an enormous task; in the late 1980s the results are apparent, as a cornucopia of women's scholarship pours from the pens and presses of the Carlos Chagas Foundation in Brazil, GRECMU in Uruguay, Pontificia Universidad Católica del Peru, Biblioteca Politica Argentina, the Colombian Association for the Population Studies (ACEP), the Interdisciplinary Women's Studies Program at El Colegio de Mexico, to name but a few.[147] In 1985 alone the State Council on the Condition of Women in São Paulo announced eight new titles: "Nineteen-eighty-five was the close of the Women's Decade but not the end of the fight for her rights. With the intention of furthering this cause, we present this collection." The titles include *Women and Work, Women's Rights, Government Politics and the Woman, Afro-Brazilian Women, Women's Health, Women's Education, Crêches and Kindergardens,* and *Women in Movement.*[148]

The topic of women and work, whether in factories, textile mills, agricultural production, or in the household, is overwhelmingly the primary focus of most of this new scholarship. Women scholars bring to the task a respect for the abilities and concerns of all women. Although few Latin American social scientists at the time identified themselves as feminist scholars, the focus on women within a careful class analysis has nonetheless contributed to an increasingly sophisticated understanding of gender difference in a wide variety of social and economic milieus.

In the mid-1980s the new women's movement was beginning to have a visible impact at the national level in several countries. Political theorist Jane Jaquette writes: "The feminist attempt to raise women's issues, though often viewed with distrust by governments, has created a new political space in a wide variety of political systems ranging from the one-party-dominant system in Mexico, to corporatist, revolutionary, and democratizing regimes."[149] The above-mentioned São Paulo State Council on the Condition of Women was the first state-level commission, "the result of promises made by the newly-elected governor to various women's groups and feminist organizations who helped in his campaign."[150] The reference is to the elections of 1982, the gubernatorial elections that inaugurated the politics of redemocratization; the candidate was a member of MDBP, the opposition party. The city of São Paulo, which is South America's largest city, with an estimated population of 17 million, also established the first all-female police station in an effort to cope with the endemic problem of violence against women, a central concern of Brazilian feminists. São Paulo's initiative inspired the creation of similar stations across the country.[151] President José Sarney courted the support of the women's movement with the establishment in 1985 of a National Council for the Rights of Women, "to ensure that policies are enacted that end discrimination against women and facilitate their participation in the political, economic and cultural life of the country."[152]

In Mexico, during the 1988 presidential campaign, each of the major candidates put out a position statement that addressed women's issues. The statements provide an interesting litmus test of the mainstream Mexican political spectrum. *Partido Mexicano Socialista* candidate Herberto Castillo Martínez reiterated his party's century-long commitment to the equality of the sexes and to equal pay for equal work; the new note was the call for the "decriminalization of abortion," the defense of the integrity of victims of rape, and "the creation of daycare centers for the children of workers, domestic servants, and students."[153] *Frenté Democrático Nacional* candidate Cuauhtémoc Cárdenas Soloranzo, who enjoyed enormous popular support and posed a serious threat to PRI, promised to create a Secretariat of Women if elected; he was more cautious on the issue of abortion, saying that "decriminalization depends on the consensus of women themselves." Cárdenas did state that "no one can and no one should impose their own criteria on others with regard to birth control."[154]

PRI candidate Carlos Salinas de Gortari, who won the election, noted that "women constitute half the human resource of the country" and promised to work to extend the rights already guaranteed in the constitution and in law to all women and to "ensure for women of the popular sectors a better quality of education and life, better urban services, health care, and greater participation in the planning and execution of these programs." Carlos Salinas did not mention either abortion or birth control in his statement but did address the issue of sexual molestation and called for the "full weight of the law" to be brought to bear in prosecuting rape cases.[155] PAN, the traditional conservative opposition party to PRI, whose members were also traditionally antifeminist, called for "strengthening the principles and values of family life" but did recognize the existence of discrimination against women and stood for equality within the family and equal opportunity for women in the work force and in education. PAN's alliance with the Mexican Catholic church virtually precluded its candidate from endorsing birth control or the right to abortion; what is perhaps significant is that it did not issue a statement condemning such practices.

The most radical platform in terms of feminist politics was that of the *Partido Revolucionario de los Trabajadores* (Worker's Revolutionary Party): "Women encounter a situation of disadvantage, discrimination, and oppression simply by being born female. In all aspects of national life their subordination is apparent: in the home, in the streets, in the work place, in villages, in schools." PRT was also exceptional in the specificity of its recommendations. Five areas were targeted:

1. "Effective rights for women." Equal rights for rural women would give them the right to land title, credit, and technical help in their own names. All women should enjoy living conditions equal to those of men, including single mothers.

2. "End violence against women." Recommendations included the establishment of refuges for battered women with adequate medical and psychological help, protection of women under arrest from beating and rape by police, and prohibition of all types of sexual molestation and blackmail in the work place, school, barrio, and home.

3. The right to voluntary maternity. Recommendations included ending forced sterilization, sex education that focuses on personal fulfillment and is not sexist, safe contraceptives that are not dangerous to the health of the woman, the manufacture of diaphragms in Mexico, and the right to "interrupt an undesired pregnancy in hygenic conditions in state hospitals without cost."

4. Day care for all Mexican children who need it.

5. The right to organize within trade unions, rural associations, neighborhoods, and student groups and to defend their rights in every way.[156]

Griselda Alvarez, who served as the first woman governor of the state of Colima in 1979, commented that "it is a race of the tortoise and the hare: Mexican women's entry into and impact on Mexican politics is slow but constant." And if the commitment of most politicians to their platforms tends to fade once elected, the involvement of women and their male supporters in trying to bring about change does not. This is most dramatically visible at the grass-roots level; in Mexico, Brazil, Peru, Guatemala, the politics of *feminismo popular*, which may be loosely translated as grass-roots feminism, is apparent in the issues raised. For example, in Mexico, as elsewhere, female migrant workers, many of whom are indigenous women, have had little or no protection, either through law or organizational support.[157] In February, 1986, a national meeting was called to discuss the violation suffered by these women at the hands of gunmen, rural headmen, and landlords, and to call for an end to forced sterilization programs, to which many indigenous women had been subjected.

In Brazil, too, poor rural women have been among the most vulnerable to every kind of exploitation and deprivation. At the July 1986 congress of the *Central Unica dos Trabalhadores* (Workers Central Union), women were well represented and well organized. Land reform, long-promised but unrealized, was the focus of the conference. Women led the move to organize a caravan to Brasília to lobby for government recognition of their status as rural workers (approximately 12 million women rural workers make up half of the rural work force) and to call for the extension of all rights to them, including the right to possess land regardless of their marital status. At the Third National Encounter of the Landless Movement, also in 1986, women rural leaders spoke out: "Could you imagine the land occupations, the encampments, the negotiations, without women? Just a little while ago, our participation was indirect, we didn't take part in decision-making. Today, we are already on the directorates and state coordination committees. We women have the potential to become the strongest base of the Movement." [158]

Lifelong activist Magda Portal, writing of women in Peru in 1983, observed that migrant indigenous women were quicker to understand the need to organize for their rights than were most middle-sector women:

In the drama of migration, the woman plays the role of worker and defender of her rights. These women, who only recently have had contact with the capital, quickly learn that they must demand respect of their rights to be treated as human beings, and how to make a place for themselves and their families in the urban society. [But] I believe that it is not too much to say that most Peruvian women continue to be unenlightened, living as if they were underage minors, under masculine direction and subject to restrictions on their liberty, conceding to the imposition of obsolete laws which impede discovery of new horizons. Their self-identification is revealing, "Profession, Housewife." [159]

The diffusion of feminist ideas among ever-broader sectors of the population is visible in the late 1980s; what is also apparent in the Latin American context is the emergence of new issues and motifs. As a reporter for *fem* put it, "At the beginning of 1980, feminism was most engaged in the debate of the specificity of woman and relations between men and women. Then, there was the question of child care and equal salaries. Only later did we begin to speak of the personal, of our body, and of sexuality." [160] One of the most important factors in this evolution was the growing presence of lesbian women, especially at the international conferences. At the first three Latin American and Caribbean *encuentros* lesbian women participated, most openly so at the Santos meeting. Lesbian women also had a significant presence in Nairobi in 1985.

In Latin American societies the subject of lesbianism was taboo, hidden. But as the feminist movement opened up the discussion of female sexuality, lesbian women found a space to claim for themselves. From October 13 to 16,

1987, lesbian women gathered in Cuernavaca, Mexico, at the *Primer Encuentro de Lesbianas Feministas Latinoamericanas y Caribenas*. Their purpose was to establish a hemisphere-wide network to work toward breaking down the social isolation of lesbians, gain strength through solidarity, and find ways of responding to discrimination against lesbians.

The Cuernavaca meeting was timed to immediately precede the *IV Encuentro Feminista Latinoamericano y del Caribe*, which convened at Taxco, Mexico, October 19–25, 1987.[161] Fifteen hundred women attended the meeting, including a large delegation of Central American women (forty-two from Nicaragua, nine from El Salvador, ten from Honduras, and fifteen from Guatemala), most of whom had not previously participated in an international feminist conference. The Nicaraguan women were greeted with "*¡No pasaran!*" (They shall not prevail!), a shout of support for the Sandinistas and of opposition to the U.S.-backed contras. Delegates from Cuba also were present for the first time. Cuban women had been unable to obtain visas from the Peruvian government to attend in Lima in 1983, and the Brazilian government had delayed their visas until the Santos conference was over. The Cuban women entered to cries of "Cuba, Sí! Yankees, No!" which others tried to change to "Cuba, Sí! Machismo, No!"

The *IV Encuentro* was notable for the increased presence of women from grass-roots groups, including textile workers, union members, peasants, and squatter-neighborhood activists. As each delegation moved into the hall, the members spoke briefly. The Nicaraguan women said, "We fought to fight," referring to their struggle to fight beside their countrymen. Salvadoran and Honduran women claimed they were not feminists but had come to discover what feminism might offer them in their revolutionary struggles. Mayan Guatemalan women spoke of their flight into Mexico to escape the devastation and murder in their homeland and of their discomfort and embarrassment at having to put aside their traditional clothing for less conspicuous clothes ("I feel naked in pants") to avoid harassment and possible arrest by Mexican officials.[162]

The Guatemalan women put forth a petition asking for the right "to try those responsible for genocide, ethnocide and the destruction of our environment," the right to demilitarize the countryside and society in general, their right as refugees to return freely to their country under international protection with their safety guaranteed, "our right to live."[163] Violence, in all of its forms, was a recurrent theme at the conference. The Mayan women's tales were of government counterinsurgency forces acting against the populace; Colombian women called attention to the violence in their country, which claimed thousands of victims "at the hands of paramilitary bands" and held captive their "hopes of democracy, of reason, of a life of love."[164] Like the Guatemalan and Colombian women, the delegates from Haiti asked for a resolution against "torture, disappearances, and violence." Rape and sexual violence against women caught up in all conflicts, and the rape and violation to which women are subject in their daily lives, were established as a topic to be addressed at forthcoming national congresses.

The political disputes of the earlier conferences between feminists who believed the movement must be autonomous and those who believed that there could not be a feminism separate from revolution, continued at Taxco but in relatively muted tones. Two things were far more striking than any polemics: first, the acceptance of diversity—"Taxco was a reunion whose principal characteristics were diversity and the conflict and richness which came out of that diversity"[165]—and second, the many new themes raised in workshops and discussions.

Mornings were devoted to discussion of the conference theme, "The Politics of Feminism in Latin America Today." A Chilean woman spoke of the changes she had observed in the feminist movement:

Many of us are coming back, as part of a growing process, back from having been "red wing squares" or "left wing squares" with all the isms. I think that, from the most radical feminism, deeply transformative ideas have emerged. The [early feminists] gave the first kick to the soccer ball, the ball is now circulating through the field and is not always controlled by the players themselves and the score is sometimes made by people who hadn't been participating, but who suddenly succeed in passing a law, do you see? On the one hand, the feminist movement appears to be marginal but on the other, it is obvious that it has permeated everything, that language is changing. People in power can't talk about women the way they used to five or six years ago.[166]

Afternoons were filled with workshops such as: "Women, Abortion, and the Catholic Church"; "Traditional Nahuatl Medicine"; "Woman and Old Age"; "Feminism and the Ecological Movement"; "Feminism and Religion." A workshop put on by the Cuban Federation of Women (FMC) was packed, with about two hundred women in attendance. It lasted four hours; what began as a question-and-answer session developed into a heated dialogue after a Venezuelan woman asked why Cuban women had not accomplished more in the twenty-seven years since Fidel Castro came to power. The Cuban women admitted that they had a long way to go: "The popular culture is as *machista* as in any Latin American culture. Our discourse with respect to the problem of woman is changing, advancing and deepening; we have to work with reality and to break down old forms and open new roads. The Cuban Revolution is not a finished process, no more than feminism is."[167]

Proposals that emerged from the workshops included ones to "include a feminist theology in liberation theology," to decriminalize abortion and "alleviate the guilt of the thousands of Christian women in Latin America who have to resort to abortion," to systematize information about women in women's studies centers, and to create health clinics for women. With regard to feminist politics, it was resolved "to combat the Marxist conception that feminism is a bourgeois aberration" and "to nourish a more open definition of feminism which will encompass both personal and group experiences."[168]

The conference concluded with declarations that invoked the hopes of the women: "If Women Are Not Present, Democracy Is Not There!" and "Somos Todos Feministas!" "We are all feminists!" A series of regional and national conferences was planned. Three international feminist congresses are scheduled to take place in 1990. One, held in the Dominican Republic, enabled more Caribbean women to participate. A second, lesbian conference was held in Costa Rica, and the Quinto Encuentro Feminista Latinoamericana y del Caribe convened in Argentina in November in celebration of the role women have taken in redemocratization in that country.

# 8. Conclusion

Queremos democracia en el país y en la casa.
—Slogan of the feminist movement in Chile.[1]

"We want democracy in the nation and in the home." The slogan of the Chilean women's movement cited by Adriana Santa Cruz, editor of the influential inter-American feminist journal *Mujer*, reflects the confluence of the two central themes of the contemporary women's movement in Latin America: the push for political, economic and social equity for women as well as men in the national community and the desire for a reworking of the domestic configurations that for so long have kept women subordinate within family and society.

In March 1990 the Pinochet regime, in power in Chile since the bloody overthrow of President Salvador Allende in 1973, bowed to the referendum that bound it to step aside in favor of an elected civilian government. For the first time in a quarter of a century the reins of government in all of the nations of southern South America—Brazil, Argentina, Uruguay, Paraguay, and Chile—rest in the hands of men elected to the presidency. In Nicaragua the March 1990 elections ousted President Ortega and the Sandinistas from office in favor of a centrist coalition, UNO, headed by Violeta Chamorro, widow of a martyr of the anti-Somoza struggles. Democracy, at least democracy interpreted as a respect for electoral politics, was on the upswing *en el país*, in the nations of Latin America as well as in Eastern Europe and the Soviet Union. However, it is important to realize that for most people in most of Latin America, hopes for truly representative and participatory democracy and greater social justice are deeply imperiled by economic conditions and ingrained cultural, political, and social attitudes.

Political

In Latin America, the women's movement of the early twentieth century as well as of the contemporary period arose as part of a critique of politics as usual. This is true of both reformist and revolutionary strands of the movement. The examination of the recent history of the women's movement in Latin America shows the integration of the ideas of the reformist women and revolutionary women. During the 1970s the equal-rights stance of the reformist feminists was permeated by the demands for social justice by the women of the political left; in the 1980s women activists' resistance to the ideological orthodoxy of the political left succeeded in bringing to bear a feminist critique of revolutionary practice. This resulted in a new, gendered understanding of Latin American reality, which is apparent in the debates on redemocratization.

Women active in the women's movements in Latin America were leaders in the redemocratization efforts in Chile, Brazil, Uruguay, Argentina, and Paraguay. There are parallels between the meaning of *revindication*, the term commonly used to describe the women's movement's efforts to gain social justice for women, and the meaning conveyed by the term *redemocratization*. Through the use of the prefix *re-* (again), the sense of a right or condition that once existed but was taken away and must now be reconquered is intensified: "Redemocratization implies that democracy existed before, that what is sought is a return to democracy. It suggests far more than the replacement of military governments by elected officials. The term implies deep, often agonizing appraisals of national character. In every country, it raises intense debate over economic vs. political democracy. And in those countries where grass roots organizations have spent years fighting for democracy, it raises an obvious question: What next? What is the role of popular participation in democratic civil society?"[2]

One of the visible measures of the degree of success of the equal rights movement—as distinct from the women's movement—has traditionally been the number of women who have achieved political office. This is a questionable measure in any political context, as the ability to be elected or appointed usually means that the woman identifies with her male-dominated party, not as a woman, much less as a feminist. However, women concerned with women's issues—divorce, abortion, protection from domestic violence—are making their voices heard and winning male allies in the legislatures of a number of countries, notably Mexico and Brazil. In Cuba women hold more than 30 percent of the seats in the national legislature, though in no other country in the Western Hemisphere do they hold more than 20 percent.

Another presumed gauge of women's increased status is the presence of a female head of state. Again, who the woman is, how she came to power, and what her alliances are must be assessed, as they would be for any political leader. In the spring of 1990, Violeta Chamorro was elected Nicaragua's "first woman president," and Ertha Pascal-Trouillot was named provisional president in Haiti, Haiti's "first woman head of state." Both women were compromise candidates. Both women have the proper credentials in terms of being associated with opposition to reviled former dictatorships: Chamorro's husband was assassinated by Somoza's henchmen, and Pascal-Trouillot's brother was permanently paralyzed in an attack by "Baby Doc" Duvalier's brutal Ton-Tons Macoutes. Both share upper-middle-class backgrounds. Chamorro heads a coalition that includes former contras as well as democratic liberals; she is a symbol, a woman who has lost her man, as so many Nicaraguan women have lost their husbands and sons and fathers in the bloody, prolonged civil war. Pascal-Trouillot is also the choice of an opposition coalition, the Unity Assembly, selected primarily because each of the Haitian men put forward as possible candidates was unacceptable to one faction or another. She is constrained to rule with an advisory state council composed of civic, church, labor, and rights groups as well as a representative from the military, and her term is limited to six months. Chamorro's authority is legitimated by victory in the most closely watched elections in historical memory; Pascal-Trouillot, placed in office by the military, does not share that authority, though the presence of the broadly based state council is an attempt to legitimate her presidency. At this juncture, neither Chamorro nor Pascal-Trouillot has control of the national military; both face a rocky political road.

It is possible to dismiss Chamorro and Pascal-Trouillot as figureheads, chosen as spokeswomen for their parties precisely because they are not perceived by the men around them as able to wield true political power. Of the two, Ertha Pascal-Trouillot is perhaps the more interesting in terms of the history of the women's movement in Latin America. She was the first and only woman on the Haitian Supreme Court, appointed in 1986, after the fall of Baby Doc. Pascal-Trouillot's assignment is to prepare Haiti for national elections, "to clean the face of Haiti." Given the volatile state of politics on the impoverished island, she faces a difficult if not impossible mission. At her inauguration she spoke alternately in French and Creole to make clear her hope to speak for all Haitians, regardless of class and racial background. Although Pascal-Trouillot is being characterized as having "a reputation for political independence," there is little equivocation about her commitment to women's issues. Two years after graduating from law school she published *The Judicial Status of Haitian Women in Social Legislation* (1973), and in the ensuing years she campaigned for equal economic and political status for women in an atmosphere in which it was illegal for a married woman or a woman under thirty to so much as open a bank account or buy property without her husband's or male guardian's written approval.

Ertha Pascal-Trouillot and the Haitian women who worked with her to improve women's status received scant support from the corrupt Duvalier administration, but they did garner support for their work from CIM and the network of Latin American and Caribbean women represented in the *en-*

cuentros feministas of the 1980s.[3] Her early work for equal rights was typical of
the initial engagement of women of her privileged background and education
in the contemporary women's movement. Like the women's movement, her
mature work shows evidence of a much more broad-based concern for the
plight of all women, and men, in her beleaguered homeland. In March 1990,
almost exactly sixty years after the decisive demonstration by Haitian women
against the occupation of Haiti by United States Marines, Pascal-Trouillot
took the oath of office in the Champs du Mars, standing beside the statue of
Dessalines, hero of Haitian Independence, declaring "I accept this heavy task
in the name of Haitian women."[4] On February 7, 1991, the Unity Assembly,
of which Pascal-Trouillot was the nominal head, turned over power to the
newly elected president, Father Jean-Bertrand Aristide.

Economic

Inflation—2300 percent in Brazil in 1989, 4924 percent in Argentina—and
the constraints of international indebtedness over the last decade have exacerbated the problems of the poorest of the poor, making their lives yet more
desperate, and have pushed the middle sectors ever closer to poverty as their
earnings evaporate in their pockets. Socioeconomic divisions within national
populations are even more pronounced. The Inter-American Development
Bank has dubbed the 1980s Latin America's "Lost Decade," in which the per
capita gross domestic product for the region fell 8 percent.

In such circumstances the effect of fifteen years of insistence on the consideration of women's specific needs in development programs and grass-
roots organizations is not always what might be expected or hoped for. Latin
American scholars have coined the term "superexploitation" to describe the
effect of hyperinflation and national indebtedness on the daily lives of women.
Payment on foreign debt and its interest has resulted in a steady transfer of
resources away from Latin American countries to Europe, Japan, and the
United States in the 1980s, with a concomitant inability to finance the domestic investment necessary to revitalize national economies. Most, if not all,
Latin American nations have adopted structural adjustment policies—that is,
wage and price indexes and currency revaluations—in their efforts to make
scheduled payments on international loans. ISIS International puts it thus,
"The policies of structural adjustment are based on a deeply gendered ideology which simultaneously minimizes the value of the tasks necessary for social
reproduction (women's traditional roles) while promoting a pattern of economic growth based on exploitation (often by multinational corporations) of
the socio-economic vulnerabilities of a female population which bears major
responsibility for both nurturance and financial support of children."[5]

Ironically, years of pointing out the importance of women in the economic life of third world countries appears to have convinced governments that women will devise a means to survive without special attention: "In the name of 'efficiency' governments are now prepared to save money on services in the confidence that the women will somehow cope."[6] UNICEF analysts describe the process as "the invisible adjustment," in which "the present crisis of social disinvestment is being financed principally from the resources of a 'social fund' provided by the superhuman efforts of poor women" to support themselves and their children.[7] The burden once again falls on the poorest of the poor—in Latin America an estimated 130 million women and children. The problems described so eloquently by Carolina María de Jesús as she tried to deal with the devastating effects of inflation on her daily life in 1960 persist.

Another undesired effect of prioritizing the needs of poor women in development projects is the degree to which women have been pushed to the front by community groups in order to gain funds and then were disregarded. Elvia Alvarado described the situation in her region of Honduras: "All the campesino organizations say they're organizing women. All of them have a position in the leadership for 'women's affairs.' But what happens with most of these women's groups is that they're really created to get international funding."[8] In these circumstances, women are able to wield little influence over spending or policy; they are the means to an end. Alvarado emphasizes that the people she works with in the land recovery movement teach women to organize on behalf of their own interests as well as the interest of the community.

The personal consequences for many of the individual women who become involved in grass-roots movements are also not always expected. A few, like Elvia Alvarado, Domitila Barrios de Chungara,[9] and Quiché-Guatemalan Rigoberta Menchú[10] have, through the auspices of the international women's movement and human rights networks, become renowned spokeswomen for their people and their causes and have traveled far beyond their local communities. For many others, heavy involvement in organizational activity, attendance at meetings, demonstrations, and adult literacy classes brings strains to bear on their relationships with their male partners. A Mexican woman working among poor urban women acknowledged, "When women become very active, problems between men and women definitely increase. Frequently a separation occurs." The result is a catch-22: If the woman decides to stay within the relationship, she will cut back or cease her organizational involvement; if she leaves the relationship, she will usually have to devote all of her time to finding support for her family.[11]

A further threat to the viability of popular political organizations comes from the church. Activist sectors of the Catholic church, in the hierarchy and at the grass-roots level, are currently under strong pressure from the Vatican to depoliticize their work. In Brazil, birthplace of liberation theology, the great human rights cardinal Dom Helder retired in 1989; in his stead Pope John Paul II named José Cardoso Sobrinho, who has denied liberation theologians access to leadership positions, forbidden them to televise their services, and is overseeing the effort to discontinue base communities, recloister nuns, and return priests to seminaries. Author Penny Lernoux dubbed the changes "a counter-reformation,"[12] designed to reassert the centrality of the European church. The struggle the church now faces in Latin America is not so much against communism or even secularism as it is against evangelical Protestantism, which has made hundreds of thousands of converts throughout the hemisphere in the 1980s. What this portends for women is yet to be seen, but both Eurocentric Catholicism and fundamentalist Protestantism have highly conservative and restrictive views of womanhood, defining women primarily in terms of their maternal role. Even during the ascension of liberation theology, Catholic doctrine never altered: it was through praxis, the practice of Freirian pedagogy, building of base communities, literacy campaigns, commitment of women religious to work directly with the poor instead of through charitable foundations, that women found community, self-realization, and political *sombra* within the church.

The Latin American Women's Movement and the International Women's Movement

In 1990 the Latin American women's movement is distinguished by several characteristics. The emphasis on individual fulfillment that characterized the mainstream women's movement in the United States in the 1970s and early 1980s remains muted in the Latin American context. In Latin America there developed a politics of conscientization, in which women sought to awaken one another's awareness and understanding of their specific historical situation while providing the analytic tools and organizational modes to participate in the transformation of social conditions. The women's attempts to raise public consciousness about the circumstances of women merged with the attempt—by socialists, liberal reformers, liberation theologians, revolutionaries such as the Tupamaros—to raise public consciousness about the plight of the poor. The fusion of a radical critique of economic, political, and social injustice with a gendered analysis has resulted in a syncretic understanding that has transformed both feminism and the politics of social change in Latin America and has deeply influenced the global women's movement.

Historically, the transnational arena has been an important means of bringing pressure to bear on national and local governments by women's groups in Latin America that found little official support at home. What has changed most notably is that the transnational arena is no longer the exclusive domain of upper- and middle-class women but has become a forum for women of all classes. This is apparent in the new organization of domestic workers of Latin America and the Caribbean, which met for the first time in Bogotá, Colombia, in 1988,[13] and in the creation of the International Day Against Violence Against Women.

Violence against women, in all of its forms, is a central concern of the contemporary women's movement in Latin America. At the *IV Encuentro Feminista* in Taxco, Mexico, in 1987, the resolution to observe an International Day Against Violence Against Women was formalized. November 25 was selected, in commemoration of six Dominican peasant women who suffered tortured deaths for resisting sexual violation by military troops. The *encuentro* resolution was intended to protest violence against women as perpetrated by the state as well as violence against women in the home. In the past three years, since the proclamation of the International Day Against Violence Against Women, thousands of women have gathered in public squares across Latin America to show their solidarity on this issue. It is a quintessential expression of Latin American feminism as it has evolved: the use—in this case, the creation—of an official, international event to make a statement in the local arena, to gather a bit of political *sombra*. Protesting state violence is a dangerous act in Guatemala, to give but one egregious example. But November 25 is also a protest against the violence women experience on a daily basis in their homes at the hands of the men with whom they share their lives, and it is a protest against the tolerance by public officials of rape and domestic battery. In Brazil it has been used to denounce the customary "right" (albeit illegal) of men to kill wives suspected of infidelity.

In instituting the International Day Against Violence Against Women, Latin American feminists did not attempt to separate public from private, national politics from domestic concerns. Their activism obviates neat distinctions between what is "feminist"—a gendered understanding of women's position within the family, for example—and the gendered expression of a larger political issue, in this case, violent political repression by the state. The blending of the political activism of women of the political left with the gendered analysis of feminists has produced a feminist expression that is profoundly ethical, from the women's demonstrations against state violence against the populace—expressed in women's voices, echoes of the mothers' movements—to the protests against the day-to-day violence women experience because they are women.

A second example of the contemporary use of the transnational arena by Latin American women may be seen in the creation of an international network of domestic workers' organizations (*Organizaciónes de Trabajadores del Hogar de America Latina y Caribe.*) The evolution of household workers' unions also demonstrates the linkage between church-supported organizational efforts among marginal workers and the international women's movement. Household workers constitute as much as 20 percent of the working female population in many Latin American countries, and they are historically among the most isolated of workers. Generally, they are young female migrants to the cities, differentiated from their employers by their background, ethnicity, speech patterns, and dress, and they are vulnerable to every kind of abuse. They have had little defense against exploitation. In the mid-1960s, several Catholic social agencies located in urban areas undertook programs to alleviate the problem, generally reaching the girls through church meetings or church-sponsored night classes, which employers were encouraged—by the church—to allow their maids to attend.

Peruvian household worker Adelinda Díaz Uriarte describes her initial encounter with the movement and tells how the priests managed to stay within their prescribed nonpolitical boundary: "We were advised by Father Alejandro Cussianovich. I owe a lot to these persons [the Catholic advisors] because they taught me much about our reality. They led me and other *compañeras* to take the step toward organizing household workers in unions. As part of a church movement, they were not allowed to get involved in the defense of workers' rights, but the union could, because we ourselves were the ones who led it." [14]

In 1984 representatives from household workers' unions in Latin America and the Caribbean were invited to participate in a Latin American Studies Association conference in Mexico City. From that meeting came international support and funding to convene the continent-wide meeting of female domestic workers in Bogotá, March 24–28, 1988. Their rallying cry is "It is not enough to have rights unless you have the understanding (*conciencia*) to organize to defend them" (*"No basta hay tener derechos hay que tener conciencia hay que organizarse para defenderlas"*).[15] The reference is to the fact that there are laws on the books in virtually every country regulating the wages, working hours, health conditions, and the like, of household workers, but they have been universally unenforced. This is, of course, but one of many spheres in which the gap between de jure recognition of rights and de facto recognition persists. It is the hope of the organizers of local household workers' unions that by organizing at the international level they can envision problems in a regional way, identify areas of common concern that cross national borders, and, in time-honored fashion among Latin American women's groups, use the international forum to bring attention to issues within their local and national communities.

A third way in which the international women's movement has been important to Latin American women is by serving as a forum for the debate of issues that might not, for various reasons, be easily raised at the local or national level. For example, although Latin American women insisted on incorporating a class analysis into the discussion of women's issues (as was discussed in chapter 7, the initial challenge by women involved in resistance movements to the formal women's movement was articulated by Domitila Barrios de Chungara at the UN International Women's Year conference in Mexico City in 1975), they were often insensitive to issues of race and ethnicity. Only very recently has there been a consistent effort to confront racism within their own communities, most notably in Brazil. The international women's conferences provide a long-established forum for continuing discussions among women from vastly different backgrounds in Latin America.

Characteristic of the contemporary women's movement in Latin America is its political intent. By and large, feminist groups arose outside of official institutions and, as is evident in the chapters on revolution and counterrevolution and redemocratization, were generally aligned with the forces of opposition—in Chile, opposition to Pinochet; in Brazil, Argentina, Uruguay, and Paraguay, with the forces of redemocratization in opposition to the military regimes.

Typically, the feminist perspective has emanated from independent research groups, such as GRECMU in Uruguay and the Centro de Flora Tristán in Peru, and spoken through alternative publications such as *Caçerola*, *Mujer*/Fempress, *fem*. In 1990 there is evidence that these formerly independent entities are moving into official relationships with educational institutions and governmental bodies. The Interdisciplinary Program for Women's Studies (PIEM, Programa Interdisciplinario de Estudios de la Mujer) at El Colegio de Mexico presents an interesting example. Several of the women now associated with PIEM were involved in founding *fem*, one of the earliest and most influential of alternative feminist journals in the hemisphere.

Their influence is clear in the projects undertaken by PIEM. In the wake of the catastrophic earthquake of 1985, PIEM got funds from UNICEF to gather information to demonstrate the absolutely crucial role of women in reconstructing neighborhoods and sustaining family groups.[16] Two points are striking: raising the question of women's role and the immediate recognition of the contributions of the women of Mexico City to the resuscitation of their communities. This is a measure of the depth and swiftness with which a gendered understanding of events has penetrated public awareness. For nearly two decades scholars and activists have painstakingly reexamined every field of human endeavor to reconquer—*reivindicar*—a space for women in history, literature, psychology, science, politics, health care—the list is inclusive. The PIEM project was not a retrieval of information or a gendered rethinking of a long-held proposition. It was an immediate, almost simultaneous response to the earthquake that proclaimed: We now know that the female experience will be different from that of her male counterpart, and we now know that experience has importance and impact beyond the individual woman, that it has political significance within the local and the national community.

Second, the PIEM project involved women of the barrios from the first, not only as describers of their experience but as analysts of what had been effective for them in organizing salvage efforts and sustaining their families. There are significant class differences between the women intellectuals who form PIEM and women of the districts whose homes were most severely damaged in the earthquake. In the past the relationship between the women could easily have been a charitable one of donor and recipient: the patrona distributing aid to the victims of a disaster. This was not the spirit of the PIEM project. The presumption is that each group of women has things of value to exchange with one another and that the process will be one of conscientization for all involved.[17] In this effort the ideals of the 1968 student movement are apparent, but through the introduction of a gendered analysis they have taken on more deeply nuanced understandings of class and race as well.

What the consequences will be for institutionalization of feminist groups remains to be seen. Unlike feminist groups, women's groups have long been organized and mobilized on behalf of governments and political parties; in the present context, many of these "women's sections" have taken on self-awareness of their own. Perhaps the most patriotic women's movements— in the sense of identifying most strongly with the national project—have emerged in Mexico, Cuba, and Sandinista Nicaragua, though even in these intensely nationalist milieus it is difficult to reconcile a feminist understanding and analysis with clearly patriarchal governmental structures and practices. In fact, what frequently occurs within officially linked women's groups may be quite contrary to governmental intentions. For example, the Sandinista government in Nicaragua organized women into committees for the defense of the revolution (GDRs). Their purpose was to broadcast the ideals of the revolution and to serve as watchers within their communities. A U.S. colleague visiting with women members of the GDRs in the mid-1980s discovered that the groups had become a network for the distribution of information on birth control, abortion, self-examination, and other practices central to women's health care and exceedingly difficult to come by through regular channels in pre- or post-Somoza Nicaragua. A tattered copy of *Our Bodies, Our Selves* had been Xeroxed, hand-copied, and reproduced by every means available. At the community level, the GDRs had transformed themselves into women's self-help groups.[18]

Democracy in the Country and in the Home

"Democracy in the country and in the home" expresses the aspirations of the contemporary women's movements in Latin America. Redemocratization, understood as a profound reassessment of economic and political participation, is a halting, uneven process that rests precariously on the willingness of the military to stay out of the political process and the ability of the civilian governments to cope with problems of inflation, health care, stagnant economies.

The ideals of *democracia en el país* and *democracia en la casa* emerge from different aspects of the women's movement.[19] If women of the political left can be credited with forcing open the narrow equal rights perspective of the early stages of the contemporary women's movement in Latin America, the push for "democracy in the home" is rooted in the reformist, or bourgeois, feminism of the middle classes. Feminist analysis and critiques of the domestic unit, seen as divisive by working class women in the past, have now been widely absorbed. A recent editorial in *Mujer*/Fempress opened with the assertion that "a striking trend among recently formed feminist groups is the attempt to address the most basic social problems . . . and to insist on a feminist stance, despite the initial resistance of women of these organizations and of the *favelas* to the term feminist."[20]

In Argentina, Nené Reynoso, founder of The Women's Library (Liberia de la Mujer), describes the persistent spread of feminist ideas in a situation of profound political and economic fragmentation:

Feminism in Argentina does not consist of a strong movement which develops permanent projects, but is made up of individuals, women from diverse parts of the social spectrum, with fragile ties to institutions and groups which disappear and regroup in order to confront specific situations as they arise. It is surprising that despite this weak structure many of our ideas have become part of the social conscience: they have permeated political discourse, the institutions of state, the world of culture, the university, the media. Nevertheless, we must recognize that this does not translate into the conversion of the majority of women to our position. There is a gap between the organic development of the movement and the diffusion of its ideas.[21]

In the present atmosphere of economic crisis, efforts to revise deeply gendered social and cultural attitudes are jeopardized. The ostensible gains of the women's movement—political citizenship for women, a focus on the double burden of poor women, greater access to schooling for girls, labor regulations that take women's work into account—are under constant threat of erosion. Identification of "the invisible adjustment" made by women as a key element that makes it possible for governments to meet international debt payments shows that a gendered understanding of poverty has emerged in the last decade, but the use to which that understanding has been put demonstrates that caring for poor, usually ethnically different women and their children is still regarded as an expendable luxury by governments.

Feminism in Latin America is not and never has been a single expression or ideology. Historically, there are multiple and contested expressions of feminism. The first editorial in *Feminaria*, an Argentine journal that began publication in 1988, catches the spirit: *"Feminaria* is feminist but is not limited to one concept of feminism." [22] Nevertheless, in its multiplicity feminism is a force in the politics of inclusion and the practice of conscientization, an essential part of the continuing search for social justice.

"We want democracy in the nation and in the home." True democracy, in which the power of governance is vested in all of the people, as distinct from any class or individuals privileged by gender, race, class, hereditary rights, or military strength, is yet to be fully realized in any area of the world. Elections are a symbolic step toward realization of this ideal. True democracy in the *patria* is a radical vision but perhaps not as radical as the concept of democracy in the home. Yet in the 1980s there was a growing recognition that for women, as Elvia Alvarado puts it, "our struggle has to begin in the home." [23]

The focus of this work is on the role of women in the impetus toward change that envisions a fuller empowerment of all people within a society. From the wars of independence to the present, women have articulated their desire to fully participate, at times utilizing whatever vehicle seemed to offer the best opportunity to do so and at other times creating their own means of expression, most clearly visible as the women's movements of the nineteenth and twentieth centuries. The struggle to be included in a full definition of the human ultimately demands that all people, male and female, of all backgrounds must be included in the polity. With this understanding, women are not coincidental to but vital to redemocratization if it is to prove viable, and they are central to overcoming seemingly implacable social and economic problems. In this effort the importance of collective memory, of bearing witness, of knowing the history of women cannot be underestimated.

Notes

Introduction (pp. xiii–xv)

1. From a speech in Bucaramanga, Santander, Colombia, November 25, 1965.
2. For discussion of Temma Kaplan's work on this topic, see Chapter 1.
3. Gerda Lerner, *The Creation of Patriarchy* (New York, Oxford: Oxford University Press, 1986), 3. Lerner also reminds us that although many groups of people, male and female, have been ignored in historical accounts, "no man has been excluded from the historical record because of his sex, yet all women were" (p. 5).

1. Women, History, and Creating a New Historical Record (pp. 1–13)

1. Words and music by Holly Near (Hereford Music, 1978).
2. re. US involvement in creating the "culture of terror": Robert MacNamara, U.S. secretary of defense, before Congress, 1963: "Our primary objective in Latin America is to aid, wherever necessary, the continual growth of the military and paramilitary forces, so that together with the police and other security forces they may provide the necessary internal security." The report of Argentine President Raúl Alfonsin's National Commission on the Disappeared, "Nunca Mas," explored "the doctrine behind the repression." Its authors quote one of the heads of the Argentine junta, General Leopoldo Galtieri, who in 1981 said that "the First World War was a confrontation between armies; the Second was between nations, and the Third is between ideologies. The United States and Argentina must stand together because of their common aspirations and concerns"; quoted in Lawrence Weschler, "A Miracle, A Universe," *The New Yorker*, 1 June 1987, pp. 84–85.
3. The exploration of the meaning of *las madres* was informed and inspired by Jean Franco's analysis of the mothers' movements in her working paper, "Gender, Death, and Resistance." See also Jean Franco, "Killing Priests, Nuns, Women and Children," in Marshall Blonsky, ed., *On Signs* (Baltimore: Johns Hopkins University Press, 1985).
4. Luisa Valenzuela, "Making Love Visible: The Women of Buenos Aires," *Vogue*, 174 (May 1984), 344–45.
5. Ariel Dorfman, "Mother's Day," *New York Times*, 7 May 1977.
6. *New York Times*, 30 March 1930, p. 1.
7. *New York Times*, 30 March 1930, p. 1.
8. Elinor Burkett explores this concept in her article "Indian Women and White Society: The Case of Sixteenth Century Peru," in *Latin American Women: Historical Perspectives*, Asunción Lavrin, ed. (Westport, Conn., Greenwood Press, 1978).

9. Quoted in Hubert Herring, *A History of Latin America from the Beginnings to the Present*, 3rd ed. (New York: Knopf, 1968), p. 426.

10. The recommendations of the Hoover Commission on its return to Washington "in favor of the restoration of the Independence of the Negro Republic" were an almost verbatim adoption of the recommendations made in *Occupied Haiti*, a report edited by Emily Green Balch ("Being the report of a Committee of Six disinterested Americans representing organizations exclusively American, who, having personally studied conditions in Haiti in 1926, favor the restoration of the Independence of the Negro Republic") (New York: The Writers Publishing Co., 1927). The Committee of Six was constituted by the Women's International League for Peace and Freedom (WILPF), which was "asked by certain of its Haitian members to look into conditions in Haiti" at the meeting of the WILPF International Executive Committee in July 1925. Members of the committee included "two members of the United States WILPF, two representative colored women, a professor of economics representing the Foreign Service Committee of the Society of Friends, and a representative of the Fellowship of Reconciliation."

11. Elena Poniatowska, *Massacre in Mexico* (New York: Viking Press, 1972) 317.

12. Ibid., 319–21. Note that November 1 is All Soul's Day, celebrated in Mexico as the Day of the Dead.

13. Ibid., 322.

14. Franco, "Gender, Death, and Resistance."

15. Ibid.

16. Ibid.

17. Elizabeth Jelin, *Los movimientos sociales en la Argentina contemporeana* (Buenos Aires: Centro Editor de América Latina, 1985.

18. Ibid.

19. Valenzuela, "Making Love Visible."

20. Quoted in *New York Times*, 12 Sept. 1977, p. 22.

21. Dorfman, "Mother's Day."

22. *New York Times*, 1 May 1981.

23. An eerie earlier instance of an Argentine military junta deliberately hiding a body exists in the strange fate of Eva Perón's embalmed remains after the overthrow of Juan Perón in 1955. Her body had been preserved with great care and was being stored in the headquarters of the Confederación General del Trabajo (CGT) pending the completion of a memorial monument. Upon discovering this fact, the military leaders of the junta were terrified that news of her whereabouts would become public and that any grave site or known storage place for her body would become a shrine to Perónism. Two attempts to bury her in an unmarked grave failed; then Carlos Eugenio Moori Koenig, head of military intelligence, was put in charge of the remains, with strict instructions not to mutilate the corpse in any way (a concern both that such an action might become public and a concession to the strong Catholicism of President Arramburu). After being on the fourth floor of the military intelligence building for over a year, the body was turned over to Father Rotger, an Argentine priest, for secret burial. See Nicholas Fraser and Marysa Navarro, *Eva Perón* (London: Andre Deutsch, 1980) esp. the chapters "Death and Its Public" and "The Body and the Myth." The intertwinings of the meaning of the body in Catholic practice and the very real possibility that if the men were perceived to have harmed or in any way desecrated the corpse they would be publicly reviled underline the heinousness of the crimes committed during the *proceso* and the need of the military to "disappear" their victims.

24. Franco, "Gender, Death and Politics," quoting Michael Taussig.

25. Ibid.

26. Lawrence Weschler, "A Miracle, A Universe," *The New Yorker*, 1 June 1987, pp. 84–85.

27. The Amnesty International report *Torture in the Eighties* lists more than sixty nations in which "torture has become a banal bureaucratic practice."

28. Quoted on "All Things Considered," National Public Radio, 10 Mar. 1985.

29. Gerda Lerner, *The Creation of Patriarchy* (New York: Oxford University Press, 1986).

2. Precursoras (pp. 14–34)

1. Quoted in Magda Portal, *Flora Tristán, Precursora.* (Lima: Editorial la Equidad, 1983), 12.

2. Jean Hawkes, *Flora Tristán: Peregrinations of a Pariah, 1833–1834* (London: Virago Press, 1986), ix.

3. Portal, *Flora Tristán*, 11.

4. Ibid. For another example of the way in which Tristán's ideas have been used as exemplary by the contemporary women's movement in Peru, see opening quote in Teresa Burga and Marie-France Cathelat, *Perfil de la mujer Peruana 1980–1981* (Lima: Editorial Ausonia, 1981).

5. For example, in the text *The People and Politics of Latin America* (Boston: Ginn and Company, 1930), Mary Wilhelmine Williams opens her discussion of "The Aborigine People" with this quote: "World wrongly called new! This clime was old when first the Spaniard came, in search of gold" (p. 17). Williams's chapter on Cortés in Mexico and Pizarro in Peru is titled "The Hispanic Invasion of Aboriginal America." Her perceptions were likely shaped by her own feminism and lifelong commitment to the principles espoused by the Women's International League for Peace and Freedom (WILPF). For further discussion of WILPF, see chaps. 4 and 5, this text. Williams's text went through three editions and was the most widely used text on Latin American history in the United States between 1930 and 1952. Williams (1878–1944) tended to be firmly on the side of the formerly colonized peoples of the hemisphere and held anti-Catholic, anti-Spanish (though not anti-Portuguese) sentiments. The rights of people to national self-determination and the rights of nations large and small were central principles in her political thinking. See Francesca Miller, "Precedent and Pedagogy: Teaching the History of Women in Latin America," *Women's Studies Quarterly*, 43 (October 1986).

6. James D. Henderson and Linda Roddy Henderson, *Ten Notable Women of Latin America* (Chicago: Nelson-Hall, 1978), xiii.

7. To gain a sense of the richness and diversity of the new literature available in the field, see K. Lynn Stoner, *Latinas of the Americas: A Source Book* (New York and London: Garland Publishing, 1989).

8. Burr C. Brundage, *Encyclopedia of Latin America*, 109.

9. Elinor C. Burkett, "Indian Women and White Society: The Case of Sixteenth Century Peru," in *Latin American Women: Historical Perspectives*, ed. Asunción Lavrin (Westport, Conn.: Westview Press, 1978), 102.

10. Norma Alarcón, "Chicana's Feminist Literature: A Re-vision Through Malinche/or Malintzin: Putting Flesh Back on the Object," in *This Bridge Called My Back: Writings by Radical Women of Color*, ed. Cherríe Moraga and Gloria Anzaldúa (New York: Kitchen Table: Women of Color Press, 1981), 182.

11. Adalzira Bittencourt, *A mulher Paulista na história* (Rio de Janeiro: Livros de Portugal, 1954), 17.

12. The concept of *limpieza pura* is complex and was redefined over time. At the time of contact, girls of the Inca nobility were highly prized for their ancestry and title to land and wealth.

13. Cesareo Fernández Duro, *La mujer Espanola en Indias: Disertación ante la Reál Academia de la Historia* (Madrid, 1902), 179. As mentioned above, Hernando Cortés's more famous liaison was with Malinche, with whom he had two children and without whose aid he would likely have failed in his effort to conquer Mexico.

14. Ibid.

15. Ibid.

16. Ibid., 173.

17. Ibid., 165–173, passim.

18. Ibid.

19. Ibid.

20. Ibid., 183.

21. June Hahner, ed., *Women in Latin American History: Their Lives and Views*, rev. ed. (Los Angeles: UCLA Latin American Center, 1980), 27.

22. Ibid.

23. Duro, *La mujer Espanola en las Indias*, 183.

24. Marietta Morrisey, *Slave Women in the New World: Gender Stratification in the Caribbean*, Lawrence: University Press of Kansas, 1989.

25. Mary Karasch, *Slave Life in Rio de Janeiro 1808–1850* (Princeton, N.J.: Princeton University Press, 1987), 4.

26. David G. Sweet and Gary B. Nash, eds., *Struggle and Survival in Colonial Latin America* (Berkeley: University of California Press, 1981).

27. Della Flushe and Eugene Korth, *Forgotten Females: Women of African and Indian Descent in Colonial Chile, 1535–1800* (Detroit: Baine Etheridge Books, 1982), v.

28. Historians Edith Couturier and Asunción Lavrin have made significant contributions to our understanding of the history of women in colonial Latin America. For example, Edith Couturier and Asunción Lavrin, "Dowries and Wills: A View of Women's Socioeconomic Role in Colonial Guadalajara and Puebla, 1640–1790," *Hispanic American Historical Review*, 59 (May 1979): 280–304. On upperclass women, see also Doris Ladd, *Mexican Women in Anahuac and New Spain: Aztec Roles, Spanish Notary Revelations, Creole Genius*. (Austin: University of Texas Institute of Latin American Studies, 1979).

29. Sor Juana Inés de la Cruz, *Carta atemagorica: Respuesta a Sor Filotea*, cited in Emilie Bergmann, "Dreaming in a Double Voice," *Women, Culture and Politics* (Berkeley and Los Angeles: University of California Press, 1990), 90.

30. Octavio Paz, *Sor Juana*, trans. Maragret Sayers Peden (Cambridge, Mass.: The Belknap Press of Harvard University Press, 1988) 3.

31. Seminar on Feminism and Culture in Latin America, "Introduction," in *Women, Culture and Politics in Latin America* (Berkeley and Los Angeles: University of California Press, 1990), 1.

32. Emilie Bergmann, "Sor Juana Inés de la Cruz: Dreaming in a Double Voice," *Women, Culture and Politics in Latin America* (Berkeley and Los Angeles: University of California Press, 1990), 151.

33. Paz, *Sor Juana*, 63.

34. Asunción Lavrin, ed., *Latin American Women*; Asuncion Lavrin, ed., *Sexuality and Marriage in Colonial Latin America* (Lincoln: University of Nebraska Press, 1989);

Silvia Marina Arrom, *The History of Women in Mexico City, 1790–1857* (Stanford, Calif.: Stanford University Press, 1985).

35. Arrom, *Women in Mexico City,* 154.

36. Elias Amador, quoted in *Enciclopedia de Mexico,* vol. 4 (1970).

37. Henderson, and Henderson, *Ten Notable Women,* 97.

38. For further discussion of her role in the Brazilian independence movement, see chap. 3.

39. Maria Dundas Graham, *Journal of a Voyage to Brazil and Residence There during Part of the Years 1821, 1822, 1823* (New York, London: Frederick A. Praeger, 1969), 292.

40. Ibid., 293.

41. Ibid.

42. Ibid.

43. Ibid., 292.

44. Robin Morgan, ed., *Sisterhood Is Global* (Garden City, NY: Anchor Press/ Doubleday, 1984), 112.

45. See, for example, Vicente Grez, *Las mujeres de la Independencia* (Santiago de Chile: Zig-Zag, 1966).

46. Amador, quoted in *Enciclopedia de Mexico,* vol. 4 (1970).

47. Ibid.

48. Flora Tristán, *The Worker's Union,* trans. Beverly Livingston (Urbana: University of Illinois Press, 1983) 77.

49. Vicente Lecuna, ed., *Documentos referentes a la creacion de Bolivia,* vol. 2, excerpted in John J. Johnson, *Simón Bolívar and Spanish American Independence* (New York: Van Nostrand Reinhold, 1986), 200.

50. Lecuna, *Documentos.*

51. Indalecio Lievano Aguirre, "Manuelita Saénz," in *La mujer en la vida del Libertador,* ed. Blanca Gaitán de Paris (Bogotá, Colombia: Cooperativa Nacional de Artes Graficas, 1980), 128.

52. In Asunción Lavrin, ed., *Latin American Women,* 219–35.

53. Ibid., 220.

54. Aguirre, "Manuelita Saénz," 130.

55. Ibid., 135.

56. Evelyn Cherpak, "The Participation of Women in the Independence Movement in Gran Colombia, 1730–1830," in Lavrin, ed., *Latin American Women,* 229–30.

3. Woman and Education in Latin America (pp. 35–67)

1. Francesca Miller, "The International Relations of Women of the Americas, 1890–1928," *The Americas: A Quarterly Review of Inter-American Cultural History,* 43 (October 1986): 174.

2. Ann Firor Scott used Woolf's question to illuminate the discrepancies in opportunities available to women and their brothers in British colonial America, and I am indebted to her for this parable. See Scott's essay in *Women's America: Refocusing the Past,* ed. Linda K. Kerber and Jane De Hart Mathews (New York: Oxford University Press, 1982), 66.

3. Luis Martín, *Daughters of the Conquistadores: Women of the Viceroyalty of Peru* (Albuquerque: University of Mexico, 1983).

4. Asunción Lavrin, "The Colonial Woman in Mexico," in *Latin American Women: Historical Perspectives,* ed. Asunción Lavrin (Westport, Conn.: Westview Press, 1978), 26–27.

5. Susan A. Soeiro, "The Feminine Orders in Colonial Bahia, Brazil: Economic, Social and Demographic Implications, 1677–1900," in *Latin American Women*, ed. Asunción Lavrin.

6. Manuel Barranco, "Mexico: Its Educational Problems—Suggestions for Their Solution" (Ph.D. diss., Columbia University, 1914), 48.

7. Francesca Miller, "Brazil's Relations with Russia, 1808–1840: A Study in the Formation of Foreign Policy" (Ph.D. diss., University of California, Davis, 1977), 7.

8. James D. Henderson and Linda Roddy Henderson, *Ten Notable Women of Latin America* (Chicago: Nelson-Hall, 1978), 124.

9. Scott, *Women's America*, 66.

10. Cynthia Jeffress Little, "Education, Philanthropy, and Feminism: Components of Argentine Womanhood, 1860–1926," in *Latin American Women*, ed. Asunción Lavrin, 236.

11. Silvia Marina Arrom, *The Women of Mexico City, 1790–1857* (Stanford, Calif.: Stanford University Press, 1985), 22.

12. Francisca Senhorinha da Motta Diniz, *O Sexo Feminino*, 1 (1873), in the archives (Raros Livros) of the Biblioteca Nacional, Rio de Janeiro.

13. Little, "Education, Philanthropy, and Feminism," 236.

14. Barbara Ganson de Rivas, "Paraguayan Lane to Lances: A History of Women in the Social and Economic Life of Paraguay" (M.A. thesis, University of Texas at Austin, 1984), 132.

15. Heleieth I. B. Saffioti, *Women in Class Society* (New York: Monthly Review Press, 1978), 165.

16. Shirlene Ann Soto, *The Mexican Woman: A Study of Her Participation in the Revolution, 1910–1940* (Palo Alto, Calif.: R & E Research Associates, 1979), 5.

17. Mary Kay Vaughan, *The State, Education, and Social Crisis in Mexico, 1880–1928* (DeKalb: Northern Illinois University Press, 1982), 204.

18. Amanda Labarca, "Educación secundaria," in *Actividades femeninas en Chile* (Santiago de Chile: Imprenta y Litografía la Ilustración, Santo Domingo, 1928), 193.

19. Ibid., 195.

20. An interesting sidelight of their success in entering educational and occupational realms previously held by men was that Chilean women popularly attributed their success to their Araucanian ancestry. The Araucanians were inscribed by the Spanish colonizers as fierce and indomitable warriors. In the 1880s, the reference to indigenous ancestry was both patriotic and a romanticization of the diminishing Indian population.

21. Kathryn Lynn Stoner, "From the House to the Streets: Women's Movement for Legal Change in Cuba, 1898–1958" (Ph.D. diss., Indiana University, 1983), 156.

22. Ibid., 159.

23. Ibid.

24. Francesca Miller, "International Relations of Women of the Americas," 173.

25. Proceedings of the *Congreso Femenino Internacional*, Buenos Aires, 1910.

26. Maximiliano Salas Marchan, "Chile," in *Educational Yearbook of the International Institute of Teachers College, Columbia University 1925* (New York: Macmillan, 1926), 72.

27. Ernesto Nelson, "Argentina," in *Educational Yearbook*, 27.

28. Ibid., 30.

29. Eduardo Monteverde, cited in Arturo Carbonell y Migal, *Escuela Uruguaya—historia, organizacion, y administracion* (Montevideo: 1924), 447.

30. Carneiro Leão, "Brazil," in *Educational Yearbook*, 63.

31. Saffioti, *Women in Class Society*, 176.

32. Ibid.
33. Barranco, *Mexico: Its Educational Problems*, 56.
34. Vaughan, *State, Education, and Social Crisis*, 202.
35. Ibid.
36. Soto, *The Mexican Woman*, 49.
37. Ibid., 75.
38. CIM, *Inter-American Commission of Women 1928–1973* (Washington, D.C.: General Secretariat, Organization of American States, 1974), 4.
39. Robert F. Arnove, Michael Chiapetta, and Sylvia Stalker, "Latin American Education," in *Latin America: Perspectives on a Region*, ed. Jack W. Hopkins (New York: Holmes & Meier, 1987), 123.
40. Saffioti, *Women in Class Society*, 176.
41. Carmen Diana Deere, "The Differentiation of the Peasantry and Family Structure: A Peruvian Case Study," *Journal of Family History* 3 (4) (1978): 426.
42. *Statistical Abstract of Latin America 1955* (Los Angeles: University of California, Latin American Center).
43. George Psacharopoulos and Antonio Zabalza, "The Destination and Early Career Performance of Secondary School Graduates in Colombia: Findings from the 1978 Cohort," *World Bank Staff Working Papers*, No. 653 (Washington, D.C.: World Bank, 1984).
44. Inter-American Development Bank, *Economic and Social Progress in Latin America 1980–81* (Washington, D.C.: Inter-American Development Bank, 1981), 137.
45. June E. Hahner ed., *Women in Latin American History, Their Lives and Views*. UCLA Latin American Studies Series, No. 51, rev. ed. (Los Angeles: University of California, Latin American Center Publications, 1980), 176.
46. Arnove et al., "Latin American Education," 129.
47. Elsa Chaney, *Supermadre: Women in Politics in Latin America*, Latin American Monographs, No. 50 (Austin: Published for Institute of Latin American Studies by University of Texas Press, 1979), 210; Ximena Bunster and Elsa Chaney, *Sellers and Servants: Working Women in Lima, Peru* (New York: Praeger, 1985).
48. Arnove et al., "Latin American Education," 123.
49. Ruth Leger Sivard, ed., *Women . . . A World Survey* (Washington, D.C.: World Priorities, 1985); also see Elsa Chaney and Ximena Bunster's discussion of this in *Sellers and Servants*.
50. Sivard, *Women . . . A World Survey*, 20.

4. Feminism and Social Motherhood (pp. 68–109)

1. Magda Portal, *Hacia la mujer nueva* (Lima, Peru, 1933).
2. Historian Karen Offen, writing of the emergence of feminism in France, posits that feminism is "the historical development of the critique and program for sociopolitical change in the status of women in a variety of cultures." Karen Offen, "Defining Feminism: A Comparative Historical Approach," *Signs: Journal of Women in Culture and Society* (1988), 2. An earlier version of this paper was published as "Toward an Historical Definition of Feminism: The Case of France" (Working Paper No. 22, Institute for Research on Women and Gender, Stanford University, 1985). Offen argues that use of the term "feminism" to describe the women's movement first came into use in France at the Congrés general des institutions feministes in Paris in 1892.
3. Janet Greenberg has found eighty women's journals published in nineteenth-century Latin America, mainly in Argentina (23), Brazil (16), and Mexico (16); Colombia, Cuba, Peru, and Puerto Rico recorded 3 or 4 each. Greenberg did not include

258Notes

in her count magazines devoted to homemaking, fashion, etc.; the content of these journals was for female education, change in legal status, the publication of women authors.

4. Francisca Senhorina da Motta Diniz, ed., *O Sexo Feminino*, 1 (7 Sept. 1873), in the archives (Raros Livros) of the Biblioteca Nacional, Rio de Janeiro.

5. *O Sexo Feminino*, no. 15 (20 Dec. 1873). June Hahner has written extensively on the feminist press in Brazil; see also Hahner, ed., *Women in Latin American History, Their Lives and Views*, rev. ed. UCLA Latin American Studies, No. 51 (Los Angeles: University of California, Latin American Center Publications, 1976), 51–55.

6. Francisca Senhorina da Motta Diniz, ed., *O Quinze de Novembro do Sexo Feminino* (26 Apr. 1890), in the archives (Raros Livros) of the Biblioteca Nacional, Rio de Janeiro.

7. Janet Greenberg, "A Working Bibliography: Towards a History of Women's Periodicals in Latin America from the Eighteenth to the Twentieth Century," in *Women, Culture and Politics in Latin America* (Berkeley and Los Angeles: University of California Press, 1990).

8. Kathryn Lynn Stoner, "From the House to the Streets: Women's Movement for Legal Change in Cuba, 1898–1958" (Ph.D. diss., Indiana University, 1983), 14.

9. Asunción Lavrin, *The Ideology of Feminism in the Southern Cone, 1900–1940*, Latin American Program Working Papers, No. 169 (Washington, D.C.: Smithsonian Institution, Latin American Program, 1986), 6.

10. Ana Macías, "Felipe Carrillo Puerto and Women's Liberation in Mexico," in *Latin American Women: Historical Perspectives*, ed. Asunción Lavrin (Westport, Conn.: Greenwood Press, 1978), 287.

11. Francesca Miller, "The International Relations of Women of the Americas 1890–1928," *The Americas: A Quarterly Review of Inter-American Cultural History*, 43 (October 1986): 175–76.

12. Miller, "International Relations," 176.

13. Maria del Carmen Feijóo, "Las Feministas," *La Vida de Nuestro Pueblo*, no. 9, (1982): 1.

14. Carolina Muzzilli, "El divorcio," *Congreso Femenino Internacional* (Buenos Aires, 1910): 417.

15. In her essay, "Trés Conferencias" (Bogotá, 1931), Teresa de la Parra explores this theme. See also Miller, "Latin American Feminism in the Transnational Arena" (paper presented at the Seventh Berkshire Conference on the History of Women, June 1987) and Karen Offen, "Defining Feminism."

16. Elvira Rawson de Dellepiane, "Modificaciones al Codigo Civil Argentino," *Congreso Femenino Internacional* (Buenos Aires, 1910): 428–79.

17. Shirlene Ann Soto, *The Mexican Woman: A Study of Her Participation in the Revolution, 1910–1940* (Palo Alto, Calif.: R & E Associates, 1979), 52. "The reasons for Yucatán's leadership in the Mexican woman's movement in this period lay in the support of socialist governor Salvador Alvarado (1915–1918), the progressive ideals of its women, its wealth from henequen production, and the fact that the Yucatán had been one of the first Mexican states to open education to women."

18. Ibid., 56.

19. Ibid., 52.

20. Ibid., 53.

21. Ibid., 55.

22. Stoner, "From the House to the Streets," 58.

23. Elsa Chaney, *Supermadre: Women and Politics in Latin America*, Latin American Monographs, No. 50 (Austin, TX: University of Texas Press, 1979), 52.

24. Elvira García y García, *Actividad femenina* (Lima: Casa Editora, 1928). Irene Matthews comments on García y García's "middle-class bias and racism"; Chaney also describes Alvarado's split with her former teacher.

25. María Jesús Alvarado Rivera, "Femenismo," *Congreso Femenino Internacional,* (Buenos Aires, 1910), 265.

26. Catt to Hay, 19 February 1923, Papers of Carrie Chapman Catt, The Arthur and Elizabeth Schlesinger Archives on the History of Women in America, Radcliffe College, Cambridge, Mass.

27. Chaney, *Supermadre,* 54.

28. Ibid., 69.

29. Eleanor Foster Lansing, "Foreword," *Bulletin of the Women's Auxiliary Committee of the United States of the Second Pan-American Scientific Congress,* no. 1 (February 1921), in Alice Park Collection, Archives of the Hoover Institution on War, Revolution and Peace, Stanford, Calif.

30. "The Second Pan American Scientific Congress," *Bulletin of the Pan-American Union,* 45 (December 1915): 762.

31. Lansing, cited in Miller, "International Relations," 175.

32. Hahner, *Women in Latin American History,* 76.

33. Comisión Interamericana de Mujeres, *Libro de Oro* (Washington D.C.: Inter-American Commission of Women, Secretariat General of the OAS, 1980), 72.

34. Susan Kent Besse, *Freedom and Bondage: The Impact of Capitalism on Women in São Paulo, Brazil* (Ph.D. diss., Yale University, 1983), 224.

35. Miller, "International Relations," 178.

36. Papers of Carrie Chapman Catt; also Mary Wilhelmine Williams, *People and Politics in Latin America,* rev. ed. (Boston: Ginn and Company, 1945), 791, 815.

37. Besse, *Freedom and Bondage,* 246.

38. *Boletín da Federacao Brasileira pelo Progresso Feminino,* 1 (November 1934), cited in Besse, *Freedom and Bondage,* 231.

39. Besse, *Freedom and Bondage,* 231.

40. Stoner, "From the House to the Streets," 111.

41. Stoner notes that the organizations ranged from the conservative "Catholic Damas Isabelitas to the more liberal Club Femenino [and] debated no less than 39 social and political issues important to women." The agendas of the Cuban women's conferences are cited in Stoner, "From the House to the Street," 111–112.

42. Stoner, "From the House to the Streets," 113.

43. Shirlene Ann Soto, *The Mexican Woman,* 83.

44. Ibid., 83.

45. Ibid., 75.

46. Ana Macías, *Against All Odds: The Feminist Movement in Mexico to 1940* (Westport, Conn.: Greenwood Press, 1982), 106; also Miller, "International Relations," 179.

47. Dawn Keremetsis, "Women Workers in the Mexican Revolution (1910–1940): Advance or Retreat?" (unpublished paper, 1981).

48. Macías, *Against All Odds,* 106.

49. Shirlene Soto discusses a number of women's congresses, as does Ana Macías. Soto, in *The Mexican Woman,* writes: "The most spectacular change in the women's movement in Mexico from 1920 to 1934 was in the increased number of women's organizations and conferences. Hundreds of women, recognizing the value in national and international organization, joined together" (p. 76).

50. Soto, *The Mexican Woman,* 79.

51. Ibid.

52. The Equal Rights Treaty was drafted by Alice Paul of the National Woman's

Party of the United States and presented to the Havana Conference by Doris Stevens.

53. James Brown Scott, *The International Conferences of American States 1889–1928* (New York: Oxford University Press, 1931), vii.

54. Francesca Miller, "Latin American Feminism," in Seminar on Women and Culture in *America, Women, Culture and Politics in Latin America* (Berkeley and Los Angeles: University of California Press, 1990).

55. Alice Park, 1928 Diary, Alice Park Collection, Archives of the Hoover Institution on War, Revolution and Peace, Stanford, Calif.

56. This idea is discussed in the work of the scholars cited above and in my own research; see also Jane Jaquette, "Female Political Participation in Latin America," in *Women in the World: A Comparative Study* (Santa Barbara, Calif.: ABC Clio Press, 1976), for an early statement of this thesis. Elsa Chaney (*Supermadre*), put it thus: "The whole struggle for the vote, just emerging as an issue at the time of these meetings, often was viewed almost exclusively as a vehicle for obtaining social reforms in favor of women, children, the old, the sick, juvenile delinquents and prostitutes."

57. Bertha Lutz, *Trexe principios basicos: Suggestões ao ante-projecto de constituição*, cited in Besse, *Freedom and Bondage*, 133. See also June Hahner, "The Beginnings of the Women's Suffrage Movement in Brazil," *Signs: Journal of Women in Culture and Society*, 5 (1979): 200–224.

58. María Luiza Bittencourt, "Report from Brazil," in Beatrice Newhart, "Woman Suffrage in the Americas," *Pan-American Union Bulletin*, 70 (April 1936): 425.

59. Stoner, "From the House to the Streets," 106.

60. Beatrice Newhart, "Woman Suffrage in the Americas," *Pan-American Union Bulletin*, 70 (April 1936): 426.

61. Soto, *The Mexican Woman*, 85.

62. Newhart, "Woman Suffrage in the Americas," 427.

63. Rollie E. Poppino, "Brazil: A New Model for National Development," *Current History* 62 (February 1972).

64. Magda Portal, *El aprismo y la mujer* (Lima: Editorial Cooperativa Aprista "ATAHUALPA," 1933), 56.

65. Portal, *El aprismo y la mujer*, 17.

66. Alicia Moreau de Justo, *El socialismo y la mujer* (Buenos Aires: La Vanguardia, 1931), 12.

67. Julietta Kirkwood, "Women and Politics in Chile," *International Social Science Journal*, 35 (1983). In her article, Julietta Kirkwood explores the especially brutal treatment of women accused of revolutionary activity.

68. María da Conceição Torres García, "O mito de Pagú, na realidade de Patricia Galvão," *Mulheres Ilustres*. I am grateful to Amnesiades Leonard for providing this article.

69. Besse, *Freedom and Bondage*, 290.

70. García, "O mito de Pagú"; Besse, *Freedom and Bondage*.

71. Quoted in Besse, *Freedom and Bondage*, 299.

72. Papers of the *Comité de las Americas de la Liga Internacional de Mujeres Pro Paz y Libertad*, 1947: "La Sección . . . ha trabajando por muchos anos contra el imperialismo norteamericano, y ha cooperado con resultados favorables por los siguientes fines: Declaracion del Gobienro de los Estados Unidos que nunca volvera a intervenir en paises extranjeros para proteger la propriedad norteamericana: . . . retiro de los marinos de Haiti, Nicaragua, y la Republica Dominicana; derogacion de la Emienda Platt en la Constitucion de Cuba. Desde 1926 ha contribuido a mejorar las relaciones entre os Estados Unidos y Mexico. . . . Ha tratado de descubrir y aminorar la exploitacion de

trabajadores en Cuba, Bolivia, Chile y otros paises" (WILPF, archives of the Hoover Institution on War, Revolution, and Peace, Stanford University).

73. Alice Park, 1928 Diary.

74. Nelly Merino Carvallo, ed., *Mujeres de America*, 1 (September–October 1933). I am grateful to Gwen Kirkpatrick for providing me with a number of copies of this journal.

75. Doris Stevens Collection, Arthur and Elizabeth Schlesinger Archives of the History of Women, Radcliffe College, Cambridge, Mass. (uncollated ms.).

76. James Brown Scott, *International Conferences*, 503.

77. Doris Stevens Collection.

78. Scott, *International Conferences*, 503.

79. Documents of the IACW, p. 39, Doris Stevens Collection. For a full discussion of IACW activities prior to 1947, see Miller, "International Relations."

80. "Pro Paz" was organized by *asociaciones femeninas y estudantiles* in Argentina; the signatories of the petition included men's and women's associations, as well as individuals; see Merino Carvallo, ed., *Mujeres de America*, 1 (September–October, 1933).

81. Ibid.

82. J. Lloyd Mecham, *A Survey of United States–Latin American Relations* (New York: Houghton Mifflin, 1965).

83. At the Montevideo Conference of 1933, Eleanor Roosevelt had Alexandra W. Wedde and Sophonisba P. Breckinridge attached to the U.S. delegation to prepare a "Confidential File on Doris Stevens." They reported Stevens's "flirtation" with the Brazilian delegate, rumors of an affair with a Peruvian diplomat: "A further cause for regret is the unpleasant impression which it is felt has been created in the minds of members of the various delegations, some of whom feel that Miss Stevens is the authentic voice of American womanhood. Your delegates therefore take pleasure in the attitude of our government in disassociating itself from this commission." U.S. Department of State, "Confidential File on Doris Stevens, December 26, 1933," in the Unprocessed Papers of the Doris Stevens Collection, Arthur and Elizabeth Schlesinger Archives of the History of Women in America, Radcliffe College, Cambridge, Mass. None of the allegations was proved, but the intention was clearly to discredit Miss Stevens.

5. Democracy and the Search for Social Justice, 1938–1958 (pp. 110–144)

1. United Nations, Charter, 25 April 1945, San Francisco, Calif.

2. Vicky Randall, *Women and Politics: An International Perspective*, 2nd ed. (Chicago: University of Chicago Press, 1987), for example, makes the assumption that feminism did not develop in third world Catholic countries. Among pioneering studies of feminism in Latin America are Asunción Lavrin, *The Ideology of Feminism in the Southern Cone, 1900–1940*, Latin American Program Working Papers, No. 169 (Washington D.C.: Smithsonian Institution, Latin American Program, 1986); June Hahner, ed., *Women in Latin American History: Their Lives and Views*, rev. ed., UCLA Latin American Studies, No. 51 (Los Angeles: University of California, Latin American Center Publications, 1980); Shirlene Ann Soto, *The Mexican Woman: A Study of Her Participation in the Revolution, 1910–1940* (Palo Alto, Calif.: R&E Research Associates, 1979); Francesca Miller, "The International Relations of Women of the Americas 1890–1928," *The Americas: A Quarterly Review of Inter-American Cultural History*, 43 (October 1986); María del Carmen Feijóo, "Las Feministas," *La Vida de Nuestro Pueblo*, No. 9 (Buenos Aires: Centro Editor de America Latina, 1982); Kathryn Lynn Stoner, "From

the House to the Streets: Women's Movement for Legal Change in Cuba 1898–1958" (Ph.D. diss., University of Indiana, 1983).

3. For the development of the idea of the use of the international arena by Latin American women activists, see Francesca Miller, "Latin American Feminism and the Transnational Arena," in Seminar on Women and Culture in Latin America, *Women, Culture and Politics in Latin America* (Berkeley and Los Angeles: University of California Press, 1990).

4. Ward W. Morton, *Woman Suffrage in Mexico* (Gainesville: University of Florida Press, 1962), 21.

5. Ibid., 23.

6. Ibid.

7. Ibid., 37.

8. Ibid., 41.

9. Lillian Estelle Fisher, "Influence of the Present Mexican Revolution upon the Status of Mexican Women," *Hispanic American Historical Review*, 22 (February 1942): 222.

10. Morton, *Woman Suffrage in Mexico*, 45.

11. "Feminismo," in *Enciclopedia de Mexico*, vol. 4 (Mexico City: Los Talleres de Offset Publicitario, 1970), 95.

12. North American Congress on Latin America, April 1974.

13. Ibid.

14. Doris Stevens Collection, Arthur and Elizabeth Schlesinger Archives of the History of Women, Radcliffe College, Cambridge, Mass. (uncollated ms.).

15. Particularly in the Caribbean and Central America, the priorities of the United States during the war years and the Good Neighbor Policy were for stability, loyalty, and the maintenance of order.

16. Mary Cannon, "Women's Organizations in Ecuador, Paraguay, and Peru," *Bulletin of the Pan-American Union*, 77 (November 1943): 604.

17. Ibid.

18. Ibid., 607.

19. Comisión Interamericana de Mujeres (CIM). *Inter-American Commission of Women 1928–1973* (Washington, D.C.: General Secretariat, Organization of American States, 1974). The women had prepared their platform at the Inter-American Conference on the Problems of War and Peace, Mexico City, February 21–March 8, 1945. In Mexico, the IACW sought full legal status "which since its inception it has enjoyed only to a certain extent" and economic support from each of the member governments. They also succeeded in having a resolution approved at a plenary session, "The Commission, which is the only women's organization of continental scope in America" recommends "that the governments of the American Republics modify their legislation . . . to abolish any existing discriminations by reason of sex." *Bulletin of the Pan American Union*, 79 (1945): 345.

20. Ibid., 356. Article re suffrage in Guatemala also notes that "voting is compulsory for literate men, optional for literate women."

21. Hubert Herring, *A History of Latin America from the Beginnings to the Present*, 3rd ed. (New York: Alfred A. Knopf, 1968), 520.

22. Lucile Palácios, elected to the Venezuelan House of Deputies and a member of the Feminine Action Committee that worked for the victory of AD and woman suffrage, wrote to the IACW thanking them for their support and notifying them of plans for the revision of the Venezuelan Civil Code; *Bulletin of the Pan-American Union*, 81 (May–June 1947): 337. In 1948, when the government of Gallegos was

overthrown and congress dissolved, Palácios went underground and joined the resistance; Comisión Interamericana de Mujeres (CIM), *Libro de oro* (Washington, D.C.: Interamerican Commission of Women, Secretariat General of the Organization of American States), 154.

23. Francesca Miller, "Constitution of 1946 (Brazil)," in *Encyclopedia of Latin America*, ed. Helen Delpar (New York: McGraw-Hill, 1974), 169. The constitution of 1946 incorporated the principle of universal male and female suffrage for the first time; previously, property and literacy requirements had effectively limited the electorate to approximately 5 percent of the population.

24. The nationalism of Mexican feminists persists in the present, and was certainly visible at the IWY meeting in Mexico City in 1975. The closest parallels come from the Cuban women after 1959 and Nicaraguan women in the 1980s. This may be a telling point about the success of these revolutions as *national* revolutions. For a discussion of feminism and patriotism vis-à-vis feminism and the nation state, see Miller, "Latin American Feminism": "Alienation from the political process within the national community should not be construed as obviating love of homeland, of place, of one's historical family." (p. 19).

25. Adela Formoso de Obregón Santacilia, *La Mujer Mexicana en la organización social del país* (Mexico City: Talleres Graficos de la Nación, 1939), 9.

26. Of the Latin American states, Colombia, Mexico, and Brazil sent troops abroad (Colombian air forces; Mexican Air Force unit to Philippines; Brazilian forces to Italy). Mexican labor was critical to the Allied war effort; it not only sustained its own agricultural production but, through the *bracero* program, kept U.S. agriculture in full production. Brazil was critical to the Allied war effort in keeping the shipping lanes of the South Atlantic open; more than 2,000 Brazilian merchant marines were killed in the line of duty.

27. Heleieth I. B. Saffiotti, *A mulher na sociedade de clases: Mito e realidad* (São Paulo: Vozes, 1976); English translation by Heleieth Saffiotti, *Women in Class Society* (New York: Monthly Review press, 1978), 215.

28. Ana Alice Costa Pinheiro, "Advances y definiciones del movimiento feminista en Brasil" (M.A. thesis, Colegio de Mexico, January 1981), points out that there were bitter splits between the women associated with the Socialist International and members of the WIDF, which was affiliated with the Communist party. In the late 1940s the Socialist International (SI) was denouncing dictatorship, supportive of the UN, and opposed to the Soviet system. The women's branch of the SI was the International Council of Social Democratic Women, with 1,700,000 members in nineteen countries; its Latin American secretariat was in Montevideo, Uruguay.

29. The WIDF was founded on December 1, 1945, in Paris, where its headquarters remained until it was expelled in 1951 and moved to East Berlin. Richard Staar, ed., *Yearbook on International Communist Affairs 1973* (Stanford, Calif.: Stanford University, Hoover Institution Press, 1973).

30. Rollie E. Poppino, *International Communism in Latin America: A History of the Movement 1917–1963* (New York: Macmillan, The Free Press, 1964), 77. According to Poppino, the Communist party was outlawed in Brazil in 1947.

31. Saffiotti, "A mulher na sociedad," 359.

32. Ibid., 216–17.

33. Magda Portal, "¿Quienes traicionaron al pueblo?" *Cuadernos de Divulgación Popular*, 1 (April 1950): 12.

34. Ibid. Women did not win the vote at the national level in Peru until 1955.

35. Ibid. See also Kathryn J. Burns, "Beyond 'That Essential Femininity': Feminist

Organizations in Peru, 1900–1950" (Senior thesis, Princeton University, 1981) for an excellent bibliography and discussion of this period.

36. Portal, "¿Quienes traicionaron?" 7, 8.

37. Magda Portal, "Yo soy Magda Portal," in *Ser mujer en el Peru*, 2nd ed, interviews collected and edited by Esther Andradi and Ana María Portugal (Lima: Takapu Editores, 1979), 209–30.

38. Irene Matthews, "Magda Portal: Poetess, Politician, Example" (unpublished paper, University of California, Davis, 1985), 25.

39. Ibid., 23.

40. See, for example, the entry on Eva Perón in *Encyclopedia of Latin America*, ed. Helen Delpar (New York: McGraw-Hill, 1974), 467; written by Noreen F. Stack, the article states, "[Eva Perón] spearheaded the movement for woman suffrage."

41. The first nation to grant woman suffrage was New Zealand in 1893. The post–World War II years saw an impressive broadening of female suffrage: France, Guatemala, Hungary, Indonesia, Japan, Panama, Trinidad, and Tobago in 1945; Benin, Italy, Liberia, Romania, and Yugoslavia in 1946; Argentina, Malta, Togo, Venezuela, and Vietnam in 1947; Belgium, Israel, North Korea, and South Korea in 1948; Chile, Costa Rica, India, and Syria in 1949. The former colonial powers of the Western Hemisphere granted female suffrage as follows: United Kingdom, 1928; Spain, 1931; France, 1945; and Portugal, 1976. In 1989 women have the legal right to suffrage in all but a few states of the Middle East (Oman, Qatar, Saudi Arabia, UAR) and South Africa, where both black women and black men are denied the vote. Kuwait specifically denies woman suffrage. In nations of the Western Hemisphere and Europe the average time lapse between the granting of male suffrage and the granting of female suffrage is forty-seven years. In the postwar independence movements in Africa, woman suffrage was generally included in the new constitutions. Worldwide, women were the last major population group to be enfranchised. See Ruth Leger Sivard, *Women . . . A World Survey*, (Washington, D.C.: World Priorities, 1985). Information collated for this text by research assistant Karen Boyd.

42. Nicholas Fraser and Marysa Navarro, *Eva Perón* (London: Andre Deutsch, 1980), 105.

43. Ibid., 106.

44. *Discurso de Eva Perón en el acto inaugural de la primera asamblea naciónal del Movimiento Perónista Femenino* (Buenos Aires: 1949), quoted in Fraser and Navarro, *Eva Perón*, 110.

45. Ibid., 111.

46. Ibid.

47. Ibid., 108.

48. U.S. Department of State, *Interamerican Conference for the Maintenance of Continental Peace and Security, Quitandinha, Brazil August 15–September 2, 1947* (Washington, D.C.: 1948).

49. The heart of the NATO Treaty reads, "The parties agree that an armed attack against one or more of them in Europe or North America shall be considered an attack against them all." For full wording, see "North Atlantic Treaty Organization," *Encyclopedia Britannica*, vol. 16 (Chicago: Encyclopaedia Britannica, Inc., William Benton, 1973), 606A; also Dean Acheson, *Present at the Creation: My Years in the State Department* (New York: Norton, 1969).

50. Papers, *Primero Congreso Interamericano de Mujeres, Celebrado en la Capital de Guatemala, del 21 de agosto de 1947* (Guatemala City: Los Talleres de Latipografia, 1948). From the Collection of Alicia Moreau de Justo, Montevideo, Uruguay. I am grate-

ful to Janet Greenberg for providing this document. For a fuller discussion of this conference, see Miller, "Latin American Feminism."

51. Ibid. The countries represented were Argentina, Bolivia, Brazil, Canada, Cuba, Colombia, Costa Rica, Chile, Ecuador, El Salvador, Haiti, Honduras, Mexico, Nicaragua, Panama, Peru, United States, Uruguay, and Venezuela. Only Paraguay and the Dominican Republic appear to have had no representation.

52. Ibid.

53. Women's International League for Peace and Freedom, Comité de las Americas de la Liga Internaciónal de Mujeres Pro Paz y Libertad, papers, 1947 (Archives of the Hoover Institution on War, Revolution, and Peace, Stanford University).

54. Ibid.

55. *Memoria del Primero Congreso Interamericano de Mujeres*, 1947, 27.

56. Ibid., 65.

57. Ibid., 37.

58. Ibid., 27.

59. Ibid.

60. Ibid., 135.

61. Ibid., 24.

62. Ibid., 117.

63. Ibid., 46.

64. Ibid.

65. Ibid., 136.

66. Pan-American Union, *Final Act of the Ninth International Congress of American States, Bogotá, Colombia, March 30–May 2, 1948* (Washington, D.C., Author, 1948), 247.

67. Adalzira Bittencourt, *A mulher Paulista na história* (Rio de Janeiro: Livros de Portugal, 1954), 300. Several founding members and former representatives to the IACW served on the first UN Commission on the Status of Women. Brazilian chronicler Adalzira Bittencourt credits Bertha Lutz with helping to create the UN commission, "Em 1952 foi a representante do Brasil na Comissão de Estatutos da Mulher das Naçoes Unidas, comissão essa criada por iniciativa sua."

68. Comision Interamericana de Mujeres (CIM), "Influence of the Commission at the International Level," in *Inter-American Commission of Women 1928–1973* (Washington, D.C.: General Secretariat, Organization of American States, 1974), 12.

69. Juan José Arévalo, *Carta politica al pueblo de Guatemala* (Guatemala City: Editorial San Antonio, 1963); see also Marie Berthe Dion, *Las ideas sociales y politicas de Arévalo*, 2nd ed. (Mexico City: Editorial America Nueva, 1958), 143: "El Arevalismo propicia un regimen democratico de socialism, contrario a los conceptos marxistas de dictadura autoritaria, lucha de clases y revolucion violenta, propugnando la descentralizacion gubernatival, la armonia social y las reformas progresivas."

70. For a scholarly history of the emergence of the Communist party of Guatemala, see Rollie E. Poppino, *International Communism*. The party reformulated (after near disintegration during the Ubico dictatorship) as the clandestine Democratic Vanguard in 1947. In 1949 the Communist party of Guatemala was formed and came into the open in 1950. On orders from Moscow, it merged with the Revolutionary Workers party in 1951 to form the Guatemalan Labor party, which attained legal status in 1952.

71. See Cole Blasier, *The Hovering Giant: U.S. Responses to Revolutionary Change in Latin America* (Pittsburgh, Pa.: University of Pittsburgh Press, 1976) and Walter LaFeber, *Inevitable Revolutions: The United States in Central America* (New York: W. W. Norton, 1983).

72. Ronald M. Schneider, *Communism in Guatemala 1944–1954*, Foreign Policy Re-

search Institute Series, No. 7 (New York: Frederick A. Praeger, 1958).

73. Ibid.

74. Schneider, *Communism in Guatemala*, 110; see also R. E. Poppino, *International Communism*, 134: "The situation in Guatemala during the period of Communist ascendancy in the early 1950s provides a clear example of the kind and range of mass-based front groups the Communists strive to exploit. There the organizations under Communist domination included the General Confederation of Workers of Guatemala, the national peasant Confederation of Guatemala, the Guatemalan Women's Alliance (AFG), the Alliance of Democratic Youth of Guatemala, the Democratic University Front, the Confederation of Secondary School Students, and the Saker-Ti Group of Young Artists and Writers."

75. Schneider, *Communism in Guatemala*, 91: "Through Viriginia Bravo the president's wife lent her name to Communist run activities among the women of Latin America."

76. See Schneider, *Communism in Guatemala*, discussion of sources, 323.

77. Poppino, *International Communism*, 36, 108: "This is a matter of continuing concern to party leaders, who emphasize the desirability and need to attract more women into the Communist ranks. Most of the parties maintain several special-interest front organizations designed to appeal to housewives, working women, female students, and women in the professions."

78. There is an intriguing story to be investigated about the involvement of women in Guatemalan politics in this era. All of the women, *arevalistas* and Communist, were centered in Guatemala City, which was a pretty small pond in this period. Guatemala had a population of approximately 3 million in 1954, of which 60 percent were indigenous and primarily rural. About 10 percent of the population lived in the environs of the capital city (ca. 290,000 in 1950). Apparently, the preponderance of the women politically active at the national level in this era was educated, Hispanized, and middle class, but there were clear ideological divisions among them. What were their interactions? How did they see themselves, their role in events? Because of U.S. involvement and the collection of vast numbers of documents by the CIA in the attempt to justify armed intervention in Guatemalan affairs, a great deal of information is readily accessible (e.g., the microfilm of the Guatemalan National Committee for the Defense against Communism ([Library of Congress]). Male politics in the era have been intensely scrutinized; what role women played remains to be researched; the information presented in this text is but the tip of the iceberg. For instance, did women play a significant role in the anti-Communist forces, through church affiliations or private charitable institutions? Or was the anti-Communist movement played out primarily through the military, an institution in which women had no voice?

79. Gloria Ardaya Salinas, "The Barzolas and the Housewives Committee," in *Women and Change in Latin America*, ed. June Nash and Helen Safa (South Hadley, Mass.: Bergen and Garvey, 1986), 328.

80. Salinas, "The Barzolas," 331.

81. Salinas quotes from Moema Viezzer, *Testimonio de Domitila* (Mexico City: Editorial Siglo Vientinuno, 1978).

82. Salinas, "The Barzolas," 323.

83. Lydia Gueiler, *La mujer y la revolucion* (La Paz: Editorial Burillo, 1959).

84. Salinas, "The Barzolas," 331.

85. Both Gueiler and Salinas support this statement; Salinas points out that after the MNR came to power, women continued to be almost completely excluded from leadership positions.

86. CIM, *Libro de oro*.
87. Gueiler, *La mujer y la revolucion*, 285.
88. Ibid.
89. Ibid., 139.
90. Ibid., 141.
91. Ibid.
92. Ibid., 14; in 1979, Lydia Gueiler Tejada served a brief term as provisional president of Bolivia, the first woman to do so. The sequence of political events that brought her to office is described in James L. Busey, *Latin American Political Guide*, 18th ed. (New York: Robert Schalkenbach Foundation, 1985), 146–47.
93. Adalzira Bittencourt, *A mulher Paulista na história*.
94. Ibid., 45.
95. Haydée Santamaria, *Moncada: Memories of the Attack That Launched the Cuban Revolution*, trans. Robert Taber (Secaucus, N.J.: Lyle Stuart, 1980), 21.
96. Ibid., 23.
97. Ibid., 52–53.
98. Ibid., 112.
99. Ibid., 113.
100. Ibid., 97.
101. Abel and Haydée Santamaria published an underground newspaper, *Son los mismos*, in response to the coup d'etat. It was through this that Abel first met Fidel Castro.
102. Santamaria, *Moncada*, 97–99.
103. Francesca Rappole Wellman (Miller), "Vice President Nixon's Trip to South America, 1958" (M.A. thesis, University of California, Davis, 1969).
104. Santamaria, *Moncada*, 108.
105. Robin Morgan, "Cuba: Paradise Gained, Paradise Lost—the Price of Integration," in *Sisterhood Is Global*, ed. Robin Morgan (Garden City, N.Y.: Anchor Press/Doubleday, 1984), 169.

6. Revolution and Counterrevolution, 1959–1973 (pp. 145–186)

1. Carolina María de Jesus, *Child of the Dark: The Diary of Carolina María de Jesus*, translated from Portugese by David St. Clair (New York: Dutton, 1962); Portuguese edition, *Quarto de despejo* (São Paulo: Livraria Francisco Alves, 1960), 96.
2. See, for example, "Activities of the Communist and Workers' Parties, Party Work Among Women: From the Experience of the Women's Movement in Argentina," *World Marxist Review*, 5 (March 1962), and "Women in the Forefront of the Struggle," *World Marxist Review*, 7 (May 1964).
3. Jane Jaquette, "Women in Revolutionary Movements in Latin America," *Journal of Marriage and the Family* 35 (May 1973): 344.
4. John Gerassi, ed., *Revolutionary Priest* (New York: Vintage Books, 1971), 310.
5. Ibid., 295–301.
6. Ibid., 15.
7. Camilo Torres, "Message to Women," *Frenté Único*, 14 Oct. 1965, quoted in John Gerassi, ed., *Revolutionary Priest*, 398–99.
8. Ibid., xiii.
9. The term *guerrilla* (little war) originated during the Spanish resistance to Napoleon in 1800–1810, from the word *guerra* (war). Over time, *guerrilla* came to be used interchangeably with *guerrillero*.
10. See, for example, *Cassell's Spanish Dictionary* (New York: Funk and Wag-

nalls, 1966).

11. Ché Guevara, *Guerrilla Warfare*, preface by I. F. Stone, trans. J. P. Morray (New York: Vintage Books, 1967), 86.

12. Ibid.

13. Ibid.

14. Ibid.

15. Ibid., 87.

16. Jaquette, "Women in Revolutionary Movements," 334–54. As was true in Guatemala, the Cuban women were the partners of male party leaders: Celia Sanchez with Fidel Castro, Espín married to Raul Castro, and Santamaria with Hart.

17. The Alliance for Progress originated in the recommendations of Milton Eisenhower, *The Wine Is Bitter* (Garden City, N.Y.: Doubleday, 1962), a special report on Latin America written in 1953; Richard M. Nixon, *Six Crises* (Garden City, N.Y.: Doubleday & Co, Inc., 1962), his response to his 1958 visit to Latin America; Juscelino Kubitschek's 1959 proposal for a multilateral approach to hemispheric problems, which became "Operation Pan-America"; and John F. Kennedy's request to the U.S. Congress to fund the Alliance for Progress. An initial $1 billion was promised. F. Miller, "Vice-President Richard M. Nixon's Trip to South America, 1958" (M.A. Thesis, University of California, Davis, 1969).

18. Edward L. Cleary, *Crisis and Change: The Church in Latin America Today* (Maryknoll, New York: Orbis Books, 1985), 32. Re dependent development: "Economic progress of their countries would take place especially to the profit of the developed world. This was so because the developed countries bought raw materials from Latin America at low prices and then sold it manufactured goods at a handsome profit. Later, as domestic industrialization took place, multinational companies of the developed world would move into the process and send profits back home." The dependency argument presented here reflects the formulations of the 1960s.

19. Ibid.

20. Ibid., chap. 1.

21. Ibid., 18.

22. Ibid., 22.

23. Carolina María de Jesus, *Child of the Dark*, 59.

24. Ibid., 43.

25. Ibid., 12.

26. Ibid., 13; translator's preface (David St. Clair). The book has also gone through numerous editions in English.

27. Ibid., 111.

28. Ibid., 28.

29. Ibid.

30. Ibid., 30.

31. Ibid., 31.

32. Poppino, *Brazil: The Land and the People* (New York: Oxford University Press, 1968), 280.

33. The State of Guanabara, formerly the Federal District, was also a new political entity, created in 1960 when the capital of Brazil was moved from Rio de Janeiro to Brasília.

34. Heleieth I. B. Saffiotti, *A Mulher na sociedad de clases: Mito e realidad* (São Paulo: Vozes, 1976); English translation: I. B. Heleieth Saffiotti, *Women in Class Society* (New York: Monthly Review Press, 1978), 217.

35. Ibid., 218.

36. Ibid., 219; see also Sônia E. Alvarez, "The Politics of Gender in Latin America: Comparative Perspectives on Women in the Brazilian Transition to Democracy," vols. 1, 2 (Ph.D diss. Yale University, 1986), 192.

37. CIM met in Rio de Janeiro in 1952 and gave impetus to Fonseca's platform.

38. Robin Morgan, ed., *Sisterhood Is Global* (Garden City, N.Y.: Anchor Books, 1984), 77.

39. Danda Prado, "Brazil: A Fertile but Ambiguous Feminist Terrain," in *Sisterhood Is Global*, ed. Robin Morgan, 81; Prado cites de Beauvoir as quoted by L. G. Ribeiro, "Simone de Beauvoir e Mulheres," *Diario de Noticias*, Rio de Janeiro, 9 Aug. 1960.

40. Prado, "Brazil," 81.

41. Ibid.

42. *The Feminine Mystique* was translated into Portuguese in 1970.

43. Poppino, *Brazil*, 281.

44. Alvarez, "Politics of Gender," 193.

45. Ibid.

46. For a discussion of the effectiveness of the right wing in mobilizing women around the most traditional aspects of their roles (wife, mother) during the 1964 coup d'etat, see Sônia Alvarez, "Politics of Gender." For discussions of women's collective actions, see Louise A. Tilly, "Women's Collective Action and Feminism in France, 1870–1914," in *Class Conflict and Collective Action*, ed. Louise A. Tilly and Charles Tilly (Beverly Hills, Calif.: Published in cooperation with the Social Science History Association, Sage Publications, 1981).

47. For an elegant analysis of women organizing around gender-based concerns, women acting to protect their ability to fulfill their perceived roles (the mother putting food on the table, providing sustenance for the family), see Temma Kaplan, "Female Consciousness and Collective Action: the Case of Barcelona, 1910–1918," *Signs*, 7 (Spring 1982).

48. Robert Wesson, *The United States and Brazil: Limits of Influence* (New York: Praeger, 1981), 43. Wesson argues, and I agree, that it is a mistake to put too much weight on the importance of U.S. manipulation in the coup d'etat of 1964. It is analytically more useful to see the United States as but one of the interests involved. Brazilians were the prime movers; many of the military men involved were glad to accept U.S. support but were deeply nationalist and unwilling to take directions from the United States.

49. Wesson, *The United States and Brazil*, 49.

50. Saffioti, *Women in Class Society*, 217.

51. de Jesus, *Child of the Dark*, 96.

52. Wesson, *The United States and Brazil*, 41.

53. Ibid. "Counterinsurgency erased the boundary between civilian and military affairs and made ambiguous the concept of the enemy."

54. Moema Viezzer's footnote in *Let Me Speak! Testimony of Domitila, A Woman of the Bolivian Mines*, by Domitila Barrios de Chungara, ed. Moema Viezzer, trans. Victoria Ortiz (New York and London: Monthly Review Press, 1978), 68; for description of the Triangular Plan, see Robert J. Alexander, "Tin Industry," in *Encyclopedia of Latin America*, ed. Helen Delpar (New York: McGraw-Hill, 1974), 583.

55. Alexander, "Tin Industry," 583.

56. Barrios de Chungara, *Let Me Speak!*, 69.

57. Ibid.

58. Ibid., 58.

59. Ibid., 72.

70 Notes

0. Ibid., 73. For fuller discussion of the *Barzolas*, see chap. 5. Domitila states, "The barzolas are part of a tragic chapter in the history of women in Bolivia."
61. San Roman was a chief of political security for the MNR government. "In his own house, San Roman had a kind of jail where he brutally tortured the people. San Roman was the terror of all political prisoners." Barrios de Chungara, *Let Me Speak!*, 68.
62. Ibid., 73.
63. Ibid., 75.
64. Ibid., 76.
65. Guevara, *Guerrilla Warfare*, 1.
66. Fanny Edelman, "Party Work among Women," *World Marxist Review* 5 (October 1962): 49.
67. Ibid., 44.
68. For a discussion of the Bay of Pigs invasion, see Cole Blaiser, *The Hovering Giant: U.S. Responses to Revolutionary Change in Latin America* (Pittsburgh, Pa.: University of Pittsburgh Press, 1976), 200–202, 229, 205.
69. *World Marxist Review* 5 (October 1962).
70. *World Marxist Review* 5 (March 1962): 45.
71. Rollie E. Poppino, *International Communism in Latin America: A History of the Movement 1917–1963* (New York: Macmillan, The Free Press, 1964), 108.
72. Morgan, *Sisterhood*, 209.
73. Ibid., 73.
74. Ibid., 719.
75. Ibid.
76. James L. Busey, *Latin American Political Guide*, 18th ed. (New York: Robert Schalkenbach Foundation, 1985), 116.
77. Morgan, *Sisterhood*, 77. See also Timothy P. Wickham-Crowley, "Winners, Losers and Also-Rans: Toward a Comparative Sociology of Latin American Guerrilla Movements" (MS) pp. 3–4. In Venezuela, "Guerrilla bands appeared in 1962, followed a year later by more systematic guerrilla movements organized with party backing: The Armed Forces of National Liberation (FALN), sponsored by the Communists, and the Revolutionary Left (MIR), organized by a splinter group of AD. From 1963 on, the guerrillas' fortunes declined as agrarian reform, elections, public distaste, efficient repression, an improving economy and amnesties gradually took the wind from their sails. Internal splits hastened the decline. By the late 1960s, the guerrillas had all but petered out of existence."
78. Comisión Interamericana de Mujeres (CIM), *Inter-American Commission of Women 1928–1973* (Washington, D.C.: General Secretariat, Organization of American States, 1974), 11.
79. Elsa Chaney, *Supermadre: Women in Politics in Latin America*, Latin American Monographs, No. 50 (Austin: Published for Institute of Latin American Studies by University of Texas Press, 1979), 91.
80. Ibid.
81. Ibid.
82. For a critical view of these appointments, see "La Silenciada," in Morgan, *Sisterhood*, 169.
83. Barbara Evans Clements, "Clara Zetkin," in *Biographical Dictionary of Modern Peace Leaders*, editor-in-chief Harold Josephson (Westport, Conn.: Greenwood Press, 1985), 1047–48.

84. James D. Henderson and Linda Roddy Henderson, *Ten Notable Women of Latin America* (Chicago: Nelson Hall, 1978), 220.

85. Daniel James, ed., *The Complete Bolivian Diaries of Ché Guevara and Other Captured Documents* (New York: Stein and Day, 1986), 26.

86. Henderson and Henderson, *Ten Notable Women*, 221.

87. Ibid., 223.

88. Quoted in *fem*, 3 (January–February 1980): 99.

89. Ibid.

90. Lee Lockwood, *Castro's Cuba, Cuba's Fidel* (New York: Vintage, 1969), 356.

91. Ibid.

92. Ibid.

93. *fem*, 3 (January–February 1980): 100.

94. Henderson and Henderson, *Ten Notable Women*, 233.

95. James, *The Complete Bolivian Diaries*, 26–27.

96. Henderson and Henderson, *Ten Notable Women*, 234.

97. Marta Rojas and Mirta Rodriguez Calderón, ed., *Tania: The Unforgettable Guerrilla*, (New York: Random House, 1971); first published as *Tania: La guerrillera involvidable* (Havana: Instituto del Libro, 1970), 199–200.

98. Antonio Arguedas, quoted in Rojas and Rodriguez Calderón, *Tania*, 918.

99. Ibid., 200.

100. Ibid., 201.

101. Henderson and Henderson, *Ten Notable Women*, 236.

102. Rojas and Rodriguez Calderón, *Tania*, 205.

103. Ibid., 207; Rojas was killed by members of the National Liberation Army of Bolivia on July 14, 1969.

104. Ibid., 207.

105. *fem*, 3 (January–February 1980): 105.

106. Lockwood, *Castro's Cuba, Cuba's Fidel*, 355.

107. Ernesto F. Betancourt, "Exporting the Revolution to Latin America," in *Revolutionary Change in Cuba*, ed. Carmelo Mesa-Lago (Pittsburgh, Pa.: University of Pittsburgh Press, 1971), 111.

108. Ibid., 112.

109. Luís E. Aguilar, ed., *Marxism in Latin America* (New York: Alfred A. Knopf, 1968), 257–58.

110. Barrios de Chungara, *Let Me Speak!*, 113.

111. Ibid., 114.

112. Ibid.

113. Carlos Marighela, *For the Liberation of Brazil*, trans. John Butt and Rosemary Sheed, Introduction by Richard Gott (New York: Penguin Books, 1971).

114. Ibid., frontispiece.

115. Ibid., 98.

116. Ibid., 33–34.

117. Ibid., 35.

118. After the kidnapping of the U.S. ambassador, which succeeded in securing the release of fifteen rebel prisoners, the military resorted to terror and torture in double measure. Marighela was killed by police on November 4, 1969; Marighela, *For the Liberation*, frontispiece.

119. See Jacquette, "Women in Revolutionary Movements," 351; also this text, chap. 1.

120. Giovanna Merola, "For as long as it takes," in *Sisterhood* edited by Robin Morgan, p. 719.

121. Angela Neves-Xavier de Brito, "Brazilian Women in Exile: The Quest for an Identity," *Latin American Perspectives* 13 (Spring 1986): 60.

122. Ibid.

123. Jacquette, "Women in Revolutionary Movements," 351.

124. María Esther Gilio, *The Tupamaro Guerrillas*, trans. Anne Edmonson, Introduction by Robert J. Alexander (New York: Ballantine Books, 1972), xii.

125. Ibid., 151.

126. Ibid., 148.

127. Ibid., xiii.

128. Ibid., 227.

129. Ibid.

130. Ibid., x.

131. Ibid., 228.

132. Ibid., 65.

133. Cleary, *Crisis and Change*, 33; Sally W. Yudelman, *Hopeful Openings: A Study of Five Women's Development Organizations in Latin America and the Carribbean*; Kumarian Press Case Studies Series (West Hartford, Conn.: Kumarian Press, 1987), 35.

134. Yudelman, *Hopeful Openings*, 5, citing Penny Lernoux.

135. Ibid.

136. Ibid.

137. Gilfeather, Sister Katherine Anne, "Women Religious, the Poor and the Institutional Church in Chile," *Journal of Interamerican Studies and World Affairs* (1979), 135; also, in one of the most influential treatises on the movement, *Theology of Liberation: History, Politics, and Salvation*, trans. and ed. by Sister Caridad Inda and John Eagleson (Maryknoll, N.Y.: Orbis Books, 1973), Gustavo Gutierrez states that his book is based on the experiences of men and women in Latin America but "makes no mention of the intrinsically unjust position of women in Latin American society, much less of their secondary position in the Catholic Church" Gilfeather, p. 145.

138. Yudelman, *Hopeful Openings*, 5–6. This questioning led directly to recognizing and questioning their status as women within their communities in the 1970s.

139. Gilfeather, "Women Religious," 136.

140. Daniel Levine, *Religion and Politics in Latin America: The Catholic Church in Venezuela and Colombia* (Princeton, N.J.: Princeton University Press, 1981), 19. For discussion of *communidades de base*, see this text, chap. 7.

141. Gilfeather, "Women Religious," 145.

142. Medea Benjamin, ed. and trans., *Don't Be Afraid, Gringo: A Honduran Woman Speaks from the Heart, The Story of Elvia Alvarado.* (San Francisco: The Institute for Food and Development Policy, 1987), 30.

143. Successive land reform laws, in 1962, 1972, and 1975 did little to change the situation.

144. Yudelman, *Hopeful Openings*, 36.

145. Ibid.

146. Yudelman, *Hopeful Openings*, quoting Safilios-Rothschild. Note that the 1962 agrarian reform law was passed in part to conform to the Alliance for Progress prescription but was greatly watered down under pressure from United Fruit Company et al.

147. Yudelman, *Hopeful Openings*, 36.

148. CAC resurfaced in 1978 with support from OXFAM/England and the Inter-American Foundation to organize FEHMUC (Federacion Hondureña de Mujeres Campesinas); Yudelman, *Hopeful Openings*, 37. Influenced by the UN Decade for Women, it was at this time that CAC adopted the slogan, "The liberation of the people begins with the liberation of women." Speaking in 1987, Elvia Alvarado was cynical about the claims of the union to organize among women *campesinos*: "All the campesino organizations say they're organizing women. All of them have a position in the leadership for 'women's affairs.' But what really happens with most of these women's groups is that they're really created to get international funding. The foreigners love to fund 'women's projects'" (Benjamin, *Don't Be Afraid, Gringo*, 87). Then, when the project is finished or fails, the women's group falls apart. Alvarado emphasized that her group seeks to teach women organizational skills so that they can identify their own needs and build their own projects around them.

149. Daphne Patai, *Brazilian Women Speak: Contemporary Life Stories* (New Brunswick, N.J.: Rutgers University Press, 1988), 40. Regarding her choice of "Sister Denise" Patai states: "In the Brazilian Northeast, the important work being done by women in the activist Roman Catholic Church could probably have been explained to me by many individuals, but I specifically wanted to learn about the experiences of an older nun, one whose life in the Church had begun before the arrival of liberation theology."

150. Patai, *Brazilian Women Speak*, 40. Sister Denise did not take this step until 1976, when she was forty-three years old.

151. Ibid., 41.

152. Ibid.

153. Ibid., 42.

154. Ibid., 47.

155. Ibid., 46.

156. Ibid., 62.

157. Brian Loveman, *Chile* (New York: Oxford University Press, 1979), 303.

158. Ibid., 302.

159. Frei Montalva, Eduardo, "The Alliance That Lost Its Way," *Foreign Affairs* 45 (April 1967), quoted in *The Quest for Change in Latin America*, ed. W. Raymond and James Nelson Goodsell (New York: Oxford University Press, 1970), 516.

160. Loveman, *Chile*, 326.

161. Ibid., 333.

162. Chaney, *Supermadre*, 337.

163. Ibid., 337.

164. Neves-Xavier de Brito, "Brazilian Women in Exile," 65.

165. Ibid.

166. Chaney, *Supermadre*, 337.

167. Elsa M. Chaney, "The Mobilization of Women in Allende's Chile," in *Women in Politics*, ed. Jane Jacquette (New York: John Wiley & Sons, 1974), 269.

168. Ibid.

169. Davis E. Hojman, "Land Reform, Female Migration and the Market for Domestic Service in Chile," *Journal of Latin American Studies*, 21:113. See also Carmen Diana Deere, "Rural Women and State Policy: The Latin American Agrarian Reform Experience," *World Development*, 13 (September 1985): 9.

170. Hojman, "Land Reform," 113.

171. Ibid.

172. Brian H. Smith, *The Church and Politics in Chile* (Princeton, N.J.: Princeton University Press, 1982), 181. "This movement began among 80 clerics active in working-class parishes in Santiago in April 1971."

173. Neves-Xavier de Brito, "Brazilian Women in Exile," 65.

174. Salvador Allende, quoted in Chaney, "The Mobilization of Women," 169.

175. Kaplan, "Female Consciousness," 175; also this text, chap. 1.

176. Michele Mattelart, "Chile: The Feminine Version of the Coup d'Etat," in *Sex and Class in Latin America: Women's Perspectives on Politics, Economics and the Family in the Third World*, ed. June Nash and Helen Icken Safa (New York: J. F. Bergin, 1980), 179.

177. Chaney, "The Mobilization of Women," 169.

178. Penny Lernoux, *Cry of the People* (Garden City, N.Y.: Doubleday, 1980; New York: Penguin Books, 1982; Levine, 19; Smith, *The Church and Politics in Chile*.

179. Levine, *Religion and Politics*, 19; Smith, *The Church and Politics in Chile*, 158.

180. Mattelart, "Chile," 183.

181. Chaney, *Supermadre*, 124. The linkage of TFP, Liberty and Fatherland, The Institute, and Poder Femenino to the CIA and to right-wing Brazilian groups was later established in U.S. congressional hearings.

182. Mattelart, "Chile," 283.

183. Ibid.

184. Quoted in Mattelart, "Chile," 285.

185. Lernoux, *Cry of the People*, 296.

186. For discussion of the Chilean National Secretariat of Women, see chap. 7.

187. Cited in Pat Garrett-Schesch, "The Mobilization of Women During the Popular Unity Government," *Latin American Perspectives* 2 (Spring 1975): 101.

188. Chaney, "The Mobilization of Women."

189. Neves-Xavier de Brito, "Brazilian Women in Exile," 66.

190. Ibid., citing Albertino Oliveira da Costa, María Teresa Porciuncula de Moraes, and Valentina da Rocha Lima's work, *Memorias—das mulheres—do exilio* (Rio de Janeiro: Paz e Terra, 1980), 110.

7. National Liberation, Redemocratization and International Feminism (pp. 187–237)

1. Quoted in *off our backs*, 18 (March 1988).

2. "Foco literally means 'the center of action' or 'detonator.' As a strategy for revolutionary change, based on the Cuban model, the foco approach assumed that a small group of militarily trained, armed professional revolutionaries was capable of creating the subjective conditions for a successful insurrection, of being the spark . . . that lights the revolutionary fire. The emphasis in foco organizations was on military and tactical, rather than political and ideological, training and as a result, they tended to be isolated from mass movements and organizations." Norma Chinchilla, *Women in Revolutionary Movements: The Case of Nicaragua*, Women in International Development Working Papers, No. 27 (East Lansing: Michigan State University, 1983), 1.

3. Sônia E. Alvarez, "The Politics of Gender in Latin America: Comparative Perspectives on Women in the Brazilian Transition to Democracy," vols. 1, 2 (Ph.D. diss., Yale University, 1986), 320.

4. Vilma Espín, "The Early Years," in *Women and the Cuban Revolution*, ed. Elizabeth Stone (New York: Pathfinder Press, 1981), 40. Speeches by Espín and Castro. Family Code of 1975 and Maternity Law for Working Women.

5. Espín, "The Early Years," 40. Note that when "federation" is used in the title of women's organizations formed after World War II, it usually signifies that they are affiliated with the International Democratic Federation of Women.

6. June Hahner, ed., *Women in Latin American History, Their Lives and Views*, rev. ed., UCLA Latin American Studies, No. 51. (Los Angeles: University of California, UCLA Latin American Center Publications, 1980), 166. Hahner excerpts an interview with Espín from Prensa Latina Feature Service, Havana, 1972.

7. Ibid., 168.

8. Zoíla Franco, "Women in the Transformation of Cuban Education," *Prospects: Quarterly Review of Education Resources* (Paris: UNESCO, 1975), 388. For fuller discussion of the Cuban literacy campaign, see chapter 3.

9. Heidi Steffens, "Cuba: The Day Women Took Over Havana," *Ms.*, 3 (April 1975): 35.

10. Ibid.

11. Latin American and Caribbean Women's Collective, *Slaves of Slaves: The Challenge of Latin American Women* (London: Zed Press, 1980), 101.

12. Jane Jaquette, "Female Political Participation in Latin America: Raising Feminist Issues," in *Women in the World: 1975–1985, The Women's Decade*, ed. Lynne B. Iglitzin and Ruth Ross (Santa Barbara, Calif.: ABC Clio Press, 1986). Jaquette points out that "Cuba has been the focus of much praise and some criticism for the way in which women have been mobilized. Praise for the Family Law . . . has been matched by criticism of the Castro regime for mobilizing women only to the extent they are needed by the national economy. There is a leftist critique of the Cuban experience centering on the issue of whether the Cuban Federation of Women is truly a mass organization, with input from below, or whether it is primarily an arm of the government, which uses it to promote decisions made at the top" (p. 261). Jaquette also discusses one of the problems faced by scholars attempting to assess the real role of women within the revolution, which is that although an enormous literature exists on the topic, most of it is laudatory rather than substantive.

13. Partido Comunista de Cuba (PCC). "Investigacion sobre la mujer y los poderes populares en Matanzas," in *Primer congreso del Partido, Tesis No. 3, Sobre el pleno ejercito de la igualdad de la mujer* (Havana: Departamento de Orientacion Revolucionaria, Comité Central, 1975). Cited in Isabel Larguia and John Dumoulin, "Women's Equality and the Cuban Revolution," in *Women and Change in Latin America*, ed. June Nash and Helen Safa (South Hadley, Mass.: Bergin and Garvey, 1986, c1985).

14. "The campaign of getting men to work in the home, inaugurated months ago with the first discussions of Cuba's new Family Code (which makes it law for men whose wives work to do half the housework and child care), was a frequent topic of discussion at the congress." Margaret Randall, "Notes on the Second National Congress of the Federacion de Mujeres Cubanos, November 25–29, 1974," *Latin American Perspectives*, 2 (1975): 111.

15. The Second Congress received substantial coverage in the feminist press in the United States (*Ms.*, etc.). Cuba and the meaning of the Cuban Revolution was of central importance among North American female intellectuals as well as male intellectuals in the 1970s.

16. Fidel Castro, "Closing Speech to the Second Congress of the Federation of Cuban Women, November 29, 1974," in *Women and the Cuban Revolution*, ed. Elizabeth Stone (New York: Pathfinder Press, 1981), 10.

17. Randall, "Notes on the Second National Congress," 114.

18. Ibid.

19. See, for example, the CIM publication *Enlace*, nos. 22 (May 1967), 23 (April 1968), 25 (1969), 26 (October 1973); also, Inter-American Commission of Women, *Report Presented to the Twenty-First Session of the United Nations Commission on the Status of Women* (Washington, D.C.: Pan-American Union, 1968); and Inter-American Commission of Women, *Report Presented to the Twenty-Second Session of the United Nations Commission on the Status of Women* (Washington, D.C.: Pan-American Union, 1969).

20. Re dissension among representatives to CIM, interview with Coralee Turbitt, who served as a delegate of the Women's International Development agency to CIM, 1971, October 21, 1988.

21. Alvarez, "The Politics of Gender," 317.

22. In the aftermath of the brutal political repression of the late 1960s, many Brazilian activists went into exile. With the political *distensão* (decompression) of the mid-1970s, some returned. For an excellent discussion of Brazilian women in exile and their return, see Angela Neves-Xavier de Brito, "Brazilian Women in Exile: The Quest for an Identity," *Latin American Perspectives*, 13 (Spring 1986): 58–80.

23. Alvarez, "The Politics of Gender," 317: When President Geisel's "political decompression" allowed for public commemorations of IWY in São Paulo, Rio de Janeiro, and Belo Horizante in 1975, this latter "more politically acceptable" (from the point of view of the left-wing political opposition) organizational form came to predominate within the nascent Brazilian feminist movement until the late 1980s. The UN's proclamation of IWY in 1975 and the newly "decompressed" regime's decision to endorse its three basic goals of "Equality, Development and Peace" enabled women who had been concerned with issues of gender inequality in Brazilian society to organize publicly for the first time. It also provided the still politically repressed left-wing opposition with a new "front" or forum for political action.

24. Alvarez, "The Politics of Gender," 317, quoting Rose Marie Muraro.

25. Ibid., 316.

26. Ibid., 321.

27. Editorial, *Brasil Mulher*, 1 (October 1975), quoted in Alvarez, "The Politics of Gender," 321.

28. Editorial, *Nos Mulheres*, no. 1 (June 1976), cited in Alvarez, "The Politics of Gender," 323.

29. Primero Encontro de Communidade, São Paulo.

30. Alvarez, "The Politics of Gender," 317.

31. Alvarez ("The Politics of Gender," 261) writes of the post-1968 church, "the Church was to act as a catalytic and prophetic force, using moral rather than temporal power to promote justice."

32. It is important to speculate as to why women were able to create a space of political dissent and to openly criticize the social, political, and economic status quo in Brazil at this time. Alfred Stepan argues that the women's activities served Geisel's program to disempower the hard-line military; that is, that the women were not allowed to demonstrate just because they were women (and Brazilian wives and mothers) but because they brought increased moral force to bear upon the military units responsible for disappearances and torture. See Alfred Stepan, ed., *Democratizing Brazil* (New York: Oxford University Press, 1989).

33. Alvarez, "The Politics of Gender," 293.

34. Martin Scurrah, "Military Reformism in Peru: Opening Pandora's Box," *LARR (Latin American Research Review)*, 21 (1), 1986.

35. The population of Peru doubled between 1960 and 1980, from 10 million to 20 million. One of the effects of the agrarian reforms was further dislocation of the

small landholders and substantial disruption of the rural economy, which forced ever greater numbers of peasants to seek work in the Lima-Callao area. In 1960 nearly 60 percent of Peruvians lived in rural areas; by 1980 that figure was reversed.

36. Jeanine Anderson de Velasco, ed., *Congreso de Investigacion Acerca de la Mujer en la Region Andina, del 7 al 10 de Junio, 1982, auspicio Universidad Católica del Peru, Organizo Asociacion Peru—Mujer* (Lima: 1983), 102. Flora Tristán was a pioneering nineteenth-century feminist.

37. Virginia Vargas, in *Congreso de Investigacion*, ed. Jeanine Anderson de Velasco, 102.

38. The term *reivindicación* also echoes Mary Wollstonecraft's title, *A Vindication of the Rights of Women: With Strictures on Political and Moral Subjects* (London, printed for J. Johnson, 1792). Two observations: (1) Wollstonecraft would have known the original meaning of vindication in reference to land rights as it was commonly used in eighteenth-century England; (2) as to the familiarity of Latin American women with Wollstonecraft's work, it was translated into Portuguese in Brazil in 1833 and was presumably available in Spanish America by the midnineteenth century. For a discussion of Pachamama, see Carol Andreas, *When Women Rebel: The Rise of Popular Feminism in Peru* (Westport, Conn.: Lawrence Hill, 1985).

39. Anderson de Velasco, *Congreso de Investigacion*, 9.

40. There are strong parallels between the Peruvian feminist movement in the early 1970s and the Italian feminist movement in the same period. In both national polities, the church and the Communist party sought women's allegiance. CEBs appear to have played a more important role in the politicization of women in Italy (there are some parallels to the Brazilian experience, although the church in Italy was not providing *sombra* to women already politically active). In Peru and Italy, by the late 1970s feminists had moved away from both the traditional left and the church to develop their own gendered critique of society. For an excellent discussion of Italian feminism, see Lucia Chiavola Birnbaum, *Liberazione della donna/Feminism in Italy* (Middletown, Conn.: Wesleyan University Press, 1986).

41. Vargas, in *Congreso de Investigacion*, 102.

42. Cornelia Butler Flora, *Socialist Feminism in Latin America*, Working Paper No. 14 (East Lansing: Michigan State University, 1982), 69.

43. Vargas, in *Congreso de Investigacion*, 102.

44. Flora, *Socialist Feminism*, 80.

45. The Velasco government established relations with the Chinese Communist party and with Cuba.

46. Sally W. Yudelman, *Hopeful Openings: A Study of Five Women's Development Organizations in Latin America and the Caribbean*, Kumarian Press Case Studies Series (West Hartford, Conn.: Kumarian Press, 1987), 3. Also, United Nations, *Meeting in Mexico, The Story of the World Conference of the International Women's Year, Mexico City, June 19–July 2, 1975* (New York: United Nations, 1975).

47. Conversation with Coralie Turbitt, December 3, 1988, re instigation for IWY. She was in Washington and working on Senator Percy's staff in 1972 and helped draft the legislation that became the Percy Amendment. The amendment tied AID money to proof on the part of the applicant government that the project give special consideration to women, especially poor women. Turbitt says this was important in the UN decision to declare plans for an IWY (which they did not fund).

48. Hanna Papanek, "The Work of Women: Postscript from Mexico City," *Signs: Journal of Women in Culture and Society*, 1 (Autumn 1975): 218.

49. UN, *Meeting in Mexico*, 37.

50. Ibid., 39.
51. Papanek, "The Work of Women," 37.
52. "Forum 85: Interview with Claudia Hinosoja," *Connexions* (Summer/Fall 1986): 17–18.
53. Domitila Barrios de Chungara, *Let Me Speak! Testimony of Domitila, A Woman of the Bolivian Tin Mines*, ed. Moema Viezzer, trans. Victoria Ortiz (New York and London: Monthly Review Press, 1978), 198.
54. Ibid., 199.
55. Ibid., 201.
56. World Plan of Action: United Nations, *Report of the World Conference of the International Women's Year, Mexico City, 19 June–2 July, 1975* (New York: United Nations, 1976), 9.
57. Ibid., 112.
58. Yudelman, *Hopeful Openings*, 3.
59. Yudelman, *Hopeful Openings*, 6.
60. Magaly Pineda, "The Spanish-Speaking Caribbean: We Women Aren't Sheep," in Robin Morgan, ed. *Sisterhood Is Global*, (Garden City, N.Y.: Anchor Press/Doubleday, 1984), 133. Pineda continues "it was in 1978 that these and others [women's groups with a feminist perspective] began to flourish. The increase and/or strengthening of women's groups was most impressive in the countryside, less so or 'marginal' urban neighborhoods, and weakest, though qualitatively important within the so-called Left."
61. Vargas, *Congreso Investigacion*, 102.
62. Flora, "Socialist Feminism in Latin America," *Women and Politics* 4 (Spring 1984):69.
63. Vargas, *Congreso Investigacion*, 102.
64. Ruth Leger Sivard, *Women . . . A World Survey* (Washington, D.C.: World Priorities, 1985), 27.
65. Vargas, *Congreso Investigacion*, 101.
66. Ibid., 103.
67. Flora, "Socialist Feminism," 90.
68. Vargas, *Congreso Investigacion*, 103.
69. Janet Greenberg, "A Working Bibliography: Towards a History of Women's Periodicals in Latin America from the Eighteenth to the Twentieth Century," in Seminar on Women and Culture in Latin America, *Women, Culture and Politics in Latin America* (Berkeley and Los Angeles: University of California Press, 1990).
70. *fem* was founded 1976. "Seven years of regularly published issues covering abortion, work, sexuality, the international woman's movement, the family, sexist language, children, mother–daughter relationships, women's history, science, housework, men, women and the Church, marriage as an institution."
71. See discussion of feminist journalism in chap. 4. Also Greenberg, "A Working Bibliography."
72. Renata Prosperpio and Ana Alice Costa, "Brasil: Se organizan las mal amadas," *fem*, (January–February 1980):34.
73. From the English-language version of "The Sunrise of the People," cited in Jane Deighton et al., *Sweet Ramparts: Women in Revolutionary Nicaragua* (London: Nicaraguan Solidarity Campaign, 1983), 104.
74. For example, *Sporadica* (Mexico), *Cacerola* (Uruguay).
75. Except in the United States, where the domestic industry has resisted adapting

the Portuguese-language films into English. Brazilian films are enormously popular throughout Latin America and in Europe, Africa, Japan, and China. Until inflation bit deeply into the economy in the 1980s, Brazil had a thriving film industry.

76. Maria Lygia Quartim de Morães, *Mulheres en movimento* (São Paulo: Camara Brasileira do Livro, 1985), 10–11; cited in Victoria Bettencourt, "Women's Movements in Brazil: The Struggle for Participation in Redemocratization" (unpublished paper, University of California, Santa Cruz, 1986).

77. The regime of General Augusto Pinochet (1973–1990) was centrally concerned with enforcing a conservative definition of womanhood that equated femaleness with motherhood and woman's role in the male-headed family. The official doctrine, put forth in *Valores patrios y valores familiares*, Cuadernos de Difusion, No. 7 (Santiago, Chile: Secretaria Nacional de la Mujer 1982), exalts the difference between male and female, including not only sex characteristics but the different roles each is to play in life: ("La mujer que no tiene clara la importancia de su misión, o de la legitimidad de sus reacciones femeninas, puede caer con mucha facilidad en alguno de los errores anteriormente descritos. Enefecto, si ella no estima como un destino superior su vocación maternal, su papel de esposa y de educadora, es facil que se situe ante el hombre en una posición, o inferior o agresiva, o bien que intenet imitario y rivalizar con el, negando su identidad femenina" (p. 24). Feminism is defined as the reverse of machismo (i.e., the desire to impose female dominance over men) (p. 23). With regard to birth control, the document states that the decisions are private (though Catholics know what the pope endorses), and the official position of the government is that Chile needs to correct its "extremely low birthrate" (p. 35). Abortion is strictly illegal: "The practice of abortion is not included in the freedom of individual decision. It is expressly condemned in our country, as much for moral reasons as for legal norms, expressed in the Constitucion Politica del Estado. His Excellency the President of the Republic has been emphatic in declaring, 'In Chile respect for life begins at the moment of conception'" (p. 36). Although this material was published in 1982, the central declarations were contained in decrees stated in 1979. Family values are identified with national values.

78. *fem*, January–February 1980, pp. 33–34.

79. Conversation with Norma Alarcón, Berkeley, California, January 1989.

80. Jane Jaquette ("Female Political Participation," 261) corroborates this observation: "The rapidity with which feminist thought has been absorbed and reworked by Latin American scholars to reflect Latin American realities is striking."

81. The experience of Nicaragua, and El Salvador and Guatemala as well, represents an important break with past conceptions of women's proper role in socialist and revolutionary struggles and with strategies for changing the attitudes of men and women about that role." Chinchilla, "Women in Revolutionary Movements," 1.

82. See Deighton et al, *Sweet Ramparts*; Chinchilla, "Women in Revolutionary Movements"; Nora Astorga, "Liberated Themselves by Liberating the People," *World Marxist Review* 25 (March 1982); "Nicaraguan Women in Struggle," *Women and Revolution: Journal of the Women's Commission of the Spartacist League* (Spring 1986), no. 31; Maxine Molyneux, "Mobilization without Emancipation? Women's Interests, the State, and Revolution in Nicaragua," *Feminist Studies* 11 (Summer 1985): 227.

83. Jaquette points out with regard to Nicaragua, "the increasing trend toward militarization of society (which can be attributed in part to U.S. policy), and the active role women are playing in that process, is raising doubts among feminist observers elsewhere in Latin America who associate feminist politics with resistance to military

rule and to militarization itself" ("Female Political Participation," 262).

84. Megan Martin and Susie Willett, eds. *Women in Nicaragua* (London: Nicaraguan Solidarity Campaign, 1980), 10.

85. Ibid., 11.

86. Ibid., 14.

87. Cited in Maxine Molyneux, "Mobilization without Emancipation," 238.

88. Molyneux, "Mobilization without Emancipation," 234. Maxine Molyneux's point is not that the Nicaraguan government could or should do more to enact a feminist agenda but that the interests of women are far broader than their interests as a gender: "The conditionality of women's unity and the fact that gender issues are not necessarily primary is nowhere more clearly illustrated than by the example of revolutionary upheaval. In such situations, gender issues are frequently displaced by class conflict, principally because although women may suffer discrimination on the basis of gender and may be aware that they do, they nonetheless suffer differentially according to their social class." Deighton et al. say the same thing in *Sweet Ramparts* (see Conclusion, pp. 158–162), but they are more critical than Molyneux.

89. Vargas, *Congreso de Investigacion*, 102.

90. *Valores patrios y valores familiares*, Cuadernos de Difusión, No. 7, (Santiago, Chile; Secretaria Nacional de la Mujer 1982), 11. The Alwin administration, which took office after the rejection of Pinochet at the polls, has created a new national women's bureau, SERNAM, and appointed women who have been active in the feminist movement in Chile.

91. Ibid., 24.

92. Gloria Bonder, "The Study of Politics from the Standpoint of Women," *International Social Science Journal*, 35 (1983): "The moral nature that Pinochet sees women as possessing performs essential functions within society—those of bringing up children in the home within the order established by the military government, and also of alleviating and enduring the sacrifices demanded of the country."

93. *Valore patrios*, 10.

94. "Former Mexican Soldier Describes Executions of Political Prisoners," *New York Times*, 19 Feb. 1989, p. 1. "In the first public acknowledgement of death squad activity in Mexico, a former Mexican Army soldier [Zacarias Osorio Cruz] is maintaining that he was part of a secret military unit that executed at least 60 political prisoners here in the late 1970s and early 1980s. . . . 'The Ministry of Defense issued official documents for such killings on a regular basis between 1977 and 1982,' he said, and the prisoners were then removed clandestinely from a military prison here, killed, and their bodies disposed of."

95. Elizabeth Stone, ed., *Women and the Cuban Revolution* (New York: Pathfinder Press, 1981), 125; speeches by Espín and Castro.

96. Charlotte Bunch, "Notes" *Ms.*, July 1980, p. 82. In several articles I found statements asserting that the regional conferences in Latin America began after Copenhagen as if they were somehow inspired by the Copenhagen meetings. The fact that the plans for the Primero Encuentro had been underway for two years seems to contravert this assumption.

97. Leni Silverstein, "The First Feminist Conference in Latin America," *International Supplement to the Women's Studies Quarterly*, 1 (January 1982):34. Silverstein points out that the decision to use only Spanish was based on financial considerations and that it "virtually excluded the participation of non-Spanish speaking Caribbean women."

98. Ibid.

99. Ibid., 35.

100. Ibid.

101. Ana María Portugal, "Hallazgos y extravios," *fem* 8 (Summer 1985):5.

102. Ibid.

103. Conversation with Lea Fletcher, publisher of *Feminaria* (Buenos Aires), Berkeley, Calif., 14 February 1989. In our discussion of publications by feminists in Chile, Fletcher pointed out that she and other Argentine women have almost no access to these publications in Argentina. She said that there is now a feminist bookstore in Buenos Aires that manages to stock some materials from the United States and Europe; but many books and journals do not make it through customs, and those that do are extraordinarily expensive, as are all imported goods, because of the weakness of the Argentine currency on the international market.

104. Masthead "Statement of Purpose," *Mujer*, no. 52 (November 1985).

105. *Mujer* (November 1985): back cover. Letter from Carmen Beatriz Ruiz, Centro de Promoción de La Mujer "Gregoria Apaza," Casilla 21170, La Paz, Bolivia.

106. It will be recalled that in the 1930s Bolivian women had a radio show that also was concerned with women of the indigenous population and feminist issues. See chap. 4.

107. That both *Mujer*/Fempress and *Isis* should be located in Santiago, Chile, presents an interesting paradox: *Isis* carries a strong revolutionary message, and many articles reprinted in *Mujer*/Fempress are socialist-feminist and all are solidly anti-authoritarian. There are two hypotheses as to why the Pinochet regime allowed this material to be produced: (1) allowing the feminist movement to publish may be used by the regime as an example of the freedom of expression in Chile, and (2) the regime views the women's work as inconsequential. The second hypothesis was suggested to me by Arnold J. Bauer on his return from Chile, January 1989. He pointed out that leftist publications were readily available in bookstores in Santiago and surmised that the regime feels unthreatened by the writings of the opposition.

108. Centro de Flora Tristán, Mujeres en Lucha, Manuela Ramos, Grupo Autonomo, Mujer y Cambio, Grupo Warmi, ALIMUPER.

109. Portugal, "Hallazgos," 8.

110. Ibid., 9.

111. Norma Fuller, "II Encuentro Feminista Latinoamericano y del Caribe," *Women's Studies International Forum*, 6 (1983): ii. See also Roxana Carrillo, "Discurso inaugural," *fem* 8 (31):6, 7.

112. Portugal, "Hallazgos," 8. "Pero no por gusto han pasado diez anos y las mismas que, curadas de excomuniones y actos de contricion, hace tiempo soltaron las amarras, '¡No mas chantajes!' (No more blackmail!) dijeron para ahogar por siempre jamas, la mala conciencia su conciencia de 'pequebu.' 'No debemos caes en el juego de las conciliacion' me digo una colombiana frenté a esa proclacion estenforea y obviamente reiferativa d un feminismo que, para contar con el nihil obstat de los comites centrales de todos los pelajes, debe declarase 'revolucionario' 'antiimperialista' 'politico' 'de masas' 'identificado con un sector de clase' 'no ajeno a la sociedad' etcetera, etcetera."

113. Fietta Jarque, "650 feministas en El Bosque," *El Observador*, 20 July 1983. Irene Campos Carr, "Second Feminist Conference of Latin America and the Caribbean: Two Reports," *Women's Studies International*, no. 3 (April 1984): 26.

114. Carr, "Second Feminist Conference," 26.

115. Carol Andreas, *When Women Rebel: The Rise of Popular Feminism in Peru* (Westport: Conn.: Lawrence Hill, 1985), 178. In 1987 it was estimated that 60 percent of *senderista* troops were females.

116. *Pueblos jovenes*, literally "young towns," is the term given to the primitive shanty towns that surround Peruvian cities, notably the port of Callao.

117. Carr, "Second Feminist Conference," 29.

118. Portugal, "Hallazgos," 9.

119. *Viva, Publicación bimestral del Central de la Mujer Peruana Flora Tristán*, no. 17.

120. Sheldon Annis and Peter Hakim, eds. *Direct to the Poor: Grassroots Development in Latin America* (Boulder, Colo.: L. Rienner, 1988).

121. Gisela Espínosa Damian, "Feminism and Social Struggle in Mexico," in *Third World/Second Sex 2*, ed. Miranda Davies (London: Zed Books, 1987) 31.

122. Ibid., 33.

123. Carmen Barroso and Cristina Bruschini, "Building Politics from Personal Lives," *Third World/Second Sex 2*, ed. Miranda Davies (London: Zed Books, 1987), 262.

124. Barroso and Bruschini, "Building Politics," 256.

125. Catherine MacKinnon, "Feminism, Marxism, Method and the State: An Agenda for Theory," *Signs*, 7 (1982):515.

126. Barroso and Bruschini, "Building Politics," 263. Several groups (SOS Corpa, Cas Mujer, Sexuality and Health, etc.) have chosen these issues as their central concern.

127. Ibid., 263.

128. The Grupo de Estudios sobre la Condición de la Mujer en Uruguay (Study Group on the Condition of Women in Uruguay) is best known by its acronym, GRECMU. Founded in 1979 and widely respected for its scholarship, it is among the best-known groups of independent women scholars in Latin America.

129. *La Cacerola, Boletín Interno de GRECMU*, 1 (April 1984).

130. Annis and Hakim, *Direct to the Poor*. Re the term "redemocratization": "During the past decade in Latin America, perhaps the most important force favoring grassroots organization has been democratization.

131. *La Cacerola*, 1 (April 1984), inside front cover.

132. Ibid.

133. Ibid., 13.

134. Janet Greenberg, "A Working Bibliography: Towards a History of Women's Periodicals in Latin America from the Eighteenth to the Twentieth Century," in *Women, Culture and Politics in Latin America* (Berkeley and Los Angeles: University of California Press, 1990).

135. Annis and Hakim, *Direct to the Poor*.

136. See discussion in chap. 6.

137. Women of ALESDA, "A Statement by Domestic Workers in Uruguay," *Third World/Second Sex*, comp. Miranda Davies (London: Zed Press, 1983), 174.

138. Mandate of the UN World Conference, cited in Charlotte Bunch, "UN World Conference in Nairobi," *Ms.*, June 1985, p. 79.

139. "Forum 85: Interview with Claudia Hinojosa," *Connexions: An International Women's Quarterly* nos. 17–18 (Summer/Fall 1986). See also "The Women's Decade" (same issue): "In general Forum '85 compared to the previous two conferences, exhibited a different tone and a stronger willingness to accept differences. In ten years the definition of feminism has broadened dramatically . . . feminism no longer represents a narrow Western view."

140. Ibid., 7.

141. "Our Feminisms," *Connexions* no. 19 (Winter 1986).

142. See, for example, the June–July 1977 issue of *Nos Mulheres*, devoted to "Racismo, uma opressão a mais."

143. There are many accounts of this incident and various interpretations. For

example, see *Connexions* no. 19 (Winter 1986); and Mercedes Sayagues, letter to the editor of *The Progressive* (November 1985); Reprinted in *Mujer* no. 55 (February 1986). Sayagues points out that "Brazil has a long history of reactionary groups manipulating poor people by sending them places to create conflict—with the press arriving first. Why were the photographers of the *Jornal do Brasil* on the beach before the bus of poor women arrived?" She is responding to the publication in *The Progressive* of an article on the Santos meeting by Jayne H. Bloch, "The Women Outside the Gates," which criticized the Organizing Commission of the Encounter.

144. Eliana Ortega and Nancy Saporta Sternbach, "Gracias de la Vida: Recounting the Third Latin American Feminist Meetings," *off our backs*, January 1986.

145. NOW meetings have frequently been disrupted by protestors, most spectacularly so during debates on the ERA and on abortion, when protestors brought dead fetuses in jars into the meetings. As was true in Santos, the disruption became the focus of coverage; the deliberations of the conference were lost.

146. International reports of the conference also reflected the biased coverage.

147. See Bibliography for an indication of the great scope of the new women's scholarship.

148. Flyer for the Conselho Estadual da Condição Feminina, São Paulo, Brazil. The production of Latin American scholars is augmented by North American and European scholars and by international agencies such as UNESCO.

149. Jane Jaquette, "Women in Revolutionary Movements in Latin America."

150. Bettencourt, "Women's Movements in Brazil: The Struggle for Participation in Redemocratization" (unpublished manuscript, University of California, Santa Cruz, 1986).

151. Maria Lygia Quartim de Morães, *Mulheres em movimiento* (São Paulo: Camara Brasileira do Livro, 1985), 10.

152. Tania Krustcka, "Brazil: Despite Formal Recognition, Women Denied Full Political Role," *Latinamerica Press*, 10 October 1985, p. 6.

153. Cited in Guadaloupe Lopez Garcia, "Las Mujeres y la Politica," *fem*, no. 67 (1988):9. The idea of day-care facilities for factory workers dates from the nineteenth century, but the inclusion of domestic workers reflects the attention all women workers have received in the past fifteen years.

154. Ibid., 10.

155. Ibid., 12.

156. Ibid., 14.

157. See Lourdes Arizpe Schlosser and Carlota Botey, "Las politicas de desarrolla agrario y su impacto sobre la mujer campesina en Mexico," in *La mujer y la politica agraria en America Latina*, ed. Magdalena Leon de Leal and Carmen Diana Deere (Bogotá, Colombia, 1986).

158. "Mulheres fortalecem," *Jornal Sem Terra*, 56 (November 1986):12–13. Cited in Bettencourt, "Women's Movements in Brazil: The Struggle for Participation in Redemocratization," 6.

159. Magda Portal, *Flora Tristán, Precursora* (Lima: Editorial La Equidad, 1983).

160. *fem*, no. 67 (1988).

161. The number of sponsoring groups for the Taxco Conference provides a comparison with the handful of women who had organized the conferences in Bogotá and then in Lima just a few years earlier. The Mexican committee included Comuncación, Intercambio y Desarrollo Humano en America Latina (CIDHAL); Centro de Desarrollo Intergrap de la Mujer (CEDIM); Terrer de Mujeres del Chopo; Mujeres para el Dialogo; Centro de Estudios de la Mujer (CED); Mujeres en Acción Syndical (MAS);

Centro de Apoyo a Mujerers Violadas A.C. (CAMVAC); Colectivo de Lucha contras la Violencia hacia las Mujers A.C. (COVAC); Cuarto Creciente; Lucero González; Julia Baco; Maria Torres; Amalia Fisher; and Eli Bartra.

162. Jennifer Chase, "Encuentro IV: 'Somos Todos Feministas,'" *off our backs*, 2 March 1988, p. 2.

163. Ibid., 34.

164. Rosa María Rodriguez e Isabel Barranco, *fem*, no. 68 (Winter 1988):5. "We, Colombian women, have brought in our suitcases, in our backpacks, in our bodies, pieces, fragments from the moment our country is living. We are a collection of differences in unity as women: The Caribbean woman, the mulatta, the Black woman, the indigenous woman, the Criolla, the Zamba. In this space we are with the Latin American and Caribbean women, who feel our daily experience of violence through this Encounter. We couldn't nor wanted to leave behind, at the border, the trace of violence in Colombia." The Colombian women proposed a Declaration of Human Rights and an International Day of Solidarity with the Right to Life in Colombia.

165. Ibid., 34.

166. *fem*, no. 68: 6.

167. *off our backs*, no. 3.

168. *fem*, no. 68: 8.

8. Conclusion (pp. 239–250)

1. Adriana Santa Cruz, Editorial, *Mujer* (Special issue: *Mujer y democracia*, (Santiago, Chile; ILET, 1985).

2. Sheldon Annis and Peter Hakim, eds. *Direct to the Poor: Grassroots development in Latin America* (Boulder, Colo.: L. Rienner, 1988).

3. See, for example, CIM report by Marie Carmel Lafontant "The Center for Haitian Studies on the Promotion of Women" (CHREPROF), in *1983 Interamerican Year of the Family* ed., Inter-American Commission of Women (Washington, D.C.: Pan-American Union, 1983).

4. *San Francisco Chronicle*, 14 March 1990, p. A-15. President Jean-Bertrand Aristide took office on February 7, 1991. The coalition of which Pascal-Trouillot was the nominal head survived a coup attempt on January 7.

5. ISIS International, March 1989.

6. Ibid.

7. UNICEF, *The Invisible Adjustment: Poor Women and the Economic Crisis* (Santiago, Chile: UNICEF, The Americas and the Caribbean Regional Office, 1989), 12.

8. Medea Benjamin, ed., *Don't Be Afraid, Gringo: A Honduran Woman Speaks from the Heart* (San Francisco: The Institute for Food and Development Policy, 1987), 87.

9. Domitila Barrios de Chungara, in *¡Aquí También Domitila!* ed., David Acebey (Mexico City: Siglo Veintiuno Editores, 1985). Domitila's experiences after publication of *Let Me Speak!*

10. Elisabeth Burgos-Debray, ed., *I . . . Rigoberta Menchú* (New York: Verso, 1984).

11. Antonieta Gimeno and Debbie Lubarr, "Mujeres Unidas: Mexico's Popular Movement," *Sojourner: The Women's Forum*, January 1990, p. 14.

12. Penny Lernoux, *Cry of the People* (Garden City, N.Y.: Doubleday, 1980).

13. Elsa M. Chaney and Mary García Castro, eds., *Muchachas No More: Household Workers in Latin America and the Caribbean*, Bibliography by Margo L. Smith. (Philadelphia: Temple University Press, 1989).

14. Chaney and García Castro, *Muchachas*, 401.

15. Posters sold to help finance the conference carried an outline of Latin America and the Caribbean emblazoned with drawings of young women's faces and the slogan "No basta hay tener derechos hay que tener conciencia hay que organizarse para defenderlas."

16. Alejandra Massolo and Martha Schteingart, eds., *Participacion Social, Reconstruccion y Mujer: El Sismo de 1985.* (Mexico City: El Colegio de Mexico, PIEM [Programa Interdisciplinario de Estudios de la Mujer] 1987).

17. The collaborative nature of the project is emblematic of much of the new work on and by women in Latin America.

18. Conversation with Ruth Rosen, 8 March 1990.

19. Both aspects of the women's movement in Latin America have been effectively articulated by women of the educated middle classes.

20. Santa Cruz, *Mujer y democracia* (1985).

21. Nené Reynoso, "Reflexiones sobre politica feminista," *Feminaria II*, 3 (April 1989):1.

22. *Feminaria I*, 1 (June 1988).

23. Alvarado, *Gringo*, 63.

Bibliographic Commentary

This commentary is designed to be an entry point to the literature on the history of women in Latin America. It is by no means comprehensive, nor does it attempt to cover the breadth of sources consulted in the making of this book. Rather, it has two modest purposes: First, to indicate new work in the field of Latin American women's history, which is appearing as this book goes to press; and second, to point out some of the sources that were important to the study. Although the book itself draws heavily on Latin American sources, emphasis in this commentary is on material available in U.S. libraries and archives.

In the six years since the writing of this book was undertaken, the availability of materials on the history of women in Latin America has expanded significantly. Superb new country studies stand ready to go to press or have just been released, including Sônia E. Alvarez, *Engendering Democracy in Brazil: Women's Movements in Transitional Politics* (Princeton, N.J.: Princeton University Press, 1990); Nestor Tomás Aúza, *Periodismo y feminismo en la Argentina 1830–1930* (Buenos Aires: Emece Editores, 1988); Florence E. Babb, *Between Field and Cooking Pot: The Political Economy of Marketwomen in Peru* (Austin: University of Texas Press, 1989); Carmen Diana Deere, *Household and Class Relations: Peasants and Landlords in Northern Peru* (Berkeley: University of California Press, 1990); Donna Guy, *Sex and Danger in Buenos Aires* (Lincoln: University of Nebraska, 1991); June E. Hahner, *Emancipating the Female Sex: The Struggle for Women's Rights in Brazil, 1850–1940* (Durham, N.C.: Duke University Press, 1991); K. Lynn Stoner, *From the House to the Streets: The Cuban Women's Movement for Legal Change, 1898–1940* (Durham, N.C.: Duke University Press, 1991), and Maria Elena Valenzuela, *La Mujer en el Chile militar: Todas ibamos reinas* (Santiago: Ediciones Chile y America [CESOC], 1987).

Edited thematic collections continue to build on the tradition of interhemispheric scholarly collaboration set by the pioneering collections of the 1970s (e.g., Ann Pescatello's *Female and Male in Iberian America* [1972], June Nash and Helen Safa's *Sex and Class in Latin America* [1976], and Asunción Lavrin's landmark *Latin American Women: A History* [1977]). The new work is distinguished by its theoretical sophistication, underlining the importance of feminist analysis to the new historiography. Among these are *The Women's Movement in Latin America* (Boston: Unwin Hyman, 1989), edited and with introductory and conclusionary chapters by political scientist

Jane Jaquette; it contains six country studies that analyze "the role of women and of feminist thought in the transition from authoritarian to democratic politics in South America in the 1980s." *Women, Culture and Politics in Latin America*, a collective work by the Seminar on Feminism and Culture in Latin America (University of California Press, 1990), posits new theoretical approaches to the field and offers a unique bibliography of women's periodical and journal publications in Latin America over a two-hundred-year period. *Muchachas No More: Household Workers in Latin America and the Caribbean*, edited by Elsa Chaney and Mary Garcia Castro, includes analyses of domestic workers' situations and biographical descriptions of their organizational efforts. *Through Her Eyes: Women's Theology from Latin America*, edited by Elsa Tamez, initiates the examination of theology from the perspective of Latin American women. *Sexuality and Marriage in Colonial Latin America*, edited by Asunción Lavrin, is emblematic of the vibrancy of new work on the colonial era. From the Programa Interdisciplinario de Estudios de Mujer at El Colegio de Mexico comes *Presencia y transparencia: La mujer en la historia de Mexico* (1987). This book, with eight articles, is an example of the fine scholarship emerging from women's studies programs and women's independent collectives in Latin America.

The growing maturity of the field of Latin American women's studies is visible in new bibliographies and source aids. *Latinas of the Americas: A Source Book*, edited by K. Lynn Stoner, picks up where Meri Knaster's *Women in Spanish America* (1977) left off and is the most comprehensive humanities and social science bibliography available to date. Each of the fifteen categories (which include biography, feminist studies, health, history, literature, religion, and development) is introduced with an overview essay. Specialized bibliographies and literature review articles are published regularly in *Latin American Research Review*. ISIS International has published two new directories to make the materials collected in the ISIS documentation and information centers accessible by computer data search: *Base de datos mujer/Women's Data Base* (Vol. 1, nos. 1–2; Santiago, Chile, 1988) and *Listado de descriptores en el tema de la mujer/ List of Descriptors on the Theme of Women* (Santiago, Chile, 1988). In 1987 the Comisión Interamericana de Mujeres/Interamerican Commission of Women undertook the task of collecting and publishing comprehensive statistical indexes on women in Latin America, a project that has not only allowed for comparative analyses, but demonstrates the degree to which accurate information on women is lacking in many regions and sectors. The *Boletín Regional Estadistico de la Mujer/Regional Statistical Bulletin on Women* is coordinated by Gloria Carlin G. at the Centro Regional de Informatica de la Mujer/Regional Information Center on Women, Santiago, Chile: OAS-CIM. An older but useful annotated bibliography on Latin American women is contained in Pamela R. Byrne and Suzanne R. Ontiveros's *Women in the Third World* (ABC-CLIO Press, 1986). In addition, most of the edited volumes mentioned above contain bibliographies specific to the field and topic; for example, Chaney and Castro's *Muchachas No More* includes a computer data–based bibliography, compiled by Margo L. Smith, on domestic service in cross-cultural perspective.

Periodicals

Though not widely accessible in the United States, feminist and women's movement periodicals published in Latin America were central to the success of the work. The following list is but a brief indication of the range of publications. Among the most important were the contemporary journals *Fem*, edited by Elena Urrutia (Mexico City: 1976–present) and the publications supported by ILET (Unidad de Comunicacion Alternativa de la Mujer), which include *mujer/fempress, Especial Mujer*

(Santiago, Chile, 1982–present) and *ISIS International*. Other journals that helped to shape the text are *La Escoba* (La Paz, Bolivia: Centro de Informacion y Desarrollo de la Mujer, 1986); *Informativo* (Lima, Peru: Centro de Documentacion sobre la Mujer, 1986–); *Ixquic: La Mujer en Guatemala* (Guatemala City, 1985–); *Somos* (Managua, Nicaragua; bimonthly bulletin of the Asociación de Mujeres Nicaraguenses Luisa Amanda Espinoza [AMNLAE]); *La Cacerola* Montevideo, Uruguay: Grupo de Estudios sobre la Condición de la Mujer en el Uruguay (GRECMU); *Quehaceres* (Santo Domingo, Dominican Republic, January 1981–); *VIVA* (Lima, Peru: Centro de la Mujer Peruana "Flora Tristán"); *Feminaria*, edited by Lea Fletcher (Buenos Aires, June 1988–present); *ISIS Boletín Internacional de la Mujeres/ISIS International Women's Journal* (Santiago, Chile and Rome, Italy, 1976–present); ISIS also publishes *Mujeres en Acción/Women in Action*. The Comision Interamericana de Mujeres/Inter-American Commission of Women, Washington, D.C., has published *Comision Interamericana de Mujeres (CIM)* since the 1970s. *FMC: Boletín de la Federación de Mujeres Cubanas* (Havana) is the journal of the Cuban women's federation. *Naciones Unidas/United Nations Publications: Noticiero sobre la Condición de la Mujer* (New York: UN Section on the Status of Women, 1976–). A number of journals from Brazil have informed the work, including *Nos Mulheres* (São Paulo, Brazil, June 1976–), a publication of the Asscoiação de Mulheres; *Mulheiro* (São Paulo, Brazil, 1981–); *Mulher em Vida* (Sao Paulo, Brazil, 1986–).

Journals published prior to the contemporary women's movement give evidence of the commitment of women in Latin America to the cause of women, feminism, and female education. For this author, the discovery in 1972 in the Livros Raros section of the Biblioteca Nacional in Rio de Janeiro of Francisca S. da Motta Diniz's journal, *O Sexo Feminino*, first published in Campanha, Minas Gerais, Brazil, on September 7, 1873, and later published in Rio de Janeiro (1875–1876) marks the beginning of the research undertaken for this book. Motta Diniz's later publications, *O Quinze de Novembro de Sexo Feminino* (November 1889) and *Primaveira* (August 29, 1880–October 1880) were also of great interest. To indicate but a few of the other early journals that informed the text, *La Siempreviva*, published by women dedicated to the idea of female education in the Yucatán, Mexico, in the 1870s and 1880s, was helpful. Of the journals published by women in the early twentieth century, *Mujeres de America* (Buenos Aires, 1933–1935), edited by Nelly Marino Carvallo, and *La Acción Argentina* (Buenos Aires) were especially useful. For an initial overview of the variety of feminist and women's movement journals published in Latin America over a two-hundred-year period, see Chapter 10, Seminar on Feminism and Culture in Latin America, "Toward a History of Women's Periodicals in Latin America: Introduction," and Chapter 11, Janet Greenberg, "Toward a History of Women's Periodicals in Latin America: A Working Bibliography" in *Women, Culture and Politics in Latin America* (Berkeley, University of California Press, 1990).

Proceedings and Reports of Meetings and Conferences

Despite the outpouring of writing on women's issues that has occurred during the last two decades and the importance of the UN Decade of the Woman, there is perhaps no area of historical literature where women—other than monarchs and Mata Haris—have been less visible than in the literature of international relations. One of the intentions of the present study is to initiate a discussion of the extent and meaning of this history through the examination of Latin American women's activism at the transnational level over the past century. The records of women's organizations, deliberations, tactics, correspondence, public statements, and delegations to designated representatives of their governments add a new dimension to the history of international relations.

The following sources are examples of the kinds of materials available for research on the extent and significance of Latin American women's use of the transnational arena. Many are held in private collections; for example, *Congreso Femenino Internacional* (425 pp.), the proceedings of the congress, were published in Buenos Aires in 1910 and preserved in the personal archives of a feminist-anarchist group in Argentina. *Primero Congreso Interamericano de Mujeres, celebrado en la Capital de Guatemala, del 21 de agosto de 1947* (Guatemala City: Los Talleres de Latipografía, 1948) is from the collection of Alicia Moreau de Justo, Montevideo, Uruguay. National diplomatic archives, such as the Arquivo Historico do Itamaraty in Rio de Janeiro hold miscellaneous materials on women involved in international activities (e.g., correspondence between Josefina Peixoto, wife of the president of Brazil, and Bertha M. Honore Palmer, organizer of the women's pavilion at the Columbian Exposition in Chicago, 1892, which discusses the work of Brazilian women artisans and women's "first time" participation in an international fair). Published documentary sources from Latin America include *Actividades femeninas en Chile* (Santiago de Chile: Imprenta y Litografía La Ilustracion, 1928); *Congreso de Investigación Acerca de la Mujer en la Region Andina*, edited by Jeanine Anderson de Velasco (Lima, Peru: Organizo Asociacion Peru-Mujer, 1983); and Bertha Lutz, *Homenagem das Senhoras Brasileiras a Illustre Presidente da União Inter-Americana de Mulheres* (Rio de Janeiro: Rodrigues & Co., 1926).

Sources for reports of meetings and congresses in translation include material in *Third World/Second Sex 2*, edited by Miranda Davies (London: Zed Books, 1983); *Hopeful Openings: A Study of Five Women's Development Organizations in Latin America and the Caribbean*, edited by Sally Yudelman (West Hartford, Conn.: Kumarian Press, 1978); *Documents of the World Congress of Women—Equality, National Independence, Peace* (Secretariat of the Women's International Democratic Federation, Prague, October 8–13, 1981 (Berlin: Unter den Linden, 1981); *Women and the Cuban Revolution*, edited by Elizabeth Stone (New York: Pathfinder Press, 1981); *The International Conferences of American States, 1889–1928*, edited by James Brown Scott (New York: Oxford University Press, 1931); Pan-American Union, *Final Act of the Ninth International Conference of American States, Bogotá, Colombia, March 30–May 2, 1948* (Washington, D.C., 1948); *Yearbook on International Communist Affairs 1973* (Stanford, Calif.: The Hoover Institution Press, 1973); U.S. Department of State, *Interamerican Conference for the Maintenance of Continental Peace and Security, Quitandinha, Brazil, August 15–September 2, 1947* (Washington, D.C.: U.S. Government Printing Office, 1948); and *The Educational Yearbook of the International Institute of Teachers College, Columbia University 1925*, which includes statistics and analyses by Carneiro Leão (Brazil), Maximilian Salas (Chile), and Ernesto Nelson (Argentina).

There are a number of archives in the United States that contain pertinent material. The Alice Park Collection at the Hoover Institution on War, Revolution and Peace, Stanford, California, contains a variety of invaluable documents, including Park's diary of her participation in the founding of the Interamerican Commission of Women at the Sixth International Conference of American States (Havana, Cuba, 1928) and numerous individual documents, such as Eleanor Foster Lansing, *Bulletin of the Women's Auxiliary Committee of the United States of the Second Pan American Scientific Congress* (no. 1, February 1921); "Second Women's Pan American Conference," *Third Pan American Scientific Congress* (Lima, Peru: Imprensa Americana, 1924). The Hoover Institution also holds miscellaneous newspaper clippings and photographs from the early Pan-American Conferences and the papers of the Comité de las Americas de la Liga Internacional de Mujeres Pro Paz y Libertad (1947).

Latin American historian Mary Wilhelmine Williams's papers are housed in the Stanford University Manuscript Collections, Green Library, Stanford, California. Williams's correspondence and journals of her seventeen-month journey through Latin America in 1927–1928 on behalf of the American Association of University Women to survey female education are part of the collection, as are diaries and photographs of her research trips to Mexico, Central America, and Brazil in 1923, 1930, 1934.

The holdings of the Arthur and Elizabeth Schlesinger Archives on the History of Women in America, Radcliffe College, Cambridge, Massachusetts, proved a rich source. The Doris Stevens Collection contains correspondence from the Latin American members of the Inter-American Commission of Women; thirty volumes of laws and statutes relating to the status of women throughout the hemisphere that were collated by the IACW in 1930; numerous pictures, brochures, and pamphlets; Stevens's manuscript biography; and a copy of the U.S. Department of State's "Confidential File of Doris Stevens, December 26, 1933." The Carrie Chapman Catt manuscript collection contains pertinent correspondence and the journals of her trip to South America in 1924–1925. Miscellaneous documents in the Schlesinger Archives, such as E. B. Swiggett, "Report of the Second Pan American Scientific Congress" (July 1, 1916), were also of interest.

Microfilm of the Women's International League for Peace and Freedom (WILPF) papers was made available by the Microfilm Collection of Green Library, Stanford University. Although not rich in Latin American material, the WILPF papers did offer clues to more productive sources and provide context.

The *Bulletin of the Pan American Union*, published monthly from 1892 to 1946 in Washington, D.C., contains a wide variety of reports of women's meetings and conferences in Latin America over a fifty-year period, as well as analytic articles by women correspondents from North and South America.

The publications of the Comisión Interamericana de Mujeres (CIM)/Inter-American Commission of Women since 1928 provide information and a sense of change over time. A small sampling will indicate the scope of CIM publications: *Report Presented to the Twenty-First Session of the United Nations Commission on the Status of Women* (1968); *Bibliografía: Esposición del libro de la mujer* (1928–1978); *Enlace*, (1960s–); *Inter-American Commission of Women, 1928–1973* (1974); *Libro de Oro* (Washington, D.C.: General Secretariat, Organization of American States, 1980).

Publications of the United Nations such as *Meeting in Mexico: The Story of the World Conference of the International Women's Year, Mexico City, June 19–July 2, 1975* (New York: United Nations, 1975), and the *World Plan of Action: Report of the World Conference of the International Women's Year, Mexico City, June 19–July 2, 1975* (New York: United Nations, 1976), provided global context and entry point information for Latin America. UNESCO has funded and published a wealth of information, especially on women and development. Many of the publications listed in the following bibliography were supported by UNESCO monies. An example of the publications they support within Latin America is *Caso de Nicaragua* (Ministerio de la Presidencia, Oficino de la Mujer: Este estudio se enmarca en el subprograma de "Estudios e investigaciones sobre los derechos fundamentales de las mujeres" de la UNESCO) (February 1987).

Information on the contemporary women's movement in Latin America is available in a wide variety of sources, including the numerous journals mentioned above, and is best gleaned from consultation of the footnotes to this text. Reports of the Encuentros Feministas Latinoamericanas y del Caribe (1981, 1983, 1985, 1987, 1990) appeared in *mujer/fempress* and *fem*, to name the most accessible of the Latin American journals. In the United States, *Ms.* magazine carried reports on the UN meetings, and *Connexions, off our backs*, and the *International Supplement to the Women's Studies Quarterly* had good coverage of the early Encuentros Feministas.

Diaries, Testimonies, Biographical Articles, and Speeches

See for example, Juan José Arévalo, *Carta Politica al Pueblo de Guatemala* (Guatemala City: Editorial San Antonio, 1963); Adalzira Bittencourt, *A Mulher Paulista na historia* (Rio de Janeiro: Livros de Portugal, 1954); Fidel Castro, "Closing Speech to the Second Congress of the Federation of Cuban Women," and Vilma Espín, "The Early Years," in *Women and the Cuban Revolution*, edited by Elizabeth Stone (New York: Pathfinder Press, 1981); Domitila Barrios de Chungara, *Let Me Speak! Testimony of Domitila, a Woman of the Bolivian Tin Mines*, edited by Moema Viezzer and translated by Victoria Ortiz (New York and London: Monthly Review Press, 1978); Barrios de Chungara's new book, with David Aceby, *¡Aquí también, Domitila!* (Mexico City: Siglo Veintiuno Editores, 1985); *Revolutionary Priest: The Story of Camilo Torres*, edited by John Gerassi (New York: Vintage Books, 1971); *The Complete Bolivian Diaries of Ché Guevara and Other Captured Documents*, edited by James Daniel (New York: Stein and Day, 1986); Nicholas Fraser and Marysa Navarro, *Eva Peron* (London: Andre Deutsch, 1980); *Mulher Brasileira: Bibliografia anotada*, 2 vols., Fundação Carlos Chagas (São Paulo: Editora Brasiliense, 1979–1981); Lydia Gueiler, *La mujer y la revolución* (La Paz, Bolivia: Editorial Burillo, 1959); *Women in Latin American History: Their Lives and Views*, edited by June Hahner (Los Angeles: UCLA Latin American Center publications, 1980); James D. and Linda Roddy Henderson, *Ten Notable Women of Latin America* (Chicago: Nelson-Hall, 1978); Latin American and Caribbean Women's Collective, *Slaves of Slaves: The Challenge of Latin American Women*, translated by Micheal Pallis (London: Zed Press, 1980); Carolina Maria de Jesus, *Child of the Dark: The Diary of Carolina Maria de Jesus*, translated by David St. Clair (New York: Dutton, 1962); Albertina Oliveira da Costa, Maria Teresa Porciuncula de Morães, and Valentina da Rocha Lima, *Memorias—das mulheres—do exilo: Obra coletiva* (Rio de Janeiro, Brazil: Paz y Terra, 1980); Daphne Patai, *Brazilian Women Speak: Contemporary Life Stories* (New Brunswick, N.J.: Rutgers University Press, 1988); *Tania: The Unforgettable Guerrilla*, edited by Marta Rojas and Mirta Rodriguez Calderon (New York: Random House, 1971); Haydée Santamaria, *Moncada: Memories of the Attack That Launched the Cuban Revolution*, translated by Robert Taber (Secaucus, N.J.: Lyle Stuart, 1980).

A Working Bibliography

Ackelsberg, Martha A. "Separate and Equal? Mujeres Libres and Anarchist Strategy for Women's Emancipation." *Feminist Studies*, Spring 1985.

Agosín, Marjorie. *Scraps of Life: Chilean Arpilleras, Chilean Women and the Pinochet Dictatorship*. Translated by Cola Frantzen. Trenton, N.J.: Red Sea Press, 1987.

Aguilar, Neuma. "Impact of Industrialization on Women's Work Roles in Northeast Brazil." *Studies in Comparative International Development* 10 (Summer 1975).

Aguilar, Luis E., ed. *Marxism in Latin America*. New York: Alfred A. Knopf, 1968.

Alarcón, Norma. "Chicana's Feminist Literature: A Re-vision Through Malinche/ or Malintzin: Putting Flesh Back on the Object." In *This Bridge Called My Back: Writings by Radical Women of Color*, edited by Cherrie Moraga and Gloria Anzaldua. New York: Kitchen Table Women of Color Press, 1981.

Alvarado, Elvia. *See* Benjamin, Medea.

Alvarez, Sônia E. *Engendering Democracy in Brazil: Women's Movements in Transitional Politics*. Princeton, N.J.: Princeton University Press, 1990.

———. "Politicizing Gender and Engendering Democracy." In *Democratizing Brazil: Problems of Transition and Consolidation*, edited by Alfred Stepan. New York: Oxford University Press, 1989.

———. *The Politics of Gender and the Brazilian Abertura Process: Alternative Perspectives on Women and the State in Latin America*. Women in International Development. East Lansing, Mich.: Michigan State University, 1987.

———. "The Politics of Gender in Latin America: Comparative Perspectives on Women in the Brazilian Transition to Democracy." Vols. 1 and 2. Ph.D. diss., Yale University, 1986.

———. "Women's Movements and Gender Politics in the Brazilian Transition." In *The Women's Movement in Latin America*, edited by Jane Jaquette, Boston: Unwin Hyman, 1989.

Alzola de Citanovic, Nilsa M. "Imagen tradicional y participación real de la mujer en la sociedad Argentina (1810–1920)." *Cuadernos del Sur* (Univ. Nacional del Sur, Istituto de Humanidades, Bahia Blanca, Argentina). 12 (July 1979).

Anderson de Velasco, Jeanine, ed. *Congreso de Investigación Acerca de la Mujer en la Region Andina. Del 7 al 10 de Junio, 1982*. Lima, Peru: Asociación Peru-Mujer, 1983.

Andreas, Carol. *When Women Rebel: The Rise of Popular Feminism in Peru*. Westport, Conn.: Lawrence Hill & Co., 1985.

Anglesey, Zoe, ed. *Ixok Amar Go: Central American Women's Poetry for Peace*. Penobscot, Me.: Granite Press, 1987.

Annis, Sheldon, and Peter Hakim, eds. *Direct to the Poor: Grassroots Development in Latin America*. Boulder, Colo.: Rienner, 1988.

Antologia de la Prensa Obrera. *La Mujer y el movimiento obrero Mexicano en el siglo XIX*. Mexico City: Centro de Estudios del Movimiento Obrero Mexicano, Año Internacional de la Mujer, 1975.

Aranda, Clara Eugenia. *La Mujer: Exploitación, lucha liberación*. Mexico City: Editorial de Nuestro Tiempo, 1976.

Arizpe Schlosser, Lourdes. "Women in the Informal Labour Sector: The Case of Mexico City." *Women and national development: the complexities of change*, edited by Center for Research on Women in Higher Education and Professions, Wellesley College. Chicago: University of Chicago Press, 1977.

Arizpe Schlosser, Lourdes, and Carlot Botey. "La Politicas de desarrolla agrario y su impacto sobre la mujer campesina en Mexico." In *La Mujer y la politica agraria en America Latina*, edited by Magdalena Leon de Leal and Carmen Diana Deere. Bogota, Colombia: Asociacion Colombiana para el Estudio de la Población. 1986.

Arnove, Robert F., Micheal Chiapetta, and Sylvia Stalker. "Latin American Education." In *Latin America: Perspectives on a Region*, edited by Jack W. Hopkins. New York: Holmes & Meier, 1987.

Arrom, Silvia Marina. "Teaching the History of Hispanic-American Women." *The History Teacher* 13 (August 1980).

———. *The Women of Mexico City, 1790–1857*. Stanford, Calif.: Stanford University Press, 1985.

Astorga, Nora. "Liberated Themselves by Liberating the People." *World Marxist Review* 25 (March 1982).

Aúza, Nestor Tomás. *Periodismo y feminismo en la Argentina 1830–1930*. Buenos Aires: Emece Editores, 1988.

Babb, Florence E. *Between Field and Cooking Pot: The Political Economy of Marketwomen in Peru*. Austin: University of Texas Press, 1989.

———. "Women and Work in Latin America," *Latin American Research Review* 25, no. 2, 1990.

Balch, Emily Greene. *Beyond Nationalism: The Social Thought of Emily Greene Balch*. edited by Mercedes M. Randall. New York: Twayne, 1972.

———, ed. *Occupied Haiti*. New York: The Writers Publishing Company, 1927.

Balmori, Diana, Miles Wortman, and Stuart Voss. *Notable Family Networks in Modern Latin America*. Chicago: University of Chicago Press, 1984.

Barranco, Manuel. "Mexico: Its Educational Problems—Suggestions for Their Solution." Ph.D. diss., Columbia University, 1914.

Barrig, Maruja. "The Difficult Equilibrium Between Bread and Roses: Women's Organizations and the Transition from Dictatorship to Democracy in Peru." In *The Women's Movement in Latin America: Feminism and the Transition to Democracy*. edited by Jane Jaquette. Boston: Unwin Hyman, 1989.

Barrios de Chungara, Domitila, with David Aceby. *¡Aqui Tambien, Domitila!* Mexico: Siglo Vientiuno Editores, 1985.

Barrios de Chungara, Domitila, with Moema Viezzer. *Let Me Speak! Testimony of Domitila, a Woman of the Bolivian mines*, translated by Victoria Ortiz. New York and London: Monthly Review Press, 1978.

Barroso, Carmen Lucia de Meco. "A Participação de mulher no desenvolvimento cientifico brasiliero." *SBPC/CC* 27 (June 1975).

Barroso, Carmen Lucia de Meco, and Cristina Bruschini. "Building Politics from Personal Lives." In *Third World/Second Sex 2*, edited by Miranda Davies. London: Zed Press, 1987.

Benería, Lourdes, ed. "Porque tão poucas mulheres exercem atitudades científicas?" *Women and Development: The Sexual Division of Labor in Rural Societies*. New York: Praeger, 1982.

Benería, Lourdes, and Martha Roldan. *The Crossroads of Class and Gender: Industrial Housework, Subcontracting, and Household Dynamics in Mexico City*. Chicago: University of Chicago Press, 1987.

Benjamin, Medea, ed. *Don't be Afraid, Gringo: A Honduran Woman Speaks from the Heart: The Story of Elvia Alvarado*. San Francisco: Institute for Food and Development Policy, 1987.

Bergmann, Emilie. "Sor Juana Inés de la Cruz: Dreaming in a Double Voice." In *Women, Culture and Politics in Latin America*. Berkeley and Los Angeles: University of California Press, 1990.

Besse, Susan Kent. "Freedom and Bondage: The Impact of Capitalism on Women in São Paulo, Brazil, 1917–1937." Ph.D. diss., Yale University, 1983.

Bettencourt, Victoria. "Women's Movements in Brazil: The Struggle for Participation in Redemocratization." Unpublished manuscript, University of California, Santa Cruz, 1986.

Biles, Robert E. "Women and Politics in Latin America." In *Latin America and the Caribbean Contemporary Record*, Vol. 3. Baltimore: John Hopkins University, 1983–84.

Birnbaum, Lucia Chiavola. *Liberazione della donna/Feminism in Italy*. Middletown, Conn.: Wesleyan University Press, 1986.

Bittencourt, Adalzira. *A Mulher Paulista na historia*. Rio de Janeiro: Livros de Portugal, 1954.

Bittencourt, Maria Luiza. "Report from Brazil." In "Woman Suffrage in the Americas," edited by Beatrice Newhart. *Pan-American Union Bulletin*. 70 (April 1936).

Blay, Eva Alterman. "The Political Participation of Women in Brazil: Female Mayors." *Signs* 5 (Autumn 1979).

———. "Social Movements and Womens' Participation in Brazil." *International Political Science Review* 6, no. 3 (1985).

Blough, William J. "Political Attitudes of Mexican Women: Support for the Political System among a Newly Enfranchised Group." *Journal of Inter-American Studies and World Affairs* 14 (May 1972).

Bonder, Gloria. "The Study of Politics from the Standpoint of Women." *International Social Science Journal* 35 (1983); translated from Gloria Bonder, "Mujer y politica: ¿Cual politica? ¿Que mujer?" *Fem* 46 (1984?).

Bossen, Laurel Herbenar. *The Redivision of Labor: Women and Economic Choice in Four Guatemalan Communities*. Albany, N.Y.: SUNY Press, 1984.

Bourque, Susan C., and Kay Barbara Warren. *Women of the Andes: Patriarchy and Social Change in Two Peruvian Towns*. Ann Arbor: University of Michigan Press, 1981.

Bronstein, Audrey. *The Triple Struggle: Latin American Peasant Women*. London: WOW, 1982.

Brown, L. Susan. "Women in Post-Revolutionary Cuba: A Feminist Critique." *The Insurgent Sociologist* (Summer 1986).

Bullrich, Silvina. *Flora Tristán, La Visionaria*. Buenos Aires: Riesa, 1982.

Bunster, Ximena, and Elsa Chaney. *Sellers and Servants: Working Women in Lima, Peru*. New York: Praeger, 1985.

Burkett, Elinor C. "Indian Women in a White Society: The Case of 16th Century Peru." In *Latin American Women: Historical Perspectives*, edited by Asunción Lavrin. Westport, Conn.: Greenwood Press, 1978.

Burns, Kathryn J. "Beyond That 'Essential Femininity': Feminist Organizations in Peru, 1900–1950." Senior thesis, Princeton University, 1981.

Calderón de la Barca, Frances. *Life in Mexico*. London, 1843.

Camp, Roderic A. "Women and Political Leadership in Mexico: A Comparative Study of Female and Male Political Elites." *Journal of Politics* 41 (1979).

Cannon, May. "Women's Organizations in Ecuador, Paraguay, and Peru." *Bulletin of the Pan-American Union*, 77 (November 1943).

Carlson, Marifran. "Feminism and Reform: A History of the Argentine Feminist Movement to 1926" Ph.D. diss., University of Chicago, 1983.

——— . *Feminismo: The Women's Movement in Argentina from Its Beginnings to Evita Peron*. Chicago: Academy Chicago Publishers, 1987.

Carr, Irene Campos. "Second Feminist Conference of Latin America and the Caribbean: Two Reports." *Women's Studies International* 3 (April 1984).

Carrillo, Roxana. "Discurso inaugural." *Fem* 8, no. 31.

Carvalho, María Lucia de. *A Mulher no mercado de trabalho brasiliero*. VOZES 66 (August 1972).

Catasús, S., A. Farnos, F. González, R. Grove, R. Hernández, and B. Morejón. *Cuban Women: Changing Roles and Population Trends*. Women, Work and Development, no. 17. Geneva: International Labor Office, 1988.

Cathelat, Marie-France, and Teresa Burga. *Perfil de la mujer peruana: 1980–1981*. Lima, Peru: Investigaciones Sociales Artisticas, n.d. [1982?]

CEPAL (Comisión Economica para America Latina). *Mujeres en America Latina: Aportes para una discusion*. Mexico City: Fondo de Cultura Economica, 1975.

Chaney, Elsa. "Old and New Feminists in Latin America: The Case of Peru and Chile." *Journal of Marriage and the Family* 35 (May 1973).

——— . *Supermadre: Women in Politics in Latin America*. Austin: University of Texas Press for Institute of Latin American Studies, 1979.

Chaney, Elsa, and Ximena Bunster. *Sellers and Servants: Working Women in Lima, Peru*. New York: Praeger, 1985.

Chaney, Elsa, and Mary García Castro, eds. *Muchachas No More: Household Workers in Latin America and the Caribbean*. Philadelphia: Temple University Press, 1989.

Chase, Jennifer. "Encuentro IV: Somos todas feministas." *off our backs* (March 1988).

Chiñas, Beverly. *The Isthmus Zapotecs: Women's Roles in Cultural Context*. New York: 1973.

Chinchilla, Norma Stoltz. "Class Conflict in Central America: Background and Overview." *Latin American Perspectives*, no. 25/26 (1980).

——— . "Industrialization, Monopoly Capital and Women's Work in Guatemala." *Signs* 3, no. 1 (1977).

——— . "Mobilizing Women: Revolution in the Revolution." *Latin American Perspectives* 3, no. 4 (1977).

——— . *Women in Revolutionary Movements: The Case of Nicaragua*. Women in International Development, Michigan State University Working Papers, no. 27. East Lansing: Michigan State University, 1983.

Chuchryk, Patricia M. "Feminist Anti-Authoritarian Politics: The Role of Women's Organizations in the Chilean Transition to Democracy." In *The Women's Movement in Latin America: Feminism and the Transition to Democracy*, edited by Jane Jaquette.

Boston: Unwin Hyman, 1989.

Cohen, Lucy M. "Woman's Entry to the Professions in Colombia: Selected Characteristics." *Journal of Marriage and the Family* 35 (May 1973).

Colón R., Consuelo. *Mujeres de Mexico*. Mexico City: 1944.

Confederación Interamericana de Educación Católica (CIEC). *Formación de la mulher en el mundo actual*. Bogotá, Colombia: Secretaria General de la CIEC, 1976.

Corvarrubias, P., and Franco, R., eds. *Chile, mujer y sociedad*. Santiago: UNICEF, 1978.

Couturier, Edith, and Asunción Lavrin. "Dowries and Wills: A View of Women's Socioeconomic Role in Colonial Guadalajara and Puebla, 1640–1790." *Hispanic American Historical Review* 59 (May 1979).

Damian, Gisela Espinosa. "Feminism and Social Struggle in Mexico." In *Third World/ Second Sex 2*, edited by Miranda Davies. London: Zed Books, 1987.

Davies, Miranda, ed. *Third World—Second Sex: Women's Struggles and National Liberation. Third World Women Speak Out*. London: Zed Press, 1983.

———, ed. *Third World—Second Sex 2*. London: Zed Books, 1987.

de Jesus, Carolina Maria. *Child of the Dark: The Diary of Carolina Maria de Jesus*, translated from Portuguese by David St. Clair. New York: Dutton, 1962. Originally published as *Quarto de Despejo* (São Paulo: Livraria Francisco Alves, 1960.

Deere, Carmen Diana. "Changing Social Relations of Production and Peruvian Peasant Women's Work." *Latin American Perspectives* 4 (Winter 1977).

———. "Developpement cooperatíf et participation feminine a la reforme agraire Nicaraguayenne." *Revue Tiers Monde* 26 (April–June 1985).

———. "The Differentiation of the Peasantry and Family Structure: A Peruvian Case Study." *Journal of Family History* 3, no. 4 (1978).

———. *Household and Class Relations: Peasants and Landlords in Northern Peru*. Berkeley: University of California Press, 1990.

Deere, Carmen Diana, and Magdalena León de Leal. *La Mujer y la politica agraria en America Latina*. Bogotá, Colombia: Asociación Colombiana para el Estudio de la Poblacion, 1986.

Deighton, Jane, Rossana Horsley, Sarah Stewart, and Cathy Cain. *Sweet Ramparts: Women in Revolutionary Nicaragua*. London: Nicaraguan Solidarity Campaign, 1983.

Domitila. *See* Barrios de Chungara.

Dorfman, Ariel. "Mother's Day." *New York Times*, 7 May 1977.

Drier, Katherine S. *Five Months in the Argentine from a Woman's Point of View, 1918 to 1919*. New York: Frederic Fairchild Sherman, 1920.

Edelman, Fanny. "Party Work among Women." *World Marxist Review* 5 (October 1962).

Elú de Leñero, María del Carmen, ed. *Perspectivas femeninas en America Latina*. Mexico City: SepSetentas 1976.

Enloe, Cynthia. "Bananas, Bases and Patriarchy: Some Feminist Questions about the Militarization of Central America." *Radical America* 19, no. 4 (1985).

Espín, Vilma. "The Early Years." In *Women and the Cuban Revolution*, edited by Elizabeth Stone. New York: Pathfinder Press, 1981.

Ewell, Judith, and William H. Beezley, eds. *The Human Tradition in Latin America: The Nineteenth Century*. Wilmington, Del.: Scholarly Resources, 1987.

Fee, Terry, and Rosalinda González, eds. *Women and Class Struggle. Latin American Perspectives* 4 (Winter 1977).

Feijóo, María del Carmen. "The Challenge of Constructing Civilian Peace: Women

298 A Working Bibliography

and Democracy in Argentina." In *The Women's Movement in Latin America: Feminism and the Transition to Democracy*, edited by Jane Jaquette. Boston: Unwin Hyman, 1989.

———. "Las Feministas." In *La Vida de Nuestro Pueblo: Una Historia de Hombres, Cosas, Trabajos, Lugares*. No. 9. Buenos Aires: Centro Editor de America Latina, 1982.

———. "La Mujer, el desarrollo y las tendencias de población en America Latina: Bibliografía comentada." *Estudios Cedes* 3, no. 1 (1980).

Feijóo, María del Carmen, and Elizabeth Jelin. "Trabajo y familia en el ciclo de vida femenino: El Case de las sectores populares de Buenos Aires." *Estudio Cedes* 3, no. 8/9 (1980).

Felstiner, Mary. "The Larrain Family in the Independence of Chile, 1730–1830." Ph.D. diss., Stanford University, 1970.

"Feminismo." *Enciclopedia de Mexico*.

Fernández-Kelly, María Patricia. *For We Are Sold, I and My People: Women and Industry in Mexico's Frontier*. Albany, N.Y.: Zulu Press–Albany, 1983.

Fisher, Lillian Estelle. "The Influence of the Present Mexican Revolution upon the Status of Mexican Women." *Hispanic American Historical Review* 22 (February 1942).

Five Studies on the Situation of Women in Latin America. Estudios e Informes de la CEPAL, no. 16. Santiago, Chile: United Nations, 1983.

Flora, Cornelia B. "Pentacostal Women in Colombia: Religious Change and the Status of Working-Class Women." *Journal of Interamerican Studies and World Affairs* 17 (November 1975).

———. *Socialist Feminism in Latin America*. Working Paper no. 14. East Lansing: Michigan State University, 1982.

———. "Socialist Feminism in Latin America." *Women and Politics* 4 (Spring 1984).

Flusche, Della M., and Eugene H. Korth. *Forgotten Females: Women of African and Indian Descent in Colonial Chile, 1535–1800*. Detroit: Wayne State Press, 1983.

Formoso de Obregón Santacilia, Adela. *La Mujer mexicana en el organización social del país*. Mexico City: 1939.

Franco, Jean. *Plotting Women: Gender and Representation in Mexico*. New York: Colombia University Press, 1989.

Franco, Zoíla. "Women in the Transformation of Cuban Education." In *Prospects: Quarterly Review of Education*. Paris: UNESCO, 1975.

Fraser, Nicholas, and Marysa Navarro. *Eva Peron*. London: Andre Deutsch, 1980.

Fuller, Norma. "II Encuentro Feminista Latinoamericana y del Caribe." *Women's Studies International Forum* 6, no. 5 (1983).

Gaitán de Paris, Blanca. *La mujer en la vida del Libertador*. Bogotá, Colombia: Co-operativa Nacional de Artes Graficas, 1980.

Ganson de Rivas, Barbara. "Paraguayan Lane to Lances: A History of Women in the Social and Economic Life of Paraguay." M.A. thesis, University of Texas at Austin, 1984.

García, Guadaloupe Lopez. "Las Mujeres y la política." *Fem*, no. 67 (1988).

García y García, Elvira. *Actividad femenina*. Lima, Peru: Casa Editora, 1928.

Garrett-Schesch, Pat. "The Mobilization of Women During the Popular Unity Government." *Latin American Perspectives* 2 (Spring 1975).

Gilfeather, Sister Katherine Anne, M.M. "Women Religious, the Poor, and the Institutional Church in Chile." *Journal of Interamerican Studies and World Affairs* 21 (February 1979).

González-Súarez, Mirta. "Barriers to Female Achievement: Gender Stereotypes in Costa Rican Textbooks." *Women's Studies International Forum* 11, no. 6 (1988).

Graham, Maria Dundas. *Journal of a Voyage to Brazil and Residence There During Part of the Years 1821, 1822, 1823.* New York and London: Frederick A. Praeger, 1969.

Graham, Sandra Lauderdale. "Protection and Obedience: *The Paternalist World of Female Domestic Servants, Rio de Janeiro, 1869–1910.* Ph.D. diss., University of Texas, 1982.

GRECMU (Grupo de Estudios sobre la Condición de la Mujer en el Uruguay). *La Mujer en el Uruguay: Ayer y hoy.* Montevideo, Uruguay: Ediciones de la Banda Oriental, 1983.

Greenberg, Janet. "A Question of Blood: The Conflict of Sex and Class in the *Autobiografía* of Victoria Ocampo." In *Women, Culture and Politics in Latin America.* Berkeley and Los Angeles: University of California Press, 1990.

————. "Toward a History of Women's Periodicals in Latin America: A Working Bibliography." In *Women, Culture and Politics in Latin America.* Berkeley and Los Angeles: University of California Press, 1990.

Grez, Vicente. *Las Mujeres de la Independencia.* Santiago, Chile: Zig-Zag, 1966.

Gueiler, Lydia. *La mujer y la revolución.* La Paz, Bolivia: Editorial Burillo, 1959.

Guerra-Cunningham, Lucía. *Mujer y sociedad en America Latina.* Irvine: University of California; Santiago, Chile: Editorial del Pacífico, 1980.

Guy, Donna. *Sex and Danger in Buenos Aires.* Lincoln: University of Nebraska Press, 1991.

Hahner, June E. "The Beginnings of the Women's Suffrage Movement in Brazil." *Signs* 5 (1979).

————. *Emancipating the Female Sex: The Struggle for Women's Rights in Brazil, 1850–1940.* Durham, N.C.: Duke University Press, 1990.

————. "Feminism, Women's Rights, and the Suffrage Movement in Brazil, 1850–1932." *Latin American Research Review* 15, no. 1 (1980).

————. "The Nineteenth Century Feminist Press and Women's Rights in Brazil." In *Latin American Women: Historical Perspectives,* edited by Asunción Lavrin. Westport, Conn.: Greenwood Press, 1978.

————. *Poverty and Politics: The Urban Poor in Brazil, 1870–1920.* Albuquerque, N.M.: University of New Mexico Press, 1986.

————. "Researching the History of Latin American Women: Past and Future Directions." *Revista Interamericana de Bibliografía/Inter-American Review of Bibliography* 33, no. 4 (1983).

————. *Women in Latin American History: Their Lives and Views,* rev. ed. UCLA Latin American Studies, no. 51. Los Angeles: UCLA Latin American Center, 1980.

————. "Women and Work in Brazil, 1850–1920: A Preliminary Investigation." In *Essays Concerning the Socioeconomic History of Brazil and Portuguese India,* edited by Dauril Alden and Warren Dean. Gainesville, Fla.: University Presses of Florida, 1977.

Halac, Ricardo. *Segunda tiempo.* Buenos Aires: Editorial Galerna, 1978.

Harkness, Shirley, and Patricia Pinzón de Lewin. "Women, the Vote and the Party in the Politics of the Colombian National Front." *Journal of Interamerican Studies and World Affairs* 17 (November 1975).

Heilbom, Anna-Britta. *La Participación cultural de las mujeres: Indias y mestizas en le Mexico precortesiano y postrevolucionario.* Stockholm: The Ethnographical Museum (Etnografiska Museet), 1967. Monograph Series, no. 10.

Henderson, James D., & Linda Roddy Henderson. *Ten Notable Women of Latin America*. Chicago: Nelson Hall, 1978.

Hernando, Diana. "Casa y Familia: Spatial Biographies in Nineteenth Century Buenos Aires." Ph.D. diss., UCLA, 1973.

Hojman, David E. "Land Reform, Female Migration and the Market for Domestic Service in Chile." *Journal of Latin American Studies* 21 (1988).

Hollander, Nancy Caro. "Women and Class Struggle: The Case of Argentina." *Latin American Perspectives* 4 (Winter 1977).

Humphrey, John. *Gender and Work in the Third World: Sexual Division in Brazilian Industry*. London and New York: Tavistock Publications, 1987.

Iglitzin, Lynne B., and Ruth Ross, eds. *Women in the World, 1975–1985: The Women's Decade*. Santa Barbara, Calif.: ABC-Clio Press, 1986.

Isis International. *Rural Women in Latin America*. Rome: Isis International, 1987.

Jaquette, Jane S. "Female Participation in Latin America." In *Women in the World: A Comparative Study*, edited by Lynne B. Iglitzin and Ruth Ross. Santa Barbara, Calif.: ABC-Clio Press, 1976.

———. "Legitimizing Political Women: Expanding Options for Female Political Elites in Latin America." In *Perspectives on Power: Women in Africa, Asia, and Latin America*, edited by Jean F. O'Barr. Durham, N.C.: Duke University, 1982.

———. "Women in Revolutionary Movements in Latin America." *Journal of Marriage and the Family* 35 (May 1973).

———. *The Women's Movement in Latin America*. Boston: Unwin Hyman, 1989.

Jelin, Elizabeth. *Los movimientos sociales en la Argentina contemporeana*. Buenos Aires: Rock Nacional, 1986.

Jelin, Elizabeth, and Maria del Carmen Feijóo. "Trabajo y familia en el ciclo de vida femenino: El Caso de las sectores populares de Buenos Aires." *Estudio Cedes* 3, no. 8/9 (1980).

Joekes, Susan R. *La mujer y la economia mundial*. Instituto Internacional de Investigaciones y Capacitacion de la Naciones Unidas para la Promoción de la Mujer (INSTRAW). Mexico City: Siglo Veintiuno Editores, 1987.

Johnson, Ann Hagerman. "The Impact of Market Agriculture on Family and Household Structure in Nineteenth Century Chile." *Hispanic American Historical Review* 59 (November 1978).

Johnson, Julie Greer. "Feminine Satire in Concolorcovo's 'El Lazarillo de Ciegos Caminantes.'" *South Atlantic Bulletin* 45 (January 1980).

Kaplan, Temma, "Female Consciousness and Collective Action: The Case of Barcelona, 1910–1918." *Signs* 7 (Spring 1982).

Karasch, Mary. *Slave Life in Rio de Janeiro 1808–1850* Princeton, N.J.: Princeton University Press 1987.

Kelly, Gail P., and Carolyn M. Elliott. *Women's Education in the Third World: Comparative Perspectives*. Albany, N.Y.: SUNY, 1982.

Keremetsis, Dawn. "Women Workers in Transition: Sexual Division of the Labor Force in Mexico and Colombia." *The Americas* (April 1984).

Keremetsis, Eileen. "The Early Industrial Worker in Rio de Janeiro, 1870–1930." Ph.D. diss., Columbia University, 1982.

Kerns, Virginia. *Women and the Ancestors: Black Carib Kinship and Ritual*. Champaign–Urbana: University of Illinois, 1983.

King, Marjorie. "Cuba's Attack on Women's Second Shift." *Latin American Perspectives* 4 (Winter 1977).

Kirkpatrick, Gwen. "The Journalism of Alfonsina Storni: A New Approach to

Women's History in Argentina." In *Women, Culture and Politics in Latin America*. Berkeley and Los Angeles: University of California Press, 1990.

Kirkwood, Julieta. "Women and Politics in Chile." *International Social Science Journal* 35, no. 4 (1983).

Krustcka, Tania. "Brazil: Despite Formal Recognition, Women Denied Full Political Role." *Latinamerica Press*, 10 October 1985.

Labarca, Amanda. "Educación Secundaria." In *Actividades femeninas en Chile*. Santiago, Chile: Imprenta y Litografia La Ilustración, Santo Domingo, 1928.

Ladd, Doris. *The Mexican Nobility at Independence, 1780–1826*. Austin: University of Texas Press, 1976.

———, ed. *Mexican Women in Anahuac and New Spain*. Austin: Institute of Latin American Studies, University of Texas at Austin, 1978.

Landes, Ruth. *City of Women*. New York: Macmillan, 1947.

Larguía, Isabel, and John Dumoulin. "Women's Equality and the Cuban Revolution." In *Women and Change in Latin America*, edited by June Nash and Helen Safa. South Hadley, Mass.: Bergin and Garvey, 1985.

Latin American and Caribbean Women's Collective. *Slaves of Slaves: The Challenge of Latin American Women*, translated by Micheal Pallis. London: Zed Press, 1980. Originally published as *Mujeres* (Paris: *des femmes*, 1977).

Lavrin, Asunción. *Female, Feminine and Feminist: Key Concepts in Understanding Women's History in Twentieth Century Latin America*. Occasional Lecture Series, no. 4. Bristol, England: University of Bristol, 1988.

———. *The Ideology of Feminism in the Southern Cone, 1900–1940*. Working Papers, no. 169, Latin American Program. Washington, D.C.: The Wilson Center, Smithsonian Institution, 1986.

———. "Recent Studies on Women in Latin America." *Latin American Research Review* 19, no. 1 (1984).

———. "Unlike Sor Juana? The Model Nun in the Religious Literature of Colonial Mexico." *University of Dayton Review* (Spring 1983).

———. "Women and Religion in Spanish America." In *Women and Religion in America*, edited by Rosemary R. Reuther and Rosemary S. Keller. San Francisco: Harper and Row, 1983.

———, ed. *Latin American Women: Historical Perspectives*. Westport, Conn.: Greenwood Press, 1978.

———, ed. *Sexuality and Marriage in Colonial Latin America*. Lincoln: University of Nebraska Press, 1989.

Leacock, Eleanor. "History, Development, and the Division of Labor by Sex: Implications for Organization." *Signs* 7 (Winter 1981).

León de Leal, Magdalena. "Personas interesadas en la problematica feminina en Perú, Argentina, Brasil, y Venezuela." *LARR 14*, no. 1 (1979)

León de Leal, Magdalena, and Carmen Diana Deere, eds. *Women and Land Reform in Latin America/La Mujer y la politica agraria en America Latina*. Bogotá, Colombia: ACEP-Siglo XXI, 1986.

Lerner, Gerda. *The Creation of Patriarchy*. New York: Oxford University Press, 1986.

Lernoux, Penny. *Cry of the People*. Garden City, N.Y.: Doubleday, 1980; New York: Penguin Books, 1982.

Lewin, Linda. "Some Historical Implications of Kinship Organization for Family-Based Politics in Northeast Brazil." *Comparative Studies in Society and History* 21 (April 1979).

Lewis, Oscar, et al. *Four Women: Living the Revolution: An Oral History of Contemporary*

Cuba. Champaign–Urbana: University of Illinois Press, 1977.

Little, Cynthia Jeffress. "Education, Philanthropy, and Feminism: Components of Argentine Womanhood, 1860–1926." In *Latin American Women: Historical Perspectives*, edited by Asunción Lavrin. Westport, Conn.: Westview Press, 1978.

Lynn, Naomi B., ed. *Women and Politics*. 4 (Spring 1984).

Machado, Leda. "The Participation of Women in the Health Movement of Jardim Nordeste, in the Eastern Zone of São Paulo, Brazil: 1976–1985." *Bulletin of Latin American Research* 7, no. 1 (1988).

Macías, Ana. *Against All Odds: The Feminist Movement in Mexico to 1940*. Westport, Conn.: Greenwood Press, 1982.

———. "Felipe Carillo and Women's Liberation in Mexico." In *Latin American Women: Historical Perspectives* edited by Asunción Lavrin. Westport, Conn.: Greenwood Press, 1978.

Madeira, Felicia R., and Paul Singer. "Structure of Female Employment and Work in Brazil, 1920–1970," *Journal of Interamerican Studies and World Affairs* 17 (November 1975).

Maier, Elizabeth. *Nicaragua, la mujer en la revolución*. Mexico City: Ediciones de Cultura Popular, 1980.

Martín, Luis. *Daughters of the Conquistadores*. Albuquerque, N.M.: University of New Mexico Press, 1983.

Martin, Megan, and Susie Willett, eds. *Women in Nicaragua*. London: Nicaraguan Solidarity Campaign, 1980.

Martinez-Alier, Verena. *Marriage, Class and Colour in Nineteenth-Century Cuba: A Study of Racial Attitudes and Sexual Values in a Slave Society*. Cambridge: Cambridge University Press, 1974.

Masiello, Francine. "Women, State and Family in Latin American Literature of the 1920s." In *Women, Culture and Politics in Latin America*. Berkeley and Los Angeles: The University of California Press, 1990.

Mathurin, Lucille. *The Arrival of Black Women*. *Jamaica Journal* 9, no. 2/3 (1975).

Mattelart, Michele. "Chile: The Feminine Version of the Coup d'Etat." In *Sex and Class in Latin America: Women's Perspectives on Politics, Economics and the Family in the Third World*, edited by June Nash and Helen Icken Safa. New York: J. F. Bergin, 1980.

Matthews, Irene. "Magda Portal: Poetess, Politician, Example." Unpublished manuscript, University of California, Davis, 1985.

McGee Deutsch, Sandra F. "The Visible and Invisible Liga Patriotica Argentina, 1919–28: Gender Roles and the Right Wing." *Hispanic American Historical Review* 64 (May 1984).

———, ed. "Women and Politics in Twentieth Century Latin America." *Journal of Third World Societies* 15 (March 1981).

Mejía, Carmen de Gómez. "Mujeres en la historia de la Independencia Colombiana." *Estudio* 1965.

Mendelson, Johanna S. R. "The Feminine Press: The View of Women in the Colonial Journals of Spanish America, 1790–1810." *Latin American Women: Historical Perspectives*, edited by Asunción Lavrin. Westport, Conn.: Greenwood Press, 1978.

Miller, Beth, ed. *Women in Hispanic Literature: Icons and Fallen Idols*. Berkeley: University of California Press, 1983.

Miller, Francesca. "Feminism and the Transnational Arena." In *Women, Culture and Politics in Latin America*. Berkeley and Los Angeles: The University of California Press, 1990.

————. "Global Feminism and the Transnational Vision of Latin American Women." In *Women in Western Heritage: Understanding Our Heritage*, edited by Frances Richardson Keller. Lewiston, N.Y.: Mellen Press, 1990.

————. "The International Relations of Women of the Americas." *The Americas: A Quarterly Review of Inter-American Cultural History* (Fall 1986).

————. "National Identity and Culinary Tradition in Brazil." *Foodtalk*, 7, nos. 2, 3 (1984); 8, no. 1 (1985).

———— (Wellman). "Vice-President Richard M. Nixon's Goodwill Trip to South America, 1958." M.A. thesis, University of California, Davis, 1969.

Miller, Linda. "Patrons, Politics, and Schools: An Arena for Brazilian Women." In *Women and Politics in Twentieth Century Latin America*. Studies in Third World Societies, no. 15. Williamsburg, Va.: College of William and Mary, 1981.

Molyneux, Maxine. "Mobilization Without Emancipation? Women's Interests, The State and Revolution in Nicaragua," *Feminist Studies* (Summer 1985).

————. "No God, No Boss, No Husband." *Latin American Perspectives* (Winter 1986).

————. "The Politics of Abortion in Nicaragua: Revolutionary Pragmatism—or Feminism in the Realm of Necessity?" *Feminist Review*, no. 29 (May 1988).

Morães, Maria Lygia Quartim de. *Mulheres em movimento*. São Paulo, Brazil: Camara Brasileira do Livro, 1985.

Moreau de Justo, Alicia. *El socialismo y la mujer*. Buenos Aires: 1931.

Morello-Frosch, Marta. "Alfonsina Storni: The Tradition of the Feminine Subject." In *Women, Culture and Politics in Latin America*. Berkeley and Los Angeles: University of California Press, 1990.

Morgan, Robin, ed. *Sisterhood Is Global*. Garden City, N.Y.: Anchor Press/Doubleday, 1984.

Morrisey, Marietta. *Slave Women in the New World: Gender Stratification in the Caribbean*. Lawrence: University Press of Kansas, 1989.

Morton, Ward. *Woman Suffrage in Mexico*. Gainesville: University of Florida Press, 1962.

Moya-Raggio, Eliana. "Arpilleras: Chilean Culture of Resistance." *Feminist Studies* 10 (Summer 1984).

NACLA (North American Congress on Latin America). "Feminismo Balaguerista: A Strategy of the Right." *NACLA Latin America and Empire Report* 8 (April 1974).

NACLA. "Latin American Women, One Myth—Many Realities." *NACLA Latin America and Empire Report* 14 (September–October 1980).

NACLA. "Women's Labor." *NACLA Latin America and Empire Report* 9 (September 1975).

Nash, June, and Helen Icken Safa, eds. *Sex and Class in Latin America*. New York: Bergin, 1980.

————. *Women and Change in Latin America*. South Hadley, Mass.: Bergin and Garvey, 1985.

Navarro, Marysa. "Research on Latin American Women," *SIGNS* 5 (Autumn 1979).

Neilson, Melinda. "Non-Traditional Education of Women in Cuetzalan, Mexico," *Resources for Feminist Research* 13 (March 1984).

Newman, Kathleen. "The Modernization of Femininity: Argentina 1916–1926." In *Women, Culture and Politics in Latin America*. Berkeley and Los Angeles: University of California Press, 1990.

Neuhouser, Kevin. "Sources of Women's Power and Status among the Urban Poor in Contemporary Brazil." *Signs* 14, no. 31 (1988).

Neves-Xavier de Brito, Angela. "Brazilian Women in Exile: The Quest for an Identity."

Latin American Perspectives 13 (Spring 1986).

Norris, William P. *The Social Networks of Impoverished Brazilian Women: Work Patterns and Household Structure in an Urban Squatter Settlement.* Working Paper no. 84. Lansing: Michigan State University, 1985.

OAS. *Inter-American Conventions on Women.* Treaty Series, no. 38. Washington, D.C.: General Secretariat, Organization of American States, 1971.

Obregón Santacilia, Adela Formoso de. *La mujer mexicana en la organizacion social del país.* Mexico City: Talleres Graficos de la Nación, 1939.

Offen, Karen. "Defining Feminism: A Comparative Historical Approach." *Signs,* 1988.

Oliveira da Costa, Albertina, Maria Teresa Porciuncula de Morães, and Valentina de Rocha Lima. *Memorias—das mulheres—do exilio: Obra coletiva. Memorias do Exilio.* Rio de Janeiro: Paz y Terra, 1980.

Ortega, Eliana, and Nancy Saporta Sternbach. "Gracias de la Vida: Recounting the Third Latin American Feminist Meetings." *off our backs,* January 1986.

Papanek, Hanna. "The Work of Women: Postscript from Mexico City." *Signs* 1 (Autumn 1975).

Patai, Daphne. *Brazilian Women Speak: Contemporary Life Stories.* New Brunswick, N.J.: Rutgers University Press, 1988.

Pescatello, Ann. *Female and Male in Latin America.* Pittsburgh, Pa.: University of Pittsburgh Press, 1973.

———. "Introductory Note." *Journal of Interamerican Studies and World Affairs* 17 (November 1975).

PIEM (Programa Interdisciplinario de Estudios de la Mujer, El Colegio de Mexico). *Presencia y transparencia: La Mujer en la historia de Mexico.* Mexico City: Impreso de Mexico, 1987.

Piñeda, Magaly. "The Spanish-Speaking Caribbean." In *Sisterhood Is Global* edited by Robin Morgan. Garden City, N.Y.: Anchor Press/Doubleday, 1984.

Pinheiro, Ana Alice Costa. "Advances y definiciones del movimiento feminista en Brasil." M.A. thesis, Colegio de Mexico, 1981.

Poniatowska, Elena. *Hasta no verte, Jesús mio.* Mexico City: Editorial Era (Biblioteca Era) 1969.

———. *Massacre in Mexico.* New York: Viking Press, 1972.

Poppino, Rollie E. *Brazil: The Land and the People.* New York: Oxford University Press, 1968.

———. *International Communism in Latin America: A History of the Movement 1917–1963.* New York: Macmillan, The Free Press, 1964.

Portal, Magda. *El Aprismo y la mujer.* Lima, Peru: Editorial Cooperative Aprista ATAHULPA, 1933.

———. *Flora Tristán, Precursora.* Lima, Peru: Editorial la Equidad, 1983.

———. "Quienes traicionaron al pueblo?" *Cuadernos de divulgación popular,* 1 (April 1950).

———. *La Trampa.* Lima, Peru: Ediciones Raíz, 1956.

———. "Yo soy Magda Portal." In *Ser mujer en el Peru,* 2nd ed. Interviews collected and edited by Esther Andradi and Ana María Portugal. Lima, Peru: Takapu Editores, 1979.

Portnoy, Alicia, ed. *You Can't Drown the Fire: Latin American Women Writing in Exile.* Pittsburgh, Pa./San Francisco: Cleis Press, 1988.

Portugal, Ana María. "Hallazgos y extravios." *Fem* 8 (Summer 1985).

Prado, Danda. "Brazil: A Fertile but Ambiguous Feminist Terrain." In *Sisterhood Is Global,* edited by Robin Morgan. Garden City, N.Y.: Anchor Books, 1984.

Pratt, Mary Louise. "Women, Literature and Brotherhood." In *Women, Culture and*

Politics in Latin America. Berkeley and Los Angeles: University of California Press, 1990.

Prieto de Zegarra, Judith. "Mujer, poder y desarrollo en el Peru." In *El Decenio de la Mujer*, 2 vols. Callao, Peru: Editorial Dorhca Representaciones, 1980.

Prosperio, Renata, and Ana Alice Costa. "Brasil: Se organizan las mal amadas." *Fem* 3 (January–February 1980).

Psacharopoulos, George, and Antonio Zabalza. *The Destination and Early Career Performance of Secondary School Graduates in Colombia: Findings from the 1978 Cohort*. World Bank Staff Working Papers, no. 653 Washington, D.C.: World Bank, 1984.

Ramos-Escandón, Carmen, et al. *Presencia y transparencia: La Mujer en la historia de Mexico*. Mexico City: El Colegio de Mexico. 1987.

Ramos, Silvina. *Maternidad en Buenas Aires: La Experiencia popular*. Buenos Aires: CEDES (Centro de Estudios de Estado y Sociedad), 1983.

Randall, Margaret. "We Need a Government of Men and Women! Notes on the Second National Congress of the Federación de Mujeres Cubanos, November 25–29, 1974." *Latin American Perspectives* 2, no. 5 (1975).

———. *Women in Cuba: Twenty Years Later*. New York: Smyrna Press, 1981.

Randall, Vicky. *Women and Politics: An International Perspective*, 2nd ed. Chicago: University of Chicago Press, 1987.

Recchini de Lattes, Zulma. *Dynamics of the Female Labour Force in Argentina*. Women in a World Perspective Series. UNESCO 1983.

Regional Conference on the Integration of Women into the Economic and Social Development of Latin America, the Caribbean and Mexico. New York: United Nations, 1983.

Rey de Miranda, Nohra. *La Mujer: Jefe de hogar*. Bogota, Colombia: CEDE, 1982.

Reyes, Chela, ed. *Mujeres chilenas cuentan*. Santiago, Chile: Zig-Zag, 1978.

Riddell, Adaljiza Soza. "Female Political Elites in Mexico: 1974." *Women in the World: A Comparative Study*. Santa Barbara, Calif.: ABC-Clio Press, 1976.

Robles, Martha. *Educación y sociedad en la historia de Mexico*, 2nd ed. Mexico City: Siglo Veintiuno Editores, 1978.

Robles de Mendoza, Margarita. *La Evolucion de la mujer en Mexico*. (Delegada de Mexico en la Comision Inter-Americana Feminina de Washington). 1931.

Rodrigues, Jessita Martins. *A Mulher operaria. Um Estudo sobre Tecelas*. São Paulo, Brazil: Editora Hucitec, 1979.

Rodriguez, Ileana. "Obstaculos a la promoción y aplicación de la 'convención sobre la Eliminacion de Todas las Formas de Discriminacion contra la Mujer.'" *Caso de Nicaraqua* (Ministerio de la Presidencia, Oficino de la Mujer: Este estudio se enmarca en el subprograma de "Estudios e investigagicones sobre los derechos fundamentales de las mujeres" de la UNESCO. February 1987.

Rojas, Marta, and Mirta Rodriguez Calderon, eds. *Tania: The Unforgettable Guerrilla*. New York: Random House, 1971. Originally published as *Tania: La guerrillera involidable* (Havana: Instituto del Libro, 1970).

Russell-Wood, A. J. R. "Female and Family in the Economy and Society of Brazil." In *Latin American Women: Historical Perspectives*, edited by Asunción Lavrin. Westwood, Conn.: Greenwood Press, 1978.

Sa Barreto, Elba Siquiera de. *Mulher Brasileira: Biblografia anotada*. São Paulo, Brazil: Editora Brasiliense, 1979.

Safa, Helen Icken. "The Changing Class Composition of the Female Labor Force in Latin America." *Latin American Perspectives* 4 (Fall 1977).

Safa, Helen Icken, and June Nash, eds. *Sex and Class in Latin America*. New York: Praeger, 1976.

———. *Women and Change in Latin America*. South Hadley, Mass.: Bergin and

Garvey, 1985.

Saffioti, Heleieth I. B. *A Mulher na sociedad de clases: Mito e realidad.* Sao Paulo: Vozes, 1976. (English translation: Heleieth I. B. Saffiotti, *Women in Class Society.* New York: Monthly Review Press, 1978).

Salgues Cargill, Maruxa. *La Imagen de la mujer en las letras hispanoamericanas: Enfogue feminista de la literature hispanoamericana.* Jaen, Spain: Grafica Nova, 1975.

Salinas, Gloria Ardaya. "The Barzolas and the Housewives Committee." In *Women and Change in Latin America,* edited by June Nash and Helen Safa. South Hadley, Mass.: Bergen and Garvey, 1986.

Santamaría, Haydée. *Moncada: Memories of the Attack That Launched the Cuban Revolution,* translated by Robert Taber. Secaucus, N.J.: Lyle Stuart, 1980.

Santos, Maria. Interview by Barabara Alpern Engel. "Women in the Nicaraguan Revolution," *Frontiers* 7, no. 2 (1983).

Schiefelbein, Ernesto, and Joseph P. Farrell. "Women, Schooling, and Work in Chile: Evidence from a Longitudinal Study." In *Women's Education in the Third World: Comparative Perspectives,* edited by Gail P. Kelly and Carolyn M. Elliott. Albany, N.Y.: SUNY Press, 1982.

Schipske, Evelyn G. "An Analysis of the Consejo Nacional de Mujeres del Peru." *Journal of Interamerican Studies and World Affairs* 17 (November 1975).

Schmidt, Steffen W. "Women in Colombia: Attitudes and Future Perspectives in the Political System." *Journal of Interamerican Studies and World Affairs* 17 (November 1975).

——. "Women, Politics and Development," *Latin American Research Review* 18, no. 1 (1983).

SECOLAS Annals. Kennesaw College, Southeastern Conference on Latin American Studies. Marietta, Ga.: Volio, 1979.

Secretariat of the Women's International Democratic Federation. *Documents of the World Congress of Women—Equality, National Independence, Peace, Prague, October 8–13, 1981.* Berlin: Unter den Linden.

Seminar on Women and Culture. "Toward a History of Women's Periodical in Latin America: Introduction." In *Women, Culture and Politics in Latin America.* Berkeley, Calif.: University of California Press, 1990.

——. *Women, Culture and Politics in Latin America.* Berkeley, Calif.: University of California Press, 1990.

Silverstein, Leni. "The First Feminist Conference in Latin America." *International Supplement to the Women's Studies Quarterly* 1 (January 1982).

Sivard, Ruth Leger, ed. *Women . . . A World Survey.* Washington, D.C.: World Priorities, 1985.

Smith, Margo. "Domestic Service as a Channel of Upward Mobility for the Lower-Class Woman: The Lima Case." In *Female and Male in Latin America,* edited by Ann Pescatello. Pittsburgh, Penn.: University of Pittsburgh Press, 1972.

Socolow, Susan M. *The Merchants of Buenos Aires, 1778–1810: Family and Commerce.* Cambridge: Cambridge University Press, 1978.

Soeiro, Susan A. "The Feminine Orders in Colonial Bahia, Brazil: Economic, Social, and Demographic Implications, 1677–1900." In *Latin American Women: Historical Perspectives,* edited by Asunción Lavrin. Westwood, Conn.: Greenwood Press, 1978.

——. "Recent Work on Latin American Women: A Review Essay." *Inter-American Studies and World Affairs* 17 (November 1975).

Soto, Shirlene. *The Mexican Woman: A Study of Her Participation in the Revolution, 1910–1940.* Palo Alto, Calif.: R&R Research Associates, 1979.

Stack, Noreen F. "Eva Perón." In *Encyclopedia of Latin America*, edited by Helen Delpar. New York: McGraw-Hill, 1974.

Steffens, Heidi. "Cuba: The Day Women Took Over Havana." *Ms.* 3 (April 1975).

Stevens, Evelyn P. "Marianismo: The Other Face of Machismo in Latin America." In *Female and Male in Latin America*, edited by Ann Pescatello. Pittsburgh, Pa., University of Pittsburgh Press, 1973.

———. "Prospects for a Women's Liberation Movement in Latin America." *Journal of Marriage and the Family* 35 (May 1973).

Stone, Elizabeth, ed. *Women and the Cuban Revolution*. New York: Pathfinder Press, 1981.

Stoner, K. Lynn. *From the House to the Streets: The Cuban Women's Movement for Legal Change, 1898–1940*. Durham, N.C.: Duke University Press, 1991.

———. "From the House to the Streets: Women's Movement for Legal Change in Cuba, 1898–1958." Ph.D. diss., University of Indiana, 1983.

———, ed. *Latinas of the Americas: A Source Book*. New York: Garland Press, 1989.

Strozzi, Ada. "Feminism in Argentina," *Bulletin of the Pan American Union* 66 (December–January 1932).

Suchliki, Jaime, ed. *Journal of Interamerican Studies* 26 (February 1984).

Sweet, David, and Gary B. Nash, eds. *Struggle and Survival in Colonial America*. Berkeley: University of California Press, 1981.

Tabak, Fanny. "UN Decade and Women's Studies in Latin America." *Women's Studies International Forum* 8, no. 2 (1985).

Tamez, Elsa. *Through Her Eyes: Women's Theology from Latin America*. Maryknoll, New York: Orbis Books, 1989.

Tiano, Susan. *Maquiladoras, Women's Work, and Unemployment in Northern Mexico*. Michigan State University Working Paper, no. 43. East Lansing, Mich.: Michigan State University, 1984.

Tilly, Louise A. "Women's Collective Action and Feminism in France, 1870–1914." In *Class Conflict and Collective Action*, edited by Louise A. Tilly and Charles Tilly. Beverly Hills, Calif.: Sage Publications, in cooperation with the Social Science History Association, 1981.

Tuñon Pablos, Julia. *Mujeres en Mexico: Una historia olvidada*. Mexico City: Planeta, 1987.

Turner, June H. ed. *Latin American Women: The Meek Speak Out*. Silver Spring, Md.: International Educational Development, 1980.

UNICEF: The Americas and the Caribbean Regional Office. *The Invisible Adjustment: Poor Women and the Economic Crisis*. Santiago, Chile: Alfabeta Impresores, 1989.

United Nations. *Meeting in Mexico: The Story of the World Conference of the International Women's Year. Mexico City, June 19–July 2, 1975*. New York: United Nations, 1975.

Valenzuela, Luisa. "Making Love Visible: The Women of Buenos Aires." *Vogue* 174 (May 1984).

Valenzuela, María Elena. *La Mujer en el Chile militar: Todas ibamos a ser reinas*. Santiago, Chile: Ediciones Chile y America, 1987.

Valores patrios y valores familiares. Cuadernos de Difusion, No. 7. Santiago, Chile: Secretaria de la Mujer, 1982.

Vargas, Virginia. In *Congreso de investigacion acerca de la mujer en la region andina*, edited by Jeanine Anderson de Velasco. Lima, Peru: 1983.

Vaughan, Mary Kay. *The State, Education, and Social Class in Mexico, 1880–1928*. DeKalb: Northern Illinois University Press, 1982.

Velagapudi, Gunvor. *La Mujer y el empleo en America Latina*. Santiago, Chile: Organición Internacional del Trabajo, Programa Regional del Empleo para America Latina y el Caribe, 1976.

Velasco, Jeanne Anderson. "The UN Decade for Women in Peru." *Women's Studies International Forum* 8, no. 2 (1985).

Viezzer, Moema, ed. *Testimonio de Domitila*. Mexico City: Editorial Siglo Vientiuno, 1978.

Wellesley College, Center for Research on Women in Higher Education and Professions, ed. *Women and National Development: The Complexities of Change*. Chicago: University of Chicago Press, 1977.

Williams, Mary Willhelmine. *People and Politics in Latin America*, rev. ed. Boston: Ginn, 1945.

Yeager, Gertrude M. "Women's Roles in Chile: Public Education Records, 1843–1883." *Latin American Research Review* 17 (1983).

Yudelman, Sally W. *Hopeful Openings: A Study of Five Women's Development Organizations in Latin America and the Caribbean*. West Hartford, Conn.: Kumarian Press, 1987.

Zakus, Debra J. "Literacy for Poor Women in Central America: A Political Struggle." *Resources for Feminist Research*. 13 (November 1984).

Index

Fed. Bras. pelo Prog. Fem. (*continued*)
[FBPF] (Brazilian Federation for the
Advancement of Women), 87–88, 97
Federação de Mulheres do Brasil (Brazilian
Women's Federation [BWF]), 119–20, 143,
152
Federación de Mujeres Cubanas (FMC), 63, 158,
188–89, 212–13, 236, 275n.12
Federación Hondureña de Mujeres Campesinas
(FEHMUC), 273n.148
Federación Inter-Americana de Mujeres (pro-
posed, 1947), 130, 131
fem, 167, 205, 207–208, 211–12, 217–18, 228, 234,
247, 278n.70
Feminaria, 250, 281n.103
Feminine (the), 74, 146–47
Feminine Action Committee (Venezuela),
262–63n.22
Feminine Amnesty Movement (Brazil), 193
Feminine Idealist party (Mexico), 112
Feminine Mystique, The (Friedan), 153, 269n.42
Feminismo popular, 67, 221, 222, 233
Feminist Action party (Dominican Republic),
113–14
Feminist Revolutionary Party (Mexico), 111
Feminism (Latin-American), 35–36; social
motherhood and, 68–109, 257–61; transnational arena, 82–109; opponents of, 91–92,
101–103; distanced from US, European,
88, 93; periodization (waves) of, 110, 138,
142–44; and Catholic church, 115, 261n.2;
in revolutionary guerrilla movements, 145,
147; international, 187–237, 275–84; use
of term, 193, 203; diffusion among ever-
broader sectors of population, 234–37;
conclusions about, 248–50. *See also* Inter-
national Feminist Congresses; Suffrage;
Women's rights; *and under specific countries*
Feministas clasistas, 218
FEMPRESS. See *Mujer / Fempress*
Fernández, Lara, 113–14
Fernández, Raoul, 128, 130
Fernández Retamar, Roberto, 141
Film industry (Brazil's), 206, 278–79n.75
Fisher, Lillian Estelle, 113
Fletcher, Lea, 281n.103
Flora, Cornelia Butler, 197
Flushe, Della, 24–25
Foco, 170, 187–88, 274n.2
Ford Foundation, 225
*Forgotten Females: Women of African and
Indian Descent in Colonial Chile* (Flushe,
Korth), 24–25
Formoso de Obregón Santacilia, Adela, 117–18

Fortuny Araña, José Manuel, 132
Fowler, Amy, 84–85
France, 257n.2
Franco, Generalissimo, 131
Franco, Jean, 7, 8, 251n.3
Fraser, Nicholas, 123
Freemasons, 39, 50
Frei, Eduardo, 178–79, 181
Freire, Paulo, 67, 149, 175, 194, 244
French Order of St. Anne's, 38
Frenté de Acción Popular (FRAP), 178
Frenté Único pro Derechos de la Mujer (United
Front for Women's Rights), 111, 113, 117
Frenté Socialista de Mujers, 203
Friedan, Betty, 153, 199, 200–201
Frondizi, Arturo, 143

Galindo, Hermila, 76, 87
Gallegos, Rómulo, 117, 262–63n.22
Galtieri, Leopoldo, 251n.2
Galvão, Patricia (Pagú), 103–104, 229–30
García, Cuca, 93
García, Refúgio, 111
García de Coronado, Domitila, 89
García Ortiz, Francisca, 76–77
García Somoza, Anastasio, 113
García y García, Elvira, 79–80, 259n.24
Garrett, Vilma de, 157
Geisel, Ernesto, 192, 194–95, 276n.22, n.32
Gender issues, 16–25, 154, 269n.46–47. *See also*
Woman question, problem (the); Women's
issues; Women's rights
Generation of 1837 (Argentina), 42
Gilfeather, Sister Katherine Anne, 175,
272n.137
Gilio, María Esther, 173
Goméz Méjia, Carmen de, xiii, xv
González, Luisa, 191
Good Neighbor Policy (US), 113, 262n.15
Goulart, Joáo, 151–52, 153, 154
Governadora (Chile), 19–20
Graham, Maria Dundas, 30–31
Gran Chaco: conflict in, 107–108
GRECMU (*Grupo de Estudios sobre la Condi-
ción de la Mujer en Uruguay*), 225, 231, 247,
282n.128
Green Berets, 165
Greenberg, Janet, 257–58n.3
Grierson, Cecilia, 73
Guanabara (Rio de Janeiro), 152, 268n.33
Guatemala, 1, 2, 9, 11, 20–21; dictator, 113;
Constitution (1945), 116, 134; revolution
(1944), 127; Communism, politics, 127,
132–34, 139, 140, 265n.70, 266n.78

UNIVERSITY PRESS OF NEW ENGLAND publishes books under its own imprint and is the publisher for Brandeis University Press, Brown University Press, Clark University Press, University of Connecticut, Dartmouth College, Middlebury College Press, University of New Hampshire, University of Rhode Island, Tufts University, University of Vermont, and Wesleyan University Press.

Library of Congress Cataloging-in-Publication Data
Miller, Francesca.
    Latin American women and the search for social justice / Francesca
Miller.
    p.   cm.
    Includes bibliographical references and index.
    ISBN 0–87451–557–2. — ISBN 0–87451–558–0 (pbk.)
    1. Women—Latin America—History.   2. Feminism—Latin America—
History.   3. Women's rights—Latin America—History.   4. Women in
politics—Latin America—History.   I. Title.
HQ1460.5.M55   1991
305.4'098—dc20   91–50371